On Core
Mathematics

Algebra 1

HOUGHTON MIFFLIN HARCOURT

Cover photo: umbrella   Jon Sheer/Flickr/Getty Images

Printed in the U.S.A.

ISBN 978-0-547-57527-8

5 6 7 8 9 10 1409 20 19 18 17 16 15 14 13 12

4500373467   B C D E F G

Contents

© Houghton Mifflin Harcourt Publishing Company

Unit 4   Linear Functions

Unit 5   Exponential Functions

Unit 6   Piecewise and Absolute Value Functions

© Houghton Mifflin Harcourt Publishing Company

© Houghton Mifflin Harcourt Publishing Company

Learning the Common Core State Standards

Has your state adopted the Common Core standards? If so, then you'll be learning both mathematical content standards and the mathematical practice standards that underlie them. The supplementary material found in *On Core Mathematics Algebra 1* will help you succeed with both.

Here are some of the special features you'll find in *On Core Mathematics Algebra 1*

INTERACTIVE LESSONS

You actively participate in every aspect of a lesson. You read the mathematical concepts in an Engage, carry out an activity in an Explore, and complete the solution of an Example. This interactivity promotes a deeper understanding of the mathematics.

7-1 Translating the Graph of $f(x) = x^2$

Essential question: *What are the effects of the constants h and k on the graph of $g(x) = (x - h)^2 + k$?*

1 ENGAGE Understanding the Parent Quadratic Function

Any function that can be written as $f(x) = ax^2 + bx + c$ where a, b, and c are constants and $a \neq 0$ is a **quadratic function**. Notice that the highest exponent of the variable x is 2.

The most basic quadratic function is $f(x) = x^2$. It is called the *parent* quadratic function. To graph the parent function, make a table of values like the one below. Then plot the ordered pairs and draw the graph. The U-shaped curve is called a **parabola**. The turning point on the parabola is called its **vertex**.

x	$f(x) = x^2$
−3	9
−2	4
−1	1
0	0
1	1
2	4
3	9

REFLECT

1a. What is the domain of $f(x) = x^2$? What is the range?

1b. What symmetry does the graph of $f(x) = x^2$ have? Why does it have this symmetry?

1c. For what values of x is $f(x) = x^2$ increasing? For what values is it decreasing?

2 EXAMPLE Graphing Functions of the Form $g(x) = x^2 + k$

Graph each quadratic function. (The graph of the parent function $f(x) = x^2$ is shown in gray.)

A $g(x) = x^2 + 2$

x	$g(x) = x^2 + 2$
−3	
−2	
−1	
0	
1	
2	
3	

B $g(x) = x^2 - 2$

x	$g(x) = x^2 - 2$
−3	
−2	
−1	
0	
1	
2	
3	

REFLECT

2a. How is the graph of $g(x) = x^2 + 2$ related to the graph of $f(x) = x^2$?

2b. How is the graph of $g(x) = x^2 - 2$ related to the graph of $f(x) = x^2$?

In general, how is the graph of $g(x) = x^2 + k$ related to the graph of $f(x) = x^2$?

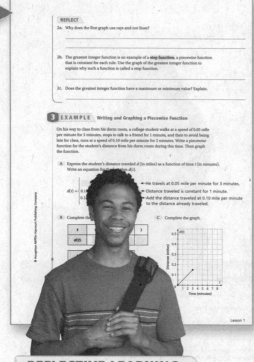

REFLECTIVE LEARNING

You learn to be a reflective thinker through the follow-up questions after each Engage, Explore, and Example in a lesson. The Reflect questions challenge you to really think about the mathematics you have just encountered and to share your understanding with the class.

TEST PREP

At the end of a unit, you have an opportunity to practice the material in multiple choice and free response formats used on standardized tests.

FOCUS ON MODELING

Special lessons that focus on modeling occur near the ends of units. They help you pull together the mathematical concepts and skills taught in a unit and apply them to real-world situations.

© Houghton Mifflin Harcourt Publishing Company

(t) Getty Images/PhotoDisc; (c) Image Source/Getty Images; (b) ImageSource/Age Fotostock

Learning the Standards for Mathematical Practice

The Common Core State Standards include eight Standards for Mathematical Practice. Here's how *On Core Mathematics Algebra 1* helps you learn those standards as you master the Standards for Mathematical Content.

① Make sense of problems and persevere in solving them.

In *On Core Mathematics Algebra 1*, you will work through Explores and Examples that present a solution pathway for you to follow. You will be asked questions along the way so that you gain an understanding of the solution process, and then you will apply what you've learned in the Practice for the lesson.

> **5 EXAMPLE** Modeling the Height of a Diver
>
> Physics students are measuring the heights and times of divers jumping off diving boards. The function that models a diver's height (in meters) above the water is
>
> $$h(t) = -5t^2 + vt + h_0$$
>
> where v is the diver's initial upward velocity in meters per second, h_0 is the diver's height above the water in meters, and t is the time in seconds. A diver who is 3 meters above the water jumps off a diving board with an initial upward velocity of 14 m/s. How many seconds will it take for the diver to hit the water? That is, when does $h(t) = 0$?
>
> A   Write the equation $h(t) = 0$, substituting in known values. $-5t^2 + \boxed{}t + \boxed{} = 0$
>
> B   Factor the left side of the equation. $(\boxed{})(\boxed{}) = 0$
>
> C   Set each factor equal to zero and solve. $t = \underline{}$ or $t = \underline{}$
>
> D   Which value of t makes sense in the context of the problem? Why?
>
> **REFLECT**
>
> 5a.   Suppose a diver who is 10 meters above the water jumps off a diving board with an initial upward velocity of 5 m/s. How many seconds will it take for the diver to hit the water? Explain your reasoning.

② Reason abstractly and quantitatively.

When you solve a real-world problem in *On Core Mathematics Algebra 1*, you will learn to represent the situation symbolically by translating the problem into a mathematical expression or equation. You will use these mathematical models to solve the problem and then state your answer in terms of the problem context. You will reflect on the solution process in order to check your answer for reasonableness and to draw conclusions.

> **2 EXAMPLE** Writing and Solving Inequalities
>
> Kristin can afford to spend at most $50 for a birthday dinner at a restaurant, including a 15% tip. Describe some costs that are within her budget.
>
> A   Which inequality symbol can be used to represent "at most"? _____
>
> B   Complete the verbal model for the situation.
>
> | Cost before tip (dollars) | | 15% | | Cost before tip (dollars) | | Budget limit (dollars) |
>
> C   Write and simplify an inequality for the model. _____
>
> **REFLECT**
>
> 2a.   Can Kristin spend $40 on the meal before the tip? Explain.
>
> 2b.   What whole dollar amount is the most Kristin can spend before the tip? Explain.

③ Construct viable arguments and critique the reasoning of others.

Throughout *On Core Mathematics Algebra 1*, you will be asked to make conjectures, construct a mathematical argument, explain your reasoning, and justify your conclusions. Reflect questions offer opportunities for cooperative learning and class discussion. You will have additional opportunities to critique reasoning in Error Analysis problems.

REFLECT

1a. Why should the parts of the domain of a piecewise function $f(x)$ have no common x-values?

REFLECT

2a. Describe how the graph of $f(x) = ab^x$ compares with the graph of $f(x) = b^x$ for a given value of b when $a > 1$ and when $0 < a < 1$.

23. **Error Analysis** A student says that the graph of $g(x) = |x + 3| - 1$ is the graph of the parent function, $f(x) = |x|$, translated 3 units to the right and 1 unit down. Explain what is incorrect about this statement.

④ Model with mathematics.

On *Core Mathematics Algebra 1* presents problems in a variety of contexts such as science, business, and everyday life. You will use mathematical models such as expressions, equations, tables, and graphs to represent the information in the problem and to solve the problem. Then you will interpret your results in context.

2 EXAMPLE Comparing Linear and Exponential Functions

Compare these two salary plans:
- Job A: $1000 for the first month with a $100 raise every month thereafter
- Job B: $1000 for the first month with a 1% raise every month thereafter

Will Job B ever have a higher monthly salary than Job A?

A   Write functions that represent the monthly salaries. Let t represent the number of elapsed months. Then tell whether the function is *linear* or *exponential*.

Job A: $S_A(t) = $ ____ + ____ t S_A is a/an _____ function.

Job B: $S_B(t) = $ ____ · ____ ^{t} S_B is a/an _____ function.

B   Graph the functions on a calculator and sketch them below. Label the functions and include the scale.

C   Will Job B ever have a higher monthly salary than Job A? If so, after how many months will this happen? Explain your reasoning.

REFLECT

2a. Revise $S_B(t)$ and use the Table feature on your graphing calculator to find the interval in which the monthly salary for Job B finally exceeds that for Job A if the growth rate is 0.1%. Use intervals of 1,000. Repeat for a growth rate of 0.01%, using intervals of 10,000.

2b. Why does a quantity increasing exponentially eventually exceed a quantity increasing linearly?

5 Use appropriate tools strategically.

You will use a variety of tools in *On Core Mathematics Algebra 1*, including manipulatives, paper and pencil, and technology. You might use manipulatives to develop concepts, paper and pencil to practice skills, and technology (such as graphing calculators, spreadsheets, or geometry software) to investigate more complicated mathematical ideas.

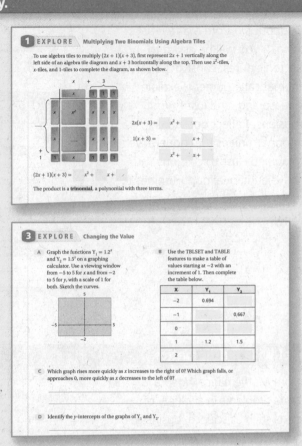

1 EXPLORE Multiplying Two Binomials Using Algebra Tiles

To use algebra tiles to multiply $(2x + 1)(x + 3)$, first represent $2x + 1$ vertically along the left side of an algebra tile diagram and $x + 3$ horizontally along the top. Then use x^2-tiles, x-tiles, and 1-tiles to complete the diagram, as shown below.

$$2x(x + 3) = \quad x^2 + \quad x$$
$$1(x + 3) = \qquad \quad x +$$
$$\qquad\qquad x^2 + \quad x +$$

$$(2x + 1)(x + 3) = \quad x^2 + \quad x +$$

The product is a **trinomial**, a polynomial with three terms.

3 EXPLORE Changing the Value

A. Graph the functions $Y_1 = 1.2^x$ and $Y_2 = 1.5^x$ on a graphing calculator. Use a viewing window from -5 to 5 for x and from -2 to 5 for y, with a scale of 1 for both. Sketch the curves.

B. Use the TBLSET and TABLE features to make a table of values starting at -2 with an increment of 1. Then complete the table below.

x	Y_1	Y_2
-2	0.694	
-1		0.667
0		
1	1.2	1.5
2		

C. Which graph rises more quickly as x increases to the right of 0? Which graph falls, or approaches 0, more quickly as x decreases to the left of 0?

D. Identify the y-intercepts of the graphs of Y_1 and Y_2.

6 Attend to precision.

Precision refers not only to the correctness of arithmetic calculations, algebraic manipulations, and geometric reasoning but also to the proper use of mathematical language, symbols, and units to communicate mathematical ideas. Throughout *On Core Mathematics Algebra 1* you will demonstrate your skills in these areas when you are asked to calculate, describe, show, explain, prove, and predict.

REFLECT

1a. Identify the property being illustrated.
- $2x + 7x = (2 + 7)x$, which equals $9x$
- $(x + 1) + 9 = x + (1 + 9)$, which equals $x + 10$
- $5 + x + 3 = x + 5 + 3$, which equals $x + 8$

1b. *Like terms* contain the same variables raised to the same power. In part a, how was the Distributive Property used to combine like terms?

1c. Constant terms are also considered like terms. In part a, how were properties used to combine constant terms?

3c. If you write only the units for the expression $100 + 12.5t$, you get $mi + \frac{mi}{h} \cdot h$ where "mi" is the abbreviation for miles and "h" is the abbreviation for hours. Explain what the following *unit analysis* shows:

$$mi + \frac{mi}{h} \cdot h = mi + mi = mi$$

7 Look for and make use of structure.

In *On Core Mathematics Algebra 1*, you will look for patterns or regularity in mathematical structures such as expressions, equations, geometric figures, and graphs. Becoming familiar with underlying structures will help you build your understanding of more complicated mathematical ideas.

This method of using the distributive property to multiply two binomials is referred to as the FOIL method. The letters of the word FOIL stand for First, Outer, Inner, and Last and will help you remember how to use the distributive property to multiply binomials.

You apply the FOIL method by multiplying each of the four pairs of terms described below and then simplifying the resulting polynomial.

- **First** refers to the first terms of each binomial.
- **Outer** refers to the two terms on the outside of the expression.
- **Inner** refers to the two terms on the inside of the expression.
- **Last** refers to the last terms of each binomial.

Now multiply $(7x - 1)(3x - 5)$ using FOIL. Again, think of $7x - 1$ as $7x + (-1)$ and $3x - 5$ as $3x + (-5)$. This results in a positive constant term of 5 because $(-1)(-5) = 5$.

$$(7x - 1)(3x - 5) = 21x^2 - 35x - 3x + 5$$

$$(7x - 1)(3x - 5) = 21x^2 - 38x + 5$$

Notice that the trinomials are written with variable terms in descending order of exponents and with the constant term last. This is a standard form for writing polynomials: Starting with the variable term with the greatest exponent, write the other variable terms in descending order of their exponents, and put the constant term last.

8 Look for and express regularity in repeated reasoning.

In *On Core Mathematics Algebra 1*, you will have the opportunity to explore and reflect on mathematical processes in order to come up with general methods for performing calculations and solving problems.

Name _____ Class _____ Date _____

8-6

Deriving the Quadratic Formula

Essential question: *What is the quadratic formula and how can you derive it from $ax^2 + bx + c = 0$?*

COMMON CORE

CC9-12.A.REI.4,
CC9-12.A.REI.4a,
CC9-12.A.REI.4b

You have learned how to solve quadratic equations by completing the square. In this lesson, you will complete the square on the general form of a quadratic equation to derive a formula that can be used to solve any quadratic equation.

1 EXPLORE   Deriving the Quadratic Formula

Solve the general form of the quadratic equation, $ax^2 + bx + c = 0$, by completing the square to find the values of x in terms of a, b, and c.

A   Subtract c from both sides of the equation.

$$ax^2 + bx = \boxed{}$$

B   Multiply both sides of the equation by $4a$ to make the coefficient of x^2 a perfect square.

$$4a^2x^2 + \boxed{}\, x = -4ac$$

C   Add b^2 to both sides of the equation to complete the square. Then write the trinomial as the square of a binomial.

$$4a^2x^2 + 4abx + b^2 = -4ac + \boxed{}$$

$$\left(\boxed{}\right)^2 = b^2 - 4ac$$

D   Apply the definition of a square root and solve for x.

$$\boxed{} = \pm\sqrt{\boxed{}}$$

$$2ax = -\boxed{} \pm \sqrt{\boxed{}}$$

$$x = \boxed{}$$

The formula $x = \dfrac{-b \pm \sqrt{b^2 - 4ac}}{2a}$ is called the **quadratic formula**. For any quadratic equation written in standard form, $ax^2 + bx + c = 0$, the quadratic formula gives the solutions of the equation.

Algebraic Modeling and Unit Analysis

Unit Focus

This unit helps you transition from performing operations with numbers to working with variables, expressions, equations, inequalities, and functions, which are the building blocks of algebra. You will apply the order of operations and the distributive property to evaluate and simplify algebraic expressions. You will also apply unit analysis as you learn to write and graph functions to model real-world situations.

Unit at a Glance

COMMON CORE

Lesson	Standards for Mathematical Content
1-1 Evaluating Expressions	CC.9-12.N.Q.1*, CC.9-12.A.SSE.1*, CC.9-12.A.SSE.1a*, CC.9-12.A.SSE.1b*
1-2 Simplifying Expressions	CC.9-12.N.Q.1*, CC.9-12.A.SSE.1*, CC.9-12.A.SSE.1a*, CC.9-12.A.SSE.2
1-3 Writing Expressions	CC.9-12.N.Q.1*, CC.9-12.N.Q.2*, CC.9-12.A.SSE.1*, CC.9-12.A.SSE.1a*, CC.9-12.A.SSE.2
1-4 Writing Equations and Inequalities	CC.9-12.N.Q.2*, CC.9-12.A.CED.1*, CC.9-12.A.CED.3*
1-5 Representing Functions	CC.9-12.N.Q.1*, CC.9-12.F.IF.1, CC.9-12.F.IF.2, CC.9-12.F.IF.5*
1-6 Modeling with Functions	CC.9-12.N.Q.1*, CC.9-12.F.IF.1, CC.9-12.F.IF.2, CC.9-12.F.IF.5*, CC.9-12.F.BF.1*, CC.9-12.F.BF.1a*
Test Prep	

UNIT 1

Unpacking the Common Core State Standards

Use the table to help you understand the Standards for Mathematical Content that are taught in this unit. Refer to the lessons listed after each standard for exploration and practice.

COMMON CORE Standards for Mathematical Content	What It Means For You
CC.9-12.N.Q.1 Use units as a way to understand problems and to guide the solution of multi-step problems; choose and interpret units consistently in formulas; **choose and interpret the scale and the origin in graphs and data displays.*** Lessons 1-1, 1-2, 1-3, 1-5, 1-6	You will see how analyzing units can help you better understand the operations involved in algebraic expressions. You will also see that choosing an appropriate scale on a graph will help you better analyze the data.
CC.9-12.N.Q.2 Define appropriate quantities for the purpose of descriptive modeling.* Lessons 1-3, 1-4	You will write expressions, equations, and inequalities to model real-world situations.
CC.9-12.A.SSE.1 Interpret expressions that represent a quantity in terms of its context.* **CC.9-12.A.SSE.1a Interpret parts of an expression, such as terms, factors, and coefficients.*** **CC.9-12.A.SSE.1b Interpret complicated expressions by viewing one or more of their parts as a single entity.*** Lessons 1-1, 1-2, 1-3	In algebra, it is important to interpret and represent parts of an expression, especially when the expression represents a real-world context. This will help you interpret more complex expressions, as well as equations and inequalities.
CC.9-12.A.SSE.2 Use the structure of an expression to identify ways to rewrite it. Lessons 1-2, 1-3	You will use the structure of an expression to help you simplify or regroup terms when you find solutions to problems.
CC.9-12.A.CED.1 Create equations and inequalities in one variable and use them to solve problems.* Lesson 1-4 (Also 1-6)	You will use verbal models to help you write equations and inequalities to represent mathematical relationships.
CC.9-12.A.CED.3 Represent constraints by equations or inequalities, and by systems of equations and/or inequalities, **and interpret solutions as viable or nonviable options in a modeling context.*** Lesson 1-4	You will see how certain input and output values may or may not result in realistic solutions to problems.
CC.9-12.F.IF.1 Understand that a function from one set (called the domain) to another set (called the range) assigns to each element of the domain exactly one element of the range. If f is a function and x is an element of its domain, then $f(x)$ denotes the output of f corresponding to the input x. The graph of f is the graph of the equation $y = f(x)$. Lessons 1-5, 1-6	You will be introduced to the concept of a function and experience a variety of situations that functions can model. You will apply these concepts throughout algebra and in future math courses.

COMMON CORE Standards for Mathematical Content	What It Means For You
CC.9-12.F.IF.2 Use function notation, evaluate functions for inputs in their domains, and interpret statements that use function notation in terms of a context. Lessons 1-5, 1-6	You will be introduced to function notation and be able to evaluate functions for certain input values. You will also be able to interpret contextual situations by writing equations to represent functions.
CC.9-12.F.IF.5 Relate the domain of a function to its graph and, where applicable, to the quantitative relationship it describes.* Lessons 1-5, 1-6	You will make a table of values, using appropriate input values for the domain, in order to graph functions. You will recognize which input values make sense for a given situation.
CC.9-12.F.BF.1 Write a function that describes a relationship between two quantities.* **CC.9-12.F.BF.1a** Determine an explicit expression, a recursive process, or steps for calculation from a context.* Lesson 1-6	You will write equations to model functions and graph functions on a coordinate grid. You will use functions to model relationships between real-world quantities.

© Houghton Mifflin Harcourt Publishing Company

UNIT 1

Evaluating Expressions

1-1

COMMON
CORE

CC.9-12.N.Q.1*,
CC.9-12:A.SSE.1*,
CC.9-12.A.SSE.1a*,
CC.9-12.A.SSE.1b*

Essential question: *How do you interpret and evaluate algebraic expressions that model real-world situations?*

1 ENGAGE   **Interpreting Expressions**

An **expression** is a mathematical phrase that contains operations, numbers, and/or variables. A **numerical expression** contains only numbers and operations, while an **algebraic expression** contains at least one variable.

A **term** is a part of an expression that is added. The **coefficient** of a term is the numerical factor of the term. A numerical term in an algebraic expression is referred to as a *constant term*.

Algebraic Expression	Terms	Coefficients
$2x^2 - 16x + 32$	$2x^2$, $-16x$, constant term 32	2 is the coefficient of $2x$. -16 is the coefficient of $-16x$.

Recall that the **order of operations** is a rule for simplifying a numerical expression:

1. **P**arentheses (simplify inside parentheses) $1 - 6 \cdot (7 - 4) + 5^2 = 1 - 6 \cdot \mathbf{3} + 5^2$

2. **E**xponents (simplify powers) $= 1 - 6 \cdot 3 + \mathbf{25}$

3. **M**ultiplication and **D**ivision (from left to right) $= 1 - \mathbf{18} + 25$

4. **A**ddition and **S**ubtraction (from left to right) $= \mathbf{8}$

REFLECT

1a. Write the expression $3m - 4n - 8$ as a sum. How does this help you identify the terms of the expression? Identify the terms.

_____

_____

1b. Explain and illustrate the difference between a term and a coefficient.

_____

_____

1c. What is the coefficient of x in the expression $x - 2$? Explain your reasoning.

_____

1d. What is the value of $1 - 18 + 25$ if you subtract then add? If you add then subtract? Why is the order of operations necessary?

_____

To **evaluate** an algebraic expression, substitute the value(s) of the variable(s) into the expression and simplify using the order of operations.

2 EXAMPLE   Evaluating Algebraic Expressions

Evaluate the algebraic expression $x(4x - 10)^3$ for $x = 2$.

A   Substitute 2 for x in the expression.

$$\boxed{} \cdot \left(4 \cdot \boxed{} - 10\right)^3$$

B   Simplify the expression according to the order of operations.

- Multiply within parentheses.   _____

- Subtract within parentheses.   _____

- Simplify powers.   _____

- Multiply.   _____

REFLECT

2a. Explain why x and $4x - 10$ are factors of the expression $x(4x - 10)^3$ rather than terms of the expression. What are the terms of the factor $4x - 10$?

_____

_____

2b. Evaluate $5a + 3b$ and $(5 + a)(3 + b)$ for $a = 2$ and $b = 4$. How is the order of the steps different for the two expressions?

_____

_____

2c. In what order would you perform the operations to correctly evaluate the expression $2 + (3 - 4) \cdot 9$? What is the result?

_____

2d. Show how to move the parentheses in the expression $2 + (3 - 4) \cdot 9$ so that the value of the expression is 9.

_____

Unit Analysis When evaluating expressions that represent real-world situations, you should pay attention to the units of measurement attached to the parts of the expression. For instance, if p people go to a restaurant and agree to split the $50 cost of the meal equally, then the units in the numerator of the expression $\frac{50}{p}$ are *dollars*, the units in the denominator are *people*, and the units for the value of the expression are *dollars per person*.

© Houghton Mifflin Harcourt Publishing Company

A Sheila is participating in a multi-day bike trip. On the first day, she rode 100 miles in 8 hours. Use the expression $\frac{d}{t}$ where d is the distance traveled and t is the travel time to find her average rate of travel. Include units when evaluating the expression.

$$\frac{d}{t} = \underline{\hspace{3cm}} = \underline{\hspace{4cm}}$$

B If Sheila continues riding at her average rate for the first day, then the expression $100 + 12.5t$ gives the total distance that she has traveled after riding for t hours on the second day. Evaluate this expression when $t = 7$, and include units.

$$100 + 12.5t = 100 \underline{\hspace{2cm}} + 12.5 \underline{\hspace{2.5cm}} \cdot \underline{\hspace{2cm}}$$

$$= \underline{\hspace{3cm}}$$

REFLECT

3a. What are the terms in the expression $100 + 12.5t$? What does each term represent in the context of Sheila's bike trip?

_____

_____

3b. What is the coefficient of the term $12.5t$? What does it represent in the context of Sheila's bike trip?

_____

_____

3c. If you write only the units for the expression $100 + 12.5t$, you get $\text{mi} + \frac{\text{mi}}{\text{h}} \cdot \text{h}$ where "mi" is the abbreviation for miles and "h" is the abbreviation for hours. Explain what the following *unit analysis* shows:

$$\text{mi} + \frac{\text{mi}}{\cancel{\text{h}}} \cdot \cancel{\text{h}} = \text{mi} + \text{mi} = \text{mi}$$

_____

_____

3d. How can you modify the expression $100 + 12.5t$ so that the units are feet when the expression is evaluated?

_____

PRACTICE

Identify the terms of each expression and the coefficient of each term.

1. $7x + 8y$

2. $a - b$

3. $3m^2 - 6n$

Evaluate each expression for $a = 2$, $b = 3$, and $c = -6$.

4. $7a - 5b + 4$

5. $b^2(c + 4)$

6. $8 - 2ab$

7. $a^2 + b^2 - c^2$

8. $(a - c)(c + 5)$

9. $12 - 2(a - b)^2$

10. $a + (b - c)^2$

11. $(a + b) - ab$

12. $5a^2 + bc^2$

13. Henry drives in town at a rate of 25 miles per hour. It takes him 15 minutes to go to the library from his house. The algebraic expression rt represents distance traveled, where r is the average rate (in miles per hour) and t is the travel time (in hours).

    a. Can you multiply 25 and 15 to find the distance Henry traveled to the library? Explain.

    b. Show how to find the distance from Henry's house to the library. Include units in your calculation.

14. Sarah works 4 hours her first week of a part-time job and earns \$60. Her total pay after the second week can be represented by the expression $60 + \frac{p}{t} \cdot s$ where p represents her pay for t hours of work and s represents the hours she works in the second week.

    a. What are the units of the fraction?

    b. Rewrite the expression substituting the given values for p and t. What are the units of each term of your new expression? Explain.

    c. Evaluate your expression for $s = 5$. Include units.

Simplifying Expressions

Essential question: *How can you rewrite algebraic expressions?*

COMMON
CORE

CC.9-12.N.Q.1*,
CC.9-12.A.SSE.1*,
CC.9-12.A.SSE.1a*,
CC.9-12.A.SSE.2

1 EXPLORE   Comparing Expressions

A soccer field has a length *l* of 105 m and a width *w* of 68 m.

A   Use the expression $2\ell + 2w$ to find the perimeter of the field.

_____

B   Using the expression $2(\ell + w)$, what is the perimeter of the field?

_____

C   What do the results suggest about $2\ell + 2w$ and $2(\ell + w)$?

_____

The Explore above illustrates the **Distributive Property**. The table below summarizes this and other important properties of real numbers.

Property	Addition	Multiplication
Commutative	$a + b = b + a$	$ab = ba$
Associative	$(a + b) + c = a + (b + c)$	$(ab)c = a(bc)$
Distributive	$a(b + c) = ab + ac$ $(b + c)a = ba + ca$	

REFLECT

1a. Identify the property being illustrated.

- $2x + 7x = (2 + 7)x$, which equals $9x$ _____

- $(x + 1) + 9 = x + (1 + 9)$, which equals $x + 10$ _____

- $5 + x + 3 = x + 5 + 3$, which equals $x + 8$ _____

1b. *Like terms* contain the same variables raised to the same power. In part a, how was the Distributive Property used to combine like terms?

_____

_____

1c. Constant terms are also considered like terms. In part a, how were properties used to combine constant terms?

_____

_____

© Houghton Mifflin Harcourt Publishing Company

1d. You can use the fact that subtracting a number is the same as adding its opposite in order to apply properties of real numbers to subtraction expressions. Identify the property being illustrated.

$$2(3x - 4) - 7x = 2(3x + (-4)) + (-7x) \qquad \text{Add the opposite.}$$

$$= 6x + (-8) + (-7x) \qquad \rule{4cm}{0.4pt}$$

$$= 6x + (-7x) + (-8) \qquad \rule{4cm}{0.4pt}$$

$$= (6 + (-7))x + (-8) \qquad \rule{4cm}{0.4pt}$$

$$= -x + (-8) \qquad \text{Add.}$$

$$= -x - 8 \qquad \text{Write without parentheses.}$$

To *simplify* an algebraic expression, you use properties of real numbers to combine like terms and eliminate any grouping symbols.

2 EXAMPLE Using Properties to Simplify Expressions

Simplify each expression.

A For a picnic, you buy p packages of chicken hot dogs at $3.99 per package and p packages of hot dog buns at $2.19 per package. The expression $3.99p + 2.19p$ can be used to represent the total cost.

$$3.99p + 2.19p = (3.99 + 2.19) \cdot \boxed{} \qquad \text{Distributive Property}$$

$$= \boxed{}$$

B Suppose that you need one more package of hot dogs than buns. Then the expression $3.99(p + 1) + 2.19p$ represents the total cost.

$$3.99(p + 1) + 2.19p = \boxed{} + \boxed{} + 2.19p \qquad \text{Distributive Property}$$

$$= 3.99p + \boxed{} + 3.99 \qquad \text{Commutative Property}$$

$$= \boxed{} + 3.99 \qquad \text{Distributive Property}$$

C Suppose that you need one more package of buns than hotdogs. Then the expression $3.99p + [2.19(p + 1)]$ represents the total cost.

$$3.99p + [2.19(p + 1)] = 3.99p + \left[\boxed{} + \boxed{} \right] \qquad \text{Distributive Property}$$

$$= \left[\boxed{} + \boxed{} \right] + 2.19 \qquad \text{Associative Property}$$

$$= \boxed{} + 2.19 \qquad \text{Distributive Property}$$

2a. What are the units of each coefficient of the expression $3.99p + 2.19p$ from the Example? What are the units of p?

_____

2b. What are the units of each term of the expression $3.99p + 2.19p$? Use unit analysis to explain.

_____

2c. What are the units of the expression $3.99p + 2.19p$? Use unit analysis to explain.

_____

2d. Explain two ways of finding the total cost of 4 packages of hot dogs and buns, using the expression $3.99p + 2.19p$.

_____

_____

PRACTICE

Identify the property being illustrated.

1. $a(9 - 7) = (9 - 7)a$

_____

2. $8m + (9m + 2) = (8m + 9m) + 2$

3. $6(5x + 2) = 30x + 12$

_____

4. $12n + 5n = (12 + 5)n$

5. $9 + (3b + 8) = (3b + 8) + 9$

_____

6. $k + 5k + 8 = (1 + 5)k + 8$

Simplify the expression.

7. $12x + 4y + 3x + y$

_____

8. $a - 4 + 7a + 11$

9. $6(n - 8) - 4n$

_____

10. $10k - (k + 3) + 2$

11. $-2(2x - 5) + 5x + 6$

_____

12. $4(x + y) - 5x - y$

13. $8b + 3(2b + c) - 3$

_____

14. $x - 5(y + 2) + (3x + 1)$

For Exercises 15–17, simplify each expression and identify the units.

15. You purchase n cans of tennis balls at $4.50 per can from an online retailer. There is a tax of 8% on your order. There are also shipping costs of $7 per order. The expression $4.5n + 0.08(4.5n) + 7$ can be used to represent the total cost.

_____

16. You and two friends all have the same meal for lunch. Each meal costs c dollars plus a tax of 6% of the cost and a tip of 20% of the cost. You use a $10 gift certificate. You can represent the total cost with the expression $3c + (0.06 + 0.20)(3c) - 10$.

_____

17. You are making n loaves of bread for a bake sale and the recipe calls for 3.25 cups of flour per loaf. You are also making $n + 1$ pies for the bake sale, and the pie recipe calls for 2 cups of flour per pie. The expression $3.25n + 2(n + 1)$ can be used to represent the total amount of flour required for the bread and the pies.

_____

18. You burn calories at a rate of 15 calories per minute when running and 6 calories per minute when walking. Suppose you exercise for 60 minutes by running for r minutes and walking for the remaining time. The expression $15r + 6(60 - r)$ represents the calories burned.

a. What units are associated with r? What units are associated with 15? What does $15r$ represent? Use unit analysis to explain.

_____

b. What does $60 - r$ represent? What units are associated with $6(60 - r)$?

_____

c. Simplify $15r + 6(60 - r)$. What units are associated with the expression? Use unit analysis to explain.

_____

19. Error Analysis A student says that the perimeter of a rectangle with side lengths $(2x - 1)$ inches and $3x$ inches can be written as $(10x - 1)$ inches, because $2(2x - 1) + 2(3x) = 10x - 1$. Explain why this statement is incorrect.

_____

_____

Writing Expressions

Essential question: *How do you write algebraic expressions to model quantities?*

CC.9-12.N.Q.1*,
CC.9-12.N.Q.2*,
CC.9-12.A.SSE.1*,
CC.9-12.A.SSE.1a*,
CC.9-12.A.SSE.2

COMMON CORE

1 ENGAGE Writing Algebraic Expressions

The table shows some words associated with the four arithmetic operations.
They can help you translate verbal phrases into algebraic expressions.

Operation	Words	Examples
addition	plus, the sum of, added to, more than, increased by, how many altogether	• the sum of a number and 3 • a number increased by 3 $n + 3$
subtraction	minus, less, less than, the difference of, subtracted from, reduced by, how many more, how many less	• the difference of a number and 3 • 3 less than a number $n - 3$
multiplication	times, multiply, the product of, twice, double, triple, percent of	• the product of 0.4 and a number • 40% of a number $0.4n$
division	divide, divided by, divide into, the quotient of, half of, one-third of, the ratio of	• the quotient of a number and 3 • one-third of a number $n \div 3$, or $\frac{n}{3}$

REFLECT

The verbal phrase "the quotient of 3 more than a number and 5" can be modeled as follows:

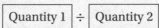

Quantity 1 ÷ Quantity 2

1a. What words in the phrase represent Quantity 1? Translate these words into an algebraic expression using *n* for the variable.

_____

1b. Write an algebraic expression to represent the overall phrase. Explain why you have to use some sort of grouping symbol.

_____

1c. Show two ways to rewrite the verbal phrase so that it could be represented by the algebraic expression $5 \div (n + 3)$.

_____

You can create a verbal model to help you translate a verbal expression into an algebraic expression.

2 EXAMPLE Modeling with Algebraic Expressions

Write an algebraic expression to model the following phrase:
the price of a meal plus a 15% tip for the meal.

A Complete the verbal model.

| Price of meal (dollars) | | 15% | | Price of meal (dollars) |

B Choose a variable for the unknown quantity. Include units.

Let _____ represent the _____.

C Write an algebraic expression for the situation. Simplify, if possible.

_____

REFLECT

2a. A 15% tip represents the ratio 15 cents to 100 cents. Why does this make 15% a *unit-less* factor?

_____

_____

2b. What units are associated with the total cost? Explain.

_____

_____

2c. What could the expression $\frac{p + 0.15p}{2}$ represent, including units?

_____

_____

_____

2d. What if the tip is 20% instead of 15%? How can you represent the total cost with a simplified algebraic expression? Identify the units for the expression.

_____

2e. What if the tip is 20% instead of 15% and 3 people are sharing the cost evenly? How can you represent the amount that each person pays with a simplified algebraic expression? Identify the units for the expression.

_____

EXAMPLE Using Unit Analysis to Guide Modeling

Lizzie has volunteered 20 hours at her town library. From now on, she plans to volunteer 5 hours per week at the library. Write an algebraic expression to represent the total number of hours she will volunteer.

A Use unit analysis to help you get the correct units for the expression.

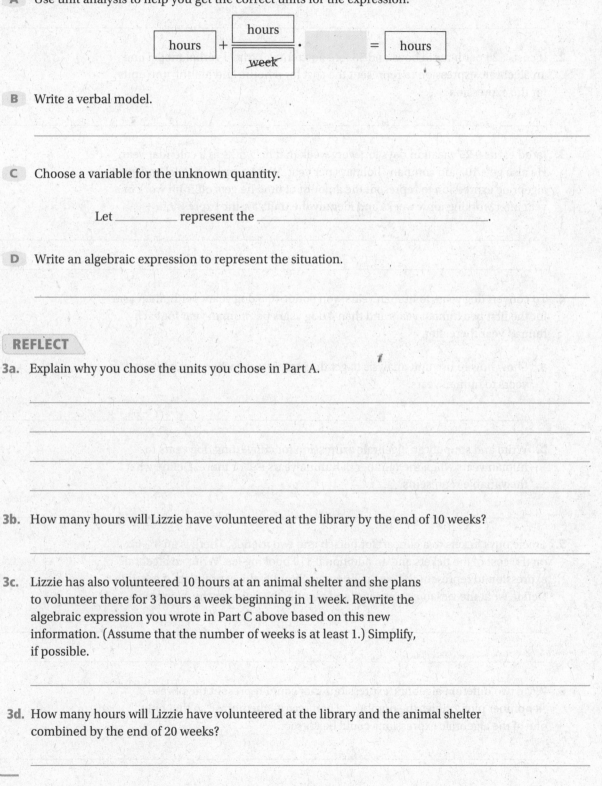

$$\boxed{\text{hours}} + \boxed{\dfrac{\text{hours}}{\text{week}}} \cdot \boxed{} = \boxed{\text{hours}}$$

B Write a verbal model.

_____

C Choose a variable for the unknown quantity.

Let _____ represent the _____.

D Write an algebraic expression to represent the situation.

_____

REFLECT

3a. Explain why you chose the units you chose in Part A.

_____

_____

_____

_____

3b. How many hours will Lizzie have volunteered at the library by the end of 10 weeks?

_____

3c. Lizzie has also volunteered 10 hours at an animal shelter and she plans to volunteer there for 3 hours a week beginning in 1 week. Rewrite the algebraic expression you wrote in Part C above based on this new information. (Assume that the number of weeks is at least 1.) Simplify, if possible.

_____

3d. How many hours will Lizzie have volunteered at the library and the animal shelter combined by the end of 20 weeks?

_____

1. Alex purchased a 6-hour calling card. He has used t minutes of access time. Write an algebraic expression to represent how many minutes he has remaining and identify the units for the expression.

_____

2. It costs $20 per hour to bowl and $3 for shoe rental. Write a verbal model and an algebraic expression to represent the cost for n hours and identify the units for the expression.

_____

3. Jared earns 0.25 vacation days for every week that he works in a calendar year. He also gets 10 paid company holidays per year. Write a verbal model and an algebraic expression to represent the amount of time he gets off from work in a year after working for w weeks and identify the units for the expression.

_____

_____

4. To convert dog years to human years, you count 10.5 dog years per human year for the first two human years and then 4 dog years per human year for each human year thereafter.

   a. Show how to use unit analysis to get the correct units when you convert dog years to human years.

   _____

   b. Write and simplify an algebraic expression for converting dog years to human years when the number of human years is 2 or more. Define what the variable represents.

   _____

5. Tracie buys tickets to a concert for herself and two friends. There is an 8% tax on the cost of the tickets and an additional $10 booking fee. Write an algebraic expression to represent the cost per person. Simplify the expression, if possible. Define what the variable represents and identify the units for the expression.

_____

_____

6. Write two different algebraic expressions that could represent the phrase "a number plus 2 times the number." Then rewrite the phrase so that only one of the algebraic expressions could be correct.

_____

_____

Writing Equations and Inequalities

COMMON CORE

CC.9-12.N.Q.2*,
CC.9-12.A.CED.1*,
CC.9-12.A.CED.3*

Essential question: *How do you represent relationships algebraically?*

An algebraic expression is a phrase. It represents a value. *Equations* and *inequalities* represent relationships between expressions. An **equation** is a mathematical statement that two expressions are equivalent. The **solution of an equation** is the value or values that make the equation true.

1 EXAMPLE Writing Equations

Leon paid $26.50 for a shirt with a sales tax of 6% included but he doesn't remember the price without tax. Write an equation to represent the situation.

A Complete the verbal model for the situation.

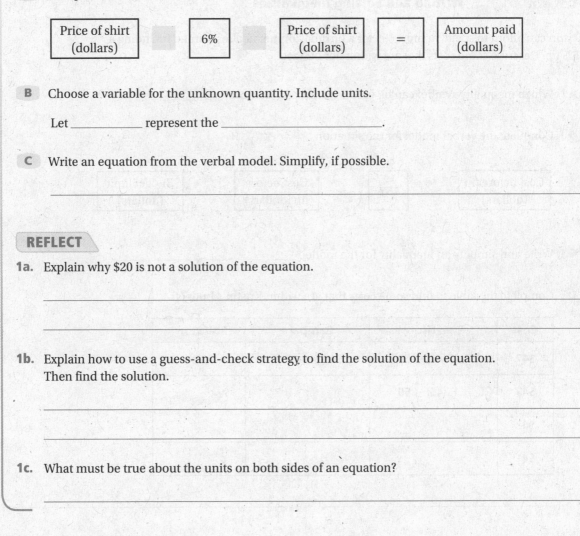

| Price of shirt (dollars) | | 6% | | Price of shirt (dollars) | = | Amount paid (dollars) |

B Choose a variable for the unknown quantity. Include units.

Let _____ represent the _____.

C Write an equation from the verbal model. Simplify, if possible.

_____

_____

REFLECT

1a. Explain why $20 is not a solution of the equation.

_____

_____

1b. Explain how to use a guess-and-check strategy to find the solution of the equation. Then find the solution.

_____

_____

1c. What must be true about the units on both sides of an equation?

_____

An **inequality** is a statement that compares two expressions that are not strictly equal by using one of the following inequality signs.

Symbol	Meaning
<	is less than
≤	is less than or equal to
>	is greater than
≥	is greater than or equal to
≠	is not equal to

A **solution of an inequality** is any value of the variable that makes the inequality true. You can find solutions by making a table.

2 EXAMPLE Writing and Solving Inequalities

Kristin can afford to spend at most $50 for a birthday dinner at a restaurant, including a 15% tip. Describe some costs that are within her budget.

A Which inequality symbol can be used to represent "at most"? _____

B Complete the verbal model for the situation.

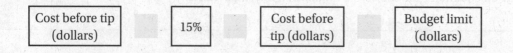

| Cost before tip (dollars) | | 15% | | Cost before tip (dollars) | | Budget limit (dollars) |

C Write and simplify an inequality for the model. _____

D Complete the table to find some costs that are within Kristin's budget.

Cost	Substitute	Compare	Solution?
$47	1.15(47) ≤ 50	54.05 ≤ 50 ✗	No
$45	1.15(45) ≤ 50		
$43			
$41			

© Houghton Mifflin Harcourt Publishing Company

2a. Can Kristin spend $40 on the meal before the tip? Explain.

_____

_____

2b. What whole dollar amount is the most Kristin can spend before the tip? Explain.

_____

_____

2c. The *solution set* of an equation or inequality consists of all values that make the statement true. Describe the whole dollar amounts that are in the solution set for this situation.

_____

_____

2d. Suppose Kristin also has to pay a 6% meal tax. Write an inequality to represent the new situation. Then identify two solutions.

_____

_____

PRACTICE

Tell whether each value of the variable is a solution of the equation $1.06p = 53$. Show your reasoning.

1. $p = 40$

_____

2. $p = 45$

_____

3. $p = 50$

_____

4. $p = 55$

_____

Tell whether each value of the variable is a solution of the equation $1.06p = 41.34$. Show your reasoning.

5. $p = 36$

_____

6. $p = 39$

_____

7. $p = 42$

_____

8. $p = 45$

_____

9. Janelle tips 20% for service at restaurants. When she left a restaurant, she saw the total she paid for her meal was $14.82.

a. Complete the verbal model for the situation.

| Price of meal (dollars) | | 20% | | Price of meal (dollars) | | = | | Amount paid (dollars) |

b. Choose a variable for the unknown quantity. Include units.

Let _____ represent the _____ .

c. Write an equation from the verbal model. Simplify, if possible.

_____

d. Solve the equation using a guess-and-check strategy. Show your work.

_____

_____

_____

10. Mark buys 5 movie tickets online for $60. The online fee for each ticket is $1.50.

a. Write a verbal model for the situation.

_____

b. Write an equation from the verbal model. Simplify, if possible.

_____

c. Solve the equation using a guess-and-check strategy. Show your work.

_____

_____

11. Ellie received a 15% discount for renewing a magazine subscription. She paid $26.35. Write an equation to find the price before the discount. Solve the equation using a guess-and-check strategy. Show your work.

_____

_____

_____

Tell whether the value is a solution of the inequality. Explain.

12. $x = 36; 3x < 100$ **13.** $m = 12; 5m + 4 > 50$ **14.** $b = 5; 60 - 10b \leq 20$

_____   _____   _____

15. Brent is ordering books for a reading group. Each book costs $11.95. If he orders at least $200 worth of books, he will get free shipping.

     a. Complete the verbal model for the situation.

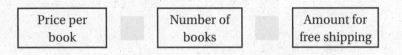

| Price per book | | Number of books | | Amount for free shipping |

     b. Choose a variable for the unknown quantity. Include units.

        Let _____ represent the _____.

     c. Write an inequality from the verbal model.

_____

     d. Complete the table to find some numbers of books Brent can order and receive free shipping.

Books	Substitute	Compare	Solution?
15	$11.95(15) \geq 200$	$179.25 \geq 200$ ✗	No
16			
17			
18			

_____

16. Farzana has a prepaid cell phone that costs $1 per day plus $.10 per minute she uses. She has a daily budget of $5 for phone costs.

     a. Write an inequality to represent the situation.

_____

     b. What is the maximum number of minutes Farzana can use and still stay within her daily budget? Show your reasoning.

_____

     c. Describe the solution set of the inequality.

_____

Representing Functions

Essential question: *How do you represent functions?*

COMMON
CORE

CC.9-12.N.Q.1*,
CC.9-12.F.IF.1,
CC.9-12.F.IF.2,
CC.9-12.F.IF.5*

1 ENGAGE   **Understanding Functions**

A *set* is a collection of items called *elements*. A **function** pairs each element in one set, called the **domain**, with exactly one element in a second set, called the **range**. For example, the function below pairs each element in the domain with its square.

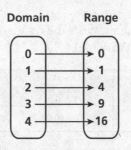

A function can be described using **function notation**. The function *f* assigns the *output* value $f(x)$ in the range to the corresponding *input* value x from the domain. The notation $f(x)$ is read as "*f* of *x*." (It does not indicate the product "*f* times *x*.") For the function shown above, $f(3) = 9$.

REFLECT

1a. The domain of the function can be written using *set notation* as {0, 1, 2, 3, 4}. Write the range of the function using set notation.

_____

1b. Tell how to read the statement $f(4) = 16$. Then interpret what it means in terms of input and output values.

_____

1c. Suppose the 3 were paired with the 4 instead of the 9. Would the pairing of the two sets still be a function? Why or why not?

_____

1d. Suppose the 3 were paired with the 4 and the 9. Would the pairing of the two sets still be a function? Why or why not?

_____

1e. If you pair each month with all the possible numbers of days in the month, will you get a function? Why or why not?

_____

_____

Functions are often used to describe a relationship between two variables. The **independent variable** represents an input value of the function and the **dependent variable** represents an output value.

An algebraic expression that defines a function is a **function rule**. For example, x^2 is the function rule for the squaring function $f(x) = x^2$. If you know a value for the independent variable, you can use a function rule to find the corresponding value for the dependent variable.

2 EXAMPLE Representing Discrete Linear Functions

The cost of sending m text messages at $0.25 per message can be represented by the function $C(m) = 0.25m$.

A Complete the table for the given domain values. Write the results as ordered pairs in the form (independent variable, dependent variable).

Independent variable, m	Dependent variable, $C(m) = 0.25m$	$(m, C(m))$
0	$0.25(0) = 0$	$(0, 0)$
1		
2		
3		
4		

B Choose a beginning, an end, and a scale for the vertical axis.

_____

C Graph the function by plotting the ordered pairs. The independent variable goes on the horizontal axis and the dependent variable on the vertical axis. Use scales that will make it easy to read points. Label the graph.

© Houghton Mifflin Harcourt Publishing Company

2a. Use function notation to represent the cost of sending 15 text messages. Evaluate the function for that value. Include units.

_____

2b. Suppose that the domain of the function is not limited as in the Example. Describe a reasonable domain of the function.

_____

_____

2c. Suppose that the domain of the function is not limited as in the Example. Describe a reasonable range of the function.

_____

_____

2d. Is the independent variable represented by the _horizontal axis_ or the _vertical axis_? Why does this make sense?

_____

_____

_____

2e. Would it make sense to connect the points on the graph with a line? Why or why not?

_____

_____

2f. The figure below shows a representation of the function rule. Explain what is being shown in the context of the situation.

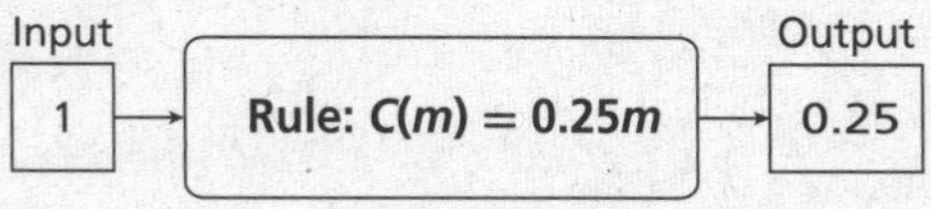

Input   Output

$1 \rightarrow$ Rule: $C(m) = 0.25m \rightarrow 0.25$

_____

_____

_____

2g. Suppose the cost per text message were $0.20 instead of $0.25. Then the cost of sending m text messages could be represented by the function $C(m) = 0.2m$. Describe a reasonable domain and range for this function.

_____

_____

Ben wants to tile part of a floor with 36 square tiles. The tiles come in whole-number side lengths from 2 to 6 inches. If s is the side length of a tile, the area that he can cover is $A(s) = 36s^2$.

A Identify the domain of the function.

B Make a table of values for this domain. Write the results as ordered pairs in the form (independent variable, dependent variable).

Independent variable, s	Dependent variable, $A(s) = 36s^2$	$(s, A(s))$

C Choose a beginning, an end, and a scale for the vertical axis.

D Graph the function by plotting the ordered pairs.

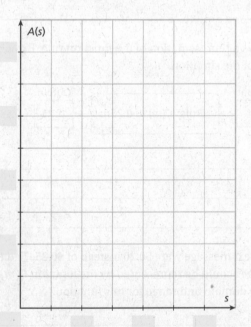

3a. Identify the range of the function.

_____

3b. What does $A(3) = 324$ mean in this context?

_____

_____

3c. Describe another reasonable beginning, end, and scale for the vertical axis. Include units.

_____

3d. Do the points appear to lie in a straight line?

_____

PRACTICE

Tell whether each pairing of numbers describes a function. If so, identify the domain and the range. If not, explain why not.

1. Each whole number from 0 to 9 is paired with its opposite.

_____

2. Each odd number from 3 to 9 is paired with the next greater whole number.

_____

3. The whole numbers from 10 to 12 are paired with their factors.

_____

_____

4. Each even number from 2 to 10 is paired with half the number.

_____

5. $\{(36, 6), (49, 7), (64, 8), (81, 9), (36, -6), (49, -7), (64, -8), (81, -9)\}$

_____

6. $\{(-64, -4), (-27, -3), (-8, -2), (-1, -1), (0, 0), (1, 1), (8, 2), (27, 3), (64, 4)\}$

_____

_____

7. Whitley has a $5 gift card for music downloads. Each song costs $1 to download. The amount of money left on the card can be represented by the function $M(d) = 5 - d$, where d is the number of songs she has downloaded.

a. Make a table and graph the function.

d.	M(d)	(d, M(d))

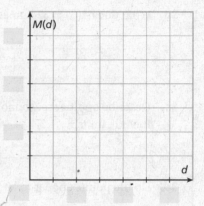

b. Identify the domain and range of the function and the units of the independent and dependent variables.

_____

_____

8. Ben wants to cover a table that has an area of 864 square inches. The function $T(s) = \frac{864}{s^2}$ gives the number of tiles he needs with side length s. The tiles come in side lengths of 1 in., 4 in., 6 in., and 12 in.

a. Make a table and graph the function.

s	T(s)	(s, T(s))

b. Identify the domain and range of the function and the units of the independent and dependent variables.

_____

_____

FOCUS ON MODELING
Modeling with Functions

Essential question: *How can you model paying off a loan using a function?*

COMMON
CORE

CC.9-12.N.Q.1*,
CC.9-12.F.IF.1,
CC.9-12.F.IF.2,
CC.9-12.F.IF.5*,
CC.9-12.F.BF.1*,
CC.9-12.F.BF.1a*

Jenna received an interest free loan of $100 to buy a new pair of running shoes. She plans to make monthly loan payments of $20 per month until the loan is paid off. At what point will Jenna pass the halfway mark with her loan payments?

1 **Write an equation for the function from the given information.**

A The balance owed is a function of the number of monthly payments. What are the units for a payment? for the number of payments?

_____

B Complete the verbal model for the balance function. Include units.

| Balance owed (dollars) | = | Loan amount (dollars) | − | | · | |

C Write a function rule for the balance function.

$B(p) =$ _____

> **REFLECT**

1a. What units are associated with the variable term in the function rule? Justify your answer using unit analysis.

_____

1b. Find the value of $B(0)$. Tell what it represents and whether it agrees with the original problem statement.

_____

_____

1c. Suppose Jenna instead makes weekly payments of $20 per week. What are the units for a payment? for the number of payments?

_____

1d. What types of numbers are appropriate for the domain of $B(p)$? _____

1e. Write a pair of inequalities that restrict the range of the function $B(p)$.

$B(p) \geq$ _____ and $B(p) \leq$ _____

2 Make a table and a graph to represent the function.

A Make a table of values for the balance function.

Independent variable, p	Dependent variable, $B(p)$	$(p, B(p))$

B Choose a beginning, an end, and a scale for the vertical axis.

_____

C Graph the balance function.

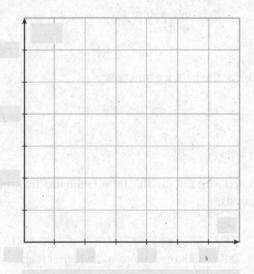

Rules

REFLECT

2a. Identify the domain of the balance function.

_____

2b. Identify the range of the balance function.

_____

3 **Analyze the balance function models.**

A Give the coordinates of the point where the dependent variable is 0. Interpret the meaning of this point in the original situation.

_____

_____

B At what value of p does $B(p)$ have its maximum value? What is the maximum value?

_____

C At what point will Jenna pass the halfway mark with her loan payments? Explain your reasoning.

_____

_____

_____

_____

REFLECT

3a. Will the balance on the loan ever be exactly $70? Why or why not?

_____

_____

3b. Is it reasonable to connect the points on the graph with a straight line? Why or why not?

_____

3c. Suppose the amount of money borrowed were $120 instead of $100. What would be the domain and the range of the balance function? How long would it take to pay off the loan?

_____

_____

3d. Suppose the monthly loan payments on the $100 loan were $10 per month instead of $20 per month. What would be the domain and the range of the balance function? How long would it take to pay off the loan?

_____

_____

1. The table shows the balance owed on an interest free loan as a function $B(p)$ of the number of monthly payments p.

   a. Identify the domain and the range of the function.

   _____

   b. What is the initial amount of the loan? What is the monthly payment? Explain.

   _____

   _____

   _____

   c. Compare this function with the function discussed in Steps 1–3?

   _____

   _____

P	(p, B(p))
0	(0, 120)
1	(1, 90)
2	(2, 60)
3	(3, 30)
4	(4, 0)

2. After Jenna pays off her loan, she deposits $20 per month into a savings account with an initial balance of $40.

   a. The account balance is a function of the number of deposits. Model this function with an equation, a table, and a graph, using selected domain values and reasonable scales. Include appropriate axis labels.

   Equation: _____

d	B(d)	(d, B(d))

   b. Describe the domain and range using set notation. In how many months will Jenna have $120 in the account? Explain.

   _____

   _____

Name _____ Class _____ Date _____

MULTIPLE CHOICE

1. Evaluate $x^2 + 3x - 18$ for $x = 3$.

   A. -6

   B. 0

   C. 6

   D. 9

2. Simplify $4n + 2(3n - 5) - 8 + n$.

   F. $8n - 13$

   G. $9n - 8$

   H. $10n - 2$

   J. $11n - 18$

3. It costs \$75 per hour plus a \$65 service fee to have a home theater system set up for you. Let t represent the number of hours. Which expression represents the total cost?

   A. $75t + 65$

   B. $65t + 75$

   C. $140t$

   D. $75t$

4. Elizabeth and her friend purchase identical team shirts to wear to a football game. There is a 7% sales tax. If c represents the cost of the two shirts without tax, which algebraic expression represents the tax for one shirt?

   F. $\frac{c}{2}$

   G. $\frac{0.07c}{2}$

   H. $\frac{1.07c}{2}$

   J. $1.07c$

5. Tia spent \$15 on skating. This included a \$5 charge for renting skates and a \$2.50 per hour fee for skating. How many hours did Tia skate?

   A. 2 hours

   B. 3 hours

   C. 4 hours

   D. 5 hours

6. Which inequality represents the situation: "Alex has at most \$45 to spend on a basketball, including 8% tax?"

   F. $p + 0.08p < 45$

   G. $p + 0.08p > 45$

   H. $p + 0.08p \geq 45$

   J. $p + 0.08p \leq 45$

7. Which set of ordered pairs represents a function?

   A. $\{(-1, 1), (0, 0), (1, 1), (2, 2)\}$

   B. $\{(3, -3), (2, -2), (1, -1), (1, 1)\}$

   C. $\{(4, 2), (4, -2), (9, 3), (9, -3)\}$

   D. $\{(-2, -1), (-2, 0), (-2, 1), (-2, 2)\}$

8. You and three friends plan to split the cost b (in dollars) of a large bag of popcorn at a movie. Which function describes the cost for each person as a function of the cost per bag?

   F. $P(b) = 3b$

   G. $P(b) = \frac{3}{b}$

   H. $P(b) = 4b$

   J. $P(b) = \frac{b}{4}$

9. The art club at Lily's school has had 300 calendars printed to sell as a fundraiser. It costs the art club $4 per calendar to have the calendars printed and the club sells them for $10 per calendar. The art club's profit $P(n)$ is given by the following function, where n represents the number of calendars sold.

$$P(n) = 10n - 1200$$

a. What does the term "$10n$" represent? What are its units? Explain your reasoning using unit analysis.

_____

_____

_____

_____

b. What does the term "1200" represent? Explain your reasoning.

_____

_____

_____

_____

c. If you were going to graph the function, what scale would you use for the horizontal axis? for the vertical axis?

_____

_____

_____

_____

10. Henry purchased a roll of 100 stamps. He uses 5 stamps each week.

a. The number of stamps at the end of each week is a function $S(w)$ of the number of weeks. Write an equation for the function.

_____

b. What types of numbers are reasonable for the domain and the range?

_____

_____

_____

c. Complete the table using selected domain values. Then graph the function.

w	S(w)	(w, S(w))

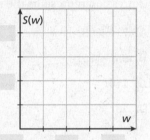

d. At the end of how many weeks will Henry have one quarter of the stamps left? Explain your reasoning.

_____

_____

Linear Equations and Inequalities

Unit Focus

In Unit 1 you learned about expressions and how to simplify terms. In this unit you will build on this skill to simplify and solve linear equations and inequalities. You will also work with literal equations and inequalities, which are related to formulas, and practice rewriting formulas so that they focus on a given quantity. Finally, you will write, solve, and graph linear equations and inequalities in two variables.

Unit at a Glance

COMMON CORE

© Houghton Mifflin Harcourt Publishing Company

UNIT 2

Unpacking the Common Core State Standards

Use the table to help you understand the Standards for Mathematical Content that are taught in this unit. Refer to the lessons listed after each standard for exploration and practice.

COMMON CORE Standards for Mathematical Content	What It Means For You
CC.9-12.N.Q.1 Use units as a way to understand problems and to guide the solution of multi-step problems; choose and interpret units consistently in formulas; choose and interpret the scale and the origin in graphs and data displays.* Lessons 2-3, 2-8	When you write equations and inequalities for real-world situations, you should consider the units attached to the variables, coefficients, and constants. Keeping units in mind can help you write equations and inequalities correctly.
CC.9-12.N.Q.2 Define appropriate quantities for the purpose of descriptive modeling.* Lessons 2-3, 2-8	When you solve real-world problems, you identify quantities that are unknown or that vary, and you use variables to represent those quantities.
CC.9-12.A.SSE.1 Interpret expressions that represent a quantity in terms of its context.* **CC.9-12.A.SSE.1a Interpret parts of an expression, such as terms, factors, and coefficients.*** Lesson 2-8	When you write expressions to represent real-world quantities, you should be able to recognize the real-world significance of the parts of the expressions.
CC.9-12.A.SSE.2 Use the structure of an expression to identify ways to rewrite it. Lessons 2-1, 2-2	A basic algebraic skill is recognizing how all the parts in an expression work together. Understanding the relationships between these parts will help you simplify or rewrite the expression.
CC.9-12.A.CED.1 Create equations and inequalities in one variable and use them to solve problems.* Lesson 2-3	Equations and inequalities in one variable can be used to solve problems that have an unknown value.
CC.9-12.A.CED.2 Create equations in two or more variables to represent relationships between quantities; graph equations on coordinate axes with labels and scales.* Lessons 2-5, 2-8	An equation in two variables represents the relationship between two quantities. Once you can express this relationship mathematically, you can graph it in a coordinate plane.
CC.9-12.A.CED.3 Represent constraints by equations or inequalities, and by systems of equations and/or inequalities, and interpret solutions as viable or nonviable options in a modeling context.* Lessons 2-3, 2-8	Variable quantities may be able to take on only certain values, and expressing those restrictions, or constraints, algebraically is an important part of modeling with mathematics.

COMMON CORE Standards for Mathematical Content	What It Means For You
CC.9-12.A.CED.4 Rearrange formulas to highlight a quantity of interest, using the same reasoning as in solving equations.* Lesson 2-5	You can apply the same skills you used in solving equations to rearrange a formula. This is good practice for geometry and the sciences, which rely heavily on formulas.
CC.9-12.A.REI.1 Explain each step in solving a simple equation as following from the equality of numbers asserted at the previous step, starting from the assumption that the original equation has a solution. Construct a viable argument to justify a solution method. Lessons 2-1, 2-2, 2-4	Algebraic properties enable you to arrive at a solution of an equation in a logical step-by-step manner. Knowing the properties of equality can not only help you reduce complex equations to simpler ones, but also give you the tools to justify your solution.
CC.9-12.A.REI.3 Solve linear equations and inequalities in one variable, including equations with coefficients represented by letters. Lessons 2-1, 2-2, 2-3, 2-4	Solving linear equations and inequalities in one variable is a basic algebraic skill. Mastering this skill will enable you to solve higher-order equations, such as quadratic equations, later in this course and in more advanced courses in the future.
CC.9-12.A.REI.10 Understand that the graph of an equation in two variables is the set of all its solutions plotted in the coordinate plane, often forming a curve (which could be a line). Lessons 2-6, 2-7	The graph of a linear equation in two variables is a line. Every point on the line is a solution to the equation. Points that are not on the line cannot be solutions to the equation.
CC.9-12.A.REI.12 Graph the solutions to a linear inequality in two variables as a half-plane (excluding the boundary in the case of a strict inequality), and graph the solution set to a system of linear inequalities in two variables as the intersection of the corresponding half-planes. Lessons 2-6, 2-7	The graph of a linear inequality in two variables shows all the possible solutions to the inequality as a shaded region on the coordinate plane. This fact becomes the basis for solving systems of linear inequalities in two variables.
CC.9-12.F.BF.1 Write a function that describes a relationship between two quantities.* **CC.9-12.F.BF.1a Determine an explicit expression ... from a context.*** Lesson 2-8	When an equation in two variables defines one variable in terms of the other, it establishes a functional relationship between the variables. You will write such equations when modeling a fundraiser for a school band.

UNIT 2

Solving Linear Equations

Essential question: *How can you use the properties of equality to support your solution to a linear equation?*

COMMON
CORE

CC.9-12.A.SSE.2,
CC.9-12.A.REI.1,
CC.9-12.A.REI.3

1 ENGAGE Equivalent Equations and the Properties of Equality

Two equations are **equivalent equations** if they have the same solution set. The equations below are equivalent because both have the solution $x = 11$.

$$x - 6 = 5 \qquad\qquad x - 11 = 0$$

$$11 - 6 = 5 \qquad\qquad 11 - 11 = 0$$

The solutions of an equation can be given as one or more equations of the form $x = s$ where s is a solution, as in $x = 11$, or listed using set notation, as in $\{11\}$.

To solve an equation, you perform a series of inverse operations to isolate the variable on one side. When these inverse operations are completed, the other side of the equation is the solution. The properties of equality listed below can be used to justify the steps taken in solving an equation.

Addition Property of Equality	If $a = b$, then $a + c = b + c$.
Subtraction Property of Equality	If $a = b$, then $a - c = b - c$.
Multiplication Property of Equality	If $a = b$, then $ac = bc$.
Division Property of Equality	If $a = b$ and $c \neq 0$, then $\frac{a}{c} = \frac{b}{c}$.

Other properties, such as the Distributive Property and the Substitution Property, are also useful when solving equations.

REFLECT

1a. How might you use the Distributive Property to help solve an equation?

_____

_____

_____

_____

1b. Are the equations $2x + 14 = 8$ and $x = -3$ equivalent? Explain.

_____

_____

_____

_____

E X A M P L E **Solving a One-Step Linear Equation**

Complete the solution to the linear equation. Justify the solution by using the properties of equality.

A

Equation	Solution step	Reason
$x + 9 = 17$	Subtract 9 from both sides.	Subtraction Property of Equality
$\dfrac{}{x =}$		
The solution set is $\{\}$.		

B

Equation	Solution step	Reason
$\dfrac{x}{6} = 12$		
$ \cdot \dfrac{x}{6} = \cdot 12$	Multiply both sides by 6.	Multiplication Property of Equality
$x = $		
The solution set is $\{\}$.		

REFLECT

2a. Which property of equality could you use to solve the equation $4x = 68$? Explain.

_____

_____

_____

2b. Give an example of an equation that could be solved using the Addition Property of Equality. Show the steps of the solution.

_____

_____

_____

2c. Solving a linear equation may take more than one step. Show how to solve $2x + 5 = 13$. Justify your steps.

_____

_____

_____

_____

_____

Justify the steps in solving $\frac{3x}{2} + 7x - 7 = 3(2x + 1)$ by using the properties of equality and other properties.

Equation	Solution steps	Reasons
$\frac{3x}{2} + 7x - 7 = 3(2x + 1)$ $\frac{3x}{2} + 7x - 7 = 6x + 3$	Distribute the 3 on the right side of the equation.	
$\frac{3x}{2} + 7x - 7 = 6x + 3$ $2 \cdot \left(\frac{3x}{2} + 7x - 7\right) = 2 \cdot (6x + 3)$ $3x + 14x - 14 = 12x + 6$	Multiply both sides of the equation by 2, then simplify.	
$3x + 14x - 14 = 12x + 6$ $(3 + 14)x - 14 = 12x + 6$ $17x - 14 = 12x + 6$	Combine like terms.	
$\begin{array}{rcr} 17x - 14 = & & 12x + 6 \\ -12x & & -12x \\ \hline 5x - 14 = & & 6 \end{array}$	Subtract 12x from both sides.	
$\begin{array}{rcr} 5x - 14 = & & 6 \\ +14 & & +14 \\ \hline 5x = & & 20 \end{array}$	Add 14 to both sides.	
$5x = 20$ $\frac{5x}{5} = \frac{20}{5}$ $x = 4$	Divide both sides by 5.	

The solution set is $\{ \}$.

REFLECT

3a. In the example, could the steps have been performed in a different order? Explain.

_____

_____

_____

3b. Would performing the steps in a different order affect the solution to the equation? Why or why not?

_____

_____

Given the functions $f(x) = 3x + 2$ and $g(x) = -x + 10$, find the set of values of x such that $f(x) = g(x)$. Justify your solution by using the properties of equality.

To find the set of values of x such that $f(x) = g(x)$, set the functions equal to one another to get $3x + 2 = -x + 10$. Now solve this equation.

Equation	Solution step	Reason
$3x + 2 = -x + 10$ ◻ ◻ ◻ $=$ ◻	Add x to both sides.	
$4x + 2 = 10$ ◻ ◻ $4x$ $=$ ◻	Subtract 2 from both sides.	
$4x = 8$ $\dfrac{4x}{◻} = \dfrac{8}{◻}$ $x = ◻$	Divide both sides by 4.	

The solution set is {◻}, so $f(x) = g(x)$ when $x = 2$.

REFLECT

4a. In the first step, suppose that you subtracted $3x$ from both sides. How would the rest of the steps change? Would the solution set be different?

_____

_____

_____

_____

4b. What is the solution set of $x = x$? Why?

_____

4c. What statement do you get if you try to solve the equation $x + 2 = x$? Is this statement true or false? What does this mean in terms of the solution set?

_____

Find the solution set for the equation. Use the properties of equality and other properties to justify your solution.

1. $2x - 3 = 9 - x$

_____

_____

_____

_____

_____

_____

_____

2. $4x - 7 = x + 5$

_____

_____

_____

_____

_____

_____

_____

3. $25 + 10(12 - x) = 5(2x - 7)$

_____

_____

_____

_____

_____

_____

_____

_____

_____

4. $\frac{1}{2}(6x + 4) = x + 2(x + 1)$

_____

_____

_____

_____

_____

_____

_____

5. Given the function $f(x) = 5x - 9$, find the set of values of x such that $f(x) = 6$. Justify your solution by using the properties of equality.

_____

_____

_____

_____

_____

_____

6. Given the functions $f(x) = -12x + 7$ and $g(x) = 4x - 9$, find the set of values of x such that $f(x) = g(x)$. Justify your solution by using the properties of equality.

_____

_____

_____

_____

_____

_____

_____

_____

© Houghton Mifflin Harcourt Publishing Company

Solving Linear Inequalities

Essential question: *How do you justify the solution to a linear inequality?*

COMMON CORE

CC.9-12.A.SSE.2,
CC.9-12.A.REI.1,
CC.9-12.A.REI.3

1 EXPLORE   Multiplying or Dividing by a Negative Number

The following two inequalities are true.

$$4 < 5 \qquad\qquad 15 > 12$$

What happens to the inequalities if you multiply both sides of the first inequality by 4 and divide both sides of the second inequality by 3?

$$4 < 5 \qquad\qquad 15 > 12$$

Both statements are still true: 16 is less than 20, and 5 is greater than 4.

Now, multiply the first inequality by -4 and divide the second inequality by -3.
Do not change the inequality symbol when you do these multiplications.

$$4 < 5 \qquad\qquad 15 > 12$$

Is -16 less than -20? No, -16 is closer to 0 than -20 is, so it is greater than -20.
Is -5 greater than -4? No, -5 is farther from 0 than -4, so it is less than -4.

Repeat the multiplication by -4 and the division by -3, but this time reverse the inequality symbol when you do.

$$4 < 5 \qquad\qquad 15 > 12$$

Do you get a true statement in each case? _____

REFLECT

1a. When solving inequalities, if you multiply by a negative number, you

must _____.

1b. When solving inequalities, if you divide by a negative number,

you must _____.

The following properties of inequality are similar to the properties of equality. They can be used to justify the steps in the solution of an inequality. These properties are also true for inequalities involving $\leq$ and $\geq$.

Addition Property of Inequality	If $a > b$, then $a + c > b + c$.
	If $a < b$, then $a + c < b + c$.
Subtraction Property of Inequality	If $a > b$, then $a - c > b - c$.
	If $a < b$, then $a - c < b - c$.
Multiplication Property of Inequality	If $a > b$ and $c > 0$, then $ac > bc$.
	If $a < b$ and $c > 0$, then $ac < bc$.
	If $a > b$ and $c < 0$, then $ac < bc$.
	If $a < b$ and $c < 0$, then $ac > bc$.
Division Property of Inequality	If $a > b$ and $c > 0$, then $\frac{a}{c} > \frac{b}{c}$.
	If $a < b$ and $c > 0$, then $\frac{a}{c} < \frac{b}{c}$.
	If $a > b$ and $c < 0$, then $\frac{a}{c} < \frac{b}{c}$.
	If $a < b$ and $c < 0$, then $\frac{a}{c} > \frac{b}{c}$.

2 EXAMPLE Justifying the Solution of an Inequality

Justify the solution to the inequality $3x - 5 > 4$ by using the properties of inequality.

Inequality	Solution steps	Reasons
$3x - 5 > 4$ $\underline{+5 \quad +5}$ $3x \quad > 9$	Add 5 to both sides.	
$3x > 9$ $\frac{3x}{3} > \frac{9}{3}$ $x > 3$	Divide both sides by 3.	

REFLECT

2a. Suppose the inequality had been $-3x - 5 > 4$. How would the solution have been different?

_____

_____

_____

2b. Give an example of an inequality that could be solved by using the Multiplication Property of Inequality where $c < 0$. Show the steps of the solution.

_____

_____

_____

2c. Compare solving a linear inequality to solving a linear equation. How are the processes similar? How are they different?

_____

_____

_____

Most linear equations have exactly one solution. Most linear inequalities have infinitely many solutions. When representing the solutions using set notation, it is not possible to list all of the solutions in braces. The solution $x \le 1$ is written in set notation as $\{x \mid x \le 1\}$. Read this solution set as "the set of all x such that x is less than or equal to 1."

$$\{ \; x \; \mid \; x \; \le \; 1 \; \}$$

the set of — all x — such that — x is less than or equal to 1

A graph on a number line can also be used to represent the solution set of a linear inequality.

- To represent < or >, mark the endpoint with an empty circle.

- To represent ≤ or ≥, mark the endpoint with a solid circle.

- Shade the part of the line that contains the solution set.

$x > 1$

$x \ge 1$

$x < 1$

$x \le 1$

3 **E X A M P L E**   **Representing the Solution of a Linear Inequality**

Complete the solution of $3x - 5 > 4$. Write the solution set using set notation, and graph your solution on a number line.

$3x - 5 > 4$

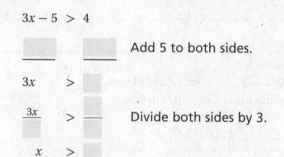

_____   _____   Add 5 to both sides.

$3x$ >   ▢

$\dfrac{3x}{\;}$ >   ▔   Divide both sides by 3.

x >   ▢

Write the solution set using set notation.

_____

Graph the solution set on a number line.

$$\xleftarrow{\quad}\;{-4}\;{-3}\;{-2}\;{-1}\;\;0\;\;1\;\;2\;\;3\;\;4\;\;5\;\;6\;\;7\;\;8\;\;9\;\xrightarrow{\quad}$$

REFLECT

3a. Is 3 in the solution set of the inequality? Why or why not?

_____

_____

3b. Name three values that are in the solution set.

_____

3c. Suppose the inequality symbol had been $\geq$. Describe the solution.

_____

_____

3d. Suppose the inequality symbol had been $\leq$. Describe the solution.

_____

_____

PRACTICE

1. Given the function $f(x) = 16 - 9x$, for what values of x is $f(x) \leq 7$? Use the properties of inequality and other properties to justify your solution.

_____

_____

_____

_____

_____

_____

Solution set: _____

2. Given the functions $f(x) = 3(x - 4)$ and $g(x) = 2(x - 3)$, for what values of x is $f(x) > g(x)$? Use the properties of inequality and other properties to justify your solution.

_____

_____

_____

_____

_____

_____

Solution set: _____

Solve the linear inequality and justify your solution. Write your answer in set notation. Graph the solution on the number line.

3. $7x - 1 > 13$

_____

_____

_____

_____

_____

Solution set: _____

4. $12 - 3x \leq 6$

_____

_____

_____

_____

_____

Solution set: _____

5. $7(3x + 4) < 10 - 3x$

_____

_____

_____

_____

_____

_____

Solution set: _____

6. $-\frac{1}{3}(x + 2) \geq 7x + 3$

_____

_____

_____

_____

_____

_____

_____

_____

Solution set: _____

$$\overset{\longleftarrow}{\underset{-6\ -5\ -4\ -3\ -2\ -1\ \ 0\ \ 1\ \ 2\ \ 3\ \ 4}{|\ \ |\ \ |\ \ |\ \ |\ \ |\ \ |\ \ |\ \ |\ \ |\ \ |}}\overset{\longrightarrow}{}$$

FOCUS ON MODELING
Modeling with One-Variable Linear Equations and Inequalities

COMMON CORE

CC.9-12.N.Q.1*,
CC.9-12.N.Q.2*,
CC.9-12.A.CED.1*,
CC.9-12.A.CED.2*,
CC.9-12.A.CED.3*,
CC.9-12.F.BF.1*

Essential question: *How can you use linear equations and inequalities to analyze a weight-loss plan?*

Jed is trying to devise a plan to help him lose weight. The weight-loss plan will be supervised by his doctor. His doctor explained to Jed that each pound of body fat is equal to 3500 Calories. So, if Jed eliminates 500 Calories per day through diet and exercise, he will lose one pound per week. The table below shows how many Calories are burned per hour of exercise for people of different weights who are walking or running at various speeds.

Calories Burned per Hour of Exercise by Body Weight				
	Body Weight			
Exercise (1 hour)	**130 lb**	**155 lb**	**180 lb**	**205 lb**
Walking 2.0 mph	148	176	204	233
Walking 3.0 mph	195	232	270	307
Walking 4.0 mph	295	352	409	465
Running, 5.0 mph	472	563	654	745
Running, 6.0 mph	590	704	817	931
Running, 6.7 mph	649	774	899	1024
Running, 7.5 mph	738	880	1022	1163
Running, 8.6 mph	826	985	1144	1303
Running, 10.0 mph	944	1126	1308	1489

Jed currently weighs 205 pounds. Using a pace calculator, he has determined that he walks at a speed of 3 miles per hour and runs at a speed of 5 miles per hour. How can Jed use the table to devise a plan for losing weight? He plans to exercise 30 minutes per day.

© Houghton Mifflin Harcourt Publishing Company

1 Write a linear function for the total number of Calories burned in each session.

A Since Jed is exercising 30 minutes per day, divide each value in the table by 60 to determine the number of Calories burned per minute. Round to the nearest hundredth.

Calories Burned per Minute of Exercise by Body Weight				
	Body Weight			
Exercise (1 min.)	**130 lb**	**155 lb**	**180 lb**	**205 lb**
Walking, 2.0 mph				
Walking, 3.0 mph				
Walking, 4.0 mph				
Running, 5 mph				
Running, 6 mph				
Running, 6.7 mph				
Running, 7.5 mph				
Running, 8.6 mph				
Running, 10 mph				

B Let t be the number of minutes Jed walks at 3.0 miles per hour. Write an expression for the number of Calories Jed burns while walking.

_____

C If Jed exercises for 30 minutes, then $30 - t$ is the number of minutes Jed runs at 5.0 miles per hour. Write an expression for the number of Calories Jed burns while running.

_____

D The number of Calories burned while Jed exercises is given below in words. Use this verbal model and your expressions from parts B and C above to write a function $C(t)$, where C is the total number of Calories burned.

Total number of Calories burned	=	Calories burned while walking	+	Calories burned while running

_____

E State the domain of the function.

_____

© Houghton Mifflin Harcourt Publishing Company

1a. Why did you divide the rates in the original table by 60 to determine the rates in the second table?

_____

_____

_____

1b. What unit of measurement does each term of $C(t)$, $5.12t$ and $12.42(30 - t)$, have? How do you know?

_____

_____

_____

1c. What unit of measurement do the values of $C(t)$ have? How do you know?

_____

_____

2 **Determine whether it is possible for Jed to burn 500 Calories per day from exercise alone.**

A Solve the equation $C(t) = 500$ for t. Justify the steps.

_____

_____

_____

_____

B Interpret the solution. Is it possible for Jed to burn 500 Calories per day by exercising for 30 minutes? Explain.

_____

_____

2a. The possible values of t range from 0 to 30. For what value of t does Jed burn the fewest number of Calories? For what value of t does Jed burn the greatest number of Calories? Explain your reasoning.

_____

_____

_____

_____

2b. Find the value of $C(0)$. How is this number relevant to the question of whether Jed can burn 500 Calories per day by exercising for 30 minutes?

_____

_____

3 Revise Jed's exercise plan so that he burns 500 Calories per day.

A If he wants to burn 500 Calories per day, one option that Jed has is to exercise for more than 30 minutes. Suppose he decides to exercise for 45 minutes. Give the new rule for $C(t)$.

_____

B Solve the equation $C(t) = 500$ for t. Show and justify the steps that you take.

_____

_____

_____

_____

C Interpret the solution. Is it possible for Jed to burn 500 Calories per day by exercising for 45 minutes? If so, how?

_____

3a. What is the minimum amount of time that Jed must exercise to burn 500 Calories per day? Explain.

_____

_____

3b. What is the maximum amount of time that Jed must exercise to burn 500 Calories per day? Explain.

_____

_____

3c. If the total number of Calories burned is held constant at 500, what happens to the amounts of time spent walking and running as exercise time increases from the minimum to the maximum?

_____

_____

4 **If Jed chooses not to exercise every day, design a diet and exercise plan that will result in a weight loss of 1 pound per week.**

A Suppose Jed decides to exercise d days per week. On days that he exercises, he will burn 500 Calories. But if he doesn't exercise *every* day, he must diet to make up for any shortfall in his goal of eliminating 3500 Calories per week. Use the verbal model below to write a function $C(d)$, where C is the number of Calories that Jed must make up through dieting.

Number of Calories eliminated through dieting	=	Weekly number of Calories to be eliminated	−	Number of Calories eliminated through exercise

_____

_____

B What is the domain of the function? Explain.

_____

_____

C Suppose Jed decides that he will eliminate at most 200 Calories per day through dieting. This means that he will eliminate at most how many Calories per week through dieting? Explain.

_____

D Based on the supposition in part C, use the function $C(d)$ to write and solve an inequality to find the number of days during a week that Jed must exercise. Show and justify the steps that you take.

_____

_____

_____

_____

4a. Interpret the solution in part D in terms of Jed's diet and exercise plan. Take into consideration what the possible values of d are.

_____

_____

EXTEND

1. Suppose Jed decides to run twice the number of minutes that he walks. How many Calories will he burn during 45 minutes of exercise? Show your work.

_____

_____

_____

2. Suppose Jed decides to eliminate at least 150 Calories per day through dieting. How many days during a week must he exercise? Show your work.

_____

_____

_____

© Houghton Mifflin Harcourt Publishing Company

Literal Equations and Inequalities

2-4

COMMON
CORE

CC.9-12.A.REI.1,
CC.9-12.A.REI.3

Essential question: *How do you solve literal equations and inequalities?*

A **literal equation** is an equation in which the coefficients and constants have been replaced by letters. In the following Explore, you will see how a literal equation can be used to represent specific equations having the same form.

1 EXPLORE Understanding Literal Equations

A For each equation given below, solve the equation by writing two equivalent equations: one where the x-term is isolated and then one where x is isolated.

$$3x + 1 = 7 \qquad -2x + 5 = 11 \qquad 4x + 3 = -1$$

_____ _____   _____

_____ _____   _____

B Identify the two properties of equality that you used in part A. List them in the order that you used them.

_____

C Each equation in part A has the general form $ax + b = c$ where $a \neq 0$. Solve this literal equation for x using the properties of equality that you identified in part B.

$ax + b = c$ Write the literal equation.

$ax = \boxed{} - \boxed{}$ Subtract b from both sides.

$x = \dfrac{\boxed{} - \boxed{}}{\boxed{}}$ Divide both sides by a.

D Show that the solution of the literal equation gives the same solution of $3x + 1 = 7$ as you found in part A. Recognize that when $a = 3$, $b = 1$, and $c = 7$, the literal equation $ax + b = c$ gives the specific equation $3x + 1 = 7$.

$x = \dfrac{\boxed{} - \boxed{}}{\boxed{}}$ Write the literal equation's solution.

$x = \dfrac{\boxed{} - \boxed{}}{\boxed{}}$ Substitute 3 for a, 1 for b, and 7 for c.

$x = \boxed{}$ Simplify.

REFLECT

1a. Why must the restriction $a \neq 0$ be placed on the literal equation $ax + b = c$?

_____

1b. Choose one of the other specific equations from part A. Show that the solution of the literal equation gives the solution of the specific equation.

_____

_____

When you solve a literal equation, you use properties of equality and other properties to isolate the variable. The result is not a number, but rather an expression involving the letters that represent the coefficients and constants.

2 EXAMPLE Solving a Literal Equation and Evaluating Its Solution

Solve the literal equation $a(x + b) = c$ where $a \neq 0$. Then use the literal equation's solution to obtain the solution of the specific equation $2(x + 7) = -6$.

A Solve $a(x + b) = c$ for x. Use the properties of equality to justify your solution steps.

Equation	Solution step	Reason
$a(x + b) = c$		
$x + b = \dfrac{}{}$	Divide both sides by a.	_____ Property of Equality
$x = \dfrac{}{} - \square$	Subtract b from both sides.	_____ Property of Equality

B Obtain the solution of $2(x + 7) = -6$ from the literal equation's solution by letting $a = 2$, $b = 7$, and $c = -6$.

$x = \dfrac{}{} - \square$ Write the literal equation's solution.

$x = \dfrac{}{} - \square$ Substitute 2 for a, 7 for b, and -6 for c.

$x = \boxed{}$ Simplify.

REFLECT

2a. When solving $a(x + b) = c$, why do you divide by a before you subtract b?

_____

_____

_____

© Houghton Mifflin Harcourt Publishing Company

2b. Write an equation that has the form $a(x + b) = c$. Find the solution of your equation using the literal equation's solution.

_____

2c. Another way to solve $a(x + b) = c$ is to start by using the Distributive Property. Show and justify the solution steps using this method.

_____

_____

_____

_____

2d. When you start solving $a(x + b) = c$ by dividing by a, you get $x = \frac{c}{a} - b$. When you start solving $a(x + b) = c$ by distributing a, you get $x = \frac{c - ab}{a}$. Use the fact that you can rewrite $\frac{c - ab}{a}$ as the difference of two fractions to show that the two solutions are equivalent.

_____

A **literal inequality** is an inequality in which the coefficients and constants have been replaced by letters. When solving a linear inequality, you need to pay attention to the restriction placed on the coefficient of the variable because it will affect the direction of the inequality symbol when you divide by that coefficient.

3 EXAMPLE   Solving a Literal Inequality and Evaluating Its Solution

Solve the literal inequality $ax + b > c$ where $a > 0$. Then use the literal inequality's solution to obtain the solution of the specific inequality $3x + 1 > -2$.

A   Solve $ax + b > c$ for x. Use the properties of inequality to justify your solution steps.

Equation	Solution step	Reason
$ax + b > c$		
$x + b > - $	Subtract b from both sides.	_____ Property of Inequality
$x > \dfrac{ - }{}$	Divide both sides by a.	_____ Property of Inequality

© Houghton Mifflin Harcourt Publishing Company

B Obtain the solution of $3x + 1 > -2$ from the literal inequality's solution by letting $a = 3, b = 1,$ and $c = -2.$

$x > \dfrac{\boxed{} - \boxed{}}{}$ Write the literal inequality's solution.

$x > \dfrac{\boxed{} - \boxed{}}{}$ Substitute 3 for a, 1 for b, and -2 for c.

$x > \boxed{}$ Simplify.

REFLECT

3a. Show and justify the steps for solving $ax + b > c$ where $a < 0.$

_____

_____

_____

3b. How is the solution of $ax + b > c$ where $a > 0$ different from the solution of $ax + b > c$ where $a < 0$? Why?

_____

_____

When the variable appears more than once in a literal inequality, you must consider the restriction on all the coefficients of the variable.

4 EXAMPLE Solving a Literal Inequality and Evaluating Its Solution

Solve the literal inequality $ax \le bx + c$ where $a > b$. Then use the literal inequality's solution to obtain the solution of the specific inequality $x \le -3x + 8.$

A Solve $ax \le bx + c$ for x. Use the properties of inequality to justify your solution steps.

Equation	Solution step	Reason
$ax \le bx + c$		
$ax - \boxed{}\, x \le c$	Subtract bx from both sides.	_____ Property of Inequality
$(\boxed{} - \boxed{})\, x \le c$	Combine like terms.	Distributive Property
$x \le \dfrac{\boxed{}}{\boxed{} - \boxed{}}$	Divide both sides by $a - b$.	_____ Property of Inequality

B Obtain the solution of $x \leq -3x + 8$ from the literal inequality's solution by letting $a = 1$, $b = -3$, and $c = 8$.

$x \leq \dfrac{}{-}$ Write the literal inequality's solution.

$x \leq \dfrac{}{-}$ Substitute 1 for a, -3 for b and 8 for c.

$x \leq \boxed{}$ Simplify.

REFLECT

4a. In solving $ax \leq bx + c$ where $a > b$, why do you *not* need to reverse the direction of the inequality symbol?

_____

_____

4b. Show and justify the steps for solving $ax \leq bx + c$ where $a < b$.

_____

_____

_____

_____

PRACTICE

1. Show and justify the steps for solving $x + a = b$. Then use the literal equation's solution to obtain the solution of $x + 2 = -4$.

_____

_____

_____

2. Show and justify the steps for solving $ax = b$ where $a \neq 0$. Then use the literal equation's solution to obtain the solution of $3x = -15$.

_____

_____

_____

3. Show and justify the steps for solving $ax = bx + c$ where $a \neq b$. Then use the literal equation's solution to obtain the solution of $2x = x + 7$.

_____

_____

_____

_____

_____

4. Show and justify the steps for solving $a(x + b) \geq c$ where $a > 0$. Then use the literal inequality's solution to obtain the solution of $5(x + 3) \geq -10$.

_____

_____

_____

_____

5. Show and justify the steps for solving $ax + b < cx + d$ where $a < c$. Then use the literal inequality's solution to obtain the solution of $-x + 4 < 2x + 13$.

_____

_____

_____

_____

_____

_____

Rewriting Formulas

COMMON CORE

CC.9-12.A.CED.2*,
CC.9-12.A.CED.4*

Essential question: *How do you rewrite formulas?*

If you study geometry, physics, economics, or many other fields, you will most likely encounter formulas relating two or more quantities. Some examples of formulas from geometry are $P = 2l + 2w$ (perimeter of a rectangle), $A = s^2$ (area of a square), and $C = 2\pi r$ (circumference of a circle). Formulas like these can be considered literal equations. As with literal equations, if you solve a formula for an unknown quantity in terms of the known quantities, you can substitute the known quantities into the rewritten formula to find the unknown quantity directly.

1 EXAMPLE   Solving a Formula for a Variable

Solve the formula for the given variable. Justify each step in your solution.

A The formula $V = lwh$ gives the volume of a rectangular prism with length l, width w, and height h. Solve the formula for h to find the height of a rectangular prism with a given volume, length, and width.

Equation	Property
$V = lwh$	
$\dfrac{V}{} = \dfrac{lwh}{}$	

$h = \dfrac{}{}$

B The formula $E = \frac{1}{2}kx^2$ gives the potential energy E of a spring with spring constant k that has been stretched by length x. Solve the formula for k to find the constant of a spring with a given potential energy and stretch.

Equation	Property
$E = \frac{1}{2}kx^2$	
$ \cdot E = \cdot \frac{1}{2}kx^2$	
$2E = kx^2$	
$\dfrac{2E}{} = \dfrac{kx^2}{}$	

$k = \dfrac{}{}$

© Houghton Mifflin Harcourt Publishing Company

1a. The formula $T = p + sp$ gives the total cost of an item with price p and sales tax s, expressed as a decimal. Describe a situation in which you would want to solve the formula for s.

_____

1b. What is true about the restrictions on the value of a variable in a formula that might not be true of other literal equations?

_____

_____

2 EXAMPLE **Writing and Rearranging a Formula**

The flower garden at the right is made up of a square and an isosceles triangle. Write a formula for the perimeter P in terms of x, and then solve for x to find a formula for the side length of the square in terms of P.

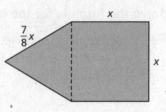

A Write a formula for the perimeter of each shape. Use only the sides of the square and the triangle that form the outer edges of the figure.

Perimeter of square = _____

Perimeter of triangle = _____

B Combine the formulas. $P = $ [   ]

C Solve the formula for x.

$P = $ [   ]   Write the combined formula.

$P = x\left(\;\square + \square\;\right)$ Distributive Property

$P = x\left(\dfrac{\square}{\square}\right)$ Find the sum. Write the result as an improper fraction.

$P\left(\dfrac{\square}{\square}\right) = x\left(\dfrac{\square}{\square}\right)\left(\dfrac{\square}{\square}\right)$ Multiplication Property of Equality

$\dfrac{\square}{\square} = x$ Simplify.

© Houghton Mifflin Harcourt Publishing Company

2a. What are the restrictions on the values of P and x? Explain.

_____

2b. How could you write a formula for the area of the square in terms of P?

_____

_____

PRACTICE

Solve the formula for the given variable.

1. Formula for distance traveled:
$d = rt$, for t

_____

_____

2. Formula for the flow of a current in an electric circuit: $V = IR$, for I

_____

_____

3. Formula for density:
$D = \frac{m}{V}$, for V

_____

_____

_____

4. Formula for the lateral surface area of a cylinder: $SA = 2\pi rh$, for r

_____

_____

_____

5. Formula for the surface area of rectangular prism: $SA = 2(lw + hw + hl)$, for w

_____

_____

_____

_____

_____

_____

6. Formula for the area of a trapezoid:
$A = \frac{1}{2}(a + b)h$, for b

_____

_____

_____

_____

_____

_____

7. An electrician sent Bonnie an invoice in the amount of a dollars for 6 hours of work that was done on Saturday. The electrician charges a weekend fee f in addition to an hourly rate r. Bonnie knows what the weekend fee is. Write a formula Bonnie can use to find r, the rate the electrician charges per hour.

_____

_____

_____

_____

8. The swimming pool below is made up of a square and two semicircles. Write a formula for the perimeter P in terms of x, and then solve for x to find a formula for the side length of the square in terms of P.

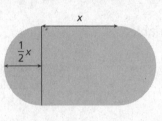

_____

_____

_____

_____

_____

9. Kai purchased a plot of land shaped like the figure below. How can he find the length of the side labeled x if he knows the area A of his lot?

_____

_____

_____

_____

_____

_____

Linear Equations in Two Variables

COMMON CORE

CC.9-12.A.REI.10

2-6

Essential question: *How do you graph the solutions to a linear equation in two variables?*

An equation in two variables x and y that can be written in the form $Ax + By = C$ for real numbers A, B, and C is a **linear equation in two variables**.

The form $Ax + By = C$ where A and B are not both 0 is called the **standard form of a linear equation**.

A **solution of an equation in two variables** x and y is any ordered pair (x, y) that makes the equation true.

1 EXPLORE   Definition of a Linear Equation in Two Variables

A Complete the table of values to find solutions of the linear equation $x + y = 5$.

B Plot the ordered pairs on a coordinate grid.

x_1	y_1	(x_1, y_1)
−2		
−1		
0		
1		
2		
3		
4		
5		
6		
7		

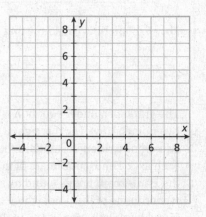

REFLECT

1a. What appears to be true about the points that are solutions of a linear equation?

_____

1b. What is the minimum number of points you would need to plot to graph a linear equation? Explain. Why should you graph more than the minimum number of points?

_____

_____

To determine whether an ordered pair (x_1, y_1) is a solution of a linear equation, substitute the values of x_1 and y_1 into the linear equation. If the two sides of the equation are equal, then the ordered pair is a solution.

2 EXAMPLE Determining Whether an Ordered Pair is a Solution

Which ordered pair is a solution to $3x + 5y = 15$?

A (0, 3)

$3(0) + 5(3) = 15$

_____

B (8, 1)

_____

_____

(0, 3) _____ a solution to $3x + 5y = 15$.

(8, 1) _____ a solution to $3x + 5y = 15$.

REFLECT

2a. What do you know about the point (0, 3) and its relationship to the graph of $3x + 5y = 15$?

_____

2b. Explain how you know that $3x + 5y = 15$ is a linear equation.

_____

The graph of a linear equation is a line. To graph a line, it is necessary to plot only two points. However, it is a good idea to plot a third point as a check. For linear equations written in standard form, two good points to plot are where the line crosses each axis. The x-coordinate of the point where the line crosses the x-axis is called the **x-intercept** and is found by substituting 0 for y in the equation of the line. The y-coordinate of the point where the line crosses the y-axis is called the **y-intercept** and is found by substituting 0 for x in the equation of the line.

3 EXAMPLE Graphing a Linear Equation in Standard Form

Graph $2x + y = 4$.

A Make a table of values. Each row in the table of values makes an ordered pair (x, y).

x	y
0	
	0
1	

B Substitute 0 for x in the equation and solve for y.

$2(0) + y = 4$

$y = $

Write the value for y next to the 0 in the first row of the table.

C Next substitute 0 for y in the equation and solve for x.

$2x + (0) = 4$

$2x = 4$

$x = $ ▢

Write the value for x before the 0 in the second row of the table.

D Choose another value for x and solve for y. It is usually easiest to choose a simple value such as 1.

$2(1) + y = 4$

▢ $+ y = 4$

$y = $ ▢

Write the value for y after the 1 in the third row of the table.

E Plot the first two points on the coordinate grid. Then plot the third point. If you have done your calculations correctly, all three points should lie on a straight line. Draw a line through the points.

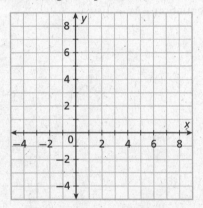

REFLECT

3a. List three other solutions to $2x + y = 4$.

_____

3b. Why should you find the x- and y-intercepts when making a table of values to graph a linear equation?

_____

_____

3c. Suppose that in part E the three points did not lie on a straight line. What would this tell you and what should you do?

_____

_____

Graph $x = 3$ and $y = -4$.

Note that the equation $x = 3$ can be written as $1x + 0y = 3$. All points with an x-value of 3 are solutions to the equation. These points lie on a vertical line that passes through $(3, 0)$.

Note that the equation $y = -4$ can be written as $0x + 1y = -4$. All points with a y-value of -4 are solutions to the equation. These points lie on a horizontal line that passes through $(0, -4)$.

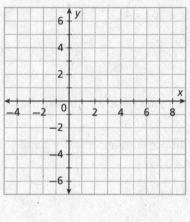

REFLECT

4a. Describe the graph of the line $y = 1$.

_____

4b. Describe the graph of the line $x = -2$.

_____

A linear equation in the form $Ax + By = C$ where $C = 0$ has a special property. To see what this property is, look below at the table and graph of the equation $-4x + 3y = 0$.

x	y
0	0
0	0
3	4

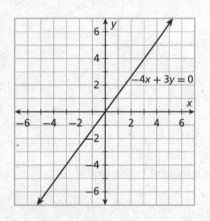

Notice that the table gives the same point for the x-intercept and for the y-intercept, namely the point $(0, 0)$. Notice also that the graph passes through the origin. This is true for any linear equation of the form $Ax + By = C$ where $C = 0$. Consequently, you cannot use the x- and y-intercepts to draw their graphs. For these equations, first plot a point at the origin. Then substitute two other values for x to locate two more points.

5 EXAMPLE Lines Through the Origin

Graph $2x - 3y = 0$.

A Complete the table of values.

B Plot the points on the coordinate grid.

C Check that all three points are collinear.

D Draw a line through the points.

x	y
0	0
1	
2	

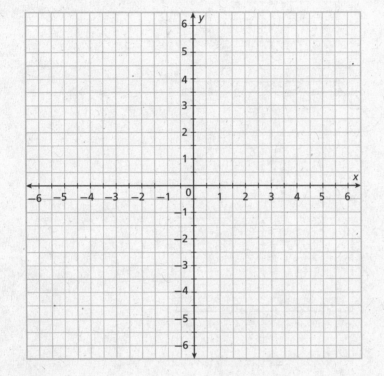

REFLECT

5a. Would it have been easier to use *x*-values of 3 and −3 to graph the line? Why or why not?

_____

_____

5b. If *C* does not equal 0, can the graph of $Ax + By = C$ pass through the origin? Why or why not?

_____

_____

PRACTICE

Tell whether the ordered pair is a solution to the equation.

1. $-5x + 2y = 4;\ (4, 8)$

_____

2. $2x - 7y = 1;\ (11, 3)$

_____

Complete the table and graph the equation.

3. $-2x + y = 3$

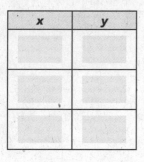

x	y

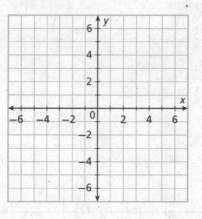

4. $3x = -6$

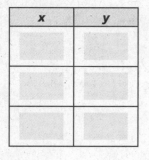

x	y

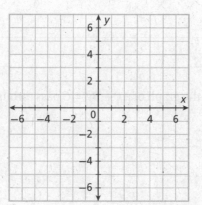

5. $4x + 5y = 0$

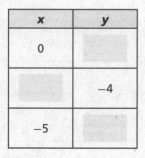

x	y
0	
	-4
-5	

Linear Inequalities in Two Variables

2-7

COMMON CORE

CC.9-12.A.REI.12

Essential question: *How do you graph a linear inequality in two variables?*

A **linear inequality in two variables**, such as $2x - 3y \geq 6$, results when you replace the $=$ sign in an equation by $<$, $>$, $\leq$, or $\geq$. A **solution of an inequality in two variables** x and y is any ordered pair (x, y) that makes the inequality true.

1 EXAMPLE Graphing a Linear Inequality

Graph the solution set for $2x - 3y \geq 6$.

A Start by graphing $2x - 3y = 6$. The inequality is true for every point on this line because the inequality symbol is less than or equal to. The line is called the *boundary line* of the solution set.

x	y
0	
	0

B Test several other points in the plane that are not on the boundary line to determine whether the inequality is true.

Point	Above or Below the Line?	Inequality	True or False?
(0, 0)	Above	$2(0) - 3(0) \geq 6$	False
(5, 0)			
(0, 3)			
(4, 2)			
(6, 1)			

The solutions of $2x - 3y \geq 6$ lie on or _____ $2x - 3y = 6$.

C Shade the set of solutions to the inequality $2x - 3y \geq 6$. The shaded region and the boundary line make up the graph of $2x - 3y \geq 6$. This area is referred to as a *half-plane*.

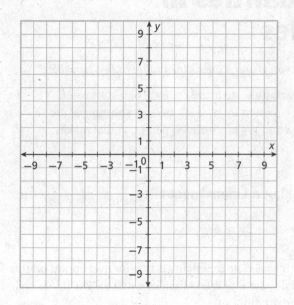

REFLECT

1a. How would the graph of $2x - 3y \leq 6$ be like the graph of $2x - 3y \geq 6$? How would it be different?

_____

_____

1b. Would the points on the boundary line $2x - 3y = 6$ be included in the graph of the inequality $2x - 3y > 6$? Why or why not?

_____

_____

1c. Error Analysis A student says that you shade above the boundary line when the inequality is > or ≥ and you shade below it when the inequality is < or ≤. Use the example to explain why this is not always true.

_____

_____

To graph a linear inequality in the coordinate plane:

1. Graph the boundary line. If the symbol is ≤ or ≥, draw a solid line. If the symbol is < or >, draw a dashed line.

2. Choose a test point (x, y) that is not on the line. Substitute the values of x and y into the inequality and determine whether it is true or false.

3. If the inequality is true for the test point, shade the half-plane on the side of the boundary line that contains the test point. If not, shade the half-plane on the opposite side of the line.

Graph the inequality $7x - y < 13$.

A Write the equation of the boundary line. _____

B Graph the boundary line. The inequality symbol is $>$, so the line will be dashed.

C Test a point that is not on the line, such as $(0, 0)$.

$7\left(\quad\right) - \boxed{} < 13$ True or false? _____

Shade the part of the plane on the correct side of the line.

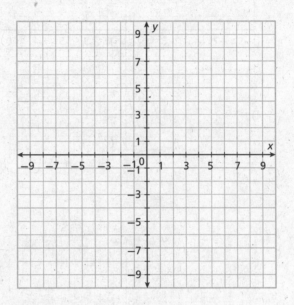

2a. Why is $(0, 0)$ a good choice for a test point? When could you not use $(0, 0)$?

_____

_____

2b. For the graph of $x \geq 4$, the boundary line is the vertical line $x = 4$. Would you shade to the left or right of the boundary? Explain.

_____

_____

_____

_____

Graph the inequality.

1. $y \geq 2$

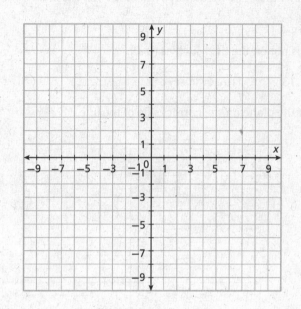

2. $x < -3$

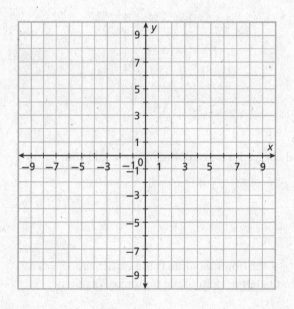

3. $x + 4y < 9$

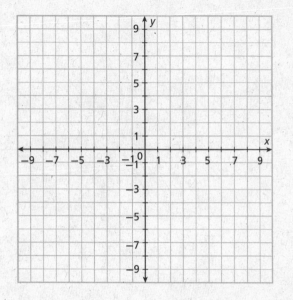

4. $2x - 2y \geq 5$

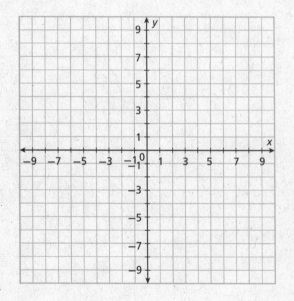

5. $-3x + 6y \geq 2$

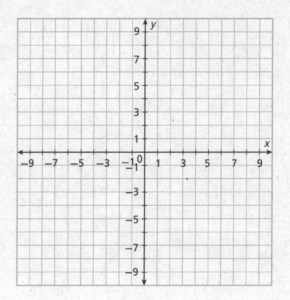

6. $7x - y > 13$

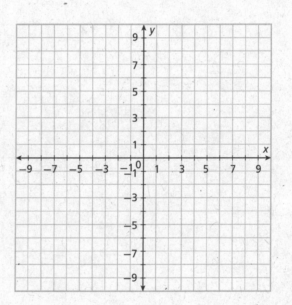

FOCUS ON MODELING

Modeling with Two-Variable Linear Equations and Inequalities

COMMON CORE

CC.9-12.N.Q.1*,
CC.9-12.N.Q.2*,
CC.9-12.A.SSE.1*,
CC.9-12.A.SSE.1a*,
CC.9-12.A.CED.2*,
CC.9-12.A.CED.3*

Essential question: *How can you use linear equations and inequalities to model the results of a fundraiser?*

The Band Booster Club is selling T-shirts and blanket wraps to raise money for a trip. The band director has asked the club to raise at least $1000 in sales. So, the booster club has set a fundraising goal of $2000 in sales.

The booster club president wants to know how many T-shirts and how many blankets wraps the club needs to sell to meet their goal of $2000. The T-shirts cost $10 each and the blanket wraps cost $25 each. How can the booster club president use the sales price of each item to help the fundraiser meet its goal?

1 **Write a linear equation to show the amount of money raised.**

A Let *x* equal the number of T-shirts sold. Write an expression for the amount of money raised from T-shirt sales. Interpret the expression.

_____

B Let *y* equal the number of blanket wraps sold. Write an expression for the amount of money raised from blanket wrap sales. Interpret the expression.

_____

C Combine the expressions and the sales goal in a linear equation.

_____

REFLECT

1a. Determine whether the booster club will meet their goal if they sell 50 T-shirts and 50 blanket wraps. Explain.

_____

1b. Determine whether the booster club will meet their goal if they sell 100 T-shirts and 40 blanket wraps. Explain.

_____

2 Graph the linear equation.

A Calculate three pairs of values for x and y. Enter your results in the table.

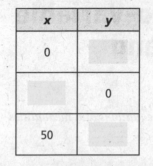

x	y
0	
	0
50	

B Plot the ordered pairs on the coordinate grid. Connect the points to graph the equation.

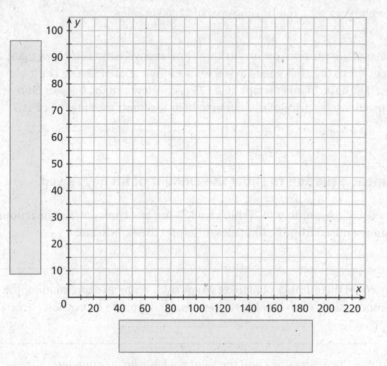

C Label the x- and y-axes in the boxes provided.

REFLECT

2a. What does the point where the line intersects the x-axis represent?

_____

_____

_____

2b. Explain what the point (100, 40) represents on this graph.

_____

_____

_____

2c. Suppose the Band Booster Club sells 25 blanket wraps during a chilly football game. Use the graph to determine about how many T-shirts they need to sell.

_____

3 Write and graph a linear inequality that shows the sales required to raise a minimum of $1000.

A Use the expressions for the amount of money raised from T-shirts and blanket wraps and the minimum goal of $1000 to write a linear inequality.

_____

B Calculate three pairs of values for x and y. Enter your results in the table. Then, graph the boundary line of the linear inequality.

x	y
0	
	0
50	

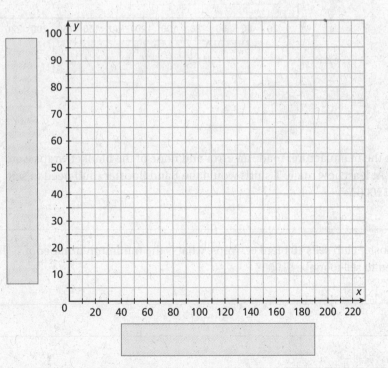

© Houghton Mifflin Harcourt Publishing Company

C Use the test point (0, 0) to determine which side of the boundary line to shade.

☐	+	☐	☐ 1000	Write the inequality.
☐	+	☐ ☐	☐ 1000	Substitute 0 for x and 0 for y.
☐	+	☐	☐ 1000	Simplify each product.
		☐ ☐	☐ 1000	Simplify the sum and check the inequality.

D Shade the correct part of the plane. Label the x- and y-axes in the boxes provided.

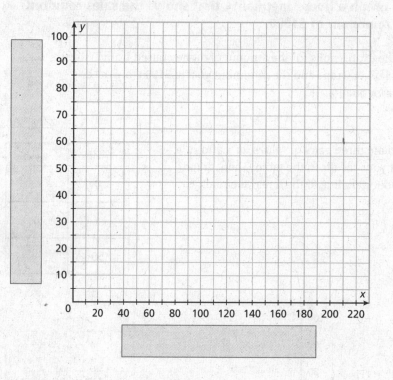

3a. Suppose the manufacturer made an error and none of the blanket wraps were sellable. At least how many T-shirts would the Band Booster Club need to sell to raise $1000?

_____

3b. If the booster club sells 18 blanket wraps, what is the minimum number of T-shirts they need to sell to make $1000?

_____

_____

_____

1. Use unit analysis to determine the unit of measurement for the expression $10x + 25y$.

   _____

   _____

2. Describe where the lines would be in relation to each other if you graphed the linear equation and the linear inequality on the same coordinate grid.

   _____

   _____

   _____

3. The booster club sold 30 more T-shirts than blanket wraps at a fundraising event and made exactly $1000. How many of each did they sell?

   _____

   _____

   _____

   _____

   _____

   _____

   _____

4. If the booster club orders at least 100 blanket wraps, they get a reduced price on them. Does it make sense for the booster club to order at least 100 blanket wraps if the goal is to raise a minimum of $1000? Explain your answer.

   _____

   _____

   _____

   _____

© Houghton Mifflin Harcourt Publishing Company

5. The booster club will earn $5 profit for every T-shirt sold and $10 profit for every blanket wrap sold. Write an inequality to show how many T-shirts and blanket wraps the club would need to sell to make a profit of at least $1000.

_____

_____

_____

6. Find a solution to the linear inequality you wrote in Problem 5. How much money would the booster club raise in *sales* if they sold that many T-shirts and blanket wraps?

_____

_____

_____

_____

_____

_____

_____

_____

_____

_____

_____

Name _____ Class _____ Date _____

MULTIPLE CHOICE

1. Which property of equality can be used to justify this step?

$$15 - 10x = 6x$$
$$\underline{+\ 10x +\ 10x}$$
$$15 = 16x$$

- **A.** Substitution Property of Equality
- **B.** Summation Property of Equality
- **C.** Addition Property of Equality
- **D.** Subtraction Property of Equality

2. Find the solution set for $8x - 3 = 2(x - \frac{1}{2})$.

- **F.** $\left\{-\frac{1}{3}\right\}$
- **H.** $\left\{\frac{1}{3}\right\}$
- **G.** $\left\{\frac{1}{5}\right\}$
- **J.** $\left\{\frac{2}{5}\right\}$

3. What is the next and most efficient step in solving the inequality for x?

$$-4x > 12$$

- **A.** $\frac{-4x}{-4} < \frac{12}{-4}$
- **C.** $\frac{-4x}{-4} > \frac{12}{-4}$
- **B.** $\frac{-4x}{4} > \frac{12}{4}$
- **D.** $\frac{-4x}{4} < \frac{12}{4}$

4. Given $-\frac{1}{3}x - \frac{2}{3} \geq 7x + 3$, which property is used below?

$$3\left(-\frac{1}{3}x - \frac{2}{3}\right) \geq 3(7x + 3)$$

- **F.** Distributive Property
- **G.** Multiplication Property of Inequality
- **H.** Subtraction Property of Inequality
- **J.** Associative Property of Multiplication

5. A 130-pound woman burns 9.83 Calories per minute while running. She burns 3.25 Calories per minute while walking during her cool-down. She runs for t minutes and exercises for a total of 45 minutes. Write an equation to find how many total Calories, C, she burns.

- **A.** $C = 9.83t + 3.25(45 - t)$
- **B.** $C = 9.83t + 3.25(t - 45)$
- **C.** $C = 9.83t + 3.25t$
- **D.** $C = 9.83(t - 45) + 3.25t$

6. It costs $5 to have a tote bag monogrammed with up to 12 letters and $.50 for each additional letter. A club has a budget of $8 maximum per tote bag. Write an inequality for the amount the club can spend on monogramming a tote bag.

- **F.** $5 + 0.5x > 8$
- **H.** $5 + 0.5x < 8$
- **G.** $5 + 0.5x \geq 8$
- **J.** $5 + 0.5x \leq 8$

7. Solve the inequality for x, given $b < c$.

$$a + bx > cx - d$$

- **A.** $x < \frac{a + d}{b - c}$
- **B.** $x < \frac{a + d}{c - b}$
- **C.** $x > \frac{a + d}{c - b}$
- **D.** $x > \frac{-d - a}{b - c}$

8. Solve $q = \frac{r}{2}(s + t)$ for t.

- **F.** $t = \frac{qr}{2} - s$
- **H.** $t = \frac{2q}{r} - s$
- **G.** $t = \frac{2q - s}{r}$
- **J.** $t = \frac{q}{2r} - s$

9. Solve $V = \frac{1}{3}\pi r^2 h$ for h.

A. $h = \frac{3V}{\pi r^2}$ **C.** $h = \frac{\pi V}{3r^2}$

B. $h = \frac{3\pi V}{r^2}$ **D.** $h = r\sqrt{\frac{3V}{\pi}}$

10. Which ordered pair is *not* a solution to $2x + 3y = 12$?

F. $(0, 4)$ **H.** $(2, 3)$

G. $(3, 2)$ **J.** $(6, 0)$

11. Which statement about the graphs of $x = 2$ and $y = 4$ is true?

A. The two lines intersect at $(2, 4)$.

B. The two lines intersect at $(4, 2)$.

C. The graph of $x = 2$ is horizontal and the graph of $y = 4$ is vertical.

D. Both lines pass through the origin $(0, 0)$.

12. Which ordered pair is a solution to $mx + ny = 0$?

F. (m, n) **H.** $(0, n)$

G. $(0, 0)$ **J.** (n, m)

13. Which description fits the graph of $x > 4$?

A. A vertical solid line, shaded to the right of the line

B. A horizontal dashed line, shaded above the line

C. A horizontal solid line, shaded above the line

D. A vertical dashed line, shaded to the right of the line

14. Which ordered pair is a solution to $-5x + 3y > 12$?

F. $(3, 9)$ **H.** $(3, -6)$

G. $(-2, -5)$ **J.** $(2, 8)$

FREE RESPONSE

15. Graph the solution to $3x - 4y \leq 1$.

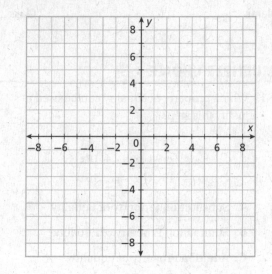

16. A charity raised $600 at a holiday bazaar selling stationery and fountain pens. A box of stationery sold for $12 and a pen sold for $20. Let x represent how many boxes of stationery were sold. Let y represent how many pens were sold.

a. Write a linear equation you can use to represent all possible numbers of boxes of stationery and pens that were sold. Identify a possible solution.

_____

b. Graph the equation on the coordinate grid. Be sure to label the graph.

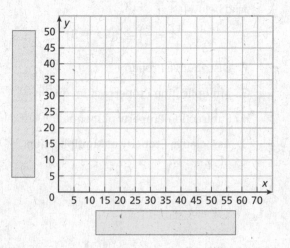

Systems of Equations and Inequalities

Unit Focus

In this unit, you will learn how to write and solve systems of linear equations and inequalities. You will begin by graphing two equations of a linear system and seeing how the solution to the system can be determined by looking at the graph. Then, you will explore different ways to solve linear systems algebraically. You will extend those skills to learn how to graph systems of linear inequalities and interpret the solutions. Finally, you will apply your knowledge to a real-world situation in which you will write and solve systems of equations and inequalities to model a shopping trip.

Unit at a Glance

COMMON CORE

UNIT 3

Unpacking the Common Core State Standards

Use the table to help you understand the Standards for Mathematical Content that are taught in this unit. Refer to the lessons listed after each standard for exploration and practice.

COMMON CORE Standards for Mathematical Content	What It Means For You
CC.9-12.N.Q.1 Use units as a way to understand problems and to guide the solution of multi-step problems; choose and interpret units consistently in formulas; **choose and interpret the scale and the origin in graphs and data displays.*** Lesson 3-6	When you model real-world situations with systems of linear equations and inequalities, it is important to check that the units of the equations and inequalities make sense. When you solve systems of linear equations and inequalities by graphing, you will need to choose appropriate units and scales for the axes in order to read your solutions from the graphs.
CC.9-12.N.Q.2 Define appropriate quantities for the purpose of descriptive modeling.* Lesson 3-6	You will write systems of linear equations and inequalities to model the relationships between quantities in real-world situations.
CC.9-12.A.CED.2 Create equations in two or more **variables to represent relationships between quantities; graph equations on coordinate axes with labels and scales.*** Lesson 3-6	You will create and graph linear systems of equations in two variables to model relationships between quantities in real-world situations.
CC.9-12.A.CED.3 Represent constraints by equations or inequalities, and by systems of equations and/or inequalities, and interpret solutions as viable or nonviable options in a modeling context.* Lesson 3-6	You will learn to create systems of linear equations and inequalities to model situations that include restrictions on the values of the variables. You will incorporate those restrictions into your model by writing equations or inequalities. In addition, you will analyze solutions to determine when they are possible in the context of a situation.
CC.9-12.A.REI.5 Prove that, given a system of two equations in two variables, replacing one equation by the sum of that equation and a multiple of the other produces a system with the same solutions. Lesson 3-4	An important strategy for solving systems of equations is to eliminate variables. You will prove that an equation in a system can be replaced with a constant multiple of itself, or the sum of itself and another equation in the system, and use this fact to eliminate variables.
CC.9-12.A.REI.6 Solve systems of linear equations exactly and approximately (e.g., with graphs), focusing on pairs of linear equations in two variables. Lessons 3-1, 3-2, 3-3, 3-4, 3-6	You will learn a variety of ways to solve systems of linear equations in two variables, including graphing, substitution, and elimination. You will learn which methods give exact solutions and which give approximate solutions.
CC.9-12.A.REI.12 Graph the solutions to a linear inequality in two variables as a half-plane (excluding the boundary in the case of a strict inequality), and graph the solution set to a system of linear inequalities in two variables as the intersection of the corresponding half-planes. Lessons 3-5, 3-6	You will solve systems of linear inequalities by representing the solution of each inequality as a shaded region of a graph. The solution of the system will be the area where the shaded regions overlap.

Solving Linear Systems by Graphing

COMMON CORE

CC.9-12.A.REI.6

Essential question: *How do you approximate the solution of a system of linear equations by graphing?*

A **system of linear equations** consists of two or more linear equations that have the same variables. A **solution of a system of linear equations** with two variables is an ordered pair that satisfies both equations in the system. The values of the variables in the ordered pair make each equation in the system true.

Systems of linear equations can be solved by graphing and by using algebra. In this lesson you will learn to solve linear systems by graphing the equations of the system and analyzing how those graphs are related.

1 EXAMPLE Solving a Linear System by Graphing

Solve the system of equations below by graphing. Check your answer.

$$\begin{cases} -x + y = 3 \\ 2x + y = 6 \end{cases}$$

A Graph each equation.

Step 1: Find the intercepts for $-x + y = 3$, plus a third point for a check. Graph the line.

x-intercept: _____ **y-intercept:** _____

Check: The y-value for $x = 2$ is $y =$ _____.

Is that point (x, y) on the line? _____

Step 2: Find the intercepts for $2x + y = 6$ and graph the line.

x-intercept: _____ **y-intercept:** _____

Check: The y-value for $x = 2$ is $y =$ _____.

Is that point (x, y) on the line? _____

B Find the point of intersection.

The two lines appear to intersect at _____.

How is the point of intersection related to the solution of the linear system?

_____

_____

C Check if the ordered pair is a solution.

The solution of the system appears to be _____.

To check, substitute the ordered pair (x, y) into each equation.

$-x + y = 3$	
$-$ ▢ $+$ ▢	3
▢	3 ✓

$2x + y = 6$	
$2\left(\ \ \right) + $ ▢	6
▢ $+$	6
▢	6 ✓

The ordered pair _____ makes both equations _____.

So, _____ is a solution of the system.

REFLECT

1a. How is the graph of each equation related to the solutions of the equation?

_____

_____

1b. Explain why the solution of a linear system with two equations is represented by the point where the graphs of the two equations intersect.

_____

_____

1c. Describe the graphs of $x = 4$ and $y = 2$. Explain how to solve the linear system by graphing.

$$\begin{cases} x = 4 \\ y = 2 \end{cases}$$

What would the graph look like? What is the solution of the linear system? Can systems of this type be solved by examining the equations without graphing them?

_____

_____

_____

_____

_____

_____

Use the graph to solve each system of linear equations.

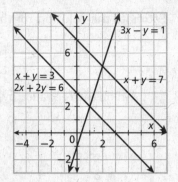

A $\begin{cases} x + y = 7 \\ 2x + 2y = 6 \end{cases}$

Is there a point of intersection? Explain.

_____

_____

Does this linear system have a solution? Use the graph to explain.

_____

_____

B $\begin{cases} 2x + 2y = 6 \\ x + y = 3 \end{cases}$

Is there a point of intersection? Explain.

_____

Does this linear system have a solution? Use the graph to explain.

_____

_____

REFLECT

2a. Use the graph to identify two lines that represent a linear system with exactly one solution. What are the equations of the lines? Explain your reasoning.

_____

2b. If each equation in a system of two linear equations is represented by a different line when graphed, what is the greatest number of solutions the system can have? Explain your reasoning.

_____

_____

2c. Identify the three possible numbers of solutions for a system of linear equations. Explain when each type of solution occurs.

_____

_____

3 EXAMPLE Estimating a Solution by Graphing

Estimate the solution for the linear system by graphing.

$$\begin{cases} x + 2y = 2 \\ 2x - 3y = 12 \end{cases}$$

A Graph each equation by finding intercepts.

$x + 2y = 2$ $2x - 3y = 12$

x-intercept: _____   *x*-intercept: _____

y-intercept: _____   *y*-intercept: _____

B Find the point of intersection.

The two lines appear to intersect at _____.

C Check if the ordered pair is an approximate solution.

$x + 2y$	$= 2$
$\boxed{} + 2 \left(\right)$	2
$\boxed{} + \boxed{}$	2
$\boxed{}$	2 ✓

$2x - 3y$	$= 12$
$2 \left(\right) - 3 \left(\right)$	12
$\boxed{} - \boxed{}$	12
$\boxed{}$	12 ✓

Does the approximate solution make both equations true? If not, explain why not and whether the approximate solution is acceptable.

_____

_____

_____

REFLECT

3a. How could you adjust the graph to make your estimate more accurate?

_____

_____

3b. Can an approximate solution make both equations true? Explain.

_____

Solve each system by graphing. Check your answer.

1. $\begin{cases} x - y = -2 \\ 2x + y = 8 \end{cases}$

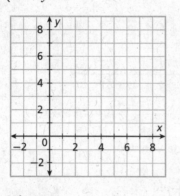

Solution: _____

2. $\begin{cases} x - y = -5 \\ 2x + 4y = -4 \end{cases}$

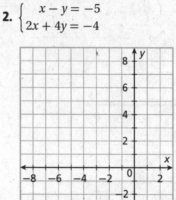

Solution: _____

3. $\begin{cases} x + 2y = -8 \\ -2x - 4y = 4 \end{cases}$

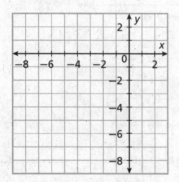

Solution: _____

4. $\begin{cases} 2x + y = 1 \\ y = -3 \end{cases}$

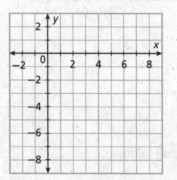

Solution: _____

5. $\begin{cases} x + 2y = 6 \\ x = 2 \end{cases}$

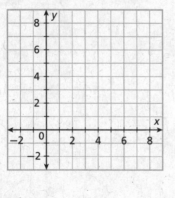

Solution: _____

6. $\begin{cases} 2x - y = -6 \\ 4x - 2y = -12 \end{cases}$

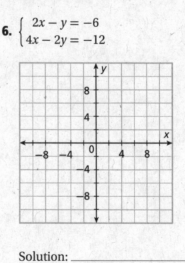

Solution: _____

Estimate the solution for the linear system by graphing. Check your answer.

7. $\begin{cases} x + y = 5 \\ x - 3y = 3 \end{cases}$

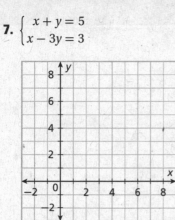

Approximate solution: _____

8. $\begin{cases} 3x = 8 \\ 2x - 2y = -3 \end{cases}$

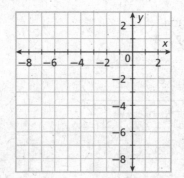

Approximate solution: _____

9. $\begin{cases} 3x - 2y = 12 \\ 2x - 6y = 9 \end{cases}$

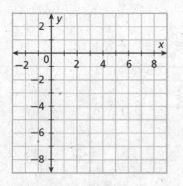

Approximate solution: _____

10. $\begin{cases} x + 2y = -6 \\ 2x + y = -4 \end{cases}$

Approximate solution: _____

Solving Linear Systems by Substitution

Essential question: *How do you use substitution to solve a system of linear equations?*

The **substitution method** is used to solve systems of linear equations by solving an equation for one variable and then substituting the resulting expression for that variable into the other equation. The steps for this method are as follows:

1. Solve one of the equations for one of its variables.

2. Substitute the expression from step 1 into the other equation and solve for the other variable.

3. Substitute the value from step 2 into either original equation and solve to find the value of the variable in step 1.

1 EXAMPLE Solving a Linear System by Substitution

Solve the system of linear equations by substitution. Check your answer.

$$\begin{cases} -3x + y = 1 \\ 4x + y = 8 \end{cases}$$

A Solve an equation for one variable.

$-3x + y = 1$ Select one of the equations.

$y = \boxed{}$ Solve for the variable y. Isolate y on one side.

B Substitute the expression for y in the other equation and solve.

$4x + \left(\boxed{} \right) = 8$ Substitute the expression for the variable y.

$\boxed{} + 1 = 8$ Combine like terms.

$\boxed{} = 7$ Subtract ____ from each side.

$x = \boxed{}$ Divide each side by ____.

C Substitute the value of x you found into one of the equations and solve for the other variable, y.

$-3\left(\boxed{} \right) + y = 1$ Substitute the value of x into the first equation.

$\boxed{} + y = 1$ Simplify.

$y = \boxed{}$ Add ____ to each side.

So, _____ is the solution of the system.

© Houghton Mifflin Harcourt Publishing Company

D Check the solution by graphing.

$-3x + y = 1$ $4x + y = 8$

x-intercept: _____   *x*-intercept: _____

y-intercept: _____   *y*-intercept: _____

The point of intersection is _____.

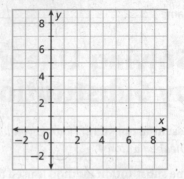

REFLECT

1a. Is it more efficient to solve $-3x + y = 1$ for x? Why or why not?

_____

1b. Is there another way to solve the system?

_____

1c. What is another way to check your solution?

_____

2 EXAMPLE   **Solving Special Systems by Substitution**

Solve each system of linear equations by substitution.

A $\begin{cases} x - y = -2 \\ -x + y = 4 \end{cases}$

Step 1 Solve $x - y = -2$ for x: $x =$

Step 2 Substitute the resulting expression into the other equation and solve.

$-\left(\right) + y = 4$ Substitute the expression for the variable *x*.

$ = 4$ Simplify.

Step 3 Interpret the solution. Graph the equations to provide more information.

What does the graph tell you about the solution?

_____

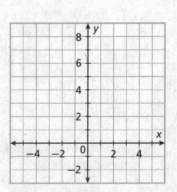

How is this solution represented algebraically when the system is solved using substitution?

_____

B $\begin{cases} 2x + y = -2 \\ 4x + 2y = -4 \end{cases}$

Step 1 Solve $2x + y = -2$ for y: $y = $ ▢

Step 2 Substitute the resulting expression into the other equation and solve.

$4x + 2\left(\right) = -4$ Substitute the expression for the variable y.

$ = -4$ Simplify.

Step 3 Interpret the solution. Graph the equations to provide more information.

What does the graph tell you about the solution?

_____

_____

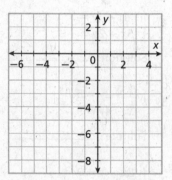

How is this solution represented algebraically when the linear system is solved using substitution?

_____

_____

_____

REFLECT

2a. If x represents a variable and a and b represent constants such that $a \neq b$, interpret what each result means when solving a system of linear equations by substitution.

$x = a$ _____

$a = b$ _____

$a = a$ _____

2b. In part B of Example 2, why is it more efficient to solve and substitute for y than to solve and substitute for x?

_____

_____

2c. Give two possible solutions of the system in part B of Example 2. How are all the solutions of this system related to one another?

_____

_____

PRACTICE

Solve each system by substitution. Check your answer.

1. $\begin{cases} x + y = 3 \\ 2x + 4y = 8 \end{cases}$

Solution: _____

2. $\begin{cases} x + 2y = 7 \\ 4x + 3y = 3 \end{cases}$

Solution: _____

3. $\begin{cases} -4x + y = 3 \\ 5x - 2y = -9 \end{cases}$

Solution: _____

4. $\begin{cases} 8x - 7y = -2 \\ -2x - 3y = 10 \end{cases}$

Solution: _____

5. $\begin{cases} 2x - 2y = 5 \\ 4x - 4y = 9 \end{cases}$

Solution: _____

6. $\begin{cases} 2x + 7y = 2 \\ 4x + 2y = -2 \end{cases}$

Solution: _____

7. $\begin{cases} 2x - y = 7 \\ 2x + 7y = 31 \end{cases}$

Solution: _____

8. $\begin{cases} x - 2y = -4 \\ 4y = 2x + 8 \end{cases}$

Solution: _____

For each linear system, tell whether it is more efficient to solve for _x_ and then substitute for _x_ or to solve for _y_ and then substitute for _y_. Explain your reasoning. Then solve the system.

9. $\begin{cases} 6x - 3y = 15 \\ x + 3y = -8 \end{cases}$

_____

_____

Solution: _____

10. $\begin{cases} \frac{x}{2} + y = 6 \\ \frac{x}{4} + \frac{y}{2} = 3 \end{cases}$

_____

_____

Solution: _____

3-3

Solving Linear Systems by Adding or Subtracting

COMMON
CORE

CC.9-12.A.REI.6

Essential question: *How do you solve a system of linear equations by adding or subtracting?*

The **elimination method** is another method used to solve a system of linear equations. In this method, one variable is *eliminated* by adding or subtracting the two equations of the system to obtain a single equation in one variable. The steps for this method are as follows:

1. Add or subtract the equations to eliminate one variable.

2. Solve the resulting equation for the other variable.

3. Substitute the value into either original equation to find the value of the eliminated variable.

1 EXAMPLE Solving a Linear System by Adding

Solve the system of equations by adding. Check your answer.

$$\begin{cases} 4x - 2y = 12 \\ x + 2y = 8 \end{cases}$$

A Add the equations.

$4x - 2y = 12$	Write the equations so that like terms are aligned.
$+\ x + 2y = 8$	Notice that the terms _____ and _____ are opposites.
$5x + 0 = 20$	Add to eliminate the variable _____.
$5x = 20$	Simplify and solve for x.
$\frac{5x}{5} = \frac{20}{5}$	Divide both sides by 5.
$x =$ ▨	Simplify.

B Substitute the solution into one of the equations and solve for y.

$x + 2y = 8$	Use the second equation.
$\left(\ \ \right) + 2y = 8$	Substitute _____ for the variable _____.
$2y =$ ▨	Subtract _____ from each side.
$y =$ ▨	Divide each side by _____.

C Write the solution as an ordered pair: _____

D Check the solution by graphing.

$4x - 2y = 12$ $x + 2y = 8$

x-intercept: _____   **x-intercept:** _____

y-intercept: _____   **y-intercept:** _____

The point of intersection is _____ .

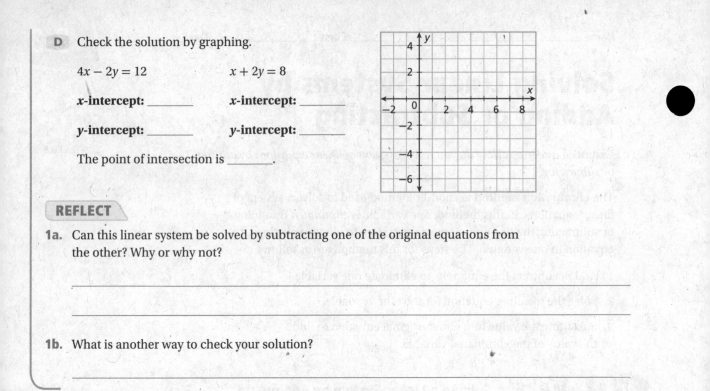

REFLECT

1a. Can this linear system be solved by subtracting one of the original equations from the other? Why or why not?

_____

_____

1b. What is another way to check your solution?

_____

---

2 EXAMPLE   Solving a Linear System by Subtracting

Solve the system of equations by subtracting. Check your answer.

$$\begin{cases} 2x + 6y = 6 \\ 2x - y = -8 \end{cases}$$

A Subtract the equations.

$2x + 6y = 6$ Write the equations so that like terms are aligned.

$- (2x - y = -8)$ Notice that both equations contain the term _____ .

$0 \ + 7y = 14$ Subtract to eliminate the variable _____ .

$7y = 14$ Simplify and solve for y.

$\frac{7y}{7} = \frac{14}{7}$ Divide both sides by 7.

$y = \boxed{}$ Simplify.

B Substitute the solution into one of the equations and solve for x.

$2x - y = -8$ Use the second equation.

$2x - (\boxed{}) = -8$ Substitute _____ for the variable _____ .

$2x = \boxed{}$ Add _____ to each side.

$x = \boxed{}$ Divide each side by _____ .

C Write the solution as an ordered pair: _____

D Check the solution by graphing.

$2x + 6y = 6$ $2x - y = -8$

x-intercept: _____   *x*-intercept: _____

y-intercept: _____   *y*-intercept: _____

The point of intersection is _____.

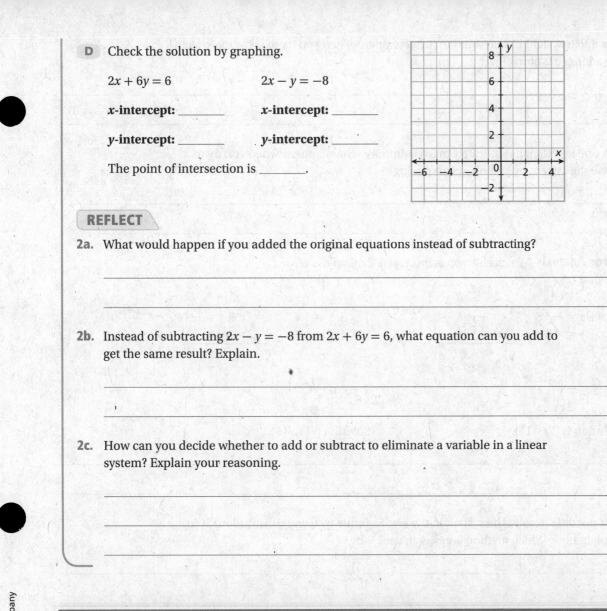

REFLECT

2a. What would happen if you added the original equations instead of subtracting?

_____

_____

2b. Instead of subtracting $2x - y = -8$ from $2x + 6y = 6$, what equation can you add to get the same result? Explain.

_____

_____

2c. How can you decide whether to add or subtract to eliminate a variable in a linear system? Explain your reasoning.

_____

_____

_____

PRACTICE

Solve each system by adding or subtracting. Check your answer.

1. $\begin{cases} -5x + y = -3 \\ 5x - 3y = -1 \end{cases}$

Solution: _____

2. $\begin{cases} 2x + y = -6 \\ -5x + y = 8 \end{cases}$

Solution: _____

3. $\begin{cases} 2x - 3y = -2 \\ 2x + y = 14 \end{cases}$

Solution: _____

4. $\begin{cases} 6x - 3y = 15 \\ 4x + 3y = -5 \end{cases}$

Solution: _____

5. $\begin{cases} -4x + y = -3 \\ 4x - y = -2 \end{cases}$

Solution: _____

6. $\begin{cases} x - 6y = 7 \\ -x + 6y = -7 \end{cases}$

Solution: _____

7. If a linear system has no solution, what happens when you try to solve the system by adding or subtracting?

_____

_____

8. If a linear system has infinitely many solutions, what happens when you try to solve the system by adding or subtracting?

_____

_____

9. Error Analysis Which solution is incorrect? Explain the error.

A

$\begin{cases} x + y = -4 \\ 2x + y = -3 \end{cases}$ $\begin{aligned} x + y &= -4 \\ -(2x + y &= -3) \\ \hline -x &= -7 \\ x &= 7 \end{aligned}$

$7 + y = -4$

$\quad y = -11$

Solution is $(7, -11)$.

B

$\begin{cases} x + y = -4 \\ 2x + y = -3 \end{cases}$ $\begin{aligned} x + y &= -4 \\ -(2x + y &= -3) \\ \hline -x &= -1 \\ x &= 1 \end{aligned}$

$1 + y = -4$

$\quad y = -5$

Solution is $(1, -5)$.

_____

_____

10. Is it possible to solve the system in the first Example by using substitution? If so, explain how. Which method is easier to use? Why?

_____

_____

_____

_____

Solving Linear Systems by Multiplying

COMMON CORE

CC.9-12.A.REI.5,
CC.9-12.A.REI.6

Essential question: *How do you solve a system of linear equations by multiplying?*

In some linear systems, neither variable can be eliminated by adding or subtracting the equations directly. In systems like these, you need to multiply one or both of the equations by a constant so that adding or subtracting the equations will eliminate one variable. The steps for this method are as follows:

1. Decide which variable to eliminate.

2. Multiply one or both equations by a constant so that adding or subtracting will eliminate that variable.

3. Solve the system using the elimination method.

1 EXPLORE Understanding Linear Systems and Multiplication

A Use the equations in the linear system below to write a third equation.

$$\begin{cases} 2x - y = 1 \\ x + y = 2 \end{cases}$$

$x + y = 2$	Write the second equation in the system.
$2(x + y = 2)$	Multiply each term in the equation by 2.
$2x + 2y = 4$	Simplify.
$+ \quad 2x - y = 1$	Write the first equation in the system.
$\underline{} x + \underline{} y = \underline{}$	Add the equations to write a third equation.

B Graph and label each equation in the original linear system.

The solution of the system is _____.

C Graph and label the third equation.

How is the graph of the third equation related to the graphs of the two equations in the original system?

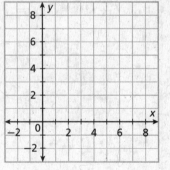

_____

_____

Is the solution of the original system also a solution of the system formed by the equation $2x - y = 1$ and the third equation? Explain.

_____

1a. Examine your results from the Explore. Does it appear that a new linear system composed of one of the equations from the original system and a new equation created by adding a multiple of one original equation to the other equation will have the same solution as the original system? Explain.

_____

_____

_____

1b. If the two equations in the original system are represented by $Ax + By = C$ and $Dx + Ey = F$, where A, B, C, D, E, and F are constants, then the third equation you wrote can be represented by doing the following:

Multiply the second equation by a nonzero constant k to get $kDx + kEy = kF$.

Then add this equation to the first equation to get the third equation.

$$
\begin{array}{l}
\ \ Ax + \ By = C \\
+\ \ kDx + kEy = kF \\
\hline
(A + kD)x + (B + kE)y = C + kF
\end{array}
$$

Complete the proof below to show that if (x_1, y_1) is a solution of the original system, then it is also a solution of the new system below.

$$
\begin{cases}
Ax + By = C \\
(A + kD)x + (B + kE)y = C + kF
\end{cases}
$$

$Ax_1 + By_1 = C$	(x_1, y_1) is a solution of $Ax + By = C$.
$Dx_1 + Ey_1 = F$	(x_1, y_1) is a solution of $Dx + Ey = F$.
$\boxed{}(Dx_1 + Ey_1) = kF$	Multiplication Property of _____
$kDx_1 + kEy_1 = kF$	_____ Property
$C + kDx_1 + kEy_1 = \boxed{} + kF$	_____ Property of Equality
$Ax_1 + \boxed{} + kDx_1 + kEy_1 = C + kF$	Substitute $Ax_1 + By_1$ for C on the left side.
$Ax_1 + kDx_1 + \boxed{} + kEy_1 = C + kF$	_____ Property of Addition
$(Ax_1 + kDx_1) + (By_1 + kEy_1) = C + kF$	Associative Property of Addition
$(A + kD)x_1 + (\boxed{} + kE)y_1 = C + kF$	Distributive Property

Since $(A + kD)x_1 + (B + kE)y_1 = C + kF$, (x_1, y_1) is a solution of the new system.

Solve the system of equations by multiplying.

$$\begin{cases} 3x + 8y = 7 \\ 2x - 2y = -10 \end{cases}$$

A Explain how to multiply one of the equations by a number so that the coefficients for one of the variables are opposites.

_____

_____

B Multiply the second equation by the constant you found in part A and add this new equation to the first equation.

⬜ $(2x - 2y = -10)$	Multiply each term in the second equation by _____ to get opposite coefficients for the y-terms.
$8x - 8y = -40$	Simplify.
$+\ 3x + 8y = \quad 7$	Add the first equation to the new equation.
$11x + 0y = -33$	Add to eliminate the variable _____.
$11x = -33$	Simplify and solve for x.
$\frac{11x}{11} = \frac{-33}{11}$	Divide both sides by 11.
$x = $ ⬜	Simplify.

C Substitute the solution into one of the equations and solve.

$3x + 8y = 7$	Use the first equation.
$3\,(\ ⬜\ ) + 8y = 7$	Substitute _____ for the variable _____.
⬜ $+ 8y = 7$	Simplify.
$8y = $ ⬜	Add _____ to each side.
$y = $ ⬜	Divide each side by _____.

D Write the solution as an ordered pair: _____

2a. How can you solve this linear system by subtracting? Which is more efficient, adding or subtracting? Explain your reasoning.

_____

_____

2b. Can this linear system be solved by adding or subtracting without multiplying? Why or why not?

_____

2c. What would you need to multiply the second equation by to eliminate x by adding? Why might you choose to eliminate y instead of x?

_____

_____

3 EXAMPLE Solving a Linear System by Multiplying Both Equations

Solve the system of equations by multiplying.

$$\begin{cases} -3x + 9y = -3 \\ 4x - 13y = 5 \end{cases}$$

A Explain how to multiply both of the equations by different integers so that the coefficients for one of the variables are opposites.

_____

_____

B Multiply both of the equations and add.

$\boxed{}(-3x + 9y = -3)$	Multiply the first equation by _____.
$\boxed{}(4x - 13y = 5)$	Multiply the second equation by _____.

$$\begin{array}{r} -12x + 36y = -12 \\ + \quad 12x - 39y = 15 \\ \hline \end{array}$$

Simplify the multiple of the first equation.
Simplify the multiple of the second equation.

$$-3y = 3$$ Add to eliminate the variable _____.

$$\frac{-3y}{-3} = \frac{3}{-3}$$ Divide both sides by -3.

$$y = \boxed{}$$ Simplify.

© Houghton Mifflin Harcourt Publishing Company

C Substitute the solution into one of the equations and solve.

$$4x - 13y = 5$$ Use the second equation.

$$4x - 13() = 5$$ Substitute _____ for the variable _____.

$$4x - () = 5$$ Simplify.

$$4x = $$ Add _____ to each side.

$$\frac{4x}{4} = \frac{-8}{4}$$ Divide each side by _____.

$$x = $$ Simplify.

D Write the solution as an ordered pair: _____

REFLECT

3a. What numbers would you need to multiply both equations by to eliminate y? Why might you choose to eliminate x instead?

_____

_____

3b. Describe how to find the numbers by which you would multiply both equations to eliminate a variable.

_____

_____

_____

3c. If both equations must be multiplied in order to eliminate a variable, how can you decide which variable will be easier to eliminate?

_____

3d. Explain what would happen if you multiplied both equations in the system $-3x + 9y = -3$ and $4x - 12y = 5$ and added them in order to eliminate a variable.

_____

_____

3e. Explain what would happen if you multiplied both equations in the system $9x - 15y = 24$ and $6x - 10y = 16$ and subtracted them to eliminate a variable.

_____

_____

PRACTICE

Solve each system by multiplying. Check your answer.

1. $\begin{cases} -2x + 2y = 2 \\ 5x - 6y = -9 \end{cases}$

Solution: _____

2. $\begin{cases} 3x + 3y = 12 \\ -6x - 11y = -14 \end{cases}$

Solution: _____

3. $\begin{cases} 4x + 3y = 11 \\ 2x - 2y = -12 \end{cases}$

Solution: _____

4. $\begin{cases} 6x + 3y = -24 \\ 7x - 5y = 6 \end{cases}$

Solution: _____

5. $\begin{cases} 3x + 8y = 17 \\ -2x + 9y = 3 \end{cases}$

Solution: _____

6. $\begin{cases} 11x + 6y = -20 \\ 15x + 9y = -33 \end{cases}$

Solution: _____

7. $\begin{cases} 2x + 3y = -6 \\ 10x + 15y = -30 \end{cases}$

Solution: _____

8. $\begin{cases} 12x - 6y = 12 \\ 8x - 16y = -16 \end{cases}$

Solution: _____

9. $\begin{cases} 5x + 9y = -3 \\ -4x - 7y = 3 \end{cases}$

Solution: _____

10. $\begin{cases} 3x - 4y = -1 \\ -6x + 8y = 3 \end{cases}$

Solution: _____

11. **Error Analysis** A linear system has two equations, $Ax + By = C$ and $Dx + Ey = F$. A student multiplies the x- and y-coefficients in the second equation by a constant k to get $kDx + kEy = F$. The student then adds the result to $Ax + By = C$ to write a new equation.

   a. What is the new equation that the student wrote?

   _____

   b. If the ordered pair (x_1, y_1) is a solution of the original system, will it also be a solution of $Ax + By = C$ and the new equation? Why or why not?

   _____

   _____

   _____

© Houghton Mifflin Harcourt Publishing Company

Solving Systems of Linear Inequalities

Essential question: *How do you solve a system of linear inequalities?*

A **system of linear inequalities** consists of two or more linear inequalities that have the same variables. The **solutions of a system of linear inequalities** are all the ordered pairs that make all the inequalities in the system true.

1 EXAMPLE Solving a System of Linear Inequalities by Graphing

Solve the system of inequalities by graphing. Check your answer.

$$\begin{cases} x + 2y > 2 \\ -x + y \le 4 \end{cases}$$

A Graph $x + 2y > 2$.

The equation of the boundary line is _____.

x-intercept: _____ **y-intercept:** _____

The inequality symbol is >, so use a _____ line.

Shade _____ the boundary line, because (0, 0) is *not* a solution of the inequality.

B Graph $-x + y \le 4$.

The equation of the boundary line is _____.

x-intercept: _____ **y-intercept:** _____

The inequality symbol is ≤, so use a _____ line.

Shade _____ the boundary line, because (0, 0) *is* a solution of the inequality.

C Identify the solutions. They are represented by the _____ shaded regions.

D Check your answer by using a point in each region. Complete the table.

Ordered Pair	Satisfies $x + 2y > 2$?	Satisfies $-x + y \le 4$?	In the overlapping shaded regions?
(0, 0)			
(2, 3)			
(−4, 2)			
(−2, 4)			

1a. How does testing specific ordered pairs tell you that the solution you graphed is correct?

_____

_____

1b. Is $(-2, 2)$ a solution of the system of inequalities? Why or why not?

_____

_____

_____

The graphs of linear inequalities in a system can have parallel boundary lines. Unlike systems of linear equations, this does not always mean the system has no solution.

2 E X A M P L E   **Graphing Systems with Parallel Boundary Lines**

Graph each system of linear inequalities.

A $\begin{cases} -x + y > 3 \\ -x + y \le -5 \end{cases}$

Describe the solutions.

_____

_____

B $\begin{cases} x + y > -4 \\ x + y > -1 \end{cases}$

Describe the solutions.

_____

_____

_____

C $\begin{cases} -x + 3y \le 3 \\ -x + 3y \ge -3 \end{cases}$

Describe the solutions.

_____

_____

_____

2a. Is $(1, -2)$ a solution of the system $x + y > -4$ and $x + y > -1$? Explain.

_____

_____

2b. Is $(3, 2)$ a solution of the system $-x + 3y \leq 3$ and $-x + 3y \geq -3$? Explain.

_____

_____

2c. Can the solution of a system of inequalities be a line? If so, give an example.

_____

_____

2d. Does the system $3x - 2y < 4$ and $3x - 2y > 4$ have a solution? Explain.

_____

_____

2e. Is it possible for a system of two linear inequalities to have every point in the plane as solutions? Why or why not?

_____

_____

_____

PRACTICE

Solve each system of linear inequalities by graphing. Check your answers.

1. $\begin{cases} x + y \leq -2 \\ -x + y > 1 \end{cases}$

2. $\begin{cases} x + 2y \geq 8 \\ x - 2y < -4 \end{cases}$

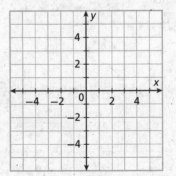

3. $\begin{cases} y \geq -2 \\ 4x + y \geq 2 \end{cases}$

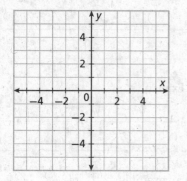

4. $\begin{cases} x < 1 \\ 2x + y > 1 \end{cases}$

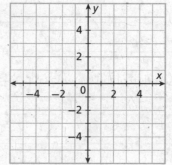

5. $\begin{cases} x - y \leq -3 \\ x - y > 3 \end{cases}$

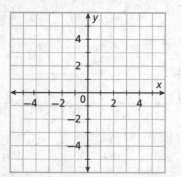

6. $\begin{cases} 4x + y \geq 4 \\ 4x + y \geq -4 \end{cases}$

7. Graph the system of linear inequalities.

$\begin{cases} x + 4y > -4 \\ x + y \leq 2 \\ x - y \geq 2 \end{cases}$

a. Describe the solutions of the system.

_____

_____

_____

b. Is (2, 0) a solution of the system? Explain your reasoning.

_____

_____

c. Is (4, −2) a solution of the system? Explain your reasoning.

_____

_____

FOCUS ON MODELING
Modeling with Linear Systems

Essential question: *How can you use systems of linear equations or inequalities to model and solve contextual problems?*

COMMON CORE

CC.9-12.N.Q.1*,
CC.9-12.N.Q.2*,
CC.9-12.A.CED.2*,
CC.9-12.A.CED.3*,
CC.9-12.A.REI.6,
CC.9-12.A.REI.12

> Y ou are purchasing jeans and T-shirts. Jeans cost $35 and T-shirts cost $15. You plan on spending $115 and purchasing a total of 5 items. How many pairs of jeans and how many T-shirts can you buy?

1 **Write a system of linear equations to model the situation.**

A Write an expression to represent the amount you will pay for x pairs of jeans at $35 per pair.

_____

B Write an expression to represent the amount you will pay for y T-shirts at $15 per shirt.

_____

C The total amount spent for jeans and T-shirts is given below in words. Use this verbal model and your expressions from Steps 1A and 1B to write an equation for the total amount you will spend.

Amount Spent for Jeans	+	Amount Spent for T-shirts	=	Total Amount Spent
_____	+	_____	=	_____

D What variable represents the number of pairs of jeans purchased?

_____

E What variable represents the number of T-shirts purchased?

_____

F Write an equation to represent the total number of items purchased.

_____

G Write a system of linear equations to model the situation.

_____

1a. What units are associated with the expressions that you wrote in 1A and 1B?

_____

_____

1b. When you add the units for the expressions representing the amounts spent on jeans and T-shirts, what units do you get for total amount spent? Are they the units you expect?

_____

_____

2 Solve the system algebraically.

A Solve an equation for one variable.

$x + y = 5$ Select one of the equations.

$y =$ [ ]   Isolate the variable y on one side.

B Substitute the expression for y into the other equation and solve.

$35x + 15 \left(\right) = 115$ Substitute the expression for the variable y.

$35x + + 75 = 115$ Use the Distributive Property.

$ + 75 = 115$ Combine like terms.

$ = 40$ Subtract ____ from each side.

$x = $ Divide each side by _____.

C Substitute the value of the variable you found in Part B into one of the equations and solve for the other variable.

$ + y = 5$ Substitute the value you found into an equation.

$y = $ Subtract ____ from each side.

So, _____ is the solution of the system.

2a. In the solution, what does the x-value of the ordered pair represent in the context of the situation? What does the y-value represent?

_____

2b. Explain why substitution is a good method to use to solve this system.

_____

_____

3 Check the solution by graphing.

A Graph each equation.

Step 1: Find the intercepts for $35x + 15y = 115$ and graph the line.

x-intercept: _____   *y*-intercept: _____

Step 2: Find the intercepts for $x + y = 5$ and graph the line.

x-intercept: _____   *y*-intercept: _____

B Find the point of intersection.

The two lines appear to intersect at _____.

T-shirts (y-axis, marked 2, 4, 6, 8); Pairs of jeans (x-axis, marked 2, 4, 6, 8)

REFLECT

3a. What units are represented on the *x*-axis?

_____

3b. What units are represented on the *y*-axis?

_____

3c. Does the solution you found by graphing confirm that the solution you found algebraically was correct? Explain.

_____

_____

3d. Was it easier to solve the system algebraically or by graphing? Explain your reasoning.

_____

_____

4 Interpret the solution.

A What does the solution tell you about the number of pairs of jeans and the number of T-shirts you can purchase?

_____

B In the context of the problem, what could be the values of *x* and *y*?

_____

C Is the solution reasonable? Explain your reasoning.

_____

_____

_____

© Houghton Mifflin Harcourt Publishing Company

4a. Is the solution you found the only solution for this linear system? Explain how you know.

_____

_____

EXTEND

1. Suppose you want to buy at least 5 items and spend no more than $115. How can you modify the system of linear equations you wrote to model this new situation?

_____

_____

2. Write an inequality to represent buying at least 5 items.

_____

3. Write an inequality to represent spending no more than $115.

_____

4. Are there any other conditions on the system, based on the context of the problem? If so, what are they?

_____

_____

5. Write a system of linear inequalities to model the situation. Include any new conditions from Question 4.

_____

6. What constraints do the additional conditions based on the context of the problem place on where in the plane the solution region will be located?

_____

7. Graph the system of inequalities.

Step 1 Graph $x + y \geq 5$.

The equation of the boundary line is _____.

***x*-intercept:** _____   ***y*-intercept:** _____

The inequality symbol is $\geq$, use a _____ line.

Shade _____ the boundary line, because $(0, 0)$
is *not* a solution of the inequality.

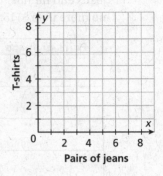

Step 2 Graph $35x + 15y \leq 115$.

The equation of the boundary line is _____.

***x*-intercept:** _____   ***y*-intercept:** _____

The inequality symbol is $\leq$, use a _____ line.

Shade _____ the boundary line line, because $(0, 0)$
is a solution of the inequality.

Step 3 Identify the solutions.

The solutions of the system are represented by the _____ shaded regions
that form a _____ to the _____ of the *y*-axis.

8. In the context of the situation, are all points in the overlapping shaded region
possible solutions? Why or why not? Explain.

_____

_____

9. Is the ordered pair that was the solution of the system of linear equations for this
situation a solution of this system of inequalities?

_____

_____

10. If you buy at least 5 items and spend no more than $115, what is the greatest number
of jeans you can buy? Explain your reasoning.

_____

_____

11. If you buy at least 5 items and spend no more than $115, what is the greatest number
of T-shirts you can buy? Explain your reasoning.

_____

_____

12. Use the graph to make a list of all the possible solutions for the number of pairs of jeans and number of T-shirts you can purchase if you buy at least 5 items and spend no more than $115.

Pairs of Jeans	T-Shirts	Total Items	Total Cost

Name _____ Class _____ Date _____

MULTIPLE CHOICE

1. Which system of linear equations is represented by the graph shown below?

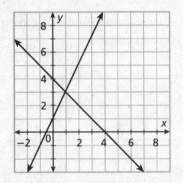

A. $\begin{cases} x + y = 4 \\ 2x + y = 1 \end{cases}$ **C.** $\begin{cases} x - y = 4 \\ 2x - y = -1 \end{cases}$

B. $\begin{cases} x + y = 4 \\ 2x - y = -1 \end{cases}$ **D.** $\begin{cases} x + y = 4 \\ x - 2y = 1 \end{cases}$

2. Katy is solving the linear system below by substitution.

$$\begin{cases} 2x + y = 7 \\ 3x - 2y = -7 \end{cases}$$

Which of the following would be a step in solving the system?

F. Substitute $y + 7$ for x in $3x - 2y = -7$.

G. Substitute $-y + 7$ for x in $3x - 2y = -7$.

H. Substitute $-2x + 7$ for y in $3x - 2y = -7$.

J. Substitute $2x - 7$ for y in $3x - 2y = -7$.

3. Which step can be taken to eliminate a variable from the linear system below?

$$\begin{cases} -4x + 2y = -2 \\ 4x - 3y = -1 \end{cases}$$

A. Add to eliminate the variable x.

B. Subtract to eliminate the variable x.

C. Add to eliminate the variable y.

D. Subtract to eliminate the variable y.

4. Frank wants to eliminate the variable y from the system below by adding.

$$\begin{cases} 7x - 6y = 8 \\ 2x + 2y = 6 \end{cases}$$

First, he will have to multiply one of the equations by a number. Which step will enable him to eliminate y by adding?

F. Multiply each term in $7x - 6y = 8$ by 3.

G. Multiply each term in $7x - 6y = 8$ by -3.

H. Multiply each term in $2x + 2y = 6$ by 3.

J. Multiply each term in $2x + 2y = 6$ by -3.

5. Which ordered pair is *not* a solution of the system of linear inequalities graphed below?

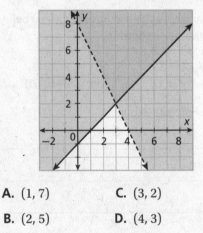

A. $(1, 7)$ **C.** $(3, 2)$

B. $(2, 5)$ **D.** $(4, 3)$

6. You are purchasing paint and paintbrushes for an art project. Tubes of paint cost $6 each and paintbrushes cost $8 each. You plan on spending $60 and purchasing a total of 9 items. Which linear system best represents the situation?

F. $\begin{cases} 6x + 8y = 9 \\ x + y = 60 \end{cases}$ **H.** $\begin{cases} 9x + 9y = 60 \\ 6x + 8y = 60 \end{cases}$

G. $\begin{cases} 6x + 9y = 60 \\ 9x + 8y = 60 \end{cases}$ **J.** $\begin{cases} x + y = 9 \\ 6x + 8y = 60 \end{cases}$

7. A system of two linear equations has no solution. Describe the graph of the system.

_____

_____

_____

8. Solve the linear system below. Describe the steps you used to solve it.

$$\begin{cases} 2x + 3y = 13 \\ x - 2y = 3 \end{cases}$$

_____

_____

_____

_____

_____

9. Pilar says that the two linear systems below have the same solution.

$$\begin{cases} 3x + 2y = 2 \\ 5x + 4y = 6 \end{cases} \qquad \begin{cases} 3x + 2y = 2 \\ 11x + 8y = 10 \end{cases}$$

Is she correct? Explain.

_____

_____

_____

_____

_____

_____

Use the information below to complete Items 10–12.

Terrance purchased a total of 10 pens and pencils for $4. Pens cost 50 cents and pencils cost 25 cents. Terrance wrote the system of equations below to represent the situation.

$$\begin{cases} x + y = 10 \\ \frac{1}{2}x + \frac{1}{4}y = 4 \end{cases}$$

10. What units are associated with the expressions in the second equation?

_____

_____

_____

_____

11. Describe the constraint that each equation places on the system.

_____

_____

_____

_____

12. Are there any other constraints on the system? If so, what are they?

_____

_____

_____

© Houghton Mifflin Harcourt Publishing Company

Linear Functions

Unit Focus

In this unit you will examine the characteristics of linear functions and their graphs. You will learn to write linear functions, perform operations with them, and find their inverses. You will also learn to model paired data using linear functions.

Unit at a Glance

COMMON CORE

Unpacking the Common Core State Standards

Use the table to help you understand the Standards for Mathematical Content that are taught in this unit. Refer to the lessons listed after each standard for exploration and practice.

COMMON CORE Standards for Mathematical Content	What It Means For You
CC.9-12.N.Q.1 Use units as a way to understand problems and to guide the solution of multi-step problems; choose and interpret units consistently in formulas; choose and interpret the scale and the origin in graphs and data displays.* Lessons 4-2, 4-3 (Also 4-5, 4-6)	Because linear functions that model real-world situations involve rates of change, it's important that you check the units involved to make sure they are compatible and give the desired units for the models.
CC.9-12.A.APR.1 Understand that polynomials form a system analogous to the integers, namely, they are closed under the operations of addition, subtraction, and multiplication; **add, subtract, and multiply polynomials.** Lesson 4-6	As you will learn later in the course, the rules for linear functions are polynomials having degree 1. You will learn to combine linear functions by adding and subtracting their rules as well as multiplying their rules by constants.
CC.9-12.A.CED.2 Create equations in two or more variables to represent relationships between quantities; graph equations on coordinate axes with labels and scales.* Lessons 4-2, 4-3, 4-5, 4-6 (Also 4-7)	You will use linear functions to model real-world situations and real-world data, and you will graph the linear models in the coordinate plane.
CC.9-12.A.REI.11 Explain why the x-coordinates of the points where the graphs of the equations $y = f(x)$ and $y = g(x)$ intersect are the solutions of the equation $f(x) = g(x)$; find the solutions approximately, e.g., using technology to graph the functions, make tables of values, or find successive approximations. **Include cases where $f(x)$ and/or $g(x)$ are linear,** polynomial, rational, absolute value, exponential, and logarithmic functions.* Lesson 4-5	You will solve real-world problems by writing two linear models and determining where their graphs intersect.
CC.9-12.F.IF.1 Understand that a function from one set (called the domain) to another set (called the range) assigns to each element of the domain exactly one element of the range. If f is a function and x is an element of its domain, then $f(x)$ denotes the output of f corresponding to the input x. The graph of f is the graph of the equation $y = f(x)$. Lessons 4-2, 4-7 (Also 4-1)	You will learn how to recognize restrictions on the domains and ranges of linear functions that model real-world situations.

UNIT 4

© Houghton Mifflin Harcourt Publishing Company

COMMON CORE Standards for Mathematical Content	What It Means For You
CC.9-12.F.IF.2 Use function notation, evaluate functions for inputs in their domains, and interpret statements that use function notation in terms of a context. Lessons 4-1, 4-2, 4-7 (Also 4-6)	You will learn to move flexibly between writing an equation in x and y and writing the equation using $f(x)$ in place of y when y is a function of x.
CC.9-12.F.IF.3 Recognize that sequences are functions, sometimes defined recursively, whose domain is a subset of the integers. Lesson 4-1	You will learn that the outputs of a discrete linear function are a sequence of numbers known as an arithmetic sequence for certain domains from the set of integers.
CC.9-12.F.IF.4 For a function that models a relationship between two quantities, interpret key features of graphs and tables in terms of the quantities, and sketch graphs showing key features given a verbal description of the relationship. Key features include: intercepts; intervals where the function is increasing, decreasing, positive, or negative; relative maximums and minimums; symmetries; end behavior; and periodicity.* Lessons 4-3, 4-4, 4-5	You will learn to graph a linear function by recognizing its slope and y-intercept from the function's rule. You will also see that a positive slope means that the function is an increasing function while a negative slope means that the function is a decreasing function.
CC.9-12.F.IF.5 Relate the domain of a function to its graph and, where applicable, to the quantitative relationship it describes.* Lessons 4-1, 4-2 (Also 4-4)	You will learn to distinguish between situations where the graph of a linear function is a set of distinct points that lie on a line and situations where the graph is an unbroken line or part of a line.
CC.9-12.F.IF.6 Calculate and interpret the average rate of change of a function (presented symbolically or as a table) over a specified interval. Estimate the rate of change from a graph.* Lessons 4-3, 4-5	You will learn that the rate of change of a linear function is constant and that it tells you the slope of the function's graph. Being able to calculate or estimate the rate of change is particularly useful when modeling real-world situations or real-world data.
CC.9-12.F.IF.7 Graph functions expressed symbolically and show key features of the graph, by hand in simple cases and using technology for more complicated cases.* **CC.9-12.F.IF.7a Graph linear** and quadratic **functions and show intercepts,** maxima, and minima.* Lessons 4-1, 4-2, 4-3, 4-5 (Also 4-7, 4-10)	You will learn to graph linear functions using slopes and y-intercepts.
CC.9-12.F.IF.9 Compare properties of two functions each represented in a different way (algebraically, graphically, numerically in tables, or by verbal descriptions). Lesson 4-2	Functions can be represented in several ways, including input-output tables, graphs, algebraic rules, and verbal descriptions. In order to compare two functions represented in different ways, you need to be able to convert them to a common representation.

UNIT 4

COMMON CORE Standards for Mathematical Content	What It Means For You
CC.9-12.F.BF.1 Write a function that describes a relationship between two quantities.* **CC.9-12.F.BF.1a** Determine an explicit expression, a recursive process, or steps for calculation from a context.* **CC.9-12.F.BF.1b** Combine standard function types using arithmetic operations.* Lessons 4-5, 4-6, 4-9 (Also 4-7)	Given a graph of a linear function, a table of function values, or a verbal description of a linear relationship, you will learn to write a function rule. You will also be able to combine function rules to create new linear functions.
CC.9-12.F.BF.2 Write arithmetic and geometric sequences both recursively and with an explicit formula, **use them to model situations,** and translate between the two forms.* Lesson 4-1	You will analyze discrete linear functions, also known as arithmetic sequences, that model real-world situations.
CC.9-12.F.BF.3 Identify the effect on the graph of replacing $f(x)$ by $f(x) + k$, $k\,f(x)$, $f(kx)$, and $f(x + k)$ **for specific values of k (both positive and negative);** find the value of k given the graphs. Experiment with cases and illustrate an explanation of the effects on the graphs using technology. Lesson 4-4	You will investigate what happens to the graph of a linear function in the form $f(x) = mx + b$ when you change the values of m and b.
CC.9-12.F.BF.4 Find inverse functions. **CC.9-12.F.BF.4a** Solve an equation of the form $f(x) = c$ for a simple function f that has an inverse and write an expression for the inverse. Lesson 4-7	You will learn to find the inverse of a linear function, and you will see that the inverse undoes, in the reverse order, the operations that the function performs on inputs to obtain outputs.
CC.9-12.F.LE.2 Construct linear and exponential **functions,** including arithmetic and geometric sequences, **given a graph, a description of a relationship, or two input-output pairs (include reading these from a table).*** Lessons 4-5, 4-6	You will write the rule for a linear function when given a graph, table, or verbal description. This is particularly useful when you fit a line to data and want to know the equation of the line.
CC.9-12.F.LE.5 Interpret the parameters in a linear or exponential **function in terms of a context.*** Lessons 4-4, 4-5, 4-6, 4-9, 4-10	A linear function has the form $f(x) = mx + b$ where the parameter m is the slope of the function's graph and the parameter b is the y-intercept of the graph. You will learn to recognize the real-world meaning of these parameters when working with linear models.

UNIT 4

COMMON CORE Standards for Mathematical Content	What It Means For You
CC.9-12.S.ID.6 Represent data on two quantitative variables on a scatter plot, and describe how the variables are related. **CC.9-12.S.ID.6a Fit a function to the data; use functions fitted to data to solve problems in the context of the data.*** **CC.9-12.S.ID.6b Informally assess the fit of a function by plotting and analyzing residuals.*** **CC.9-12.S.ID.6c Fit a linear function for a scatter plot that suggests a linear association.*** Lessons 4-9, 4-10	You will learn to model real-world data using linear functions. The models will allow you to make predictions, and the goodness of fit will, to some degree, determine the accuracy of your predictions.
CC.9-12.S.ID.7 Interpret the slope (rate of change) and the intercept (constant term) of a linear model in the context of the data.* Lessons 4-9, 4-10	Once you have a linear model for a set of data, you should be able to recognize what the model is telling you about the data.
CC.9-12.S.ID.8 Compute (using technology) and interpret the correlation coefficient of a linear fit.* Lessons 4-8, 4-10	The correlation coefficient is a measure of the strength of a linear relationship between two variables. It helps you decide whether it makes sense to model data using a linear function.
CC.9-12.S.ID.9 Distinguish between correlation and causation.* Lesson 4-8	Just because two real-world variables have a strong correlation does not mean that a change in one variable causes a change in the other variable. You must be cautious when moving from correlation to causation.
CC.9-12.S.IC.6 Evaluate reports based on data.* Lesson 4-8	You will decide whether two sets of data show correlation, causation, or neither.

UNIT 4

Discrete Linear Functions

Essential question: *What are the characteristics of a discrete linear function?*

COMMON CORE

CC.9-12.F.IF.2,
CC.9-12.F.IF.3,
CC.9-12.F.IF.5*,
CC.9-12.F.IF.7*,
CC.9-12.F.IF.7a*,
CC.9-12.F.BF.2*

1 EXPLORE Analyzing a Discrete Real-World Function

You buy a printer for $80 and then pay $15 for each ink cartridge that you use. A function relating the cost, C (in dollars), of operating the printer to the number of cartridges used, n, is $C(n) = 15n + 80$.

A Complete the table to represent the total cost for 0 to 4 cartridges.

Number of cartridges, n	Cost, C (dollars)
0	
1	
2	
3	
4	

B Graph the function from Part A. Specify the scale you use.

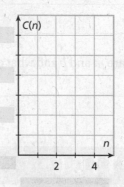

C What is the initial value of the cost function? What does it represent? What number of cartridges corresponds to the initial cost?

_____

D Compare the differences in cost with each unit increase in the number of cartridges purchased.

_____

REFLECT

1a. Identify the domain and range for the function $C(n)$ using set notation.

Domain: _____   Range: _____

1b. Describe the pattern formed by the points in the graph.

_____

1c. How do your answers change if the price of the printer is $90?

_____

_____

A function whose output values have a *common difference* for each unit increase in the input values is a *linear function*. A **linear function** can be represented by the equation $f(x) = mx + b$, where m and b are constants. The graph of a linear function forms a straight line.

When a linear function is *discrete*, its graph consists of isolated points along a straight line. If a discrete linear function has inputs that are a set of equally spaced integers, then its outputs are a sequence of numbers called an *arithmetic sequence*.

REFLECT

2a. Give three reasons why the cost function in the Explore is linear.

_____

_____

_____

2b. What are m and b and what do they represent for the cost function?

_____

PRACTICE

1. Andrea receives a $40 gift card to use a town pool. It costs her $8 per visit to swim. A function relating the value of the gift card, v, to the number of visits, n, is $v(n) = 40 - 8n$.

a. Graph the function. Label axes and scales.

b. What is the initial value?

_____

c. What is the difference between a given card value and the previous card value?

_____

d. Identify the domain and the range of the function using set notation.

_____

e. Is the function a discrete linear function? Are its outputs an arithmetic sequence? Why or why not?

_____

_____

Continuous Linear Functions

Essential question: *How are discrete and continuous linear functions alike, and how are they different?*

COMMON
CORE

CC.9-12.N.Q.1*,
CC.9-12.F.IF.1,
CC.9-12.F.IF.2,
CC.9-12.F.IF.5*,
CC.9-12.F.IF.9

1 **EXPLORE** **Comparing Linear Functions**

A Avocados cost $1.50 each. Green beans cost $1.50 per pound. The total cost of a avocados is $C(a) = 1.5a$ and the total cost of g pounds of green beans is $C(g) = 1.5g$. Complete the tables to find a few values.

Cost of Avocados		
a	$C(a) = 1.5a$	$(a, C(a))$
0	0	(0, 0)
1		
2		
3		

Cost of Green Beans		
g	$C(g) = 1.5g$	$(g, C(g))$
0	0	(0, 0)
1		
2		
3		

B What is a reasonable domain for $C(a)$? for $C(g)$? Explain.

_____

_____

C Graph the two cost functions for all appropriate domain values from the given scales below.

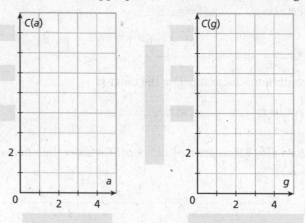

D Compare the graphs. How are they alike? How are they different?

_____

_____

_____

1a. Describe the range for $C(a)$ and for $C(g)$.

_____

_____

1b. How do the units of a and g imply that their graphs will be different?

_____

_____

_____

1c. A function whose graph is unbroken is a *continuous* function. Tell which cost function is *continuous* and which is *discrete*.

_____

2 EXAMPLE Comparing Functions Given a Table and a Rule

The functions $f(x)$ and $g(x)$ below are linear. Find the initial value and the range of each function. Then compare the functions.

- The table gives the values of the function $f(x)$. The domain of $f(x)$ is $\{4, 5, 6, 7\}$.
- Let the domain of the function $g(x) = 2x + 3$ be all real numbers such that $4 \leq x \leq 7$.

x	f(x)
4	8
5	10
6	12
7	14

A The initial value is the output that is paired with the least input.

The initial value of $f(x)$ is $f(\underline{\quad}) = \underline{\quad}$.

The initial value of $g(x)$ is $g(\underline{\quad}) = \underline{\quad}$.

B The range of $f(x)$ is _____.

Because $g(x)$ is a continuous linear function the range is

$g(4) \leq g(x) \leq g(7)$, or $\{g(x) \mid \underline{\quad} \leq g(x) \leq \underline{\quad}\}$.

C How are the functions alike? How are they different? Consider their domains, initial values, and ranges.

_____

_____

_____

_____

_____

_____

2a. Find and compare the common differences per unit increase in the input values for the functions $f(x)$ and $g(x)$ in the Example.

_____

_____

2b. How can you tell that $f(x)$ and $g(x)$ in the Example are linear?

_____

_____

3 **E X A M P L E** **Comparing Descriptions and Graphs of Functions**

Compare the following functions.

- A heavy rainstorm lasted for 2.5 hours during which time it rained at a steady rate of 0.5 inches per hour. The function $A_h(t)$ represents the amount of rain that fell in t hours.
- The graph at the right shows the amount of rain that fell during a violent rainstorm $A_v(t)$ (in inches) as a function of time t (in hours).

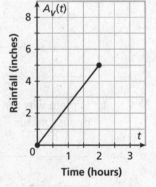

A How long did each storm last? Explain your reasoning.

_____

_____

B Calculate the amount of rainfall during the heavy storm. Then compare the amounts of rainfall for the two storms.

Heavy rainfall: (_____ inches per hour) • (_____ hours) = _____ inches of rain

_____

_____

C Calculate how many inches of rain fell per hour during the violent rainstorm. Then compare the rainfall rates for the two storms.

Violent rainfall rate: (_____ inches) ÷ (_____ hours) = _____ inches per hour

_____

REFLECT

3a. How would the graphs of $A_h(t)$ and $A_v(t)$ compare with one another?

_____

_____

1. The functions $f(x)$ and $g(x)$ are defined by the table and graph below.

x	f(x)
0	−2
1	1
2	4
3	7
4	10
5	13

a. Compare the domains, initial values, and ranges of the functions.

_____

_____

_____

b. Explain why the functions are linear. Tell whether each function is *discrete* or *continuous*

_____

_____

_____

_____

2. Grace works between 10 and 20 hours per week while attending college. She earns $9.00 per hour. Her hours are rounded to the nearest quarter hour. Her roommate Frances also has a job. Her pay for t hours is given by the function $f(t) = 10t$, where $5 \leq t \leq 15$. Her hours are not rounded.

a. Find the domain and range of each function.

_____

_____

_____

b. Compare their hourly wages and the amount they each earn per week.

_____

_____

Using Slope

Essential question: *What is the slope of a linear function and how can you use it to graph the function?*

COMMON CORE

CC.9-12.N.Q.1*,
CC.9-12.A.CED.2*,
CC.9-12.F.IF.4*,
CC.9-12.F.IF.6*,
CC.9-12.F.IF.7*,
CC.9-12.F.IF.7a*

If $f(x)$ is a linear function, then its graph is a line. The ordered pairs $(x_1, f(x_1))$ and $(x_2, f(x_2))$ can be used to name two points on the line. The change in the independent variables between these points is $x_2 - x_1$. The change in the dependent variables is $f(x_2) - f(x_1)$.

1 EXPLORE Changes in Independent and Dependent Variables

A Use the function $f(x) = 2x + 1$ to complete the table for each interval.

Interval	From $x = 1$ to $x = 2$	From $x = 1$ to $x = 3$	From $x = 1$ to $x = 4$
Change in x, the independent variable	$2 - 1 = 1$		
Change in $f(x)$, the dependent variable	$f(2) - f(1) =$ $5 - 3 = 2$		
$\dfrac{\text{Change in } f(x)}{\text{Change in } x}$	$\dfrac{2}{1} = 2$	$\dfrac{}{} = \square$	$\dfrac{}{} = \square$

B The ratio $\dfrac{f(x_2) - f(x_1)}{x_2 - x_1}$ over each interval simplifies to _____.

REFLECT

1a. What is the relationship between the ratio of $f(x_2) - f(x_1)$ to $x_2 - x_1$ and the function rule?

_____

1b. Is the ratio of $f(x_2) - f(x_1)$ to $x_2 - x_1$ the same over the interval from $x = 2$ to $x = 4$? Explain.

_____

1c. Suppose the function rule was $f(x) = 2x + 5$ instead of $f(x) = 2x + 1$. Would the ratio of $f(x_2) - f(x_1)$ to $x_2 - x_1$ remain the same? Explain.

_____

_____

_____

© Houghton Mifflin Harcourt Publishing Company

The ratio of $f(x_2) - f(x_1)$ to $x_2 - x_1$ for a linear function $f(x)$ is the **rate of change** of $f(x)$ with respect to x. The rate of change is the same for any two points on the graph of a given linear function.

You can interpret the rate of change of a linear function $f(x)$ geometrically as the *slope* of its graph. The diagram at the right shows the graph of $f(x)$, where the vertical axis represents the function values. The **rise** is the change in function values, $f(x_2) - f(x_1)$, and the **run** is the change in x-values, $x_2 - x_1$. The **slope** of the line is the ratio of the rise to the run.

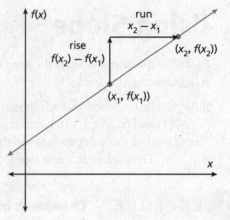

Several ways of expressing the slope of a line are given below.

$$\text{slope} = \frac{\text{rise}}{\text{run}} = \frac{f(x_2) - f(x_1)}{x_2 - x_1} = \frac{\text{change in } f(x)}{\text{change in } x}$$

REFLECT

2a. Complete the following to show that the y-intercept of the graph of a linear function $f(x)$ is the value of b in the equation $f(x) = mx + b$.

The y-intercept of the graph of an equation occurs where $x = 0$.

So, the y-intercept of the graph of $f(x) = mx + b$ is as follows.

$$f(0) = m \cdot \boxed{} + b$$

$$f(0) = \boxed{} + b$$

$$f(0) = b$$

2b. Complete the following to show that the slope of the graph of a linear function $f(x)$ is the value of m in the equation $f(x) = mx + b$.

To find the slope of the graph of $f(x) = mx + b$, choose any two points on the line. Two convenient points are $(x_1, f(x_1)) = (0, b)$ and $(x_2, f(x_2)) = (1, m + b)$.

$$\frac{f(x_2) - f(x_1)}{x_2 - x_1} = \frac{\boxed{} - \boxed{}}{\boxed{} - \boxed{}} = \frac{\boxed{}}{\boxed{}} = m$$

2c. Show that the y-intercept of the graph of the function $f(x) = 4x + 1$ is 1 and that the rate of change of $f(x)$ with respect to x is 4.

_____

_____

© Houghton Mifflin Harcourt Publishing Company

The slope of a line, can be positive, negative, 0, or undefined. If the slope is undefined, the line is not the graph of a function.

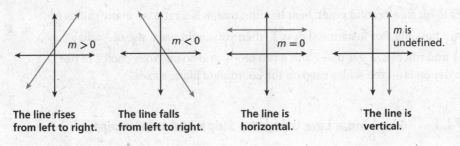

The line rises from left to right.   The line falls from left to right.   The line is horizontal.   The line is vertical.

3a. When you move from left to right between two points on a line with a positive slope, is the rise *positive*, *negative*, or 0? Is the run *positive*, *negative*, or 0? Use your answers to explain why the slope of a line that rises from left to right is positive.

_____

_____

3b. When you move from left to right between two points on a line with a negative slope, is the rise *positive*, *negative*, or 0? Is the run *positive*, *negative*, or 0? Use your answers to explain why the slope of a line that falls from left to right is negative.

_____

_____

3c. When you move from left to right between two points on a horizontal line, is the rise *positive*, *negative*, or 0? Is the run *positive*, *negative*, or 0? Use your answers to explain why the slope of a horizontal line is 0.

_____

3d. When you move up from one point to another on a vertical line, is the rise *positive*, *negative*, or 0? Is the run *positive*, *negative*, or 0? Use your answers to explain why the slope of a vertical line is undefined.

_____

_____

3e. A **constant function** is a function that has a rate of change of 0. Describe the graph of a constant function and the form of its equation.

_____

© Houghton Mifflin Harcourt Publishing Company

Graphing Lines You can graph the linear function $f(x) = mx + b$ using only the slope m and the y-intercept b. First, locate the point $(0, b)$ on the y-axis. Next, use the rise and run of the slope to locate another point on the line. Draw the line through the two points.

When using m to locate a second point, bear in mind that m is a ratio, so many values of rise and run are possible. For instance, if $m = \frac{1}{2}$, then you could use a rise of $\frac{1}{2}$ and a run of 1, a rise of 1 and run of 2, a rise of -2 and a run of -4, and so on. Your choice of rise and run often depends on the scales used on the coordinate plane's axes.

4 EXAMPLE Graphing a Line Using the Slope and y-Intercept

Graph each function.

A $f(x) = -\frac{2}{3}x + 4$

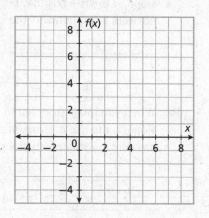

• The y-intercept is _____. Plot the point that corresponds to the y-intercept.

• The slope is _____. If you use -2 as the rise, then the run is _____.

• Use the slope to move from the first point to a second point. Begin by moving down _____ units, because the rise is negative. Then move right _____ units, because the run is positive. Plot a second point.

• Draw the line through the two points.

• The domain is the set of _____ numbers.

  The range is the set of _____ numbers.

B A pitcher with a maximum capacity of 4 cups contains 1 cup of apple juice concentrate. A faucet is turned on filling the pitcher at a rate of 0.25 cup per second. The amount of liquid in the pitcher (in cups) is a function $A(t)$ of the time t (in seconds) that the water is running.

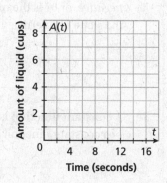

• The y-intercept is the initial amount in the pitcher at time 0, or _____ cup. Plot the point that corresponds to the y-intercept.

• The slope is the rate of change: _____ cup per second, or 1 cup in _____ seconds. So, the rise is _____ and the run is _____.

• Use the rise and run to move from the first point to a second point on the line by moving up _____ unit and right _____ units. Plot a second point.

• Connect the points and extend the line to the maximum value of the function, where $A(t) =$ _____ cups.

• The domain is the set of numbers _____ $\leq t \leq$ _____.

  The range is the set of numbers _____ $\leq A(t) \leq$ _____.

© Houghton Mifflin Harcourt Publishing Company

4a. How could you use the slope and *y*-intercept to graph the function $f(x) = 3$?

_____

_____

4b. What are the units of the rise in Part B? What are the units of the run?

_____

4c. How long does it take to fill the pitcher? Explain.

_____

4d. Why is the function rule $A(t) = \frac{1}{4}t + 1$? Use units to justify your answer.

_____

_____

_____

_____

PRACTICE

1. Calculate the rate of change of the function in the table. _____

Tickets for rides	10	12	14	16
Total cost of carnival ($)	12.50	14.00	15.50	17.00

Estimate the change in the dependent variable over the given interval from the domain of the independent variable. Estimate the rate of change.

2.

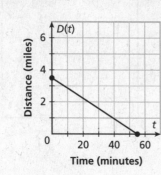

Given interval: $20 \le t \le 40$

Change in $D(t)$: _____

Rate of change: _____

3.

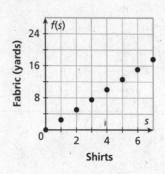

Given interval: $3 \le s \le 5$

Change in $f(s)$: _____

Rate of change: _____

Graph each linear function.

4. $f(x) = 3x - 4$

5. $f(x) = \frac{1}{2}x + 2$

6. $f(x) = -1$

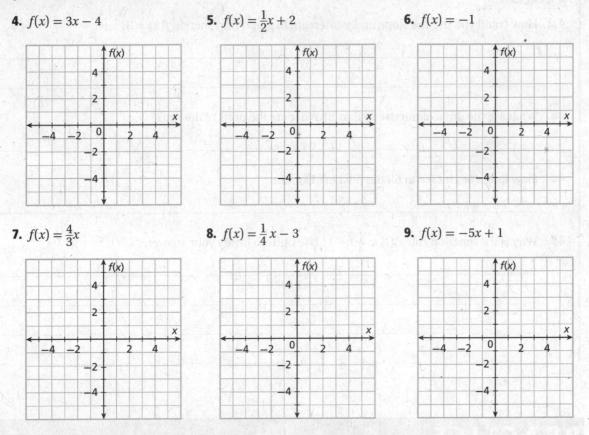

7. $f(x) = \frac{4}{3}x$

8. $f(x) = \frac{1}{4}x - 3$

9. $f(x) = -5x + 1$

Graph each linear function and answer the question. Explain your answer.

10. A plumber charges $50 for a service call plus $75 per hour. The total of these costs (in dollars) is a function $C(t)$ of the time t (in hours) on the job. For how many hours will the cost be $200? $300?

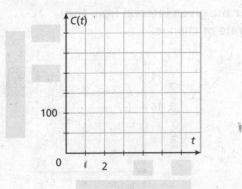

11. A bamboo plant is 10 centimeters tall at noon and grows at a rate of 5 centimeters every 2 hours. The height (in centimeters) is a function $h(t)$ of the time t it grows. When will the plant be 20 centimeters tall?

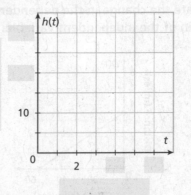

Changing the Values of *m* and *b* in $f(x) = mx + b$

COMMON CORE

CC.9-12.F.IF.4*,
CC.9-12.F.BF.3,
CC.9-12.F.LE.5*

Essential question: *How do the values of m and b affect the graph of the function* $f(x) = mx + b$?

1 EXPLORE   Changing the Value of *b* in $f(x) = x + b$

Investigate what happens to the graph of $f(x) = x + b$ when you change the value of *b*.

A   Use a graphing calculator. Start with the standard viewing window, which you can obtain by pressing ZOOM and selecting ZStandard. Because the distances between consecutive tick marks on the *x*-axis and on the *y*-axis are not equal, you can make them equal by pressing ZOOM again and selecting ZSquare.

What interval on each axis does the viewing window now show? (Press WINDOW to find out.)

_____

B   Graph the function $f(x) = x$ by pressing Y= and entering the function's rule next to $Y_1 =$. As shown, the graph of the function is a line that makes a 45° angle with each axis.

What are the slope and *y*-intercept of the graph of $f(x) = x$?

_____

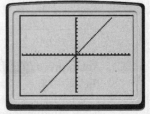

C   Graph other functions of the form $f(x) = x + b$ by entering their rules next to $Y_2 =$, $Y_3 =$, and so on. Be sure to choose both positive and negative values of *b*. For instance, graph $f(x) = x + 2$ and $f(x) = x - 3$. What do the graphs have in common? How are they different?

_____

REFLECT

1a. A *vertical translation* moves all points on a figure the same distance either up or down. Use the idea of a vertical translation to describe what happens to the graph of $f(x) = x + b$ when you increase the value of *b* and when you decrease the value of *b*.

_____

_____

Investigate what happens to the graph of $f(x) = mx$ when you change the value of *m*.

A Use a graphing calculator. Press [Y=] and clear out all but the function $f(x) = x$ from the previous Explore. Then graph other functions of the form $f(x) = mx$ by entering their rules next to $Y_2 =$, $Y_3 =$, and so on. Use only values of *m* that are greater than 1. For instance, graph $f(x) = 2x$ and $f(x) = 6x$.

What do the graphs have in common? How are they different?

_____

As the value of *m* increases from 1, does the graph become more vertical or more horizontal?

_____

B Again press [Y=] and clear out all but the function $f(x) = x$. Then graph other functions of the form $f(x) = mx$ by entering their rules next to $Y_2 =$, $Y_3 =$, and so on. This time use only values of *m* that are less than 1 but greater than 0. For instance, graph $f(x) = 0.5x$ and $f(x) = 0.2x$.

As the value of *m* decreases from 1 toward 0, does the graph become more vertical or more horizontal?

_____

C Again press [Y=] and clear out all but the function $f(x) = x$. Then graph the function $f(x) = -x$ by entering its rule next to $Y_2 =$.

What are the slope and *y*-intercept of the graph of $f(x) = -x$?

_____

How are the graphs of $f(x) = x$ and $f(x) = -x$ geometrically related?

_____

D Again press [Y=] and clear out all the functions. Graph $f(x) = -x$ by entering its rule next to $Y_1 =$. Then graph other functions of the form $f(x) = mx$ where $m < 0$ by entering their rules next to $Y_2 =$, $Y_3 =$, and so on. Be sure to choose values of *m* less than -1 as well as values of *m* between -1 and 0.

Describe what happens to the graph of $f(x) = mx$ as the value of *m* decreases from -1 and as it increases from -1 to 0.

_____

© Houghton Mifflin Harcourt Publishing Company

2a. A function $f(x)$ is called an *increasing function* when the value of $f(x)$ always increases as the value of x increases. For what values of m is the function $f(x) = mx$ an increasing function? How can you tell from the graph of a linear function that it is an increasing function?

_____

2b. A function $f(x)$ is called a *decreasing function* when the value of $f(x)$ always decreases as the value of x increases. For what values of m is the function $f(x) = mx$ a decreasing function? How can you tell from the graph of a linear function that is a decreasing function?

_____

2c. When $m > 0$, increasing the value of m results in an increasing linear function that increases *faster*. What effect does increasing m have on the graph of the function?

_____

2d. When $m > 0$, decreasing the value of m toward 0 results in an increasing linear function that increases *slower*. What effect does decreasing m have on the graph of the function?

_____

2e. When $m < 0$, decreasing the value of m results in a decreasing linear function that decreases *faster*. What effect does decreasing m have on the graph of the function?

_____

2f. When $m < 0$, increasing the value of m toward 0 results in a decreasing linear function that decreases *slower*. What effect does increasing m have on the graph of the function?

_____

2g. The *steepness* of a line refers to the absolute value of its slope. A steeper line is more vertical; a less steep line is more horizontal. Complete the table to summarize, in terms of steepness, the effect of changing the value of m on the graph of $f(x) = mx$.

How the Value of m Changes	Effect on the Graph of $f(x) = mx$
Increase m when $m > 0$.	
Decrease m toward 0 when $m > 0$.	
Decrease m when $m < 0$.	
Increase m toward 0 when $m < 0$.	

3 EXAMPLE Modeling with Changes in *m* and *b*

A gym charges a one-time joining fee of $50 and then a monthly membership fee of $25. The total cost C of being a member of the gym is given by the function $C(t) = 25t + 50$ where t is the time (in months) since joining the gym. For each situation described below, *sketch* a graph using the given graph of $C(t) = 25t + 50$ as a reference.

A The gym decreases its one-time joining fee. (Remember: You are not graphing a specific function for this situation. Rather, you are sketching a representative graph of a function related to $C(t) = 25t + 50$, whose graph is shown.)

What change did you make to the graph of $C(t) = 25t + 50$ to obtain the graph that you drew?

_____

_____

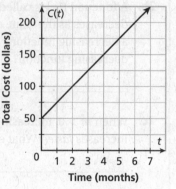

B The gym increases its monthly membership fee.

What change did you make to the graph of $C(t) = 25t + 50$ to obtain the graph that you drew?

_____

_____

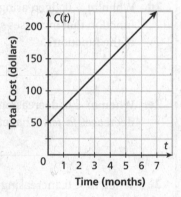

 REFLECT

3a. Suppose the gym increases its one-time joining fee *and* decreases its monthly membership fee. Describe how you would alter the graph of $C(t) = 25t + 50$ to illustrate the new cost function.

_____

_____

_____

3b. Suppose the gym increases its one-time joining fee *and* decreases its monthly membership fee, as in Question 3a. Does this have any impact on the domain of the function? Does this have any impact on the range of the function? Explain your reasoning.

_____

_____

_____

© Houghton Mifflin Harcourt Publishing Company

1. A salesperson earns a base monthly salary of $2000 plus a 10% commission on sales. The salesperson's monthly income I (in dollars) is given by the function $I(s) = 0.1s + 2000$ where s is the sales (in dollars) that the salesperson makes. Sketch a graph to illustrate each situation using the graph of $I(s) = 0.1s + 2000$ as a reference.

   a. The salesperson's base salary is increased.

   b. The salesperson's commission rate is decreased.

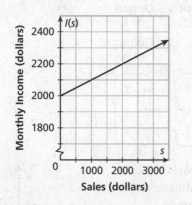

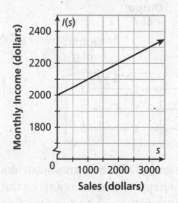

2. Mr. Resnick is driving at a speed of 40 miles per hour to visit relatives who live 100 miles away from his home. His distance d (in miles) from his destination is given by the function $d(t) = 100 - 40t$ where t is the time (in hours) since his trip began. Sketch a graph to illustrate each situation.

   a. He increases his speed to get to his destination sooner.

   b. He encounters a detour that increases the driving distance.

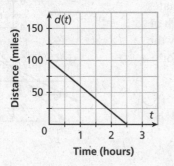

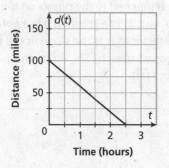

3. Use the graph of $d(t) = 100 - 40t$ in Exercise 2 to identify the domain and range of the function. Then tell whether the domain, the range, neither, or both are affected by the changes described in each part.

   _____

   _____

© Houghton Mifflin Harcourt Publishing Company

Transformations In Exercises 4 and 5, use the following information.

Given a linear function $f(x) = mx + b$, you can create new linear functions by using a constant k in combination with the rule for $f(x)$. For instance, you can create the functions $g(x) = f(x) + k$ and $h(x) = f(kx)$. The graph of each of these new functions is geometrically related to the graph of f through transformations.

Consider the function $f(x) = x + 1$ as well as the related functions $g(x) = f(x) + 2$ and $h(x) = f\left(\frac{x}{2}\right)$. In the case of g, adding 2 is performed on the *output* of f. In the case of h, dividing by 2 is performed on the *input* of f. Each of these cases is illustrated below using -2, 0, and 2 as a few sample inputs of f.

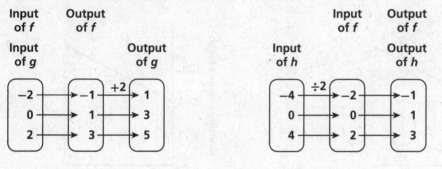

4. The graphs of f and g are shown along with arrows to indicate what happened to the points on the graph of f with x-coordinates -2, 0, and 2. The graph of g is a *vertical translation* of the graph of f. Is the slope or the y-intercept of f affected by the vertical translation? Show that this is true by writing the rule for $g(x) = f(x) + 2$.

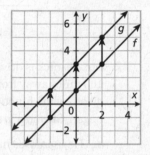

_____

5. The graphs of f and h are shown along with arrows to indicate what happened to the points on the graph of f with x-coordinates -2, 0, and 2. The graph of h is a *horizontal stretch* of the graph of f by a factor of 2. Is the slope or the y-intercept of f affected by the horizontal stretch? Show that this is true by writing the rule for $h(x) = f\left(\frac{x}{2}\right)$.

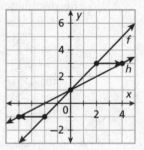

_____

Writing Linear Functions

COMMON
CORE

Essential question: *How can you represent a function symbolically from a graph, a verbal description, or a table of values?*

CC.9-12.A.CED.2*,
CC.9-12.A.REI.11*,
CC.9-12.F.IF.4*,
CC.9-12.F.IF.6*,
CC.9-12.F.BF.1*,
CC.9-12.F.LE.2*

1 EXAMPLE Writing a Linear Function

Write the linear function *f* using the given information.

A The graph of the function has a slope of 3 and a *y*-intercept of −1.

A linear function has the form $f(x) = mx + b$ where *m* is the slope and

b is the *y*-intercept. Substitute _____ for *m* and _____ for *b*.

So, the function is $f(x) = $ _____ .

B A different function has the values shown in the table.

First calculate the slope using any two ordered pairs
from the table. For instance, let $(x_1, f(x_1)) = (-1, 5)$ and
$(x_2, f(x_2)) = (3, -3)$.

x	f(x)
−1	5
3	−3
7	−11

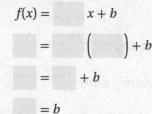

$m = \dfrac{f(x_2) - f(x_1)}{x_2 - x_1}$ Write the slope formula.

$= \dfrac{\boxed{} - \boxed{}}{\boxed{} - (\boxed{})}$ Substitute values.

$= $ ____   Simplify numerator and denominator.

$= \boxed{}$ Simplify fraction.

Then find the value of *b* using the fact that $m = $ _____ and $f(-1) = 5$.

$f(x) = \boxed{}\, x + b$ Write the function with the known value of *m*.

$\boxed{} = \boxed{}\left(\boxed{}\right) + b$ Substitute −1 for *x* and 5 for *f*(*x*).

$\boxed{} = \boxed{} + b$ Simplify the right side of the equation.

$\boxed{} = b$ Solve for *b*.

So, the function is $f(x) = $ _____ .

REFLECT

1a. In Part B, use the ordered pair (7, −11) to check your answer.

_____

The graph shows the increase in pressure (measured in pounds per square inch) as a scuba diver descends from a depth of 10 feet to a depth of 30 feet.

Pressure is the result of the weight of the column of water above the diver as well as the weight of the column of Earth's atmosphere above the water. Pressure is a linear function of depth.

What is the pressure on the diver at the water's surface?

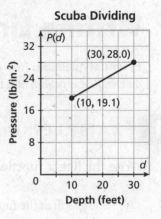

Scuba Dividing

Pressure (lb/in.²) — Depth (feet)

(30, 28.0)
(10, 19.1)

A Interpret the question.

Let d represent depth and P represent pressure. At the water's surface, $d =$ _____. For this value of d, what meaning does $P(d)$ have in terms of the line that contains the line segment shown on the graph?

_____

B Find the value of m in $P(d) = md + b$. Use the fact that $P(10) = 19.1$ and $P(30) = 28.0$.

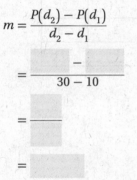

$m = \dfrac{P(d_2) - P(d_1)}{d_2 - d_1}$ Write the slope formula.

$= \dfrac{\boxed{} - \boxed{}}{30 - 10}$ Substitute values.

$= \boxed{}$ Simplify numerator and denominator.

$= \boxed{}$ Write in decimal form.

C Find the value of b in $P(d) = md + b$. Use the value of m from Part B as well as the fact that $P(10) = 19.1$.

$P(d) = \boxed{} d + b$ Write the function with the known value of m.

$\boxed{} = \boxed{} \left(\boxed{} \right) + b$ Substitute 10 for d and 19.1 for $P(d)$.

$\boxed{} = \boxed{} + b$ Simplify the right side of the equation.

$\boxed{} \approx b$ Solve for b. Round to the nearest tenth.

So, the pressure at the water's surface is $P(0) = b \approx$ _____ lb/in.²

2a. Interpret the value of m in the context of the problem.

_____

2b. Write the function $P(d) = md + b$ using the calculated values of m and b. Use the function to find the pressure on the diver at a depth of 20 feet.

_____

3 EXAMPLE   Writing and Solving a System of Equations

Mr. Jackson takes a commuter bus from his suburban home to his job in the city. He normally gets on the bus in the town where he lives, but today he is running a little late. He gets to the bus stop 2 minutes after the bus has left. He wants to catch up with the bus by the time it gets to the next stop in a neighboring town 5 miles away.

The speed limit on the road connecting the two stops is 40 miles per hour, but Mr. Jackson knows that the bus travels the road at 30 miles per hour. He decides to drive at 40 miles per hour to the next stop. Does he successfully catch the bus there?

A Identify the independent and dependent variables, how they are measured, and how you will represent them.

The independent variable is _____, measured in minutes. Let t represent the time since Mr. Jackson began driving to the next bus stop.

The dependent variable is _____, measured in miles. Let d represent the distance traveled. Since you need to track the distances traveled by both Mr. Jackson and the bus, use subscripts: d_J will represent the distance traveled by Mr. Jackson, and d_B will represent the distance traveled by the bus.

B Write a distance-traveled function for Mr. Jackson and for the bus.

Each function has the form $d(t) = rt + d_0$ where r is the rate of travel and d_0 is any initial distance. Although you know the rates of travel, they are given in miles per hour, which is incompatible with the unit of time (minutes). So, you need to convert miles per hour to miles per minute. In the conversions below, express the miles as simplified fractions.

Mr. Jackson: $\dfrac{40 \text{ miles}}{\text{hour}} \cdot \dfrac{1 \text{ hour}}{60 \text{ minutes}} = $ [ ] mile per minute

Bus: $\dfrac{30 \text{ miles}}{\text{hour}} \cdot \dfrac{1 \text{ hour}}{60 \text{ minutes}} = $ [ ] mile per minute

Continued on next page

© Houghton Mifflin Harcourt Publishing Company

At the moment Mr. Jackson begins driving to the next bus stop, the bus has traveled for 2 minutes. If you use Mr. Jackson's position as the starting point, then the initial distance for Mr. Jackson is 0 miles, and the initial distance for the bus is [   ] $\cdot 2 =$ [   ].

So, the distance-traveled functions are:

Mr. Jackson: $d_J(t) =$ [   ] $t +$ [   ]   Bus: $d_B(t) =$ [   ] $t +$ [   ]

C Determine the value of t for which $d_J(t) = d_B(t)$. You can do this by graphing the two functions and seeing where the graphs intersect. Carefully draw the graphs on the coordinate plane below, and label the intersection point.

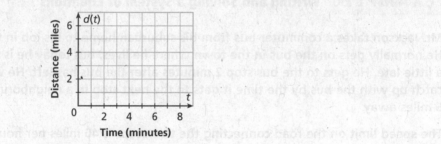

The t-coordinate of the point of intersection is _____, so

Mr. Jackson catches up with the bus in _____.

D Check the result against the conditions of the problem, and then answer the problem's question.

The problem states that the next bus stop is _____ miles away, and the

graph shows that Mr. Jackson catches up with the bus in _____ miles.

So, does Mr. Jackson successfully catch the bus? _____

REFLECT

3a. Explain how you can use algebra rather than a graph to find the time when Mr. Jackson catches up with the bus. Then show that you get the same result.

_____

_____

3b. In terms of the context of the problem, explain why the t-coordinate of the intersection point (and not some other point) determines how long it takes Mr. Jackson to catch up with the bus.

_____

_____

_____

Write the linear function f using the given information.

1. The graph of the function has a slope of 4 and a y-intercept of 1.

_____

2. The graph of the function has a slope of 0 and a y-intercept of 6.

_____

3. The graph of the function has a slope of $-\frac{2}{3}$ and a y-intercept of 5.

_____

4. The graph of the function has a slope of $\frac{7}{4}$ and a y-intercept of 0.

_____

5.

x	f(x)
−3	8
0	5
3	2

_____

6.

x	f(x)
0	−3
2	0
4	3

_____

7.

x	f(x)
1	−1
2	5
3	11

_____

8.

x	f(x)
5	−2
10	−6
15	−10

_____

9.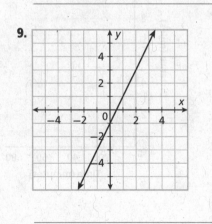

_____

10.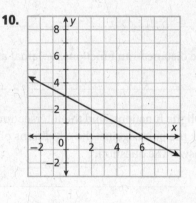

_____

11. The graph shows the amount of gas remaining in the gas tank of Mrs. Liu's car as she drives at a steady speed for 2 hours. How long can she drive before her car runs out of gas?

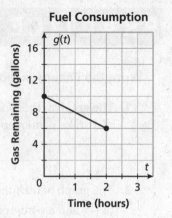

Fuel Consumption

a. Interpret the question by describing what aspect of the graph would answer the question.

_____

_____

b. Write a linear function whose graph includes the segment shown.

_____

c. Describe how to use the function to answer the question, and then answer the question.

_____

12. Jamal and Nathan exercise by running one circuit of a basically circular route that is 5 miles long and takes them past each other's home. The two boys run in the same direction, and Jamal passes Nathan's home 12 minutes into his run. Jamal runs at a rate of 7.5 miles per hour while Nathan runs at a rate of 6 miles per hour. If the two boys start running at the same time, when, if ever, will Jamal catch up with Nathan before completing his run?

a. Identify the independent and dependent variables, how they are measured, and how you will represent them.

_____

_____

_____

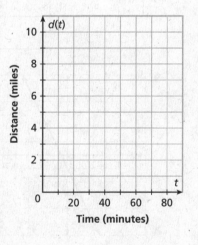

b. Write distance-run functions for Jamal and Nathan.

_____

c. Graph the functions, find the intersection point, and check the point against the conditions of the problem to answer the question.

_____

Operations with Linear Functions

Essential question: *How can you use operations to combine functions that model real-world situations?*

COMMON CORE

CC.9-12.A.APR.1,
CC.9-12.A.CED.2*,
CC.9-12.F.BF.1*,
CC.9-12.F.BF.1b*,
CC.9-12.F.LE.2*,
CC.9-12.F.LE.5*

Just as you can perform operations with numbers, you can perform operations with functions. In this lesson you will add and subtract linear functions as well as multiply a linear function by a nonzero constant function. Performing an operation on two functions $f(x)$ and $g(x)$ produces a new function $h(x)$.

1 EXAMPLE Performing Operations with Functions

A Given $f(x) = 3x - 1$ and $g(x) = -2x + 2$, find $h(x) = f(x) + g(x)$.

$h(x) = f(x) + g(x)$	Write the general form of $h(x)$.
$= (3x - 1) + \left(\right)$	Substitute the rules for $f(x)$ and $g(x)$.
$= \left(3x + \right) + \left(-1 + \right)$	Collect like terms for adding.
$= + $	Simplify.

B Given $f(x) = x + 5$ and $g(x) = 4x - 2$, find $h(x) = f(x) - g(x)$.

$h(x) = f(x) - g(x)$	Write the general form of $h(x)$.
$= (x + 5) - \left(\right)$	Substitute the rules for $f(x)$ and $g(x)$.
$= \left(x - \right) + \left(5 - \right)$	Collect like terms for subtracting.
$= + $	Simplify.

C Given $f(x) = 3$ and $g(x) = \frac{1}{3}x - 2$, find $h(x) = f(x) \cdot g(x)$.

$h(x) = f(x) \cdot g(x)$	Write the general form of $h(x)$.
$= \left(\frac{1}{3}x - 2\right)$	Substitute the rules for $f(x)$ and $g(x)$.
$= - $	Multiply using the distributive property.

REFLECT

1a. The table shows the values of the sum $f(x) + g(x)$ for several values of x using the functions $f(x)$ and $g(x)$ from part A. Use the rule that you found for $h(x)$ in part A to complete the third column of the table. What do you notice?

_____

x	f(x) + g(x)	h(x)
−2	−7 + 6 = −1	
−1	−4 + 4 = 0	
0	−1 + 2 = 1	
1	2 + 0 = 2	
2	5 + (−2) = 3	

1b. Error Analysis A student wrote the rule for $h(x)$ in part A as $5x + 1$. After letting $x = 0$ and observing that $f(0) + g(0) = -1 + 2 = 1$ and $h(0) = 1$, the student concluded that the rule must be correct. Describe what is incorrect about the student's reasoning, and describe what the student should have done to check the rule for $h(x)$.

_____

_____

_____

2 EXAMPLE Adding Linear Models

For the initial year of a soccer camp, 44 girls and 56 boys enrolled. Each year thereafter, 5 more girls and 8 more boys enrolled in the camp. Let t be the time (in years) since the camp opened. Write a rule for each of the following functions:

- $g(t)$, the number of girls enrolled as a function of time t
- $b(t)$, the number of boys enrolled as a function of time t
- $T(t)$, the total enrollment as a function of time t

A For the function $g(t)$, the initial value is _____ and the rate of

change is _____. So, $g(t) =$ _____.

B For the function $b(t)$, the initial value is _____ and the rate of

change is _____. So, $b(t) =$ _____.

C The total enrollment is the sum of the functions $g(t)$ and $b(t)$.

$T(t) = g(t) + b(t)$ Write the general form of $T(t)$.

$= $ _____ $+$ _____   Substitute the rules for $g(t)$ and $b(t)$.

$= $ _____   Simplify.

REFLECT

2a. Use unit analysis to show that the rule for $g(t)$ makes sense.

_____

_____

_____

For the soccer camp in the previous example, the cost per child each year was $200. Let t be the time (in years) since the camp opened. Write a rule for each of the following functions:

- $C(t)$, the cost per child of the camp as a function of time t
- $R(t)$, the revenue generated by the total enrollment as a function of time t

A For the function $C(t)$, the initial value is _____ and the rate of change

is _____. So, $C(t) =$ _____.

B The revenue generated by the total enrollment is the product of the cost function $C(t)$ and the total enrollment function $T(t)$, which was found in the previous example.

$R(t) = C(t) \cdot T(t)$ Write the general form of $R(t)$.

= [____] · ([_____])   Substitute the rules for $C(t)$ and $T(t)$.

= [_____]   Multiply using the distributive property.

REFLECT

3a. Explain why $C(t)$ is a constant function.

_____

3b. Use unit analysis to explain why you multiply the cost function $C(t)$ and the enrollment function $T(t)$ to get the revenue function $R(t)$.

_____

_____

_____

3c. What was the initial revenue for the camp? What was the annual rate of change in the revenue?

_____

3d. The camp's organizer had initial expenses of $18,000, which increased each year by $2,500. Write a rule for the expenses function $E(t)$. Then write a rule for the profit function $P(t)$ based on the fact that profit is the difference between revenue and expenses.

_____

1. Given $f(x) = -2x$ and $g(x) = 4x - 8$, find $h(x) = f(x) + g(x)$.

   _____

2. Given $f(x) = 3x - 5$ and $g(x) = -2x + 1$, find $h(x) = f(x) - g(x)$.

   _____

3. Given $f(x) = -2$ and $g(x) = 5x - 6$, find $h(x) = f(x) \cdot g(x)$.

   _____

4. Given $f(x) = 4$, $g(x) = x + 1$, and $h(x) = x$, find $j(x) = f(x) \cdot [g(x) + h(x)]$.

   _____

5. To raise funds, a club is publishing and selling a calendar. The club has sold $500 in advertising and will sell copies of the calendar for $20 each. The cost of printing each calendar is $6. Let c be the number of calendars to be printed and sold.

   a. Write a rule for the function $R(c)$, which gives the revenue generated by the sale of the calendars.

   _____

   b. Write a rule for the function $E(c)$, which gives the expense of printing the calendars.

   _____

   c. Describe how the function $P(c)$, which gives the club's profit from the sale of the calendars, is related to $R(c)$ and $E(c)$. Then write a rule for $P(c)$.

   _____

6. The five winners of a radio station contest will spend a day at an amusement park with all expenses paid. The per-person admission cost is $10, and each person can spend $20 on food. The radio station will pay for all rides, which cost $2 each. Assume that each person takes the same number r of rides.

   a. Write a rule for the function $C(r)$, which gives the cost per person.

   _____

   b. Write a rule for the function $P(r)$, which gives the number of people.

   _____

   c. Describe how the function $T(r)$, which gives the radio station's total cost, is related to $C(r)$ and $P(r)$. Then write a rule for $T(r)$.

   _____

Linear Functions and Their Inverses

COMMON CORE

CC.9-12.F.IF.1,
CC.9-12.F.IF.2,
CC.9-12.F.BF.4,
CC.9-12.F.BF.4a

Essential question: *What is the inverse of a function, and how can you find the inverse of a linear function?*

Recall that inverse operations are operations that undo each other. Similarly, the **inverse of a function** is another function that undoes everything that the original function does.

---

1 EXPLORE   Using Inverse Operations to Find Inverse Functions

Find the inverse of $f(x) = 2x + 1$ using inverse operations.

A List the operations that the function performs on an input value x in the order that the function performs them. Illustrate these steps using $x = 3$.

x ⟶ Multiply by 2. ⟶ _____

3 ⟶ $2 \cdot 3 = 6$ ⟶ _____

B List the *inverse operations* in the *reverse order*. Illustrate these steps using $x = 7$.

x ⟶ Subtract 1. ⟶ _____

7 ⟶ $7 - 1 = 6$ ⟶ _____

C Write a rule for the function $g(x)$ that performs the inverse operations in the reverse order. Check your rule by finding $g(7)$.

$$g(x) = \frac{x - \boxed{}}{\boxed{}}, \text{ so } g(7) = \frac{7 - \boxed{}}{\boxed{}} = \boxed{}$$

REFLECT

1a. The first table at the right shows some input-output pairs for the function f. The outputs of f are then listed as inputs for the function g in the second table. Complete the second table.

x	f(x)
−2	−3
0	1
2	5

x	g(x)
−3	
1	
5	

1b. The function g is the inverse of the function f. If $f(a) = b$, then what is $g(b)$?

_____

1c. Is it reasonable to describe f as the inverse of g? Explain.

_____

To find the rule for the inverse of a linear function f, let $y = f(x)$ and solve for x in terms of y. Whatever sequence of operations f performs on x to obtain y, the process of solving for x will introduce the inverse operations in the reverse order. You now have a function g where $g(y) = x$. Since x is commonly used as a function's input variable and y as its output variable, as a final step switch x and y to obtain $g(x) = y$.

2 EXAMPLE   Finding the Inverse by Solving $y = f(x)$ for x

Find the inverse of $f(x) = \frac{1}{2}x - 1$.

A   Let $y = f(x)$. Solve for x in terms of y.

$y = \boxed{}$ Write $y = f(x)$.

$y + \boxed{} = \boxed{}$ Add 1 to both sides.

$\boxed{}\left(y + \boxed{}\right) = \boxed{}$ Multiply both sides by 2.

$\boxed{}\,y + \boxed{} = \boxed{}$ Distribute.

B   Switch x and y and then write the rule for the inverse function g.

$\boxed{}\,x + \boxed{} = \boxed{}$ Switch x and y.

The inverse of $f(x) = \frac{1}{2}x - 1$ is $g(x) = $ _____.

REFLECT

2a. Find $f(4)$. Then use this value as the input x for $g(x)$. What output value do you get? Why is this expected?

_____

_____

2b. When solving $y = f(x)$ for x, you multiplied both sides by 2 instead of dividing both sides by $\frac{1}{2}$. In other words, instead of using an *inverse operation*, you used a *multiplicative inverse*. Why is this acceptable?

_____

_____

2c. When you switch x and y to find the inverse function, are you solving the function for y? Why or why not?

_____

_____

2d. The graph of $f(x) = \frac{1}{2}x - 1$ is shown. Graph the inverse function g. Also graph $y = x$ as a dashed line. How are the graphs of f and g related to the line $y = x$?

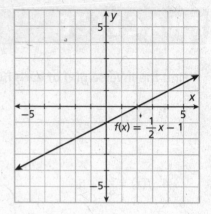

$f(x) = \frac{1}{2}x - 1$

_____

_____

2e. The point $(4, 1)$ is on the graph of f. What is the corresponding point on the graph of g? In general, if (a, b) is a point on the graph of f, what is the corresponding point on the graph of g?

_____

3 **EXAMPLE**   Finding Inverses of Real-World Functions

The function $A(r) = 2r + 30$ gives the total amount A that you will spend at an amusement park if you spend \$30 on admission and food and you go on r rides that cost \$2 each. Find the inverse function.

$A = 2r + 30$ Write the function using A for $A(r)$.

$A - \boxed{} = \boxed{}$ Subtract 30 from both sides.

$\dfrac{A - \boxed{}}{\boxed{}} = r$ Divide both sides by 2.

REFLECT

3a. Write the inverse function using function notation.

_____

3b. Explain how the inverse function would be useful if you have a fixed amount of money that you can spend at the amusement park.

_____

_____

_____

3c. When finding the inverse of a real-world function, why shouldn't you switch the variables as the final step?

_____

_____

Find the inverse $g(x)$ of each function.

1. $f(x) = x - 1$

2. $f(x) = -x + 4$

3. $f(x) = 2x - 3$

_____

_____

_____

4. $f(x) = \frac{2}{3}x + 6$

5. $f(x) = 3x - \frac{3}{4}$

6. $f(x) = -\frac{5}{2}x - \frac{15}{2}$

_____

_____

_____

7. The formula to convert a temperature F measured in degrees Fahrenheit to a temperature C measured in degrees Celsius is $C = \frac{9}{5}(F - 32)$. You can think of this formula as function $C(F)$. Find the inverse function $F(C)$ and describe what it does.

_____

8. A cylindrical candle 10 inches tall burns at rate of 0.5 inch per hour.

a. Write a rule for the function $h(t)$, the height (in inches) of the candle at time t (in hours since the candle was lit). State the domain and range of the function.

_____

b. Find the inverse function $t(h)$. State the domain and range of the function.

_____

c. Explain how the inverse function is useful.

_____

_____

9. Prove that the inverse of a non-constant linear function is another non-constant linear function by starting with the general linear function $f(x) = mx + b$ where $m \neq 0$ and showing that the inverse function $g(x)$ is also linear. Identify the slope and y-intercept of the graph of $g(x)$.

_____

10. Can a constant function have an inverse function? Why or why not?

_____

_____

Correlation

Essential question: *How can you decide whether a correlation exists between paired numerical data?*

1 ENGAGE   Understanding Correlation

When two real-world variables (such as height and weight or latitude and average temperature) are measured from the same things (the same people, places, etc.), you obtain a set of paired numerical data that you can plot as points in the coordinate plane to create a data display called a *scatter plot*. Sometimes the scatter plot will show a linear pattern. When it does, the linear pattern may be tight (that is, the points lie very close to a line), or it may be loose (that is, the points are more dispersed about a line). The degree to which a scatter plot shows a linear pattern is an indicator of the strength of a **correlation** between the two variables.

Mathematicians have defined a measure of the direction and magnitude of a correlation. This measure is called the **correlation coefficient** and is denoted by r. When the points in a scatter plot all lie on a line that is not horizontal, r has a value of 1 if the line has a positive slope and a value of -1 if the line has a negative slope. The correlation coefficient takes on values between -1 and 1 in cases where the points are not perfectly linear.

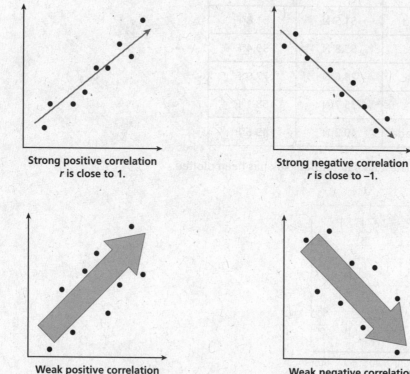

Strong positive correlation
r is close to 1.

Strong negative correlation
r is close to -1.

Weak positive correlation
r is closer to 0.5 than to 0 or 1.

Weak negative correlation
r is closer to -0.5 than to 0 or -1.

1.a. What conclusion would you draw about the value of *r* for the scatter plot shown at the right? Why?

_____

_____

1b. If the variables *x* and *y* have a strong positive correlation, what generally happens to *y* as *x* increases? What if *x* and *y* have a strong negative correlation?

_____

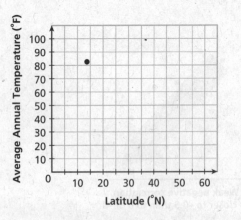

---

2 E X A M P L E   **Estimating Correlation Coefficients**

The table lists the latitude and average annual temperature for various cities in the Northern Hemisphere. Describe the correlation and estimate the correlation coefficient.

City	Latitude	Avg. Annual Temperature
Bangkok, Thailand	13.7°N	82.6°F
Cairo, Egypt	30.1°N	71.4°F
London, England	51.5°N	51.8°F
Moscow, Russia	55.8°N	39.4°F
New Delhi, India	28.6°N	77.0°F
Tokyo, Japan	35.7°N	58.1°F
Vancouver, Canada	49.2°N	49.6°F

A   Make a scatter plot. The data pair for Bangkok has been plotted.

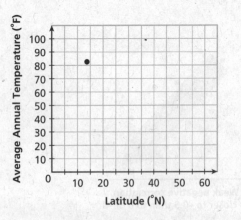

B   Describe the correlation, and estimate the correlation coefficient.

Because the plotted points appear to lie very close to a line with a _____ slope, the scatter plot shows a _____ correlation. So, the correlation coefficient is close to _____.

© Houghton Mifflin Harcourt Publishing Company

2a. Mexico City, Mexico, is at latitude 19.4°N and has an average annual temperature of 60.8°F. If you include this data pair in the data set, how would it affect the correlation? Why?

_____

_____

Correlation and Causation In the preceding example, you would expect that a city's latitude has an effect on the city's average annual temperature. While it does, there are other factors that contribute to a city's weather, such as whether a city is located on a coast or inland.

A common error when interpreting paired data is confusing correlation and causation. If a correlation exists between two variables, this does not necessarily mean that one variable causes the other. When one variable increases, the other variable may increase (or decrease) as a result of other variables not being considered. Such variables are sometimes called _lurking variables_.

3 **E X A M P L E** \ **Distinguishing Causation from Correlation**

Read the article. Decide whether correlation implies causation in this case.

A Identify the two variables that the scientists correlated. Was the correlation positive or negative?

_____

_____

B Decide whether correlation implies causation in this case. Explain your reasoning.

_____

_____

_____

_____

_____

_____

_____

_____

_____

BRAIN'S AMYGDALA CONNECTED TO SOCIAL BEHAVIOR

An almond-shaped part of the brain called the amygdala has long been known to play a role in people's emotional states. Now scientists studying the amygdala have discovered a connection between its size and the size of a person's social network. The scientists used a brain scanner to determine the size of the amygdala in the brains of 58 adults. They also gave each person a survey that measured the size of the person's social network. Their analysis of the data found that there is a correlation between the two: People with larger amygdalas tend to have larger social networks.

3a. Suppose scientists study a group of people over time and find that those who increased the size of their social networks also had an increase in the size of their amygdalas. Does this result establish a cause-and-effect relationship? Explain.

_____

_____

PRACTICE

1. The table lists the heights and weights of the six wide receivers who played for the New Orleans Saints during the 2010 football season.

Wide Receiver	Height (inches)	Weight (pounds)
Arrington	75	192
Colston	76	225
Henderson	71	200
Meachem	74	210
Moore	69	190
Roby	72	189

a. Make a scatter plot.

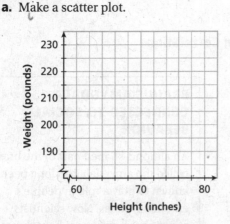

b. Describe the correlation, and estimate the correlation coefficient using one of these values: −1, −0.5, 0, 0.5, 1.

_____

2. Read the article shown at the right. Describe the correlation and decide whether correlation implies causation in this case. Explain your reasoning.

_____

_____

_____

_____

_____

_____

WALKING SPEED MAY PREDICT LIFE SPAN

Researchers who looked at data from nearly 35,000 senior citizens discovered that an elderly person's walking speed is correlated to that person's chance of living 10 more years. For instance, the researchers found that only 19 percent of the slowest-walking 75-year-old men lived for 10 more years compared with 87 percent of the fastest-walking 75-year-old men. Similar results were found for elderly women.

© Houghton Mifflin Harcourt Publishing Company

Fitting Lines to Data

Essential question: *How do you find a linear model for a set of paired numerical data, and how do you evaluate the goodness of fit?*

COMMON
CORE

CC.9-12.F.LE.5*,
CC.9-12.S.ID.6*,
CC.9-12.S.ID.6a*,
CC.9-12.S.ID.6b*,
CC.9-12.S.ID.6c*,
CC.9-12.S.ID.7*

When paired numerical data have a strong positive or negative correlation, you can find a linear model for the data. The process is called *fitting a line to the data* or *finding a line of fit for the data*.

1 EXAMPLE Finding a Line of Fit for Data

The table lists the median age of females living in the United States based on the results of the U.S. Census over the past few decades. Determine whether a linear model is reasonable for the data. If so, find a linear model for the data.

Year	Median Age of Females
1970	29.2
1980	31.3
1990	34.0
2000	36.5
2010	38.2

A Identify the independent and dependent variables, and specify how you will represent them.

The independent variable is time, so use the variable t. Rather than let t take on the values 1970, 1980, and so on, define t as the number of years since 1970.

The dependent variable is the median age of females. Although you could simply use the variable a, you can use F as a subscript to remind yourself that only median *female* ages are being considered. So, the dependent variable is a_F.

B Make a table of paired values of t and a_F. Then draw a scatter plot.

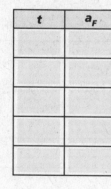

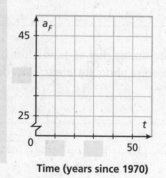

Time (years since 1970)

C Draw a line of fit on the scatter plot.

Using a ruler, draw a line that passes as close as possible to the plotted points. Your line does not necessarily have to pass through any of the points, but you should try to balance points above and below the line.

D Find the equation of the line of fit.

Suppose that a student drew a line of fit that happens to pass through the data points (20, 34.0) and (30, 36.5). Complete the steps below to find the equation of the student's line. (Note that x and y are used as the independent and dependent variables for the purposes of finding the line's slope and y-intercept.)

1. Find the slope.

$$m = \frac{y_2 - y_1}{x_2 - x_1}$$

$$m = \frac{\rule{2cm}{0.4pt} - \rule{2cm}{0.4pt}}{\rule{2cm}{0.4pt} - \rule{2cm}{0.4pt}}$$

$$m = \rule{2cm}{0.4pt}$$

2. Find the y-intercept using (20, 34.0).

$$y = mx + b$$

$$\rule{2cm}{0.4pt} = \rule{2cm}{0.4pt} \left(\rule{1cm}{0.4pt} \right) + b$$

$$\rule{2cm}{0.4pt} = \rule{0.8cm}{0.4pt} + b$$

$$\rule{2cm}{0.4pt} = b$$

So, in terms of the variables t and a_F, the equation of the line of fit is

_____.

Perform similar calculations to find the equation of your line of fit.

Equation of your line of fit: _____

REFLECT

1a. What type of correlation does the scatter plot show?

_____

1b. Before you placed a ruler on the scatter plot to draw a line of fit, you may have thought that the plotted points were perfectly linear. How does the table tell you that they are not?

_____

_____

_____

_____

1c. For your line of fit, interpret the slope and a_F-intercept in the context of the data.

_____

_____

_____

Residuals You can evaluate a linear model's goodness of fit using *residuals*. A **residual** is the difference between an actual value of the dependent variable and the value predicted by the linear model. After calculating residuals, you can draw a **residual plot**, which is a scatter plot of points whose *x*-coordinates are the values of the independent variable and whose *y*-coordinates are the corresponding residuals.

Whether the fit of a line to data is suitable and good depends on the distribution of the residuals, as illustrated below.

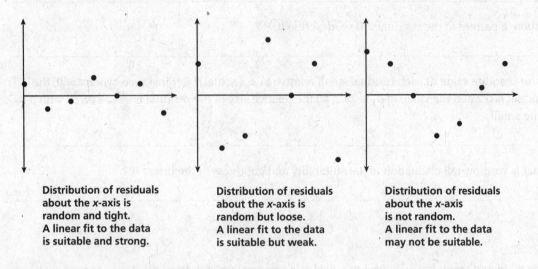

Distribution of residuals about the *x*-axis is random and tight. A linear fit to the data is suitable and strong.

Distribution of residuals about the *x*-axis is random but loose. A linear fit to the data is suitable but weak.

Distribution of residuals about the *x*-axis is not random. A linear fit to the data may not be suitable.

2 EXAMPLE   Creating a Residual Plot and Evaluating Fit

A student fit the line $a_F = 0.25t + 29$ to the data in the previous example. Make a residual plot and evaluate the goodness of fit.

A Calculate the residuals. Substitute each value of t into the equation to find the value predicted for a_F by the linear model. Then subtract predicted from actual to find the residual.

t	a_F actual	a_F predicted	Residual
0	29.2	29.0	0.2
10	31.3		
20	34.0		
30	36.5		
40	38.2		

B Plot the residuals.

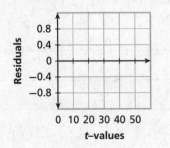

© Houghton Mifflin Harcourt Publishing Company

C Evaluate the suitability of a linear fit and the goodness of the fit.

• Is there a balance between positive and negative residuals?

_____

_____

_____

• Is there a pattern to the residuals? If so, describe it.

_____

• Is the absolute value of each residual small relative to a_F (actual)? For instance, when $t = 0$, the residual is 0.2 and the value of a_F is 29.2, so the relative size of the residual is $\frac{0.2}{29.2} \approx 0.7\%$, which is quite small.

_____

• What is your overall evaluation of the suitability and goodness of the linear fit?

_____

REFLECT

2a. Use the table and graph below to find the residuals for your line of fit from the first Example and then make a residual plot.

t	a_F actual	a_F predicted	Residual
0	29.2		
10	31.3		
20	34.0		
30	36.5		
40	38.2		

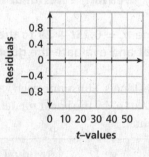

2b. Evaluate the suitability and goodness of the fit for your line of fit.

_____

_____

_____

2c. Suppose the line of fit with equation $a_F = 0.25t + 29$ is changed to $a_F = 0.25t + 28.8$. What effect does this change have on the residuals? On the residual plot? Is the new line is a better fit to the data? Explain.

_____

_____

_____

Making Predictions A linear model establishes the dependent variable as a linear function of the independent variable, and you can use the function to make predictions. The accuracy of a prediction depends not only on the model's goodness of fit but also on the value of the independent variable for which you're making the prediction.

A model's domain is determined by the least and greatest values of the independent variable found in the data set. For instance, the least and greatest t-values for the median age data are 0 (for 1970) and 40 (for 2010), so the domain of any model for the data is $\{t \mid 0 \le t \le 40\}$. Making a prediction using a value of the independent variable from *within* the model's domain is called **interpolation**. Making a prediction using a value from *outside* the domain is called **extrapolation**. As you might expect, you can have greater confidence in an interpolation than in an extrapolation.

3 EXAMPLE Making Predictions Using a Linear Model

Using the model $a_F = 0.25t + 29$, predict the median age of females in 1995 and in 2015. Identify each prediction as an interpolation or as an extrapolation.

A To make a prediction about 1995, let $t =$ _____. Then to the nearest

tenth, the predicted value of a_F is $a_F = 0.25 \left(\right) + 29 \approx$ _____.

Because the t-value falls _____ the model's domain,

the prediction is an _____.

B To make a prediction about 2015, let $t =$ _____. Then to the nearest

tenth, the predicted value of a_F is $a_F = 0.25 \left(\right) + 29 \approx$ _____.

Because the t-value falls _____ the model's domain, the

prediction is an _____.

REFLECT

3a. Use your linear model to predict the median age of females in 1995 and 2015.

_____

_____

3b. The Census Bureau gives 35.5 as the median age of females for 1995 and an estimate of 38.4 for 2015. Which of your predictions using your linear model was more accurate? Explain.

_____

_____

1. The table lists the median age of males living in the United States based on the results of the U.S. Census over the past few decades.

Year	1970	1980	1990	2000	2010
Median Age of Males	26.8	28.8	31.6	34.0	35.5

a. Let t represent time (in years since 1970), and let a_M represent the median age of males. Make a table of paired values of t and a_M. Then draw a scatter plot.

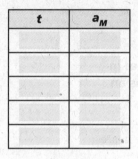

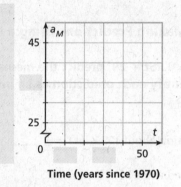

Time (years since 1970)

b. Draw a line of fit on the scatter plot and find an equation of the line.

_____

c. Calculate the residuals, and make a residual plot.

t	a_M actual	a_M predicted	Residual

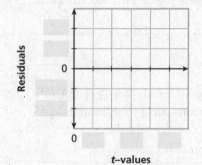

t–values

d. Evaluate the suitability of a linear fit and the goodness of the fit.

_____

_____

© Houghton Mifflin Harcourt Publishing Company

e. Predict the median age of males in 1995 and 2015. Identify each prediction as an interpolation or an extrapolation, and then compare the predictions with these median ages of males from the Census Bureau: 33.2 in 1995 and an estimated 35.9 in 2015.

_____

_____

_____

2. Compare the equations of your lines of fit for the median age of females and the median age of males. When referring to any constants in those equations, be sure to interpret them in the context of the data.

_____

_____

_____

_____

3. Explain why it isn't reasonable to use linear models to predict the median age of females or males far into the future.

_____

_____

_____

_____

4. The table lists, for various lengths (in centimeters), the median weight (in kilograms) of male infants and female infants (ages 0–36 months) in the United States.

Length (cm)	50	60	70	80	90	100
Median Weight (kg) of Male Infants	3.4	5.9	8.4	10.8	13.0	15.5
Median Weight (kg) of Female Infants	3.4	5.8	8.3	10.6	12.8	15.2

a. Let l represent an infant's length in excess of 50 centimeters. (For instance, for an infant whose length is 60 cm, $l = 10$.) Let w_M represent the median weight of male infants, and let w_F represent the median weight of female infants. Make a table of paired values of l and either w_M or w_F (whichever you prefer).

l						
w						

b. Draw a scatter plot of the paired data.

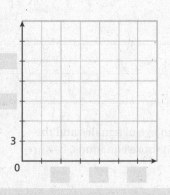

3

0

c. Draw a line of fit on the scatter plot and find the equation of the line. According to your model, at what rate does weight change with respect to length?

_____

_____

_____

d. Calculate the residuals, and make a residual plot.

l	w actual	w predicted	Residual

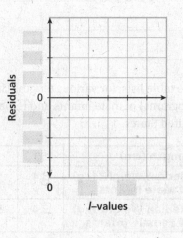

Residuals

0

0

l–values

e. Evaluate the suitability of a linear fit and the goodness of the fit.

_____

_____

_____

Linear Regression

Essential question: *How can you use a graphing calculator to perform linear regression on a set of paired numerical data?*

You can use a graphing calculator to fit a line to a set of paired numerical data that have a strong positive or negative correlation. The calculator uses a method called **linear regression**, which involves minimizing the sum of the squares of the residuals.

COMMON CORE

CC.9-12.F.LE.5*,
CC.9-12.S.ID.6a*,
CC.9-12.S.ID.6b*,
CC.9-12.S.ID.6c*,
CC.9-12.S.ID.7*,
CC.9-12.S.ID.8*

1 EXPLORE Comparing Sums of Squared Residuals

In Lesson 4-9 you fit a line to the data in the table at the right. Because each person in your class fit a line by eye, any two people are likely to have gotten slightly different lines of fit. Suppose one person came up with the equation $a_F = 0.25t + 29.0$ while another came up with $a_F = 0.25t + 28.8$ where, in each case, t is the time in years since 1970 and a_F is the median age of females.

Time	Median Age of Females
1970	29.2
1980	31.3
1990	34.0
2000	36.5
2010	38.2

A Complete each table below in order to calculate the squares of the residuals for each line of fit.

$a_F = 0.25t + 29.0$				
t	a_F (actual)	a_F (predicted)	Residuals	Square of Residuals
0	29.2	29.0	0.2	0.04
10	31.3			
20	34.0			
30	36.5			
40	38.2			

$a_F = 0.25t + 28.8$				
t	a_F (actual)	a_F (predicted)	Residuals	Square of Residuals
0	29.2	28.8	0.4	0.16
10	31.3			
20	34.0			
30	36.5			
40	38.2			

B Find the sum of the squared residuals for each line of fit.

Sum of squared residuals for $a_F = 0.25t + 29.0$: _____

Sum of squared residuals for $a_F = 0.25t + 28.8$: _____

C Identify the line that has the smaller sum of the squared residuals.

_____

REFLECT

1a. Complete the table to calculate the squares of the residuals and then the sum of the squares for your line of fit from Lesson 4-9.

t	a_F (actual)	a_F (predicted)	Residuals	Square of Residuals
0	29.2			
10	31.3			
20	34.0			
30	36.5			
40	38.2			

Sum of squared

residuals: _____

1b. If you use a graphing calculator to perform linear regression on the data, you obtain the equation $a_F = 0.232t + 29.2$. Complete the table to calculate the squares of the residuals and then the sum of the squares for this line of fit.

$a_F = 0.232t + 29.2$				
t	a_F (actual)	a_F (predicted)	Residuals	Square of Residuals
0	29.2	29.2	0	0
10	31.3			
20	34.0			
30	36.5			
40	38.2			

Sum of squared

residuals: _____

1c. Explain why the model $a_F = 0.232t + 29.2$ is a better fit to the data than $a_F = 0.25t + 29.0$, $a_F = 0.25t + 28.8$, and even your own model.

_____

_____

Because linear regression produces an equation for which the sum of the squared residuals is as small as possible, the line obtained from linear regression is sometimes called the *least-squares regression line*. It is also called the *line of best fit*. Not only will a graphing calculator automatically find the equation of the line of best fit, but it will also give you the correlation coefficient and display the residual plot.

2 EXAMPLE Performing Linear Regression on a Graphing Calculator

The table gives the distances (in meters) that a discus was thrown by men to win the gold medal at the Olympic Games from 1920 to 1964. (No Olympic Games were held during World War II.) Use a graphing calculator to find the line of best fit, to find the correlation coefficient, and to evaluate the goodness of fit.

A Identify the independent and dependent variables, and specify how you will represent them.

The independent variable is time. Since the graphing calculator uses the variables x and y, let x represent time. To simplify the values of x, define x as years since 1920 so that, for instance, $x = 0$ represents 1920 and $x = 44$ represents 1964. Then $x = $ _____ represents 1924, $x = $ _____ represents 1928, $x = $ _____ represents 1932, and so on.

The dependent variable is the distance that won the gold medal for the men's discus throw. Let y represent that distance.

Year of Olympic Games	Men's Gold Medal Discus Throw (meters)
1920	44.685
1924	46.155
1928	47.32
1932	49.49
1936	50.48
1940	No Olympics
1944	No Olympics
1948	52.78
1952	55.03
1956	56.36
1960	59.18
1964	61.00

B Enter the paired data into two lists, L_1 and L_2, on your graphing calculator after pressing [STAT].

Do the distances increase or decrease over time? What does this mean for the correlation?

_____

_____

C Create a scatter plot of the paired data using STAT PLOT. The calculator will choose a good viewing window and plot the points automatically if you press ZOOM and select ZoomStat.

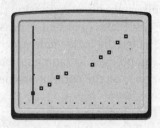

Describe the correlation.

_____

_____

_____

D Perform linear regression by pressing STAT and selecting LinReg $(ax + b)$ from the CALC menu. The calculator reports the slope a and y-intercept b of the line of best fit. It also reports the correlation coefficient r.

Does the correlation coefficient agree with your description of the correlation in Part C? Explain.

_____

_____

_____

E Graph the line of best fit by pressing Y= , entering the equation of the line of best fit, and then pressing GRAPH . You should round the values of a and b when entering them so that each has at most 4 significant digits.

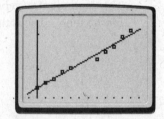

What is the equation of the line of best fit?

_____

F Create a residual plot by replacing L_2 with RESID in STAT PLOT as the choice for Ylist. (You can select RESID from the NAMES menu after pressing 2nd STAT .)

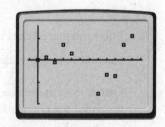

Evaluate the suitability and goodness of the fit.

_____

_____

_____

2a. Interpret the slope and *y*-intercept of the line of best fit in the context of the data.

_____

_____

2b. Use the line of best fit to make predictions about the distances that would have won gold medals if the Olympic Games had been held in 1940 and 1944. Are the predictions interpolations or extrapolations?

_____

2c. Several Olympic Games were held prior to 1920. Use the line of best fit to make a prediction about the distance that would have won a gold medal in the 1908 Olympics. What value of *x* must you use? Is the prediction an interpolation or an extrapolation? How does the prediction compare with the actual value of 40.89 meters?

_____

_____

PRACTICE

Throughout these exercises, use a graphing calculator.

1. The table gives the distances (in meters) that a discus was thrown by men to win the gold medal at the Olympic Games from 1968 to 2008.

a. Find the equation of the line of best fit.

_____

b. Find the correlation coefficient.

_____

c. Evaluate the suitability and goodness of the fit.

_____

_____

d. Does the slope of the line of best fit for the 1968–2008 data equal the slope of the line of best fit for the 1920–1964 data? If not, speculate about why this is so.

_____

_____

Year of Olympic Games	Men's Gold Medal Discus Throw (meters)
1968	64.78
1972	64.40
1976	67.50
1980	66.64
1984	66.60
1988	68.82
1992	65.12
1996	69.40
2000	69.30
2004	69.89
2008	68.82

2. Women began competing in the discus throw in the 1928 Olympic Games. The table gives the distances (in meters) that a discus was thrown by women to win the gold medal at the Olympic Games from 1928 to 1964.

Year of Olympic Games	Women's Gold Medal Discus Throw (meters)
1928	39.62
1932	40.58
1936	47.63
1940	No Olympics
1944	No Olympics
1948	41.92
1952	51.42
1956	53.69
1962	55.10
1964	57.27

a. Find the equation of the line of best fit.

_____

b. Find the correlation coefficient.

_____

c. Evaluate the suitability and goodness of the fit.

_____

_____

_____

3. Research the distances that a discus was thrown by women to win the gold medal at the Olympic Games from 1968 to 2008. Explain why a linear model is not appropriate for the data.

_____

4. The table lists the median heights (in centimeters) of girls and boys from age 2 to age 10. Choose either the data for girls or the data for boys.

Age (years)	Median Height (cm) of Girls	Median Height (cm) of Boys
2	84.98	86.45
3	93.92	94.96
4	100.75	102.22
5	107.66	108.90
6	114.71	115.39
7	121.49	121.77
8	127.59	128.88
9	132.92	133.51
10	137.99	138.62

a. Identify the real-world variables that x and y will represent.

_____

b. Find the equation of the line of best fit.

_____

_____

c. Find the correlation coefficient.

_____

d. Evaluate the suitability and goodness of the fit.

_____

_____

Name _____ **Class** _____ **Date** _____

MULTIPLE CHOICE

1. Which function is represented by the graph?

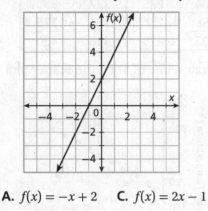

A. $f(x) = -x + 2$ **C.** $f(x) = 2x - 1$

B. $f(x) = x - 1$ **D.** $f(x) = 2x + 2$

2. Jorge bought a mechanical pencil for $8. A lead and eraser refill pack costs $2. Write a linear function to describe the cost of using the pencil as a function of the number of refill packs.

F. $C(r) = 8r - 2$ **H.** $C(r) = 2r$

G. $C(r) = 2r + 8$ **J.** $C(r) = 8r + 2$

3. The function $A(t) = 99t$ describes the cost of Cell Phone Plan A (in dollars) for t months. The table shows the cost of Cell Phone Plan B for t months. Which plan will cost more for 6 months, and which function describes the cost of Plan B?

t	1	2	3
B(t)	$150	$200	$250

A. Plan B; $B(t) = 100t + 50$

B. Plan B; $B(t) = 50t + 100$

C. Plan A; $B(t) = 100t + 50$

D. Plan A; $B(t) = 50t + 100$

4. Pat pays $250 to be a gym member for 2 months and $550 to be a member for 6 months. What is the monthly cost of a gym membership?

F. $50   **H.** $150

G. $75   **J.** $300

5. For $f(x) = -\frac{2}{5}x + 3$, find the slope and y-intercept, and determine whether the graph is increasing or decreasing.

A. $m = -\frac{2}{5}$, $b = 3$, decreasing

B. $m = -\frac{2}{5}$, $b = 3$, increasing

C. $m = 3$, $b = -\frac{2}{5}$, decreasing

D. $m = 3$, $b = -\frac{2}{5}$, increasing

6. The graph shows the distance Tiana walks as a function of time. How would the graph change if she walked 1 mi/h faster?

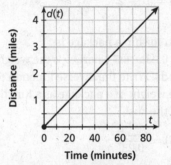

F. The line in the graph would not change.

G. The line would be less steep.

H. The line would be steeper.

J. The line would shift up on the y-axis.

7. How would the graphs of $f(x) = 2x + 6$ and $g(x) = 2x + 3$ compare if graphed on the same coordinate plane?

A. The graphs would intersect at $(0, 2)$.

B. The graph of $f(x)$ would be twice as steep as the graph of $g(x)$.

C. The graph of $f(x)$ would be 3 units above the graph of $g(x)$.

D. The graph of $f(x)$ would be 6 units above the graph of $g(x)$.

8. Gary works no more than 9 hours on weekends and gets paid $10 per hour. He works whole-hour shifts. His pay P is a function of the number of hours he works n. What is the range of this function?

F. $0 \leq n \leq 9$

G. $0 \leq P \leq 90$

H. $\{0, 1, 2, 3, 4, 5, 6, 7, 8, 9\}$

J. $\{0, 10, 20, 30, 40, 50, 60, 70, 80, 90\}$

9. Given $f(x) = 3x + 2$ and $g(x) = -2x - 4$, find $h(x) = f(x) - g(x)$.

A. $h(x) = x - 2$

B. $h(x) = x + 6$

C. $h(x) = 5x + 6$

D. $h(x) = 5x - 2$

10. The cost to ship a package is $C(w) = 0.23w + 7$ where w is the weight in pounds. Write the inverse function to find the weight of a package as a function $w(C)$ of the cost.

F. $w(C) = \dfrac{C - 7}{0.23}$

G. $w(C) = \dfrac{C + 7}{0.23}$

H. $w(C) = 0.23C + 7$

J. $w(C) = -0.23C - 7$

11. Which number best approximates the correlation coefficient for the data below?

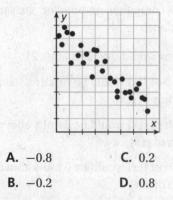

A. -0.8 **C.** 0.2

B. -0.2 **D.** 0.8

FREE RESPONSE

12. The table shows the temperature T displayed on an oven while it was heating as a function of the amount of time a since it was turned on.

a (sec)	T (°F)	a (sec)	T (°F)
31	175	250	300
61	200	285	325
104	225	327	350
158	250	380	375
202	275	428	400

a. Draw a line of fit on the scatter plot.

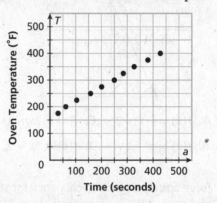

b. Find an equation of your line of fit.

_____

c. Perform linear regression to find the equation of the line of best fit and the correlation coefficient.

_____

d. Create a residual plot on a graphing calculator. Evaluate the suitability and goodness of fit of the regression equation.

_____

_____

_____

_____

e. Is the model a good predictor of the initial value? Why or why not?

_____

_____

_____

Exponential Functions

Unit Focus

In this unit you will learn what exponential functions are and use them for modeling and solving problems that involve increasing or decreasing quantities. You will learn how the graph of an exponential function changes when the function rule changes in certain ways. You will learn how to solve exponential equations. You will learn how to use a graphing calculator to write an exponential function model for data that are approximately exponential. You will learn how an exponential function compares with a linear function.

Unit at a Glance

COMMON
CORE

UNIT 5

Unpacking the Common Core State Standards

Use the table to help you understand the Standards for Mathematical Content that are taught in this unit. Refer to the lessons listed after each standard for exploration and practice.

COMMON CORE Standards for Mathematical Content	What It Means For You
CC.9-12.A.CED.1 Create equations and inequalities **in one variable and use them to solve problems.*** Lesson 5-5	You will write and solve exponential equations to solve problems such as when a sales goal will be achieved or when a changing population will reach a certain number.
CC.9-12.A.CED.2 Create equations in two or more variables to represent relationships between quantities; graph equations on coordinate axes with labels and scales.* Lessons 5-1, 5-5, 5-6, 5-8 (Also 5-2, 5-3, 5-4)	A function is often in the form of an equation in two variables, such as $y = 3x$, or the alternate form $f(x) = 3x$. You will write and graph functions and use those skills to solve problems throughout this unit.
CC.9-12.A.REI.11 Explain why the x**-coordinates of the points where the graphs of the equations** $y = f(x)$ **and** $y = g(x)$ **intersect are the solutions of the equation** $f(x) = g(x)$**; find the solutions approximately, e.g., using technology to graph the functions,** make tables of values, or find successive approximations. **Include cases where** $f(x)$ **and/or** $g(x)$ **are** linear, polynomial, rational, absolute value, **exponential** and logarithmic **functions.*** Lessons 5-5, 5-8	One way to solve an equation is to graph two functions and find where the graphs intersect. For example, you could solve the equation $2x = x + 4$ by graphing the functions $f(x) = 2x$ and $g(x) = x + 4$ and then finding where the graphs intersect. You will apply this idea to solving exponential equations with a graphing calculator. You will also solve exponential equations using paper-and-pencil techniques.
CC.9-12.F.IF.1 Understand that a function from one set (called the domain) to another set (called the range) assigns to each element of the domain exactly one element of the range. If f **is a function and** x **is an element of its domain, then** $f(x)$ **denotes the output of** f **corresponding to the input** x**. The graph of** f **is the graph of the equation** $y = f(x)$**.** Lesson 5-2 (Also 5-1)	A function is a set of ordered pairs, usually denoted (x, y) or $(x, f(x))$. The domain is the set of all x-values. The range is the set of all y-values (or $f(x)$-values). You will represent exponential functions in several different ways: by a list of the ordered pairs, by an equation that tells the function rule, and by a graph.
CC.9-12.F.IF.2 Use function notation, evaluate functions for inputs in their domains, and interpret statements that use function notation in terms of a context. Lesson 5-1	You will use function notation as you model situations with exponential functions. You will revisit the fact that $f(x)$ means the value of the function for the given value of x.
CC.9-12.F.IF.3 Recognize that sequences are functions, sometimes defined recursively, whose domain is a subset of the integers. Lesson 5-1	You will be introduced to discrete exponential functions, which are one type of sequence where the ratio between consecutive values is constant.

COMMON CORE **Standards for Mathematical Content**	**What It Means For You**
CC.9-12.F.IF.4 For a function that models a relationship between two quantities, interpret key features of graphs and tables in terms of the quantities, and sketch graphs showing key features given a verbal description of the relationship.* Lessons 5-3, 5-4 (Also 5-2)	You will use graphs and tables as models to help solve problems. You will learn to interpret key features of exponential graphs. One key feature is end behavior, which concerns the shape of the graph as you move infinitely far left or right.
CC.9-12.F.IF.5 Relate the domain of a function to its graph and, where applicable, to the quantitative relationship it describes.* Lessons 5-1, 5-2, 5-8 (Also 5-3)	For a function denoted by $f(x)$, the domain is a set of x-values. You will learn that in many cases, there are x-values in a domain that do not make sense for the problem you are working on. In those cases, you need to choose an appropriate domain by deciding what x-values make sense in context.
CC.9-12.F.IF.7 Graph functions expressed symbolically and show key features of the graph, by hand in simple cases and using technology for more complicated cases.* **CC.9-12.F.IF.7e** Graph exponential and logarithmic **functions, showing intercepts and end behavior,** and trigonometric functions, showing period, midline, and amplitude.* Lessons 5-1; 5-2, 5-3, 5-8	You will graph exponential functions and then compare the graphs with each other. You will learn how a graph changes when the function rule changes in certain ways, and you will describe those changes by discussing intercepts and end behavior.
CC.9-12.F.BF.1 Write a function that describes a relationship between two quantities.* **CC.9-12.F.BF.1a** Determine an explicit expression, a recursive process, or steps for calculation from a context.* Lessons 5-5, 5-6, 5-8 (Also 5-2, 5-3)	When you write a function rule, you are determining an explicit expression. You will use the recursive nature of exponential growth to write expressions for real-world situations.
CC.9-12.F.BF.3 Identify the effect on the graph of replacing $f(x)$ by $f(x) + k$, $kf(x)$, $f(kx)$, and $f(x + k)$ for specific values of k (both positive and negative); find the value of k given the graphs. **Experiment with cases and illustrate an explanation of the effects on the graphs using technology.** Lesson 5-4	You will explore the effects of changing key parameters of an exponential function to see how they affect the behavior of the graph.

UNIT 5

COMMON CORE Standards for Mathematical Content	What It Means For You
CC.9-12.F.LE.1 Distinguish between situations that can be modeled with linear functions and with exponential functions.* **CC.9-12.F.LE.1a Prove that linear functions grow by equal differences over equal intervals, and that exponential functions grow by equal factors over equal intervals.*** **CC.9-12.F.LE.1b Recognize situations in which one quantity changes at a constant rate per unit interval relative to another.*** **CC.9-12.F.LE.1c Recognize situations in which a quantity grows or decays by a constant percent rate per unit interval relative to another.*** Lessons 5-2, 5-3, 5-6, 5-7, 5-8	You will use properties of equations and properties of exponents to prove key facts about the behavior of linear and exponential functions over intervals of the same size. You will learn to distinguish linear growth from exponential growth. You will learn to recognize exponential growth by comparing consecutive function values and looking for a constant ratio.
CC.9-12.F.LE.2 Construct linear and **exponential functions, including** arithmetic and **geometric sequences, given a graph, a description of a relationship, or two input-output pairs (include reading these from a table).*** Lessons 5-1, 5-2, 5-3, 5-5, 5-8	You will write function rules for discrete and continuous exponential functions based on a verbal description of the relationship or given values from which you can calculate the key parameters and write the function.
CC.9-12.F.LE.3 Observe using graphs and tables that a quantity increasing exponentially eventually exceeds a quantity increasing linearly, quadratically, or (more generally) as a polynomial function.* Lesson 5-7	You will graph an increasing linear function and an exponential growth function on the same viewing window of a graphing calculator. Then you will experiment with different window sizes to see that the exponential function always rises above the linear function.
CC.9-12.F.LE.5 Interpret the parameters in a linear or exponential function in terms of a context.* Lessons 5-2, 5-3, 5-6, 5-8	In the function $y = mx + b$, the slope, m, and the y-intercept, b, are called *parameters*. Exponential functions also have parameters. You will identify those parameters and describe what they represent in different situations.
CC.9-12.S.ID.6 Represent data on two quantitative variables on a scatter plot, and describe how the variables are related.* **CC.9-12.S.ID.6a Fit a function to the data; use functions fitted to data to solve problems in the context of the data.*** **CC.9-12.S.ID.6b Informally assess the fit of a function by plotting and analyzing residuals.*** Lessons 5-6, 5-8	You will use a graphing calculator to find best-fit exponential functions for data sets and then use those functions to solve problems. You will use residuals to assess (judge) fit. A residual is the difference between an actual data value and a corresponding model function value. You will learn to make a scatter plot to show all the residuals for a data set and its model. Then, by looking at the scatter plot, you can assess how well the model fits the data.

UNIT 5

Discrete Exponential Functions

Essential question: *What are discrete exponential functions and how can you represent them?*

COMMON
CORE

CC.9-12.A.CED.2*,
CC.9-12.F.IF.2,
CC.9-12.F.IF.3,
CC.9-12.F.IF.5*,
CC.9-12.F.IF.7e*,
CC.9-12.F.LE.2*

1 ENGAGE Understanding Discrete Exponential Functions

Recall that a discrete function has a graph that consists of isolated points. The function shown is a discrete *linear* function, because the isolated points lie along a line. Note that the *differences* of successive output values are all equal.

Tickets	Dollars
0	0
1	10
2	20
3	30
4	40
5	50

10
10
10
10
10

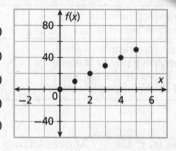

The function shown here is a discrete *exponential* function relating attendance at an annual event to the number of years since the initial event. Note that the *ratios* of successive output values are equal.

Events	Attendance
0	3
1	6
2	12
3	24
4	48
5	96

×2
×2
×2
×2
×2

REFLECT

1a. Describe the limitations on the domains of these discrete functions.

_____

1b. How are the graphs alike? How are they different?

_____

_____

_____

1c. What was the attendance at the initial seminar? What is the ratio of successive output values? How has attendance grown over time?

_____

A function whose successive output values have a *constant ratio* for each unit increase in the input values is an *exponential function*. An **exponential function** can be represented by the equation, $f(x) = ab^x$, where x is a real number, $a \neq 0$, $b > 0$, and $b \neq 1$. The constant ratio is the base b.

If a discrete exponential function has inputs that are a set of equally spaced integers, then its outputs are a sequence of numbers called a *geometric sequence*.

When evaluating exponential functions, you will need to remember these properties of exponents.

Zero and Negative Exponents		
Words	**Algebra**	**Example**
Any nonzero number raised to the zero power is 1.	$c^0 = 1, c \neq 0$	$12^0 = 1$
Any nonzero number raised to a negative power is equal to 1 divided by the number raised to the opposite power.	$c^{-n} = \frac{1}{c^n}, c \neq 0$	$2^{-3} = \frac{1}{2^3} = \frac{1}{8}$

2 EXAMPLE Representing an Exponential Function

Make a table for the function $f(x) = 2\left(\frac{2}{3}\right)^x$ for the domain $\{-2, -1, 0, 1, 2, 3\}$. Then graph the function for this domain.

A Complete the following to calculate $f(-2)$.

$$2\left(\frac{2}{3}\right)^{-2} = 2\left(\frac{1}{\left(\right)}\right) = 2\left(\frac{1}{}\right) = 2\left(\right) = $$

B Complete the table of values.

x	f(x)	(x, f(x))

C Graph the function.

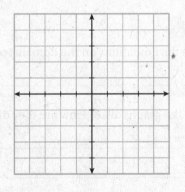

2a. Identify the values of a and b for the function $f(x) = 2\left(\frac{2}{3}\right)^x$.

_____

2b. Describe how the value of the function changes as x increases.

_____

2c. Explain why each of the following statements is true.

- For $0 < b < 1$ and $a > 0$, the function $f(x) = ab^x$ *decreases* as x increases.

_____

_____

_____

- For $b > 1$ and $a > 0$, the function $f(x) = ab^x$ *increases* as x increases.

_____

_____

_____

_____

Writing Equations You can write an equation for an exponential function as long as you can identify or calculate the values of a and b. The value of a is the value of the function where x is 0, because $f(0) = ab^0 = a \cdot 1 = a$. The value of b is the factor that is the ratio of successive function values.

3 EXAMPLE   Writing an Equation from a Verbal Description

When a piece of paper is folded in half, the total thickness doubles. Suppose an unfolded piece of paper is 0.1 millimeter thick. Write an equation for the total thickness, t, as a function of the number of folds, n.

A The value of a is the thickness before any folds are made, or _____.

B Because the thickness doubles with each fold, the value of b is _____.

C An equation for the function is $t(n) =$ _____.

3a. Why is the exponential function in Part A of the Example discrete?

_____

3b. If the paper were twice as thick to begin with, what would be an equation for the function?

_____

_____

© Houghton Mifflin Harcourt Publishing Company

4 **EXAMPLE** Writing an Equation from Input-Output Pairs

The height, h, of a dropped ball is an exponential function of the number of bounces, n. On its first bounce, a certain ball reached a height of 15 inches. On its second bounce, the ball reached a height of 7.5 inches. Write an equation for the height of the ball as a function of the number of bounces.

A Divide successive function values, or heights, to find the value of b.

$b = \boxed{} \div \boxed{} = \boxed{}$

B Use your value for b and a known ordered pair to find the value of a.

$h(n) = ab^n$ Write the general form.

$h(n) = a\left(\boxed{}\right)^n$ Substitute the value for b.

$\boxed{} = a\left(\boxed{}\right)^1$ Substitute the input and output values for the first bounce.

$\boxed{} = \boxed{}\, a$ Simplify.

$\boxed{} = a$ Solve for a.

C An equation for the function is _____.

REFLECT

4a. Use unit analysis to explain why b is a unit-less factor in Part B above.

_____

_____

4b. Show that using the values for the second bounce will give the same result for a.

_____

4c. What was the initial height? What was the height for the fifth bounce? Explain.

_____

_____

4d. What is the ratio of the height on the fifth bounce to the initial height? How is this ratio related to the constant ratio for this exponential function? Explain.

_____

_____

_____

Make a table of values and a graph for each function.

1. $f(x) = 2^x$

x	f(x)
−3	
−2	
−1	
0	
1	
2	
3	

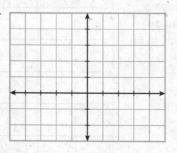

2. $f(x) = 2\left(\frac{3}{4}\right)^x$

x	f(x)
−3	
−2	
−1	
0	
1	
2	
3	

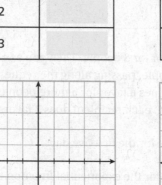

3. $f(x) = 0.9(0.6)^x$

x	f(x)
−3	
−2	
−1	
0	
1	
2	
3	

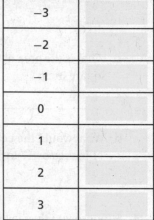
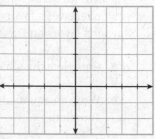

Use two points to write an equation for each function shown.

4.

x	−3	−2	−1	0
f(x)	8	4	2	1

_____

5.

x	1	2	3	4
f(x)	8	6.4	5.12	4.096

_____

6.

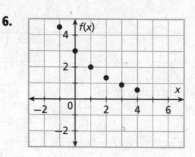

_____

7.

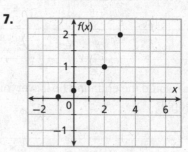

_____

8. The area of the top surface of an 8.5 inch by 11 inch piece of paper is a function of the number of times it is folded in half.

a. Write an equation for the function that models this situation. Explain why this is an exponential function.

_____

b. Identify the value of a. What does it represent in this situation?

_____

c. What is the area of the top surface after 4 folds? Round to the nearest tenth of a square inch.

_____

d. What would the equation be if the original piece of paper had dimensions 11 inches by 17 inches? Compare this equation with the equation in Part (a).

_____

9. Suppose you do a favor for 3 people. Then you ask each of them to do a favor for 3 more people, passing along the request that each person who receives a favor does a favor for 3 more people. Suppose you do your 3 favors on Day 1, each recipient does 3 favors on Day 2, and so on.

Day n	Favors $f(n)$
1	3
2	9
3	
4	
5	

a. Complete the table for the first five days.

b. Write an equation for the exponential function that models this situation.

_____

c. Describe the domain and range of this function.

_____

_____

d. According to the model, how many favors will be done on Day 10? _____

e. How is the number of favors done on Day 10 related to the number done on Day 5? Explain your reasoning.

_____

_____

f. What would the equation be if everyone did a favor for 4 people rather than 3 people?

_____

Exponential Growth Functions

COMMON
CORE

CC.9-12.F.IF.1,
CC.9-12.F.IF.5*,
CC.9-12.F.IF.7e*,
CC.9-12.F.LE.1c*,
CC.9-12.F.LE.2*,
CC.9-12.F.LE.5*

Essential question: *How do you write, graph, and interpret an exponential growth function?*

When you graph a function $f(x)$ in a coordinate plane, the x-axis represents the independent variable and the y-axis represents the dependent variable. Therefore, the graph of $f(x)$ is the same as the graph of the equation $y = f(x)$. You will use this form when you use a calculator to graph functions.

1 EXPLORE   Describing End Behavior of a Function

A Use a graphing calculator to graph the exponential function $f(x) = 200(1.10)^x$ using Y_1 for $f(x)$. Use a viewing window from -20 to 20 for x, with a scale of 2, and from -100 to 1000 for y, with a scale of 50. Make a copy of the curve below.

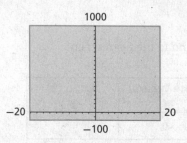

B To describe the *end behavior* of a function, you describe the function values as x increases or decreases without bound. Using the TRACE feature, move the cursor to the right along the curve. Describe the end behavior as x increases without bound.

_____

C Using the TRACE feature, move the cursor to the left along the curve. Describe the end behavior as x decreases without bound.

_____

REFLECT

1a. Describe the domain and the range of the function.

_____

1b. Identify the y-intercept of the graph of the function. _____

1c. An *asymptote* of a graph is a line the graph approaches more and more closely. Identify an asymptote of this graph _____

1d. Why is the value of the function always greater than 0?

_____

A function of the form $y = ab^x$ represents exponential growth when $a > 0$ and $b > 1$. If b is replaced by $1 + r$ and x is replaced by t, then the function is the **exponential growth model** $y = a(1 + r)^t$, where a is the *initial amount*, the base $(1 + r)$ is the *growth factor*, r is the *growth rate*, and t is the *time interval*. The value of the model increases with time.

2 EXAMPLE Modeling Exponential Growth

Alex buys a rare trading card for \$4. The value of the card increases 40% per year for four years.

A Identify the initial amount and the growth rate.

$$a = \underline{\hspace{4cm}}$$

$$r = \underline{\hspace{4cm}}$$

B Write an exponential growth equation for this situation:

$$y = \boxed{} \left(1 + \boxed{}\right)^t$$

C Copy and complete the table. Round to the nearest cent.

Time (years) t	Value ($) y
0	
1	
2	
3	
4	

D Graph the points from the table using appropriate scales. Draw a smooth curve connecting the points. Label the axes.

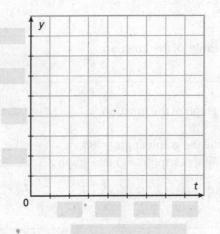

2a. Identify the *y*-intercept of the graph. What does it represent?

_____

2b. What is the growth factor $(1 + r)$ written as a percent? _____

2c. Use the graph to estimate the value of the card in 3.5 years. Then explain why it makes sense to connect the points from the table with a smooth curve when graphing this function.

_____

_____

2d. Describe the domain and range of the function $y = 4(1.4)^t$ outside of the context of this problem. Do all of these values make sense in the context of this situation? Why or why not?

_____

_____

_____

PRACTICE

Complete the table for each function.

	Function	Initial Amount	Growth Rate	Growth Factor
1.	$y = 1250(1 + 0.02)^t$			
2.	$y = 40(1 + 0.5)^t$			
3.	$y = 50(1.06)^t$			

Write an equation for each exponential growth function.

4. Eva deposits $1500 in an account that earns 4% interest each year. _____

5. Lamont buys a house for $255,000. The value of the house increases 6% each year. _____

6. Brian invests $2000. His investment grows at a rate of 16% per year. _____

7. Sue is a coin collector. At the end of 2005 she bought a coin for $2.50 whose value had been growing 20% per year for 3 years. The value continued to grow at this rate until she sold the coin 4 years later.

  a. Write an exponential growth equation for this situation, using the amount Sue paid as the value at time 0. _____

  b. Complete the table.

Time (years) t	Value ($) y
−3	
−2	
−1	
0	
1	
2	
3	
4	

  c. Graph and connect the points.

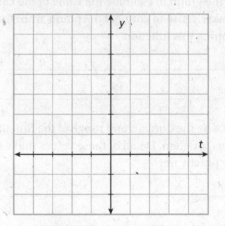

  d. Describe the domain and range for this situation.

  _____

  _____

  e. Identify the y-intercept. What does it represent?

  _____

  f. What was the value of the coin at the end of 2003? at the time Sue sold the coin? Explain your reasoning.

  _____

  _____

  _____

8. Suppose you invest $1600 on your 16th birthday and your investment earns 8% interest each year. What will be the value of the investment on your 30th birthday? Explain your reasoning.

  _____

© Houghton Mifflin Harcourt Publishing Company

Exponential Decay Functions

Essential question: *How do you write, graph, and interpret an exponential decay function?*

COMMON CORE

CC.9-12.F.IF.4*,
CC.9-12.F.IF.7*,
CC.9-12.F.IF.7e*,
CC.9-12.F.LE.1c*,
CC.9-12.F.LE.2*,
CC.9-12.F.LE.5*

1 EXPLORE Describing End Behavior of a Decay Function

A Use a graphing calculator to graph the exponential function $f(x) = 500(0.8)^x$ using Y_1 for $f(x)$. Use a viewing window from -10 to 10 for x, with a scale of 1, and from -500 to $5{,}000$ for y, with a scale of 500. Make a copy of the curve below.

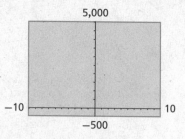

B Using the TRACE feature, move the cursor to the right along the curve. Describe the end behavior as x increases without bound.

_____

C Using the TRACE feature, move the cursor to the left along the curve. Describe the end behavior as x decreases without bound.

_____

REFLECT

1a. Describe the domain and the range of the function.

_____

1b. Identify the y-intercept of the graph of the function. _____

1c. Identify an asymptote of this graph. Why is this line an asymptote?

_____

A function of the form $f(x) = ab^x$ represents exponential decay when $a > 0$ and $0 < b < 1$. If b is replaced by $1 - r$ and x is replaced by t, then the function is the **exponential decay model** $y = a(1 - r)^t$, where a is the *initial amount*, the base $(1 - r)$ is the *decay factor*, r is the *decay rate*, and t is the *time interval*.

© Houghton Mifflin Harcourt Publishing Company

2 EXAMPLE Modeling Exponential Decay

You pay $12,000 for a car. The value then depreciates at a rate of 15% per year.
That is, the car loses 15% of its value each year.

A Write an exponential decay equation for this situation.

$$y = \boxed{}\left(1 - \boxed{}\right)^{t}$$

B Complete the table. Round to the nearest dollar.

Time (years) t	Value ($) y
0	
1	
2	
3	
4	
5	
6	

C Graph the points and connect them with a smooth curve. Label the axes.

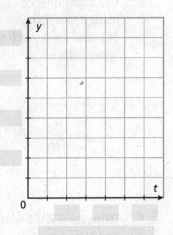

REFLECT

2a. Identify the *y*-intercept of the graph. What does it represent?

_____

2b. What is the decay factor $(1 - r)$ written as a percent?

_____

2c. What values make sense for the domain and range of this function?

_____

_____

2d. Predict the value of the car after 10 years.

_____

2e. In how many years was the value of the car $8000?

_____

2f. Explain why exponential functions of this type are referred to as exponential *decay* functions.

_____

© Houghton Mifflin Harcourt Publishing Company

E X A M P L E   Comparing Exponential Growth and Exponential Decay

The graph shows the value of two different shares of stock over the period of four years since they were purchased. The values have been changing exponentially. Describe and compare the behaviors of the two stocks.

A   The model for the graph representing

Stock A is an exponential _____ model.

The initial value is _____ and the

decay factor is ☐ ÷ ☐ = ☐ .

B   The model for the graph representing Stock B

is an exponential _____ model. The initial

value is _____ and the growth factor is ☐ ÷ ☐ = ☐ .

C   The value of Stock A is going _____ over time. The value of Stock B is going

_____ over time. The initial value of Stock A is _____ than the initial value

of Stock B. However, after about _____ years, the value of Stock A becomes less

than the value of Stock B.

REFLECT

3a.   What is the growth rate for the increasing function above? Explain your reasoning.

_____

3b.   What is the decay rate for the decreasing function above? Explain your reasoning.

_____

3c.   How did the values of the stocks compare initially? after four years?

_____

_____

3d.   In how many years was the value of Stock A about equal to the value of Stock B? Explain your reasoning.

_____

3e.   In how many years was the value of Stock A about twice the value of Stock B? Explain your reasoning.

_____

_____

PRACTICE

1. Identify the initial amount, the decay factor, and the decay rate for the function $y = 2.50(0.4)^t$. Explain how you found the decay rate.

   _____

2. Mr. Nevin buys a car for $18,500. The value depreciates 9% per year. Write an equation for this function _____

3. You are given a gift of $2,500 in stock on your 16th birthday. The value of the stock declines 10% per year.

   a. Write an exponential decay equation for this situation. _____

   b. Complete the table.

Time (years), t	Value ($), y
0	
1	
2	
3	
4	
5	

   c. Graph and connect the points. Label the axes.

   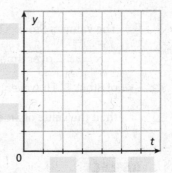

   d. Predict the value of the stock on your 22nd birthday. _____

4. The value of two parcels of land has been changing exponentially in the years since they were purchased, as shown in the graph. Describe and compare the values of the two parcels of land.

   _____

   _____

   _____

   _____

   _____

   _____

   _____

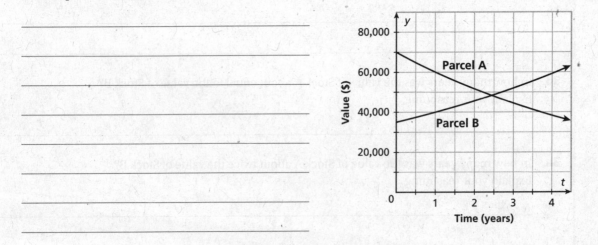

Changing the Values of *a* and *b* in $f(x) = ab^x$

COMMON
CORE

CC.9-12.F.IF.4*,
CC.9-12.F.BF.3,

Essential question: *How does the graph of $f(x) = ab^x$ change when a and b are changed?*

1 **ENGAGE** **Stretching Figures**

Recall that when you *dilate* a figure on a coordinate plane, its coordinates are all multiplied by the same scale factor. In other words, the figure is stretched horizontally and vertically by the same scale factor so that the new figure is similar to the original. If you stretch a figure in only one direction, vertically or horizontally, you do not produce a dilation.

Dilation

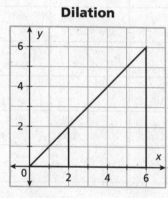

Vertical Stretch

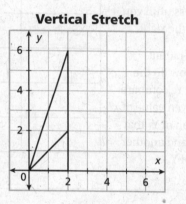

Horizontal Stretch

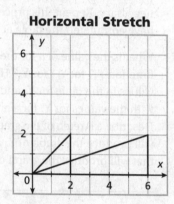

REFLECT

1a. Use the scale factor in the dilation above to help you complete the ordered pair to describe the dilation.

$(x, y) \longrightarrow \left(\boxed{}, \boxed{} \right)$

1b. Describe in words what happens to the *x*- and *y*-coordinates when the small triangle is stretched vertically. Then complete the ordered pair.

_____

_____

$(x, y) \longrightarrow \left(\boxed{}, \boxed{} \right)$

1c. Describe in words what happens to the *x*- and *y*-coordinates when the small triangle is stretched horizontally. Then complete the ordered pair.

_____

_____

$(x, y) \longrightarrow \left(\boxed{}, \boxed{} \right)$

1d. What happens to the points on the side of the figure that is on the *x*-axis when the small triangle is stretched vertically? Explain.

_____

_____

A *family* of functions is a group of functions that all have something in common. For exponential functions, every different base determines a different *parent function* for its own family of functions. You can explore the behavior of an exponential function by examining *parameters a* and *b*.

2 EXPLORE Transforming a Parent Function

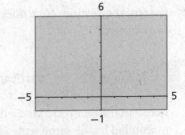

A Graph parent function $Y_1 = (1.5)^x$ and functions $Y_2 = 2\,(1.5)^x$ and $Y_3 = 3(1.5)^x$ on a graphing calculator. Use a viewing window from −5 to 5 for x and from −1 to 6 for y, using a scale of 1. Sketch the curves.

B Use the CALC feature while viewing the graphs to calculate the value of Y_1 when $x = -2$. Then use the up and down arrow keys to jump to the other curves and calculate their values when $x = -2$. Round to the nearest thousandth if necessary. Repeat this process until you have completed the table at the right.

X	Y_1	Y_2	Y_3
−2			
−1			
0			
1			
2			

C What is the value of a for the parent function Y_1? for Y_2? for Y_3? How do the values in the table for Y_2 and Y_3 compare with the values for Y_1 for a given value of x? Describe a stretch of the graph of Y_1 that will produce the graph of Y_2 and another that will produce the graph of Y_3.

_____

_____

_____

D Graph the function $Y_4 = 0.5(1.5)^x$. Explain why it is considered a vertical *shrink* of the parent function $Y_1 = (1.5)^x$.

_____

_____

REFLECT

2a. Describe how the graph of $f(x) = ab^x$ compares with the graph of $f(x) = b^x$ for a given value of b when $a > 1$ and when $0 < a < 1$.

_____

_____

_____

© Houghton Mifflin Harcourt Publishing Company

A Graph the functions $Y_1 = 1.2^x$ and $Y_2 = 1.5^x$ on a graphing calculator. Use a viewing window from -5 to 5 for x and from -2 to 5 for y, with a scale of 1 for both. Sketch the curves.

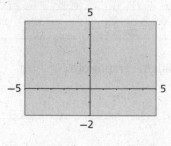

B Use the TBLSET and TABLE features to make a table of values starting at -2 with an increment of 1. Then complete the table below.

X	Y_1	Y_2
-2	0.694	
-1		0.667
0		
1	1.2	1.5
2		

C Which graph rises more quickly as x increases to the right of 0? Which graph falls, or approaches 0, more quickly as x decreases to the left of 0?

_____

_____

D Identify the y-intercepts of the graphs of Y_1 and Y_2.

_____

E Using the same window as above, graph the functions $Y_3 = 0.6^x$ and $Y_4 = 0.9^x$. Sketch the curves.

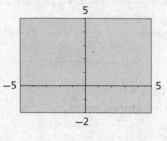

F Make a table of values starting at -2 with an increment of 1. Then complete the table.

X	Y_3	Y_4
-2	2.778	
-1		1.111
0		
1	0.6	0.9
2		

G Which graph rises more quickly as x decreases to the left of 0? Which graph falls more quickly as x increases to the right of 0?

_____

_____

H Identify the y-intercepts of the graphs of Y_3 and Y_4.

_____

3a. Consider the function $Y_5 = 1.3^x$. How will its graph compare with the graphs of Y_1 and Y_2? Discuss end behavior and the *y*-intercept.

_____

_____

_____

_____

3b. Consider the function $Y_6 = 0.7^x$. How will its graph compare with the graphs of Y_3 and Y_4? Discuss end behavior and the *y*-intercept.

_____

_____

_____

_____

3c. Describe how the graph of $f(x) = ab^x$ changes for a given positive value of *a* as you increase the value of *b* when $b > 1$. Discuss end behavior and the *y*-intercept.

_____

_____

_____

3d. Describe how the graph of $f(x) = ab^x$ changes for a given positive value of *a* as you decrease the value of *b* when $0 < b < 1$. Discuss end behavior and the *y*-intercept.

_____

_____

_____

3e. Consider the functions $Y_1 = (1.02)^x$ and $Y_2 = (1.03)^x$. Which function increases more quickly as *x* increases to the right of 0? How do the growth factors support your answer?

_____

_____

_____

3f. Consider the functions $Y_1 = (0.94)^x$ and $Y_2 = (0.98)^x$. Which function decreases more quickly as *x* increases to the right of 0? How do the decay factors support your answer?

_____

_____

_____

Solving Equations Involving Exponents

COMMON
CORE

CC.9-12.A.CED.1*,
CC.9-12.A.CED.2*,
CC.9-12.A.REI.11*,
CC.9-12.F.BF.1*,
CC.9-12.F.BF.1a*,
CC.9-12.F.LE.2*

Essential question: *How can you solve problems modeled by equations involving variable exponents?*

You can apply the properties of equations you already know to solve equations involving exponents. You will also need the following property.

Equating Exponents when Solving Equations		
Words	**Algebra**	**Example**
Two powers with the same positive base other than 1 are equal if and only if the exponents are equal.	If $b > 0$ and $b \neq 1$, then $b^x = b^y$ if and only if $x = y$.	If $2^x = 2^9$, then $x = 9$. If $x = 9$, then $2^x = 2^9$.

1 EXAMPLE Solving Equations by Equating Exponents

Solve each equation.

A $\frac{5}{2}(2)^x = 80$

$\boxed{} \cdot \frac{5}{2}(2)^x = \boxed{} \cdot 80$ Multiply to isolate the power $(2)^x$.

$(2)^x = 32$ Simplify.

$(2)^{\boxed{}} = 2^{\boxed{}}$ Write 32 as a power of 2.

$x = \boxed{}$ $b^x = b^y$ if and only if $x = y$.

B $4\left(\frac{5}{3}\right)^x = \frac{500}{27}$

$\boxed{} \cdot 4\left(\frac{5}{3}\right)^x = \boxed{} \cdot \frac{500}{27}$ Multiply to isolate the power.

$\left(\frac{5}{3}\right)^x = \frac{125}{27}$ Simplify.

$\left(\frac{5}{3}\right)^x = \left(\frac{5}{3}\right)^{\boxed{}}$ Write the fraction as a power of $\frac{5}{3}$.

$x = \boxed{}$ $b^x = b^y$ if and only if $x = y$.

1a. How can you check a solution?

_____

1b. How can you work backward to write $\frac{125}{27}$ as a power of $\frac{5}{3}$?

_____

1c. Is it possible to solve the equation $2^x = 96$ using the method in the Example? Why or why not?

_____

Some equations can't be solved using the method in the Example because it isn't possible to write both sides of the equation as a whole number power of the same base. Instead, you can consider the expressions on either side of the equation as the rules for two different functions. You can then solve the original equation in one variable by graphing the two functions. The solution is the input value for the point where the two graphs intersect.

2 EXAMPLE Writing an Equation and Solving by Graphing

A town has 78,918 residents. The population is increasing at a rate of 6% per year. The town council is offering a prize for the best prediction of how long it will take for the population to reach 100,000. Make a prediction.

A Write an exponential model to represent the situation. Let y represent the population and x represent time (in years).

$$y = 78{,}918\left(1 + \boxed{}\right)^x$$

B Write an equation in one variable to represent the time, x, when the population reaches 100,000.

$$\boxed{} = 78{,}918\left(1 + \boxed{}\right)^x$$

C Write functions for the expressions on either side of the equation.

$$f(x) = \boxed{}$$

$$g(x) = 78{,}918\left(1 + \boxed{}\right)^x$$

D What type of function is $f(x)$? What type of function is $g(x)$?

_____

E   Graph the functions on a graphing calculator. Let $Y_1 = f(x)$ and $Y_2 = g(x)$. Sketch the graph of Y_2 below. (Y_1 is already graphed for you.) Include the missing window values.

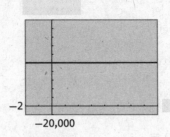

-2

$-20{,}000$

F   Use the intersect feature on the CALC menu to find the input value where the graphs intersect. (Do not round.)

_____

G   Make a prediction as to the number of years until the population reaches 100,000.

_____

REFLECT

2a. Suppose the contest is announced on January 1, and the town has 78,918 residents on that date. Explain how to predict *the date* on which the population will be 100,000.

_____

_____

_____

2b. Explain why the *x*-coordinate of the point where the graphs of $Y_1 = f(x)$ and $Y_2 = g(x)$ intersect is the solution of the equation in Part B.

_____

_____

_____

_____

_____

_____

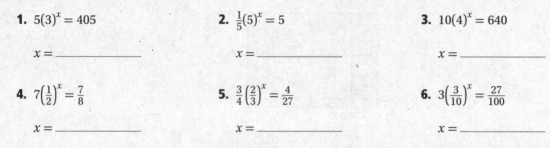

Solve each equation without graphing.

1. $5(3)^x = 405$

$x =$ _____

2. $\frac{1}{5}(5)^x = 5$

$x =$ _____

3. $10(4)^x = 640$

$x =$ _____

4. $7\left(\frac{1}{2}\right)^x = \frac{7}{8}$

$x =$ _____

5. $\frac{3}{4}\left(\frac{2}{3}\right)^x = \frac{4}{27}$

$x =$ _____

6. $3\left(\frac{3}{10}\right)^x = \frac{27}{100}$

$x =$ _____

Solve each equation by graphing. Round to the nearest hundredth.

7. $6^x = 150$

$x \approx$ _____

8. $5^x = 20$

$x \approx$ _____

9. $(2.5)^x = 40$

$x \approx$ _____

10. Last year a debate club sold 972 fundraiser tickets on their most successful day. This year the 4 club officers plan to match that number on a single day as follows:

To start off, on Day 0, each of the 4 officers of the club will sell 3 tickets and ask each buyer to sell 3 more tickets the next day. Every time a ticket is sold, the buyer of the ticket will be asked to sell 3 more tickets the next day.

If the plan works, on what day will the number of tickets sold be 972?

a. Write an equation in one variable to model the situation. _____

b. If the plan works, on what day will the number sold be 972? _____

11. There are 175 deer in a state park. The population is increasing at the rate of 12% per year. At this rate, when will the population reach 300?

a. Write an equation in one variable to model the situation. _____

b. How long will it take for the population to reach 300?

_____

c. Suppose there are 200 deer in another state park and that the deer population is increasing at a rate of 10% per year. Which park's deer population will reach 300 sooner? Explain.

_____

_____

12. A city has 642,000 residents on July 1, 2011. The population is decreasing at the rate of 2% per year. At that rate, in what month and year will the population reach 500,000? Explain how you found your answer.

_____

_____

Performing Exponential Regression

Essential question: *How can you use exponential regression to model data?*

COMMON CORE

CC.9-12.A.CED.2*,
CC.9-12.F.BF.1a*,
CC.9-12.F.LE.1c*,
CC.9-12.F.LE.5*,
CC.9-12.S.ID.6a*,
CC.9-12.S.ID.6b*

1 EXAMPLE Fitting a Function to Data

The table shows the number of internet hosts from 2001 to 2007.

Number of Internet Hosts							
Years since 2001	0	1	2	3	4	5	6
Number (millions)	110	147	172	233	318	395	490

A Enter the data from the table on a graphing calculator, with years since 2001 in List 1 and number of internet hosts in List 2. Then set up a scatter plot of the data, as shown, and graph it. Copy the points below.

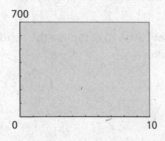

B The data fall along a curve, so an exponential function might fit the data. Use your calculator's statistical calculation features to find the exponential regression model. Record the results rounded to three significant digits.

Function *y* = _____ Correlation coefficient *r* = _____

REFLECT

1a. What does the correlation coefficient suggest about the model?

_____

1b. Use your rounded function model to predict the number of internet hosts in 2010 and in 2020. Round to three significant digits.

2010: _____ 2020: _____

1c. Are these predictions likely to be accurate? Explain.

_____

_____

Residuals You have used residuals to assess how well a linear model fits a data set. You can also use residuals for exponential and other models. Remember that if (x, y_d) is a data point and the corresponding point on the model is (x, y_m), then the corresponding *residual* is the difference $y_d - y_m$.

Recall that a model is a good fit for the data when the following are true:

- The numbers of positive and negative residuals are roughly equal.
- The residuals are randomly distributed about the *x*-axis, with no pattern.
- The absolute values of the residuals are small relative to the data.

2 EXAMPLE   Plotting and Analyzing Residuals

Continue working with the data from the first Example to plot and analyze the residuals.

A Enter the regression equation from your calculator as the rule for equation Y_1. (It can be found with the statistical variables on the variables menu.) Then view the table to find the function values y_m for the model. Record the results in the table at the right. Round to three significant digits.

B Use the results of Part A to complete the residuals column of the table.

Number of Internet Hosts (millions)			
x	**y_d**	**y_m**	**Residual** $y_d - y_m$
0	110	110	0
1	147	142	5
2	172		
3	233		
4	318		
5	395		
6	490		

C Set up a residual scatter plot of the data, as shown, and graph it. Adjust the viewing window as needed. Copy the points below.

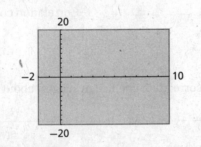

D At first glance, does the model fit the data well? Explain.

_____

_____

2a. Use the model $y = 110(1.29)^x$ from Part B of the first Example to find the function value for $x = 4$. Round to three significant digits. Compare the result with the value in the table above and with the actual value.

_____

_____

2b. Are the residuals in the calculator plotted on the residual plot exactly the same as the residuals in the table? Why or why not?

_____

_____

2c. One reason the model is a good fit for the data is that the absolute values of the residuals are small relative to the data. What does this claim mean? Give examples from the table to support this claim.

_____

_____

2d. Another reason the model fits the data well is that the residuals are randomly distributed about the *x*-axis with no pattern. Use a graphing calculator to find a *linear* regression model for these data. Describe the residual plot. What does it tell you about the model?

_____

_____

_____

2e. Describe what the parameters *a* and *b* in the model represent. Is the number of internet hosts growing or decaying? Explain your reasoning. What is the growth or decay rate?

_____

_____

_____

The first two columns of the table show the population of Arizona (in thousands) in census years from 1900 to 2000.

1. Find an exponential function model for the data. Round to four significant digits.

_____

2. Identify the parameters in the model, including the growth or decay rate, and explain what they represent.

_____

_____

_____

3. Use the more precise model stored on your calculator to complete the third column of the table with population values based on the model. Round to three significant digits.

4. Use the results of Exercise 3 to complete the residuals column of the table.

5. Use your model from Exercise 1 to predict the population of Arizona in 1975 and in 2030, to the nearest thousand. Discuss the accuracy of the results. Which result is likely to be more accurate? Why?

_____

_____

_____

Arizona Population y (in thousands) in Years x Since 1900			
x	y_d	y_m	$y_d - y_m$
0	123		
10	204		
20	334		
30	436		
40	499		
50	750		
60	1,302		
70	1,771		
80	2,718		
90	3,665		
100	5,131		

6. Make a residual plot. Does the model fit the data well? Explain.

_____

_____

_____

_____

_____

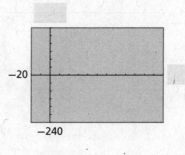

Comparing Linear and Exponential Functions

COMMON CORE

CC.9-12.F.LE.1*,
CC.9-12.F.LE.1a*,
CC.9-12.F.LE.1b*,
CC.9-12.F.LE.1c*,
CC.9-12.F.LE.3*

Essential question: *How can you recognize, describe, and compare linear and exponential functions?*

1 ENGAGE — Comparing Constant Change and Constant Percent Change

Suppose you are offered a job that pays $1000 the first month with a raise every month after that. You can choose a $100 raise or a 10% raise. Which option would you choose? What if the raise were 8%, 6%, or 4%?

A Work in groups and use multiple calculators to find the monthly salaries by following the steps described below. For the first three months, record the results in the table below, rounded to the nearest dollar.

- For the $100 raise, enter 1000, press ENTER, enter +100, press ENTER, and then press ENTER repeatedly.
- For the 10% raise, enter 1000, press ENTER, enter ×1.10, press ENTER, and then press ENTER repeatedly.
- For the other raises, replace 1.10 with these factors: 1.08, 1.06, and 1.04.

	Monthly Salary After Indicated Monthly Raise				
Month	$100	10%	8%	6%	4%
0	$1000	$1000	$1000	$1000	$1000
1	$1100	$1100	$1080	$1060	$1040
2					
3					

B Continue until you find the number of months it takes for each salary with a percent raise to exceed that month's salary with the $100 raise. Record the number of months in the table below.

	Number of Months Until Salary with Percent Raise Exceeds Salary with $100 Raise				
$100	10%	8%	6%	4%
---------	2			

© Houghton Mifflin Harcourt Publishing Company

1a. What is the change per unit interval in monthly salary for each option? Which of these is a constant rate of change in dollars per month? Explain your reasoning.

_____

_____

1b. Why are the differences from row to row in each percent column not constant? What *is* constant about the changes from row to row?

_____

_____

2 EXAMPLE   **Comparing Linear and Exponential Functions**

Compare these two salary plans:

* Job A: $1000 for the first month with a $100 raise every month thereafter
* Job B: $1000 for the first month with a 1% raise every month thereafter

Will Job B ever have a higher monthly salary than Job A?

A Write functions that represent the monthly salaries. Let t represent the number of elapsed months. Then tell whether the function is *linear* or *exponential*.

Job A: $S_A(t) = \boxed{} + \boxed{}\, t$ S_A is a/an _____ function.

Job B: $S_B(t) = \boxed{} \cdot \boxed{}^{\,t}$ S_B is a/an _____ function.

B Graph the functions on a calculator and sketch them below. Label the functions and include the scale.

C Will Job B ever have a higher monthly salary than Job A? If so, after how many months will this happen? Explain your reasoning.

_____

_____

2a. Revise $S_B(t)$ and use the Table feature on your graphing calculator to find the interval in which the monthly salary for Job B finally exceeds that for Job A if the growth rate is 0.1%. Use intervals of 1,000. Repeat for a growth rate of 0.01%, using intervals of 10,000.

_____

2b. Why does a quantity increasing exponentially eventually exceed a quantity increasing linearly?

_____

_____

_____

2c. The table shows values for the monthly salary functions in four-month intervals rather than one-month intervals.

t	$S_A(t)$	$S_B(t)$
0	1000	1000.00
4	1400	1040.60
8	1800	1082.86
12	2200	1126.83
16	2600	1172.58
20	3000	1220.19

• Does $S_A(t)$ grow by equal differences over each four-month interval? Explain your reasoning.

_____

_____

• Does $S_A(t)$ grow by the same difference over the first eight-month interval as it does over the first four-month interval? Explain your reasoning.

_____

_____

• Does $S_B(t)$ grow by equal factors over each four-month interval? Explain your reasoning.

_____

_____

• Does $S_B(t)$ grow by the same factor over the first eight-month interval as it does over the first four-month interval? Explain your reasoning.

_____

_____

Later you will prove that linear functions grow by the same difference over equal intervals and that exponential functions grow by equal factors over equal intervals.

PRACTICE

Tell whether each quantity is changing at a *constant rate* per unit of time, at a *constant percent rate* per unit of time, or *neither*.

1. Amy's salary is $40,000 in her first year on a job with a $2,000 raise every year thereafter.

   _____

2. Carla's salary is $50,000 in her first year on a job plus a 1% commission on all sales.

   _____

3. Enrollment at a school is 976 students initially and then it declines 2.5% each year thereafter.

   _____

4. Companies X and Y each have 50 employees. If Company X increases its workforce by 2 employees per month, and Company Y increases its workforce by 2% per month, will Company Y ever have more employees than Company X? If so, when?

   _____

5. Centerville and Easton each have 2500 residents. Centerville's population decreases by 80 people per year, and Easton's population decreases by 3% per year. Will Centerville ever have a greater population than Easton? If so, when? Explain your reasoning.

   _____

   _____

   _____

Complete each statement with the correct function from the table at the right.

x	f(x)	g(x)
0	50	100
1	54	104
2	58	108
3	63	112
4	68	116
5	73	120

6. _____ grows at a constant rate per unit interval.

7. _____ grows at a constant percent rate per unit interval.

8. An equation for the linear function is as follows:

   _____

9. An equation for the exponential function is as follows:

   _____

10. Complete the proof that linear functions grow by equal differences over equal intervals.

Given: $x_2 - x_1 = x_4 - x_3$,
            f is a linear function of the form $f(x) = mx + b$.

Prove: $f(x_2) - f(x_1) = f(x_4) - f(x_3)$

Proof:

$x_2 - x_1 = x_4 - x_3$	Given
$m(x_2 - x_1) = \boxed{}(x_4 - x_3)$	Mult. Prop. of Equality
$mx_2 - \boxed{} = mx_4 - \boxed{}$	Distributive Property
$mx_2 + b - mx_1 - b = mx_4 + \boxed{} - mx_3 - \boxed{}$	Add. and Subt. Prop. of Equality
$(mx_2 + b) - (mx_1 + b) = \underline{\hspace{3cm}}$	Distributive Property
$f(x_2) - f(x_1) = \underline{\hspace{3cm}}$	Definition of $f(x)$

11. Complete the proof that exponential functions grow by equal factors over equal intervals.

Given: $x_2 - x_1 = x_4 - x_3$
            g is an exponential function of the form $g(x) = ab^x$.

Prove: $\dfrac{f(x_2)}{f(x_1)} = \dfrac{f(x_4)}{f(x_3)}$

Proof:

$x_2 - x_1 = x_4 - x_3$	Given
$b^{x_2 - x_1} = b^{x_4 - x_3}$	If $x = y$, then $b^x = b^y$.
$\dfrac{b^{x_2}}{b^{x_1}} = \dfrac{b^{x_4}}{\boxed{}}$	Quotient of Powers Prop.
$\dfrac{ab^{x_2}}{ab^{x_1}} = \dfrac{ab^{x_4}}{\boxed{}}$	Mult. Prop. of Equality
$\dfrac{f(x_2)}{f(x_1)} = \underline{\hspace{2cm}}$	Definition of $f(x)$

5-8

FOCUS ON MODELING

Modeling with Exponential Functions

COMMON CORE

CC.9-12.A.REI.11*,
CC.9-12.F.BF.1a*,
CC.9-12.F.LE.1c*,
CC.9-12.F.LE.2*,
CC.9-12.F.LE.5*,
CC.9-12.S.ID.6a*

Essential question: *How can you model changes in population using an exponential function?*

The table shows the population y of Middleton, where x is the number of years since the end of 2000.

The director of Middleton's planning committee needs a model for the data to make predictions. What model should the director use? How can the director justify that the model is a good one?

Years since 2000, x	Population, y
0	5,005
1	6,010
2	7,203
3	8,700
4	10,521
5	12,420
6	14,982
7	18,010

1 **Choose and write a model for the function.**

A What are the differences between consecutive y-values?

_____

B What are the approximate ratios between consecutive y-values?

_____

C What type of model makes sense for these data? Explain your reasoning.

_____

_____

D Describe in words how the population has been changing during this time period.

_____

_____

E Write an equation that models this function.

_____

1a. Identify the parameters of the function and explain what they represent in this situation.

_____

_____

1b. Did the population grow at a constant rate per year or at a constant percent rate per year? Identify the growth rate.

_____

1c. If you assume that the function you wrote in Step 1 applies only to the time period in the table, what are the domain and range of the function?

_____

_____

1d. If you assume that the function you wrote in Step 1 applies beyond the time period in the table, what are the domain and range of the function?

_____

_____

1e. The population of Brookville was 3500 in the year 2000. Brookville had the same growth rate as Middleton from 2000 to 2007. Assume that both populations continue to grow at that rate indefinitely.

- Write an equation to model the growth of Brookville's population.

_____

- How does the population graph of Brookville compare with that of Middleton over time? Discuss the y-intercepts and end behavior.

_____

_____

_____

_____

_____

2 Use a calculator to fit a function to the data.

A Use a graphing calculator to make a scatter plot of the data in Step 1. Copy the points below. Label the axes with their minimum and maximum values.

B Find the exponential regression model and the correlation coefficient. Round values to four significant digits.

Function $y =$ _____

Correlation coefficient $r =$ _____

C Enter the regression equation from the Variables menu on your calculator as the rule for equation Y_1. Graph it with the scatter plot.

(Note: Save the data and function on your calculator for later use.)

D How can the director of Middleton's planning committee justify that this model fits the data well based on the results of Parts B and C?

_____

_____

REFLECT

2a. By the end of 2005, what is the actual population of Middleton? the population based on the model in Step 1? the population based on the regression model stored in your calculator? Round to four significant digits. What do your answers suggest about the accuracy of the models? Explain your reasoning.

_____

_____

_____

_____

2b. Use the stored regression model to predict the population at the end of 2015 and at the end of 2030. Round to four significant digits. Which prediction is likely to be more accurate? Explain your reasoning.

_____

_____

3 Solve an equation using a graph to make a decision.

Suppose Middleton's town council decides to build a new high school when its population exceeds 25,000. When will the population likely exceed 25,000?

A Write an equation in one variable to represent the time x when the population will reach 25,000.

_____

B Enter the function $y = 25{,}000$ as Y_2 on your graphing calculator. Graph Y_1 and Y_2 together. Sketch the graphs below. Label the axes with their minimum and maximum values.

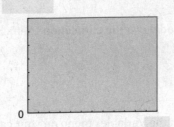

C Find the point of intersection (x, y). _____

D Make a prediction as to the number of years until the population reaches 25,000.

_____

REFLECT

3a. What does x represent in this situation?

_____

3b. During what year does the population reach 25,000? Explain your reasoning.

_____

_____

3c. Suppose the town will need a new high school already in place when the population reaches 25,000. How will the prediction above help the town make plans?

_____

_____

Step 1 shows that an exponential model is better than a linear model for the data given at the beginning of the lesson, based on comparing differences between consecutive y-values and comparing factors between consecutive y-values. Below are some other ways to evaluate the fit of a model.

1. Perform a linear regression on the given data. Round a, b, and r to four significant digits.

Function $y =$ _____   Correlation coefficient $r =$ _____

2. Based on the correlation coefficients, which model is a better fit? Explain your reasoning.

_____

_____

3. Use the exponential and linear regression models with rounded parameters. Predict the population for 2005 to four significant digits. Based on the results, which model is a better fit? Explain your reasoning.

_____

_____

_____

4. Complete the residual plots below. Label the axes with their minimum and maximum values. Use them to decide which model is a better fit. Explain your reasoning. (*Note:* The residuals list on a graphing calculator stores the residuals for the most recent regression model calculated.)

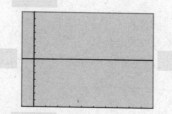

Residuals for linear model

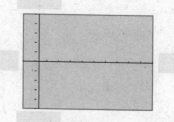

Residuals for exponential model

_____

_____

_____

_____

Name _____ **Class** _____ **Date** _____

MULTIPLE CHOICE

1. The table shows the number of people who have participated in an annual conference since it began in 2007.

Years since 2007, n	1	2	3
Participants, $p(n)$	12	36	108

Which function represents this situation?

A. $p(n) = \frac{1}{3}(4)^n$

B. $p(n) = 4(3)^n$

C. $p(n) = 4\left(\frac{1}{3}\right)^n$

D. $p(n) = 3(4)^n$

2. Amber buys a car for $17,500. The car depreciates (loses value) 8% each year. Which function shows y, the value of the car (in dollars) in t years?

F. $y = 17,500(0.08)^t$

G. $y = 17,500(0.8)^t$

H. $y = 17,500(0.92)^t$

J. $y = 17,500(1.08)^t$

3. Which statement is **NOT** true about the functions $f(x) = 1.2(1.05)^x$ and $g(x) = 1.2(1.07)^x$?

A. As x increases without bound, $f(x)$ and $g(x)$ both increase without bound.

B. As x increases to the right of 0, the value of $g(x)$ is greater than the value of $f(x)$ for every value of x.

C. The y-intercept of $g(x)$ is greater than the y-intercept of $f(x)$.

D. The y-intercept of $g(x)$ is equal to the y-intercept of $f(x)$.

4. Solve the equation $2\left(\frac{2}{3}\right)^x = \frac{8}{9}$.

F. $x = 1$

G. $x = 2$

H. $x = 3$

J. $x = 4$

5. An online music sharing club has 5,060 members. The membership is increasing at a rate of 2% per month. In approximately how many months will the membership reach 10,000?

A. 3.7 months

B. 34.4 months

C. 48.8 months

D. 98.8 months

6. The table shows attendance at games for a sports team from 2005 to 2009.

Years since 2005, x	Attendance, y
0	320,143
1	300,656
2	283,752
3	265,700
4	250,978

Kion performs an exponential regression to find a model for the data set. Then he makes a scatter plot of the residuals. What is the approximate residual for 2008?

F. −720

G. −357

H. 184

J. 334

7. Which of the following can be represented by an exponential function?

  A. Ben deposits $20 in a savings account. Then he deposits $2 each month for the next 6 months.

  B. Leslie deposits $20 in a savings account. Then she makes a deposit each month for the next 6 months, putting in $2 more with each deposit.

  C. Dan runs a mile in 9 minutes. Then he runs a mile each day for the next 4 days, reducing his time by 6 seconds each day.

  D. Rick runs a mile in 8 minutes. Then he runs a mile each day for the next 4 days, reducing his time by 1.5% each day.

8. Keenville and Westbrook each have 1500 residents. The population of Keenville increases by 3% every year. The population of Westbrook increases by 80 residents every year. How long will it take for the population of Keenville to exceed the population of Westbrook?

  F. 1.1 years

  G. 1.8 years

  H. 36.7 years

  J. 45 years

9. Mr. Turner bought stock for $15,000. If the value of the stock decreases 4% each year, when will it be worth 80% of the original purchase price?

  A. in 5.5 years

  B. in 7.5 years

  C. in 20 years

  D. in 39 years

FREE RESPONSE

10. The table shows the number of phone calls made per day (in millions) in years since 1940.

Years, x	0	10	20	30	40
calls, y	98.8	171	288	494	853

  a. Fit a function to the data using four significant digits. Tell whether it is exponential or linear.

  _____

  b. Graph the function below. Label the axes.

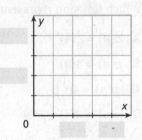

  c. Identify what the y-intercept represents.

  _____

  d. Use a graphing calculator to make a residual plot. Does the model fit the data well? Explain.

  _____

  _____

  _____

  _____

  e. Predict the calls per day in 1975 and in 1995. Which is more likely to be accurate? Explain.

  _____

  _____

  _____

  _____

Piecewise and Absolute Value Functions

Unit Focus

In this unit you will learn that a piecewise function has two or more parts in its rule, creating two or more pieces in its graph. Two special cases of piecewise functions are step functions, whose graphs look like steps, and absolute value functions, whose graphs are V-shaped. You will learn about transforming the graphs of absolute value functions, solving absolute value equations, and modeling with absolute value functions.

Unit at a Glance

COMMON CORE

Lesson		Standards for Mathematical Content
6-1	Piecewise Functions	CC.9-12.A.CED.2*, CC.9-12.F.IF.2, CC.9-12.F.IF.4*, CC.9-12.F.IF.5*, CC.9-12.F.IF.7b*, CC.9-12.BF.1*
6-2	Translating the Graph of $f(x) = \|x\|$	CC.9-12.A.CED.2*, CC.9-12.F.IF.2, CC.9-12.F.IF.7*, CC.9-12.F.IF.7b*, CC.9-12.F.BF.1*, CC.9-12.F.BF.3
6-3	Stretching, Shrinking, and Reflecting the Graph of $f(x) = \|x\|$	CC.9-12.A.CED.2*, CC.9-12.F.IF.2, CC.9-12.F.IF.7*, CC.9-12.F.IF.7b*, CC.9-12.F.BF.1*, CC.9-12.F.BF.3
6-4	Combining Transformations of the Graph of $f(x) = \|x\|$	CC.9-12.A.CED.2*, CC.9-12.F.IF.2, CC.9-12.F.IF.7*, CC.9-12.F.IF.7b*, CC.9-12.F.BF.1*, CC.9-12.F.BF.3
6-5	Solving Absolute Value Equations	CC.9-12.A.CED.1*, CC.9-12.A.CED.2*, CC.9-12.A.REI.11*
6-6	Modeling with Absolute Value Functions	CC.9-12.A.CED.2*, CC.9-12.F.IF.2, CC.9-12.F.IF.4*, CC.9-12.F.IF.5*, CC.9-12.F.IF.7b*, CC.9-12.F.BF.1*
	Test Prep	

Unpacking the Common Core State Standards

Use the table to help you understand the Standards for Mathematical Content that are taught in this unit. Refer to the lessons listed after each standard for exploration and practice.

COMMON CORE Standards for Mathematical Content	What It Means For You
CC.9-12.A.CED.1 Create equations and inequalities **in one variable and use them to solve problems.*** Lesson 6-5	You will use absolute value functions to write absolute value equations in one variable, and you will solve the equations by graphing or by using algebra.
CC.9-12.A.CED.2 Create equations in two or more **variables to represent relationships between quantities; graph equations on coordinate axes with labels and scales.*** Lessons 6-1, 6-2, 6-3, 6-4, 6-5, 6-6	You will graph piecewise and absolute value functions from their equations, and you will write equations for them when given their graphs.
CC.9-12.A.REI.11 Explain why the x**-coordinates of the points where the graphs of the equations** $y = f(x)$ **and** $y = g(x)$ **intersect are the solutions of the equation** $f(x) = g(x)$; find the solutions approximately, e.g., using technology to graph the functions, make tables of values, or find successive approximations. **Include cases where** $f(x)$ **and/or** $g(x)$ **are linear,** polynomial, rational, **absolute value, exponential** and logarithmic **functions.*** Lessons 6-5	One way to solve an equation in one variable is to treat each side of the equation as a function, graph the functions, and find where the graphs intersect. You will use this method to solve absolute value equations.
CC.9-12.F.IF.2 Use function notation, evaluate functions for inputs in their domains, and interpret statements that use function notation in terms of a context. Lessons 6-1, 6-2, 6-3, 6-4, 6-6 (Also 6-5)	You will write piecewise and absolute value functions using function notation, and you will interpret the notation when using those functions to solve real-world problems.
CC.9-12.F.IF.4 For a function that models a relationship between two quantities, interpret key features of graphs and tables **in terms of the quantities, and sketch graphs showing key features given a verbal description of the relationship.*** Lessons 6-1, 6-6 (Also 6-2, 6-3, 6-4, 6-5)	You will learn that the graph of an absolute value function has the shape of a V or an inverted V. The symmetry of the graph is particularly useful as a model for the path of a rolling ball that strikes a flat surface and bounces off.

UNIT 6

COMMON CORE Standards for Mathematical Content	What It Means For You
CC.9-12.F.IF.5 Relate the domain of a function to its graph and, where applicable, to the quantitative relationship it describes.* Lessons 6-1, 6-6 (Also 6-2, 6-3, 6-4)	When writing equations for piecewise functions whose graphs are given, you must pay close attention to the domain for each piece of the graph because the domain becomes part of the function's rule. Also, although absolute value functions are defined for all real numbers, the domain may be restricted when using the functions to model real-world situations.
CC.9-12.F.IF.7 Graph functions expressed symbolically and show key features of the graph, by hand in simple cases and using technology for more complicated cases.* **CC.9-12.F.IF.7b Graph** square root, cube root, and **piecewise-defined functions, including step functions and absolute value functions.*** Lessons 6-1, 6-2, 6-3, 6-4, 6-6 (Also 6-5)	You will graph piecewise functions, including two important special cases: step functions and absolute value functions. For absolute value functions, you will learn to identify the vertex, a key feature of their graphs.
CC.9-12.F.BF.1 Write a function that describes a relationship between two quantities.* **CC.9-12.F.BF.1a Determine an explicit expression,** a recursive process, or steps for calculation **from a context.*** Lessons 6-1, 6-2, 6-3, 6-4, 6-6	When you write a rule for an absolute value function in this unit, you will be finding an expression of the form $a\|x - h\| + k$ where a, h, and k are constants.
CC.9-12.F.BF.3 Identify the effect on the graph of replacing $f(x)$ **by** $f(x) + k$**,** $kf(x)$**,** $f(kx)$**, and** $f(x + k)$ **for specific values of** k **(both positive and negative); find the value of** k **given the graphs.** Experiment with cases and illustrate an explanation of the effects on the graphs using technology. Lessons 6-2, 6-3, 6-4	By comparing equations and graphs of absolute value functions, you will learn how changes in an equation cause a graph to be translated, vertically stretched or shrunk, reflected in the x-axis, or some combination of these transformations. Learning these concepts will enable you to graph an absolute value function without the need to create a table of values. In particular, you will be able to immediately identify the vertex and tell whether the graph's shape is a V or an inverted V.

UNIT 6

Piecewise Functions

Essential question: *How are piecewise functions and step functions different from other functions?*

COMMON
CORE

CC.9-12.A.CED.2*,
CC.9-12.F.IF.2,
CC.9-12.F.IF.4*,
CC.9-12.F.IF.5*,
CC.9-12.F.IF.7b*,
CC.9-12.F.BF.1*

A **piecewise function** has different rules for different parts of its domain. The **greatest integer function** is a piecewise function whose rule is denoted by $[\![x]\!]$, which represents the greatest integer less than or equal to x. To evaluate a piecewise function for a given value of x, substitute the value of x into the rule for the part of the domain that includes x.

1 EXAMPLE Evaluating Piecewise Functions

A Find $f(-3), f(-0.2), f(0)$, and $f(2)$ for $f(x) = \begin{cases} -x & \text{if } x < 0 \\ x + 1 & \text{if } x \geq 0 \end{cases}$.

$-3 < 0$, so use the rule $f(x) = -x$: $\qquad$ $f(-3) = -(-3) = $ _____

$-0.2 < 0$, so use the rule _____: $\qquad$ $f(-0.2) = -(-0.2) = $ _____

$0 \geq 0$, so use the rule $f(x) = x + 1$: $\qquad$ $f(0) = 0 + 1 = $ _____

$2 \geq 0$, so use the rule _____: $\qquad$ $f(2) = $ _____ $= $ _____

B Find $f(-3), f(-2.9), f(0.7)$, and $f(1.06)$ for $f(x) = [\![x]\!]$.

The greatest integer function $f(x) = [\![x]\!]$ can also be written as shown below. Complete the rules for the function before evaluating it.

$$f(x) = \begin{cases} \vdots & \\ -3 & \text{if } -3 \leq x < -2 \\ & \text{if } -2 \leq x < -1 \\ -1 & \text{if } \leq x < \\ & \text{if } 0 \leq x < 1 \\ 1 & \text{if } \leq x < \\ 2 & \text{if } \leq x < \\ \vdots & \end{cases}$$

For any number x that is less than -2 and greater than or equal to -3, the greatest of the integers less than or equal to x is -3.

-3 is in the interval $-3 \leq x < -2$, so $f(-3) = -3$.

-2.9 is in the interval $-3 \leq x < -2$, so $f(-2.9) = $ _____.

0.7 is in the interval _____, so $f(0.7) = $ _____.

1.06 is in the interval _____, so $f(1.06) = $ _____.

1a. Why should the parts of the domain of a piecewise function $f(x)$ have no common x-values?

_____

_____

1b. For positive numbers, how is applying the greatest integer function different from the method of rounding to the nearest whole number?

_____

_____

_____

2 EXAMPLE Graphing Piecewise Functions

Graph each function.

A $f(x) = \begin{cases} -x & \text{if } x < 0 \\ x+1 & \text{if } x \geq 0 \end{cases}$

Complete the table. Use the values to help you complete the graph. Extend the pattern to cover the entire domain on the grid.

x	−3	−2	−1	−0.9	−0.1
f(x)	3	2		0.9	

x	0	0.1	0.9	1	2
f(x)	1	1.1			3

The transition from one rule, $-x$, to the other, $x + 1$, occurs at $x = 0$. Show an open dot at $(0, 0)$ because the point is not part of the graph. Show a closed dot at $(0, 1)$ because the point is part of the graph.

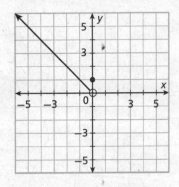

B $f(x) = [\![x]\!]$

Complete the table. Use the values to help you complete the graph. Extend the pattern to cover the entire domain on the grid.

x	−4	−3.9	−3.1	−3	−2.9
f(x)	−4	−4		−3	

x	−2.1	−2	−1.5	−1	0
f(x)		−2			0

x	1	1.5	2	3	4
f(x)					4

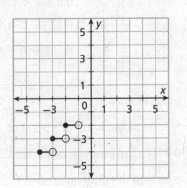

© Houghton Mifflin Harcourt Publishing Company

2a. Why does the first graph use rays and not lines?

_____

_____

2b. The greatest integer function is an example of a **step function**, a piecewise function that is constant for each rule. Use the graph of the greatest integer function to explain why such a function is called a step function.

_____

2c. Does the greatest integer function have a maximum or minimum value? Explain.

_____

3 **EXAMPLE** Writing and Graphing a Piecewise Function

On his way to class from his dorm room, a college student walks at a speed of 0.05 mile per minute for 3 minutes, stops to talk to a friend for 1 minute, and then to avoid being late for class, runs at a speed of 0.10 mile per minute for 2 minutes. Write a piecewise function for the student's distance from his dorm room during this time. Then graph the function.

A Express the student's distance traveled d (in miles) as a function of time t (in minutes). Write an equation for the function $d(t)$.

$$d(t) = \begin{cases} \boxed{}\, t & \text{if } 0 \le t \le 3 \quad \text{←He travels at 0.05 mile per minute for 3 minutes.} \\ 0.15 & \text{if } 3 < t \le \boxed{} \quad \text{←Distance traveled is constant for 1 minute.} \\ 0.15 + 0.10\,(t-4) & \text{if } 4 < t \le \boxed{} \quad \text{←Add the distance traveled at 0.10 mile per minute to the distance already traveled.} \end{cases}$$

B Complete the table.

t	0	1	2	3
$d(t)$				

t	4	5	6
$d(t)$			

C Complete the graph.

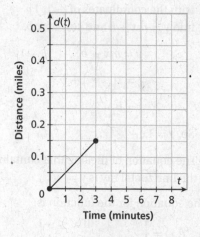

© Houghton Mifflin Harcourt Publishing Company

3a. Why is the second rule for the function $d(t) = 0.15$ instead of $d(t) = 0$?

_____

3b. Why is the third rule for the function $d(t) = 0.15 + 0.10(t - 4)$?

_____

_____

4 EXAMPLE   Writing a Function When Given a Graph

Write the equation for each function whose graph is shown.

A

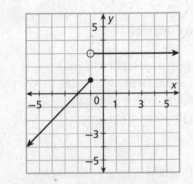

B

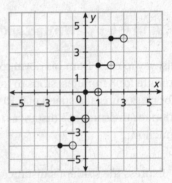

Find the equation for each ray:

- Find the slope m of the line that contains the ray on the left. Use $(-4, -2)$ and $(-1, 1)$.

$$m = \frac{1 - (\quad)}{-1 - (\quad)} = \frac{3}{3} = 1$$

Substitute this value of m along with the coordinates of $(-1, 1)$ into $y = mx + b$ and solve for b.

$$y = mx + b$$

$$\boxed{} = 1(\boxed{}) + b$$

$$\boxed{} = b$$

So, $y = 1x + \boxed{}$.

- The equation of the line that contains the horizontal ray is $y = \boxed{}$.

The equation for the function is:

$$f(x) = \begin{cases} \boxed{} & \text{if } x \leq -1 \\ \boxed{} & \text{if } x > -1 \end{cases}$$

Write a rule for each horizontal line segment.

$$f(x) = \begin{cases} -4 & \text{if } -2 \leq x < -1 \\ \boxed{} & \text{if } -1 \leq x < 0 \\ 0 & \text{if } 0 \leq x < 1 \\ \boxed{} & \text{if } 1 \leq x < 2 \\ \boxed{} & \text{if } 2 \leq x < 3 \end{cases}$$

Although the graph shows the function's domain to be $-2 \leq x < 3$, assume that the domain consists of all real numbers and that the graph continues its stair-step pattern for $x < -2$ and $x \geq 3$.

Notice that each function value is _____ times the corresponding value of the greatest integer function.

The equation for the function is:

$$f(x) = \boxed{} \; [\![x]\!]$$

4a. When writing a piecewise function from a graph, how do you determine the domain of each rule?

_____

_____

4b. How can you use y-intercepts to check that your answer in part A is reasonable?

_____

_____

PRACTICE

Graph each function.

1. $f(x) = \begin{cases} -x + 1 & \text{if } x < 0 \\ x & \text{if } x \geq 0 \end{cases}$ **2.** $f(x) = \begin{cases} -1 & \text{if } x < 1 \\ 2x - 2 & \text{if } x \geq 1 \end{cases}$ **3.** $f(x) = [\![x]\!] + 1$

Write the equation for each function whose graph is shown.

4.
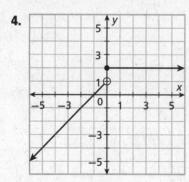

5.
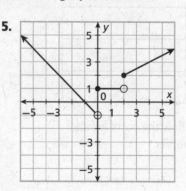

6.
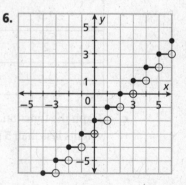

_____   _____   _____

7. A garage charges the following rates for parking (with an 8 hour limit):

   $4 per hour for the first 2 hours

   $2 per hour for the next 4 hours

   No additional charge for the next 2 hours

a. Write a piecewise function that gives the parking cost C (in dollars) in terms of the time t (in hours) that a car is parked in the garage.

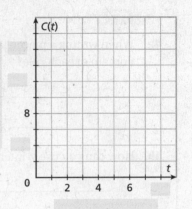

_____

b. Graph the function. Include labels to show what the axes represent and to show the scales on the axes.

8. The cost to send a package between two cities is $8.00 for any weight less than 1 pound. The cost increases by $4.00 when the weight reaches 1 pound and again each time the weight reaches a whole number of pounds after that.

a. For a package having weight w (in pounds), write a function in terms of $[\![w]\!]$ to represent the shipping cost C (in dollars).

_____

b. Complete the table.

Weight (pounds) w	Cost (dollars) C(w)
0.5	
1	
1.5	
2	
2.5	

c. Graph the function. Show the costs for all weights less than 5 pounds.

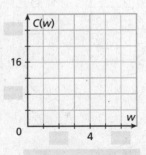

Translating the Graph of $f(x) = |x|$

COMMON
CORE

CC.9-12.A.CED.2*,
CC.9-12.F.IF.2,
CC.9-12.F.IF.7*,
CC.9-12.F.IF.7b*,
CC.9-12.F.BF.1*,
CC.9-12.F.BF.3

Essential question: *What are the effects of the constants h and k on the graph of $y = |x - h| + k$?*

1 ENGAGE   **Understanding the Parent Absolute Value Function**

The most basic **absolute value function** is a piecewise function given by the following rule.

$$f(x) = |x| = \begin{cases} x & \text{if } x \geq 0 \\ -x & \text{if } x < 0 \end{cases}$$

This function is sometimes called the *parent* absolute value function.

To graph the function, you can make a table of values like the one shown below, plot the ordered pairs, and draw the graph.

x	$f(x) = |x|$
−3	3
−2	2
−1	1
0	0
1	1
2	2
3	3

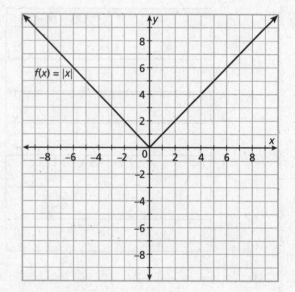

As shown at the right, the function's V-shaped graph consists of two rays with a common endpoint at $(0, 0)$. This point is called the *vertex* of the graph.

REFLECT

1a. What is the domain of $f(x) = |x|$? What is the range?

_____

1b. If you fold the graph of $f(x) = |x|$ over the y-axis, the two halves of the graph match up perfectly. The graph is said to be *symmetric* about the y-axis. Explain why it makes sense that the graph of $f(x) = |x|$ is symmetric about the y-axis.

_____

1c. For what values of x is the function $f(x) = |x|$ increasing? decreasing?

_____

Graph each absolute value function. (The graph of the parent function $f(x) = |x|$ is shown in gray.)

A $g(x) = |x| + 2$

x	g(x) = |x| + 2
−3	
−2	
−1	
0	
1	
2	
3	

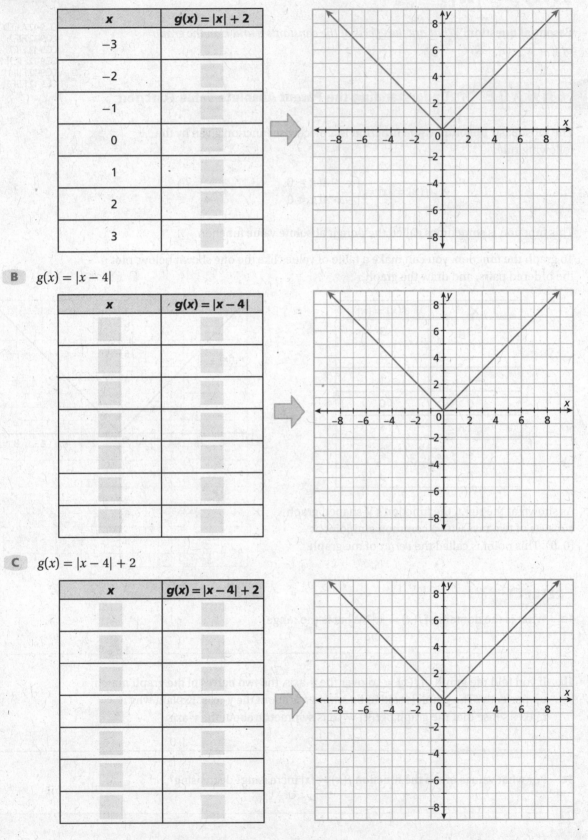

B $g(x) = |x - 4|$

x	g(x) = |x − 4|

C $g(x) = |x - 4| + 2$

x	g(x) = |x − 4| + 2

2a. How is the graph of $g(x) = |x| + 2$ related to the graph of the parent function $f(x) = |x|$?

_____

2b. How do you think the graph of $g(x) = |x| - 2$ would be related to the graph of the parent function $f(x) = |x|$?

_____

2c. How is the graph of $g(x) = |x - 4|$ related to the graph of the parent function $f(x) = |x|$?

_____

2d. How do you think the graph of $g(x) = |x + 4|$ would be related to the graph of the parent function $f(x) = |x|$?

_____

2e. How is the graph of $g(x) = |x - 4| + 2$ related to the graph of the parent function $f(x) = |x|$?

_____

_____

2f. Predict how the graph of $g(x) = |x + 3| - 5$ is related to the graph of the parent function $f(x) = |x|$. Then check your prediction by making a table of values and graphing the function. (The graph of $f(x) = |x|$ is shown in gray.)

_____

_____

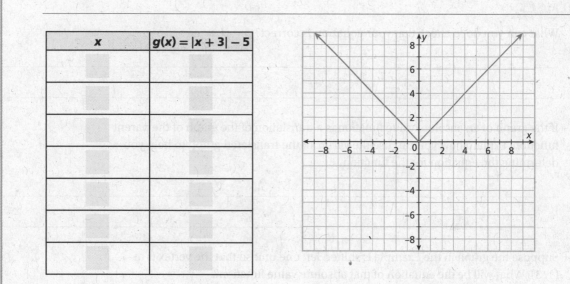

2g. In general, how is the graph of $g(x) = |x - h| + k$ related to the graph of $f(x) = |x|$?

_____

_____

Write the equation for the absolute value function whose graph is shown.

A   Compare the given graph to the graph of the parent
function $f(x) = |x|$.

Complete the table to describe how the parent function
must be translated to get the graph shown here.

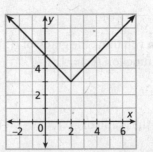

Type of Translation	Number of Units	Direction
Horizontal Translation		
Vertical Translation		

B   Determine the values of h and k for the function $g(x) = |x - h| + k$.

- h is the number of units that the parent function is translated horizontally.
  For a translation to the right, h is positive; for a translation to the left,
  h is negative.

- k is the number of units that the parent function is translated vertically.
  For a translation up, k is positive; for a translation down, k is negative.

So, $h =$ _____ and $k =$ _____. The function is _____.

REFLECT

3a. What can you do to check that your equation is correct?

_____

_____

3b. If the graph of an absolute value function is a translation of the graph of the parent
function, explain how you can use the vertex of the translated graph to help you
determine the equation for the function.

_____

_____

3c. Suppose the graph in the Example is shifted left one unit so that the vertex is at
$(1, 3)$. What will be the equation of that absolute value function?

_____

Graph each absolute value function.

1. $g(x) = |x| + 5$

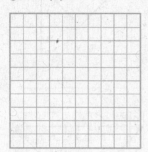

2. $g(x) = |x| - 6$

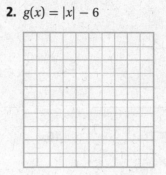

3. $g(x) = |x| - 4$

4. $g(x) = |x| + 3$

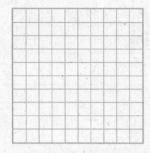

5. $g(x) = |x + 3|$

6. $g(x) = |x - 2|$

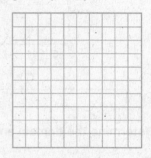

7. $g(x) = |x + 1|$

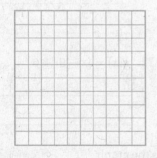

8. $g(x) = |x - 5|$

9. $g(x) = |x + 1| + 1$

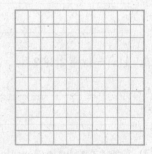

10. $g(x) = |x - 4| + 2$

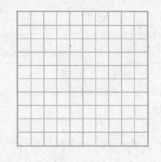

11. $g(x) = |x - 3| - 5$

12. $g(x) = |x + 7| - 1$

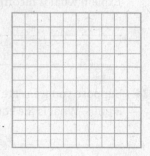

Write the equation of each absolute value function whose graph is shown.

13.

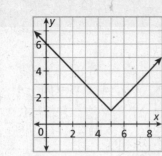

_____

14.

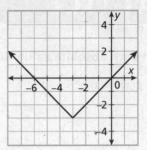

_____

15.

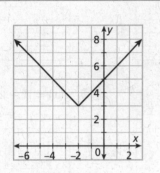

_____

16.

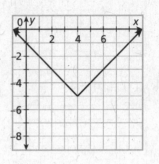

_____

Determine the domain and range of each function.

17. $g(x) = |x| - 7$

_____

_____

18. $g(x) = |x - 2|$

_____

_____

19. $g(x) = |x + 3| - 1$

_____

_____

20. $g(x) = |x + 2| + 2$

_____

_____

21. $g(x) = |x| + 1$

_____

_____

22. $g(x) = |x - 9| + 6$

_____

_____

23. Error Analysis A student says that the graph of $g(x) = |x + 3| - 1$ is the graph of the parent function, $f(x) = |x|$, translated 3 units to the right and 1 unit down. Explain what is incorrect about this statement.

_____

_____

24. Suppose you translate the graph of $g(x) = |x - 2| + 1$ to the left 4 units and down 3 units. What is the equation of the resulting function $h(x)$? Explain.

_____

_____

© Houghton Mifflin Harcourt Publishing Company

Stretching, Shrinking, and Reflecting the Graph of $f(x) = |x|$

COMMON CORE

CC.9-12.A.CED.2*,
CC.9-12.F.IF.2,
CC.9-12.F.IF.7*,
CC.9-12.F.IF.7b*,
CC.9-12.F.BF.1*,
CC.9-12.F.BF.3

Essential question: *What is the effect of the constant a on the graph of* $g(x) = a|x|$?

To understand the effect of the constant a on the graph of $g(x) = a|x|$, you will graph the function using various values of a.

1 EXAMPLE Graphing $g(x) = a|x|$ when $|a| > 1$

Graph each absolute value function using the same coordinate plane. (The graph of the parent function $f(x) = |x|$ is shown in gray.)

A $g(x) = 2|x|$

x	−3	−2	−1	0	1	2	3
g(x) = 2|x|							

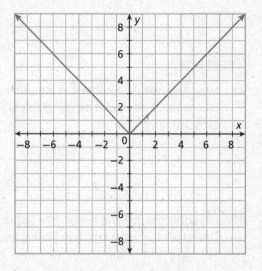

B $g(x) = -2|x|$

x	−3	−2	−1	0	1	2	3
g(x) = −2|x|							

REFLECT

1a. The graph of the parent function $f(x) = |x|$ includes the point $(-1, 1)$ because $f(-1) = |-1| = 1$. The corresponding point on the graph of $g(x) = 2|x|$ is $(-1, 2)$ because $g(-1) = 2|-1| = 2$. In general, how does the y-coordinate of a point on the graph of $g(x) = 2|x|$ compare with the y-coordinate of a point on the graph of $f(x) = |x|$ when the points have the same x-coordinate?

_____

_____

1b. Describe how the graph of $g(x) = 2|x|$ compares with the graph of $f(x) = |x|$. Use either the word *stretch* or *shrink*, and include the direction of the movement.

_____

_____

1c. What other transformation occurs when the value of a in $g(x) = a|x|$ is negative?

_____

© Houghton Mifflin Harcourt Publishing Company

Graph each absolute value function using the same coordinate plane. (The graph of the parent function $f(x) = |x|$ is shown in gray.)

A $g(x) = \frac{1}{4}|x|$

x	−8	−4	0	4	8
$g(x) = \frac{1}{4}|x|$					

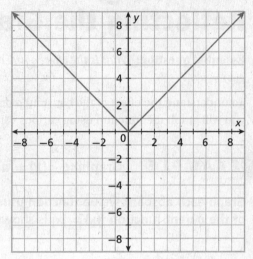

B $g(x) = -\frac{1}{4}|x|$

x	−8	−4	0	4	8
$g(x) = -\frac{1}{4}|x|$					

REFLECT

2a. How does the y-coordinate of a point on the graph of $g(x) = \frac{1}{4}|x|$ compare with the y-coordinate of a point on the graph of $f(x) = |x|$ when the points have the same x-coordinate?

_____

_____

2b. Describe how the graph of $g(x) = \frac{1}{4}|x|$ compares with the graph of $f(x) = |x|$. Use either the word *stretch* or *shrink*, and include the direction of the movement.

_____

2c. What other transformation occurs when the value of a in $g(x) = a|x|$ is negative?

_____

2d. Compare the domain and range of $g(x) = a|x|$ when $a > 0$ and when $a < 0$.

_____

_____

_____

2e. Summarize your observations about the graph of $g(x) = a|x|$.

Value of a	Vertical stretch or shrink?	Reflection across x-axis?
$a > 1$	Vertical stretch	No
$0 < a < 1$		
$-1 < a < 0$		
$a < -1$		

An absolute value function whose graph's vertex is at $(0, 0)$ has the form $g(x) = a|x|$. To write the equation for the function, you can use the coordinates of a point (x_1, y_1) on the graph to write $g(x_1) = a|x_1| = y_1$ and then solve for a.

3 EXAMPLE   Writing the Equation for an Absolute Value Function

Write the equation for the absolute value function whose graph is shown.

Use the point $(-4, -3)$ to find a.

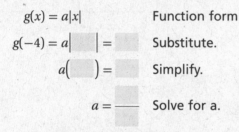

$g(x) = a\|x\|$	Function form
$g(-4) = a\left\|\right\| = $	Substitute.
$a\left(\right) = $	Simplify.
$a = \dfrac{}{}$	Solve for a.

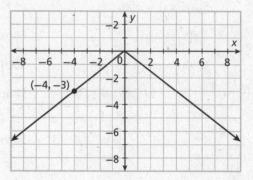

The equation for the function is _____.

REFLECT

3a. The fact that the given graph lies on or below the x-axis tells you what about the value of a? Does this agree with the value of a that you found? Explain.

_____

3b. The angle between the two rays that make up the graph of the parent function $f(x) = |x|$ is a right angle. What happens to this angle when the graph is vertically stretched? When the graph is vertically shrunk?

_____

3c. Based on your answer to Question 3b, does the given graph represent a vertical stretch or a vertical shrink of the graph of the parent function? Does this fact agree with the value of a that you found? Explain.

_____

Modeling with Absolute Value Functions When a rolling ball, such as a billiard ball, strikes a flat surface, such as an edge of the billiard table, the ball bounces off the surface at the same angle at which the ball hit the surface. (The angles are measured off a line perpendicular to the surface, as shown in the diagram.) A ray of light striking a mirror behaves in the same way.

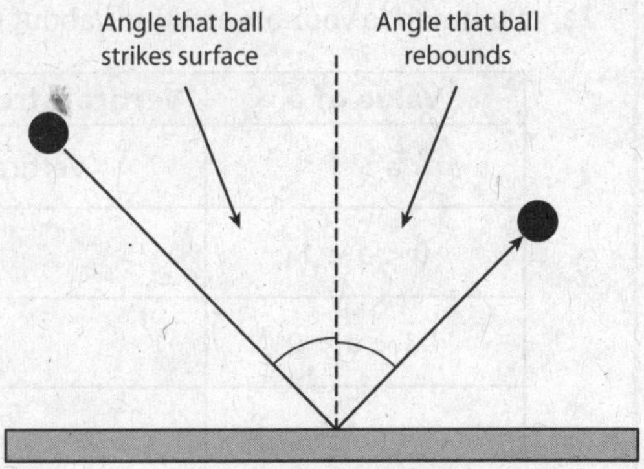

The symmetry of the graph of an absolute value function makes the graph a perfect model for the path of a rolling ball or a ray of light.

Angle that ball strikes surface

Angle that ball rebounds

4 EXAMPLE Modeling a Real-World Situation

Inez is playing miniature golf. Her ball is at point $A(-4, 6)$. She wants to putt the ball into the hole at $C(2, 3)$ with a bank shot, as shown. If the ball hits the edge at $B(0, 0)$, find the equation for the absolute value function whose graph models the path of the ball. How does the equation tell you whether the ball will go into the hole (if the ball is hit with sufficient force)?

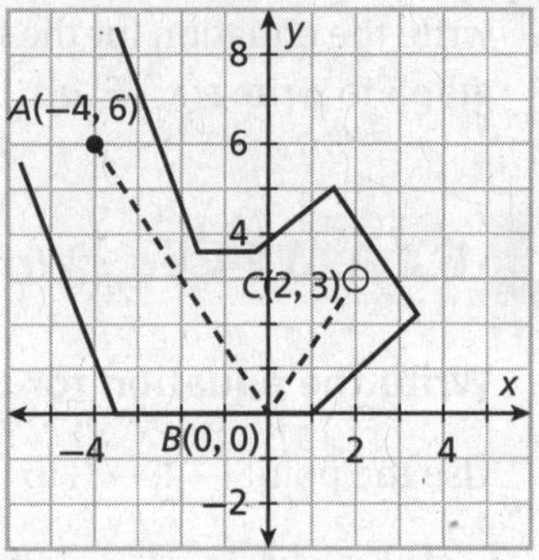

A Use the point $A(-4, 6)$ to write the equation for a function of the form $g(x) = a|x|$.

$g(x) = a|x|$ Function form

$g(-4) = a\ \boxed{} = \boxed{}$ Substitute.

$a\left(\boxed{}\right) = \boxed{}$ Simplify.

$a = \dfrac{\boxed{}}{\boxed{}}$ Solve for a.

So, the equation for the function is _____.

B Check to see whether the point $C(2, 3)$ lies on the path of the ball.

$g(2) = \frac{3}{2}|2| = \boxed{}$, so the ball _____ go into the hole.

REFLECT

4a. If you reflect point C in the x-axis, what do you notice about points A, B, and the reflection of C? Explain why this is so.

_____

_____

_____

_____

© Houghton Mifflin Harcourt Publishing Company

PRACTICE

Graph each absolute value function.

1. $g(x) = 3|x|$

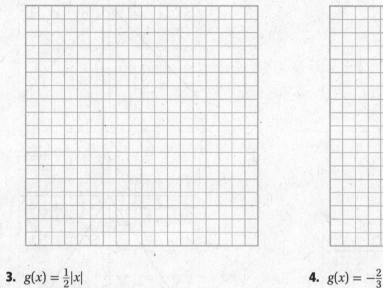

2. $g(x) = -2.5|x|$

3. $g(x) = \frac{1}{2}|x|$

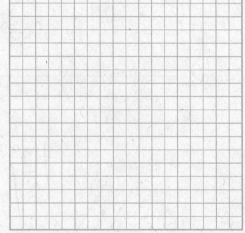

4. $g(x) = -\frac{2}{3}|x|$

5. a. Complete the table and graph all the functions on the same coordinate plane.

x	−6	−3	0	3	6
$g(x) = \frac{1}{3}|x|$					
$g(x) = \left|\frac{1}{3}x\right|$					
$g(x) = -\frac{1}{3}|x|$					
$g(x) = \left|-\frac{1}{3}x\right|$					

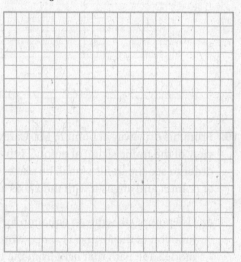

b. How do the graphs of $f(x) = a|x|$ and $g(x) = |ax|$ compare?

Write the equation of each absolute value function whose graph is shown.

6.

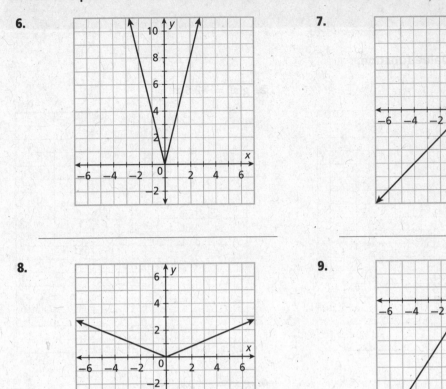

_____

7.

_____

8.

_____

9.

_____

10. From his driveway at point *P*, Mr. Carey's direct view of the traffic signal at point *Q* is blocked. In order to see the traffic signal, he places a mirror at point *R* and aligns it with the *x*-axis as shown.

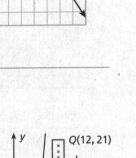
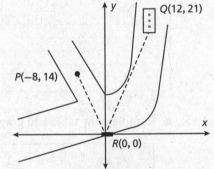

a. Use point *Q* to write an equation for a function of the form $g(x) = a|x|$ whose graph models the path that light from the traffic signal takes when it strikes the mirror at *R*.

_____

b. Explain why the mirror is positioned correctly.

_____

_____

Combining Transformations of the Graph of $f(x) = |x|$

COMMON
CORE

CC.9-12.A.CED.2*,
CC.9-12.F.IF.2,
CC.9-12.F.IF.7*,
CC.9-12.F.IF.7b*,
CC.9-12.F.BF.1*,
CC.9-12.F.BF.3

Essential question: *What are the effects of the constants a, h, and k on the graph of* $g(x) = a|x - h| + k$?

1 **EXAMPLE** Graphing $g(x) = a|x - h|$ and $g(x) = a|x| + k$

Graph each absolute value function. (The graph of the parent function $f(x) = |x|$ is shown in gray.)

A $g(x) = \frac{1}{2}|x - 3|$

x	−3	−1	1	3	5	7	9
y							

B $g(x) = 3|x| - 7$

x	−3	−2	−1	0	1	2	3
y							

REFLECT

1a. How is the graph of $g(x) = \frac{1}{2}|x - 3|$ related to the graph of $f(x) = |x|$?

_____

_____

1b. How is the graph of $g(x) = 3|x| - 7$ related to the graph of $f(x) = |x|$?

_____

_____

1c. How is the graph of $g(x) = \frac{1}{2}|x - 3|$ affected if you replace $\frac{1}{2}$ with $-\frac{1}{2}$ and 3 with −3?

_____

_____

Graph $g(x) = -2|x + 1| + 3$. (The graph of the parent function $f(x) = |x|$ is shown in gray.)

x	−4	−3	−2	−1	0	1	2
y							

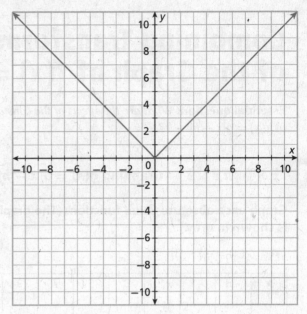

REFLECT

2a. How is the graph of $g(x) = -2|x + 1| + 3$ related to the graph of $f(x) = |x|$?

_____

_____

2b. How is the graph of $g(x) = -2|x + 1| + 3$ affected if you replace 3 with −3?

_____

2c. Complete the table to summarize how you can obtain the graph of $g(x) = a|x - h| + k$ from the graph of the parent function $f(x) = |x|$.

Obtaining the graph of $g(x) = a\|x - h\| + k$ from the graph of $f(x) = \|x\|$
Vertically stretch or shrink the graph by a factor of |a|. Also reflect the graph across the x-axis if the value of a is negative.
• If |a| >1, _____ the graph of $f(x) = \|x\|$ vertically by a factor of |a|.
• If |a| <1, _____ the graph of $f(x) = \|x\|$ vertically by a factor of |a|.
• If a < _____, reflect the graph across the x-axis.
Translate the graph h units horizontally.
• If h > 0, translate _____.
• If h < 0, translate _____.
Translate the graph k units vertically.
• If k is positive, translate _____.
• If k is negative, translate _____.

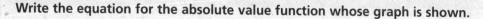

3 EXAMPLE Writing the Equation for an Absolute Value Function

Write the equation for the absolute value function whose graph is shown.

To write the equation in the form $g(x) = a|x - h| + k$, you
need to find the values of a, h, and k.

A Use the coordinates of the vertex to determine the
values of h and k.

The vertex is at _____ , so $h =$ _____ and

$k =$ _____ . Substituting these values into the

general equation for $g(x)$ gives $g(x) = a|x - \boxed{}| + \boxed{}$.

B Use the coordinates of another point on the graph to determine the value of a.

From the graph you can see that $g(0) =$ _____ . Substituting 0 for x and

_____ for $g(x)$ into the equation from part A and solving for a gives:

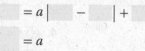

$$\boxed{} = a$$

C Write the simplified equation for the function: _____

© Houghton Mifflin Harcourt Publishing Company

REFLECT

3a. The graph of $g(x)$ opens down. In what way does this fact help you check that your
equation is reasonable?

_____

3b. The graph of $g(x)$ passes through the point $(-9, -3)$. Show how you can use this
fact to check the accuracy of your equation.

_____

_____

3c. If you know the coordinates of the vertex of the graph of an absolute value function,
then you know how the graph of the parent function has been translated. Explain
why this is so.

_____

_____

_____

Graph each absolute value function.

1. $g(x) = \frac{3}{4}|x + 2|$

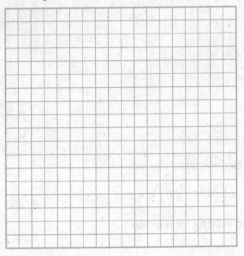

2. $g(x) = 2|x| - 4$

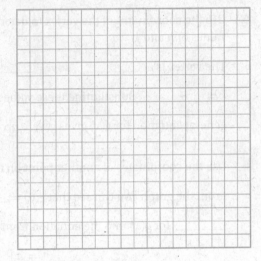

3. $g(x) = -\frac{1}{2}|x + 1|$

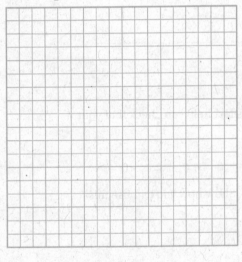

4. $g(x) = -3|x - 3| + 5$

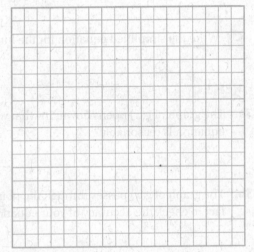

5. $g(x) = 1.5|x - 2| - 3$

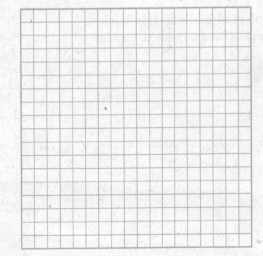

6. $g(x) = \frac{5}{3}|x + 3| - 5$

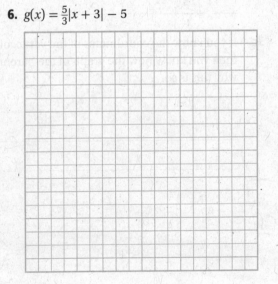

Write the equation for each absolute value function whose graph is shown.

7.

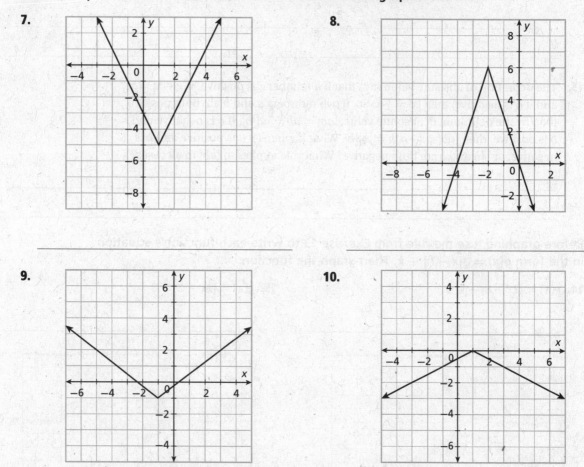

8.

_____

9.

10.

_____

11. The functions that you graphed in Exercises 1–6 are listed in the table below. State the domain and range of each function.

Function	Domain	Range
$g(x) = \frac{3}{4}\lvert x + 2\rvert$		
$g(x) = 2\lvert x\rvert - 4$		
$g(x) = -\frac{1}{2}\lvert x + 1\rvert$		
$g(x) = -3\lvert x - 3\rvert + 5$		
$g(x) = 1.5\lvert x - 2\rvert - 3$		
$g(x) = \frac{5}{3}\lvert x + 3\rvert - 5$		

12. Describe the domain and range of any function of the form $g(x) = a|x - h| + k$.

_____

_____

13. The definition of absolute value says that if a number x is positive, then $|x| = x$, and if it is negative, then $|x| = -x$. So, if two numbers a and b are both positive, then by the definition of absolute value, $|ab| = ab = |a||b|$. If a is negative and b is positive, then $|ab| = (-a)b = |a||b|$. What happens if a is positive and b is negative, or if a and b are both negative? What rule applies to $|ab|$ in all cases?

_____

_____

Before graphing, use the rule from Exercise 13 to write each function's equation in the form $g(x) = a|x - h| + k$. Then graph the function.

14. $g(x) = |2x + 8| - 1$

15. $g(x) = \left|\frac{1}{2}x - 2\right| + 3$

_____   _____

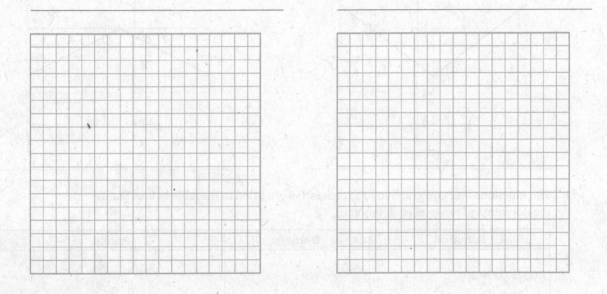

16. Does the value of a affect the location of the vertex for the graph of $g(x) = a|x - h| + k$? Why or why not?

_____

_____

_____

17. Suppose you vertically shrink the graph of $g(x) = 2|x + 3|$ by a factor of 0.5 and then translate the result 3 units right. What function has the resulting graph?

_____

Solving Absolute Value Equations

6-5

COMMON CORE

CC.9-12.A.CED.1*,
CC.9-12.A.CED.2*,
CC.9-12.A.REI.11*

Essential question: *How can you use graphing to solve equations involving absolute value?*

The equation $2|x - 3| + 1 = 5$ is an example of an *absolute value equation*.

1 EXAMPLE Solving an Absolute Value Equation by Graphing

Solve the equation $2|x - 3| + 1 = 5$ by graphing.

A Treat the left side of the equation as the absolute value function $f(x) = 2|x - 3| + 1$. Graph the function by following these steps.

- Identify and plot the vertex: _____.
- If you move 1 unit to the left or right of the vertex, describe how must you move vertically to get to a point on the graph. Give the coordinates of these points and then plot them.

_____

- Use the three plotted points to draw the complete graph.

B Treat the right side of the equation as the constant function $g(x) = 5$. Draw the graph of $g(x)$ on the same coordinate plane as the graph of $f(x)$.

C Identify the x-coordinate of each point where the graphs of $f(x)$ and $g(x)$ intersect. Show that each x-coordinate is a solution of $2|x - 3| + 1 = 5$.

_____

_____

REFLECT

1a. Use transformations to justify the steps taken when graphing $f(x)$.

_____

_____

_____

_____

_____

_____

Solve the equation $2|x - 3| + 1 = 5$ using algebra.

A Isolate the expression $|x - 3|$.

$2|x - 3| + 1 = 5$ Write the equation.

$\dfrac{}{} \quad \dfrac{}{}$ Subtract 1 from both sides.

$2|x - 3| = \boxed{}$ Simplify.

$\dfrac{2|x - 3|}{\boxed{}} = \dfrac{\boxed{}}{}$ Divide both sides by 2.

$|x - 3| = \boxed{}$ Simplify.

B Interpret the equation $|x - 3| = 2$: What numbers have an absolute value equal to 2?

_____

C Set the expression inside the absolute value bars equal to each of the numbers from Part B and solve for x.

$x - 3 = \boxed{}$ or $x - 3 = \boxed{}$ Write an equation for each value of $x - 3$.

$\dfrac{\boxed{}\ \boxed{}}{}$ $\dfrac{\boxed{}\ \boxed{}}{}$ Add 3 to both sides of each equation.

$x = \boxed{}$ or $x = \boxed{}$ Simplify.

REFLECT

2a. The left side of the equation is the function $f(x) = 2|x - 3| + 1$. Evaluate this function for each solution of the equation. How does this help you check the solutions?

_____

_____

_____

_____

2b. Suppose the number on the right side of the equation was -5 instead of 5. What solutions would the equation have? Why? When answering these questions, you may want to refer to the graph of $f(x) = 2|x - 3| + 1$.

_____

_____

Sal exercises by running east 3 miles along a road in front of his home and then reversing his direction to return home. He runs at a constant speed of 0.1 mile per minute. Write and graph a model that gives his distance d (in miles) from home as a function of the elapsed time t (in minutes). Use the graph to find the time(s) at which Sal is 1 mile from home.

A Determine the three key values of the distance function:

- When Sal begins his run ($t = 0$ minutes), he is _____ miles from home,

  so $d(0) =$ _____.

- When Sal is reverses direction, he is _____ miles from home.

  He reaches this point in $t = \dfrac{\boxed{} \text{ miles}}{0.1 \text{ mile per minute}} =$ _____ minutes, so

  $d($_____$) =$ _____.

- When Sal returns home, he is _____ miles from home. Because he has

  run a total of 6 miles, he reaches this point in $t = \dfrac{\boxed{} \text{ miles}}{0.1 \text{ mile per minute}} =$

  _____ minutes, so $d($_____$) =$ _____.

B Add axis labels and scales to the coordinate plane shown, then plot the points $(t, d(t))$ using the time and distance values from part A. The function $d(t)$ is an absolute value function, and the vertex of the function's graph is the point that represents when Sal reverses direction. Draw the complete graph of $d(t)$ and then write the equation for the function.

_____

C To find the time(s) when Sal is 1 mile from home, draw the graph of $d(t) = 1$. Find the t-coordinate of each point where the two graphs intersect.

_____

REFLECT

3a. Show how to use algebra to find the time(s) when Sal is 1 mile from home.

_____

_____

Solve each absolute value equation by graphing.

1. $-2|x + 1| + 4 = -4$

2. $0.5|x - 3| + 2 = 4$

3. $|x + 2| - 2 = -2$

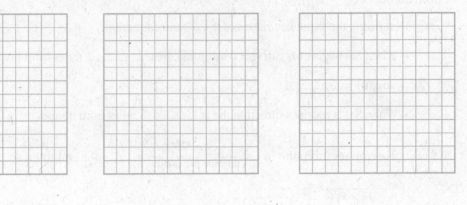

_____   _____   _____

Solve each absolute value equation using algebra.

4. $4|x + 3| - 7 = 5$

5. $0.8|x + 4| - 3 = 1$

6. $-3|x - 1| + 5 = 8$

_____   _____   _____

7. The number of shoppers in a store is modeled by $s(t) = -0.5|t - 288| + 144$ where t is the time (in minutes) since the store opened at 10:00 A.M.

a. For what values of t are there 100 shoppers in the store? _____

b. At what times are there 100 shoppers in the store? _____

c. What is the greatest number of shoppers in the store? _____

d. At what time does the greatest number of shoppers occur? _____

8. On January 1, 2010, Joline deposits $1000 in a bank account that does not earn interest. For the next 12 months she deposits $25 each month. Then she withdraws $25 each month for the next 12 months. On January 1, 2010, Sofia deposits $1100 in an account that earns 0.25% interest each month.

a. Write two models: one for the amount in Joline's account and one for the amount in Sophia's account. State what the variables in your models represent.

_____

_____

b. In what months and years do the accounts have approximately the same amount, and what are the amounts?

_____

_____

FOCUS ON MODELING

Modeling with Absolute Value Functions

COMMON CORE

CC.9-12.A.CED.2*,
CC.9-12.F.IF.2,
CC.9-12.F.IF.4*,
CC.9-12.F.IF.5*,
CC.9-12.F.IF.7b*,
CC.9-12.F.BF.1*

Essential question: *How can you use an absolute value function to plan a bank shot when playing pool?*

When a ball hits a rail on a pool table, it bounces off the rail, forming a V-shaped path. The path is symmetric about a line perpendicular to the rail at the point of contact.

Brad is improving his pool-playing skills by taking practice shots on a playing surface that measures 50 inches by 100 inches. The 2-ball is positioned as shown below. Brad wants to get the 2-ball into the lower-right corner pocket by taking a bank shot. He decides to take a bank shot off the upper rail. Where on the upper rail should the 2-ball hit in order to rebound into the lower-right pocket?

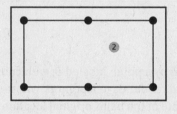

1 **Place a coordinate system on the playing surface.**

A The coordinate system shown below has horizontal and vertical grid lines every 10 inches. The lower-left pocket is the origin with coordinates (0, 0).

State the coordinates of the center of each of the following pockets: lower right, upper left, and upper right.

_____

B State the coordinates of the center of the 2-ball.

_____

1a. Suppose you place the origin of the coordinate system at the center of the side (middle) pocket on the lower rail instead. How does this change the coordinates of the centers of the corner pockets? The coordinates of the center of the 2-ball?

_____

_____

1b. Using the original coordinate system shown, sketch the path of the 2-ball as it hits the upper rail and rebounds into the lower-right pocket. Explain why the graph of an absolute value function is a good model for the path.

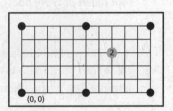

_____

_____

_____

1c. Using the original coordinate system, estimate the coordinates of the point where the 2-ball must hit in order to rebound into the lower-right corner pocket.

_____

_____

2 **Examine a special case.**

A In the diagram below, a ball is represented by a point, labeled B, with coordinates (x_1, y_1). The ball strikes a rail at point A and rebounds to a point B' whose y-coordinate is the same as the y-coordinate of the ball's original location. Write the y-coordinate of B' on the diagram.

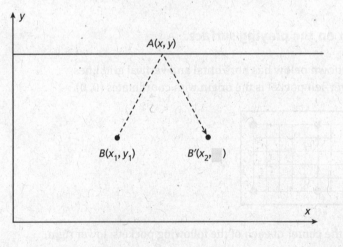

B State the x-coordinate of point A in terms of x_1 and x_2. Explain your reasoning.

_____

_____

2a. The figure at the right is another representation of the situation. Knowing that m∠BAC = m∠B′AC, what can you say about △BAC and △B′AC? Explain.

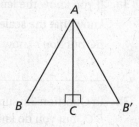

_____

_____

2b. In the figure, is it correct to say that △B′AC is a dilation of △BAC after △ACB is reflected across the line through points A and C? If so, what is the scale factor of the dilation?

_____

3 **Examine the general case.**

A In the diagram below, the ball at point B strikes a rail at point A and rebounds to a point B′ whose y-coordinate is not the same as the y-coordinate of the ball's original location. Write the y-coordinate of B′ on the diagram.

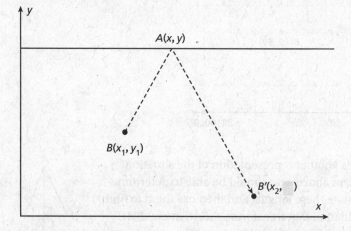

B The diagram at the right is another representation of the situation. Because m∠BAC = m∠B′AC′, you can reflect △BAC across the line through points A and C and then dilate the reflection by a certain scale factor to obtain △B′AC′. Explain how to determine the scale factor if you know the side lengths of the two triangles.

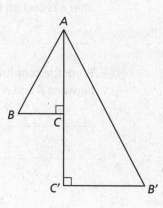

_____

_____

3a. If you know the lengths AC and AC' in the diagram from Step 3B, then you know that the scale factor f for the dilation is $f = \frac{AC'}{AC}$. If you also know the length BC but *don't* know the length $B'C'$, how can you use BC and f to find $B'C'$?

_____

3b. In Question 3a, suppose you don't know either the length BC or the length $B'C'$, but you do know the sum S of those lengths. How can you express S only in terms of BC and the scale factor f?

_____

4 **Apply the general case to the real-world problem.**

A The coordinate system for the pool table is shown below. Write the y-coordinate of A on the diagram.

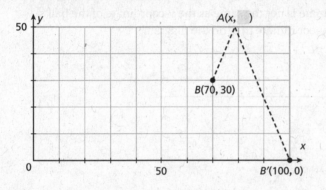

B The diagram at the right is another representation of the situation. From the coordinate system above, you should be able to determine the lengths AC and AC'. State these lengths and then use them to find the scale factor f for the dilation that transforms $\triangle BAC$ into $\triangle B'AC'$ after a reflection in the line through the points A and C.

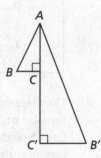

_____

C From the coordinate system above, determine the *horizontal* distance between B and B'. Explain how you obtained your answer.

_____

_____

D Find the length BC by recognizing that the sum of BC and $B'C'$ equals the horizontal distance that you found in the previous step.

$BC + B'C' = \boxed{}$ Equation for horizontal distance

$BC + \boxed{} BC = \boxed{}$ Use the scale factor to replace $B'C'$.

$\boxed{} BC = \boxed{}$ Combine like terms.

$BC \approx \boxed{}$ Solve for BC.

E Find the x-coordinate of point A. Explain your reasoning.

_____

_____

REFLECT

4a. Compare your answer for Step 4E with your estimate from Reflect Question 1b. Are your calculated value and your estimate reasonably close?

_____

5 **Write the equation for the path of the ball.**

A In Lesson 6-3 you learned that the path of a rolling ball that strikes and bounces off a flat surface can be modeled by the graph of the function $f(x) = a|x - h| + k$. You now know the values of h and k. Write the function using those values.

_____

B Find the value of a by using point $B(70, 30)$.

$f(x) = a\left|x - \boxed{}\right| + \boxed{}$ Write the function.

$\boxed{} = a\left|\boxed{} - \boxed{}\right| + \boxed{}$ Substitute for x and $f(x)$ using the coordinates of B.

$\boxed{} = a\left|\boxed{}\right| + \boxed{}$ Simplify inside the absolute value.

$\boxed{} = \boxed{} a + \boxed{}$ Find the absolute value.

$\boxed{} = \boxed{} a$ Subtract 50 from both sides.

$\boxed{} \approx a$ Divide both sides by 8.6.

C Write the function whose graph models the path of the 2-ball. Use the function and the point $B'(100, 0)$ to show that the ball does go into the lower-right corner pocket.

_____

_____

© Houghton Mifflin Harcourt Publishing Company

5a. In Step 5B, the value of *a* is negative. Explain why this is expected.

_____

_____

5b. In Step 5C, the value of the function was not exactly 0. Explain why not.

_____

_____

EXTEND

1. Write the absolute value function whose graph models the path of the 2-ball as a piecewise function.

_____

_____

2. For the absolute value function whose graph models the path of the 2-ball, state the domain and range of the function based on the initial and final positions of the ball.

_____

_____

3. Graph the absolute value function whose graph models the path of the 2-ball on a graphing calculator. Use a viewing window that shows $0 \leq x \leq 100$ and $0 \leq y \leq 50$. How is the function's graph different from the actual path of the ball? Why?

_____

_____

_____

4. Suppose Brad wants to get the 2-ball into the upper-left corner pocket with a bank shot off the lower rail. Find the coordinates of the point on the lower rail that the ball must hit, and give the equation of the absolute value function whose graph models the path of the ball.

_____

_____

Name _____ Class _____ Date _____

MULTIPLE CHOICE

1. The function $C(t)$ gives the cost C of buying t tickets to a museum exhibit when a group discount is offered.

$$C(t) = \begin{cases} 20t \text{ if } 0 \leq t < 10 \\ 18t \text{ if } t \geq 10 \end{cases}$$

Which statement describes what $C(10)$ represents?

- **A.** 10 tickets cost $200.
- **B.** 10 tickets cost $180.
- **C.** 10 tickets cost $20.
- **D.** 10 tickets cost $18.

2. Which of the following describes a way to graph the function $g(x) = -2|x|$?

- **F.** Stretch the graph of $f(x) = |x|$ vertically by a factor of 2. Then reflect the result across the x-axis.
- **G.** Shrink the graph of $f(x) = |x|$ vertically by a factor of $\frac{1}{2}$. Then reflect the result across the x-axis.
- **H.** Translate the graph of $f(x) = |x|$ down 2 units.
- **J.** Translate the graph of $f(x) = |x|$ right 2 units.

3. What are the coordinates of the vertex of the graph of $f(x) = 3|x + 1| - 4$?

- **A.** $(1, 4)$
- **B.** $(1, -4)$
- **C.** $(-1, 4)$
- **D.** $(-1, -4)$

For Items 4–6, refer to the graph of an absolute value function $f(x)$ shown below.

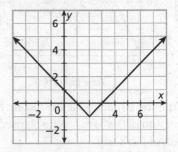

4. What is the equation for $f(x)$?

- **F.** $f(x) = |x - 1| - 2$
- **G.** $f(x) = |x - 2| + 1$
- **H.** $f(x) = |x + 2| - 1$
- **J.** $f(x) = |x - 2| - 1$

5. What are the domain and range of $f(x)$?

- **A.** Domain: $\{x \mid x \geq -1\}$
  Range: {real numbers}
- **B.** Domain: $\{x \mid x \leq -1\}$
  Range: {real numbers}
- **C.** Domain: {real numbers}
  Range: $\{y \mid y \geq -1\}$
- **D.** Domain: {real numbers}
  Range: $\{y \mid y \leq -1\}$

6. What are the solutions of $f(x) = g(x)$ where $g(x) = 1$?

- **F.** $x = 2$
- **G.** $x = 1$ and $x = 3$
- **H.** $x = 0$ and $x = 4$
- **J.** No solutions

7. The graph shows Jim's distance from shore as he rows a boat to an island and back to shore.

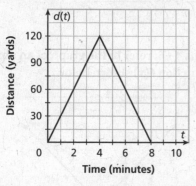

Time (minutes)

a. Write the equation for the distance function $d(t)$ where t is the elapsed time of Jim's trip.

_____

_____

b. What is the domain for this function? What does the maximum domain value represent?

_____

_____

8. a. Graph the function $g(x) = \frac{1}{2}|x + 1| - 4$.

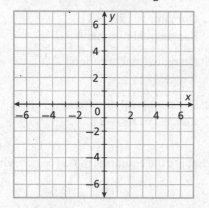

b. Describe how to transform the graph of $f(x) = |x|$ to obtain the graph of $g(x) = \frac{1}{2}|x + 1| - 4$.

_____

_____

_____

_____

9. A taxicab driver charges $6.00 for any distance less than 1 mile. For distances of 1 mile or more, he charges $6.00 plus $3.00 for each complete mile.

a. Write the equation for the function $C(d)$, which gives the cost C (in dollars) of riding in the taxicab for a distance d (in miles).

_____

b. Graph the function to show the costs for all distances less than 5 miles. Include labels and scales on your graph.

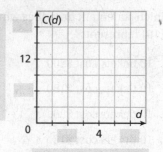

10. Student enrollment in a county's schools during a 16-year period is modeled by the function $s(t) = -0.3|t - 8| + 11$ where $s(t)$ is the number of students (in thousands) at time t (in number of years since 1990).

a. What was the enrollment in 1990? Show how you found your answer.

_____

_____

b. In what year(s) was the enrollment closest to 10,000? Explain how to find the answer.

_____

_____

_____

_____

Quadratic Functions of the Form $f(x) = a(x - h)^2 + k$

Unit Focus

This unit introduces you to quadratic functions and their graphs, called parabolas. You will learn how transformations affect the characteristics of those graphs, such as the location of the vertex and whether the parabola opens up or down. You will also learn how to solve quadratic equations, obtained by setting a quadratic function equal to a constant, both by using graphs and by using square roots. Finally, you will apply all that you have learned about quadratic functions by using them as models for real-world situations.

Unit at a Glance

COMMON CORE

Lesson		Standards for Mathematical Content
7-1	Translating the Graph of $f(x) = x^2$	CC.9-12.F.IF.2, CC.9-12.F.IF.4*, CC.9-12.F.IF.5*, CC.12.F.IF.7a*, CC.9-12.F.BF.1*, CC.9-12.F.BF.3
7-2	Stretching, Shrinking, and Reflecting the Graph of $f(x) = x^2$	CC.9-12.A.CED.2*, CC.9-12.F.IF.2, CC.9-12.F.IF.4*, CC.9-12.F.IF.7a*, CC.9-12.F.BF.1*, CC.9-12.F.BF.3
7-3	Combining Transformations of the Graph of $f(x) = x^2$	CC.9-12.A.CED.2*, CC.9-12.F.IF.2, CC.9-12.F.IF.4*, CC.9-12.F.IF.7a*, CC.9-12.F.BF.1*, CC.9-12.F.BF.3
7-4	Solving Quadratic Equations Graphically	CC.9-12.A.CED.1*, CC.9-12.A.CED.2*, CC.9-12.A.REI.11*
7-5	Solving Quadratic Equations Using Square Roots	CC.9-12.A.CED.1*, CC.9-12.A.REI.4b
7-6	Modeling with Quadratic Functions	CC.9-12.N.Q.1*, CC.9-12.N.Q.2*, CC.9-12.A.CED.2*, CC.9-12.F.IF.2, CC.9-12.F.IF.4*, CC.9-12.F.BF.1*
	Test Prep	

UNIT 7

Unpacking the Common Core State Standards

Use the table to help you understand the Standards for Mathematical Content that are taught in this unit. Refer to the lessons listed after each standard for exploration and practice.

COMMON CORE Standards for Mathematical Content	What It Means For You
CC.9-12.N.Q.1 Use units as a way to understand problems and to guide the solution of multi-step problems; choose and interpret units consistently in formulas; **choose and interpret the scale and the origin in graphs and data displays.*** Lesson 7-6 (Also 7-3)	When making a scatter plot of paired data, you need to consider the least and greatest values of each variable in order to establish an appropriate scale on each axis.
CC.9-12.N.Q.2 Define appropriate quantities for the purpose of descriptive modeling.* Lesson 7-6 (Also 7-3)	When using a function to model real-world data, you need to identify the independent and dependent variables before you can write a rule relating them.
CC.9-12.A.CED.1 Create equations and inequalities **in one variable and use them to solve problems.*** Lessons 7-4, 7-5 (Also 7-6)	You will use quadratic functions to write quadratic equations in one variable, and you will solve the equations using graphs or square roots.
CC.9-12.A.CED.2 Create equations in two or more **variables to represent relationships between quantities; graph equations on coordinate axes with labels and scales.*** Lessons 7-1, 7-2, 7-3, 7-4, 7-6	You will learn to graph functions of the form $f(x) = a(x - h)^2 + k$ and to write equations in this form given the graphs of quadratic functions.
CC.9-12.A.REI.4 Solve quadratic equations in one variable. **CC.9-12.A.REI.4b Solve quadratic equations by inspection (e.g., for $x^2 = 49$), taking square roots,** completing the square, the quadratic formula and factoring, as appropriate to the initial form of the equation. Recognize when the quadratic formula gives complex solutions and write them as $a \pm bi$ for real numbers a and b. Lesson 7-5 (Also 7-6)	You will learn that every positive number has two square roots, and you will solve quadratic equations of the form $a(x - h)^2 + k = c$ by isolating the expression $(x - h)^2$ and using the definition of a square root.
CC.9-12.A.REI.11 Explain why the x-**coordinates of the points where the graphs of the equations** $y = f(x)$ **and** $y = g(x)$ **intersect are the solutions of the equation** $f(x) = g(x)$**; find the solutions approximately, e.g., using technology to graph the functions,** make tables of values, or find successive approximations. Include cases where $f(x)$ and/or $g(x)$ are linear, polynomial, rational, absolute value, exponential, and logarithmic functions.* Lesson 7-4	You will solve quadratic equations graphically by finding the points where the graphs of a quadratic function and a constant function intersect. You will do this by hand as well as by using a graphing calculator.

UNIT 7

© Houghton Mifflin Harcourt Publishing Company

COMMON CORE Standards for Mathematical Content	What It Means For You
CC.9-12.F.IF.2 **Use function notation, evaluate functions for inputs in their domains,** and interpret statements that use function notation in terms of a context. Lessons 7-1, 7-2, 7-3, 7-6	You will write quadratic functions using function notation, and you will evaluate them when graphing and modeling.
CC.9-12.F.IF.4 **For a function that models a relationship between two quantities, interpret key features of graphs and tables in terms of the quantities,** and sketch graphs showing key features given a verbal description of the relationship.* Lessons 7-1, 7-2, 7-3, 7-6 (Also 7-4)	You will learn that the graph of any quadratic function either decreases and then increases or increases and then decreases. The turning point is called the vertex, and the y-coordinate of the vertex is either the function's minimum value or its maximum value. You will also see that the graph of a quadratic function can intersect the x-axis in 0, 1, or 2 points.
CC.9-12.F.IF.5 **Relate the domain of a function to its graph and, where applicable, to the quantitative relationship it describes.*** Lesson 7-1 (Also 7-3, 7-4)	Quadratic functions are defined for all real numbers. The domain may be restricted, however, in real-world situations modeled by quadratic functions.
CC.9-12.F.IF.7 **Graph functions expressed symbolically and show key features of the graph, by hand in simple cases and using technology for more complicated cases.*** **CC.9-12.F.IF.7a** **Graph** linear and **quadratic functions and show intercepts, maxima, and minima.*** Lessons 7-1, 7-2, 7-3 (Also 7-4)	You will find the maximum and minimum values of quadratic functions as well as the intercepts of those functions. You will discover when quadratic functions increase and when they decrease and use the symmetry of their graphs to help you solve problems.
CC.9-12.F.BF.1 **Write a function that describes a relationship between two quantities.*** **CC.9-12.F.BF.1a** **Determine an explicit expression,** a recursive process, or steps for calculation **from a context.*** Lessons 7-1, 7-2, 7-3, 7-6	You will write equations for quadratic functions that model real-world situations.
CC.9-12.F.BF.3 **Identify the effect on the graph of replacing $f(x)$ by $f(x) + k$, $kf(x)$, $f(kx)$, and $f(x + k)$ for specific values of k (both positive and negative); find the value of k given the graphs.** Experiment with cases and illustrate an explanation of the effects on the graph using technology. Lessons 7-1, 7-2, 7-3 (Also 7-6)	You will investigate how the values of a, h, and k affect the graph of $f(x) = a(x - h)^2 + k$, and you will learn which quadratic functions are even functions.

UNIT 7

Translating the Graph of $f(x) = x^2$

COMMON
CORE

Essential question: *What are the effects of the constants h and k on the graph of* $g(x) = (x - h)^2 + k$?

CC.9-12.F.IF.2,
CC.9-12.F.IF.4*,
CC.9-12.F.IF.5*,
CC.9-12.F.IF.7a*,
CC.9-12.F.BF.1*,
CC.9-12.F.BF.3

1 ENGAGE — Understanding the Parent Quadratic Function

Any function that can be written as $f(x) = ax^2 + bx + c$ where *a*, *b*, and *c* are constants and $a \neq 0$ is a **quadratic function**. Notice that the highest exponent of the variable *x* is 2.

The most basic quadratic function is $f(x) = x^2$. It is called the *parent* quadratic function. To graph the parent function, make a table of values like the one below. Then plot the ordered pairs and draw the graph. The U-shaped curve is called a **parabola**. The turning point on the parabola is called its **vertex**.

x	$f(x) = x^2$
−3	9
−2	4
−1	1
0	0
1	1
2	4
3	9

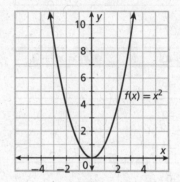

REFLECT

1a. What is the domain of $f(x) = x^2$? What is the range?

_____

1b. What symmetry does the graph of $f(x) = x^2$ have? Why does it have this symmetry?

_____

_____

1c. For what values of *x* is $f(x) = x^2$ increasing? For what values is it decreasing?

_____

_____

Graph each quadratic function. (The graph of the parent function $f(x) = x^2$ is shown in gray.)

A $g(x) = x^2 + 2$

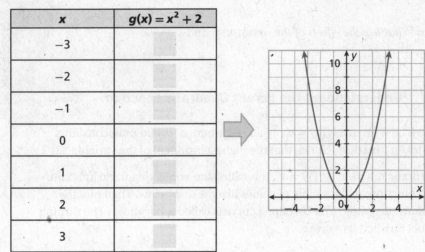

x	$g(x) = x^2 + 2$
−3	
−2	
−1	
0	
1	
2	
3	

B $g(x) = x^2 - 2$

x	$g(x) = x^2 - 2$
−3	
−2	
−1	
0	
1	
2	
3	

REFLECT

2a. How is the graph of $g(x) = x^2 + 2$ related to the graph of $f(x) = x^2$?

_____

2b. How is the graph of $g(x) = x^2 - 2$ related to the graph of $f(x) = x^2$?

_____

2c. In general, how is the graph of $g(x) = x^2 + k$ related to the graph of $f(x) = x^2$?

_____

© Houghton Mifflin Harcourt Publishing Company

3 EXAMPLE Graphing Functions of the Form $g(x) = (x - h)^2$

Graph each quadratic function. (The graph of the parent function $f(x) = x^2$ is shown in gray.)

A $g(x) = (x - 1)^2$

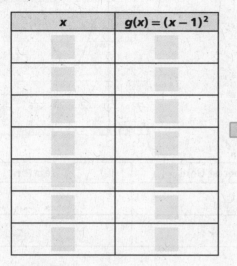

x	$g(x) = (x - 1)^2$

B $g(x) = (x + 1)^2$

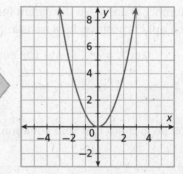

x	$g(x) = (x + 1)^2$

REFLECT

3a. How is the graph of $g(x) = (x - 1)^2$ related to the graph of $f(x) = x^2$?

_____

3b. How is the graph of $g(x) = (x + 1)^2$ related to the graph of $f(x) = x^2$?

_____

3c. In general, how is the graph of $g(x) = (x - h)^2$ related to the graph of $f(x) = x^2$?

_____

EXAMPLE   Writing Equations for Quadratic Functions

Write the equation for the quadratic function whose graph is shown.

A   Compare the given graph to the graph of the parent function $f(x) = x^2$.

Complete the table below to describe how the parent function must be translated to get the graph shown here.

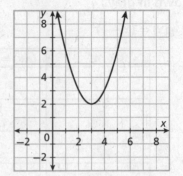

Type of Translation	Number of Units	Direction
Horizontal Translation		
Vertical Translation		

B   Determine the values of h and k for the function $g(x) = (x - h)^2 + k$.

- h is the number of units that the parent function is translated horizontally. For a translation to the right, h is positive; for a translation to the left, h is negative.

- k is the number of units that the parent function is translated vertically. For a translation up, k is positive; for a translation down, k is negative.

So, $h =$ _____ and $k =$ _____. The equation is _____.

REFLECT

4a. What can you do to check that your equation is correct?

_____

4b. If the graph of a quadratic function is a translation of the graph of the parent function, explain how you can use the vertex of the translated graph to help you determine the equation for the function.

_____

_____

4c. **Error Analysis** A student says that the graph of $g(x) = (x + 2)^2 + 1$ is the graph of the parent function translated 2 units to the right and 1 unit up. Explain what is incorrect about this statement.

_____

_____

Graph each quadratic function.

1. $f(x) = x^2 + 4$

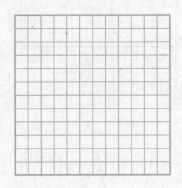

2. $f(x) = x^2 - 5$

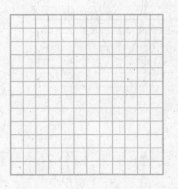

3. $f(x) = (x - 2)^2$

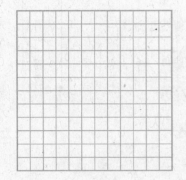

4. $f(x) = (x + 3)^2$

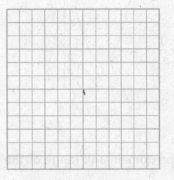

5. $f(x) = (x - 5)^2 - 2$

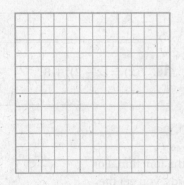

6. $f(x) = (x - 1)^2 + 1$

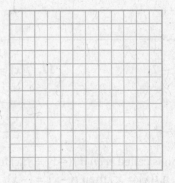

7. $f(x) = (x + 4)^2 + 3$

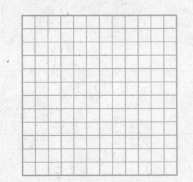

8. $f(x) = (x + 2)^2 - 4$

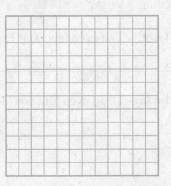

Write a rule for the quadratic function whose graph is shown.

9.

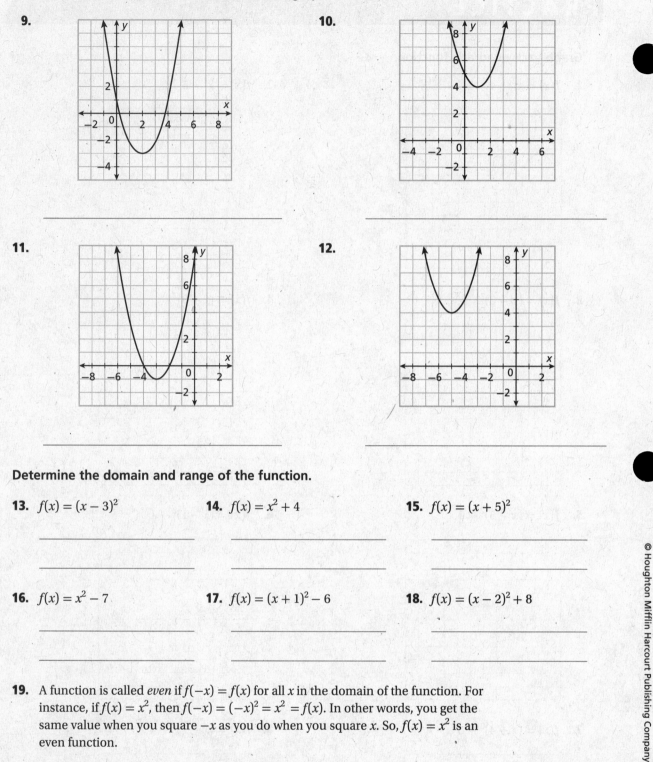

10.

_____

11.

12.

_____

Determine the domain and range of the function.

13. $f(x) = (x - 3)^2$

14. $f(x) = x^2 + 4$

15. $f(x) = (x + 5)^2$

_____ _____ _____

_____ _____ _____

16. $f(x) = x^2 - 7$

17. $f(x) = (x + 1)^2 - 6$

18. $f(x) = (x - 2)^2 + 8$

_____ _____ _____

_____ _____ _____

19. A function is called *even* if $f(-x) = f(x)$ for all x in the domain of the function. For instance, if $f(x) = x^2$, then $f(-x) = (-x)^2 = x^2 = f(x)$. In other words, you get the same value when you square $-x$ as you do when you square x. So, $f(x) = x^2$ is an even function.

  a. Is $f(x) = x^2 - 1$ an even function? Explain.

_____

  b. Is $f(x) = (x - 1)^2$ an even function? Explain.

_____

© Houghton Mifflin Harcourt Publishing Company

Stretching, Shrinking, and Reflecting the Graph of $f(x) = x^2$

COMMON CORE

CC.9-12.A.CED.2*,
CC.9-12.F.IF.2,
CC.9-12.F.IF.4*,
CC.9-12.F.IF.7a*,
CC.9-12.F.BF.1*,
CC.9-12.F.BF.3

Essential question: *What is the effect of the constant a on the graph of $g(x) = ax^2$?*

To understand the effect of the constant a on the graph of $g(x) = ax^2$, you will graph the function using various values of a.

1 **EXAMPLE** Graphing $g(x) = ax^2$ when $a > 0$

Graph each quadratic function. (The graph of the parent function $f(x) = x^2$ is shown in gray.)

A $g(x) = 2x^2$

x	$g(x) = 2x^2$
−3	
−2	
−1	
0	
1	
2	
3	

B $g(x) = \frac{1}{2}x^2$

x	$g(x) = \frac{1}{2}x^2$
−3	
−2	
−1	
0	
1	
2	
3	

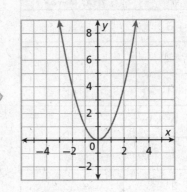

REFLECT

1a. The graph of the parent function $f(x) = x^2$ includes the point $(-1, 1)$ because $f(-1) = (-1)^2 = 1$. The corresponding point on the graph of $g(x) = 2x^2$ is $(-1, 2)$ because $g(-1) = 2(-1)^2 = 2$. In general, how does the y-coordinate of a point on the graph of $g(x) = 2x^2$ compare with the y-coordinate of a point on the graph of $f(x) = x^2$ when the points have the same x-coordinate?

_____

_____

1b. Describe how the graph of $g(x) = 2x^2$ compares with the graph of $f(x) = x^2$. Use either the word *stretch* or *shrink*, and include the direction of the movement.

_____

1c. How does the y-coordinate of a point on the graph of $g(x) = \frac{1}{2}x^2$ compare with the y-coordinate of a point on the graph of $f(x) = x^2$ when the points have the same x-coordinate?

_____

_____

1d. Describe how the graph of $g(x) = \frac{1}{2}x^2$ compares with the graph of $f(x) = x^2$. Use either the word *stretch* or *shrink*, and include the direction of the movement.

_____

2 EXAMPLE Graphing $g(x) = ax^2$ when $a < 0$

Graph each quadratic function. (The graph of the parent function $f(x) = x^2$ is shown in gray.)

A $g(x) = -2x^2$

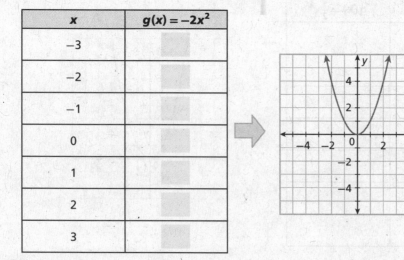

x	$g(x) = -2x^2$
-3	
-2	
-1	
0	
1	
2	
3	

© Houghton Mifflin Harcourt Publishing Company

B $g(x) = -\frac{1}{2}x^2$

x	$g(x) = -\frac{1}{2}x^2$
-3	
-2	
-1	
0	
1	
2	
3	

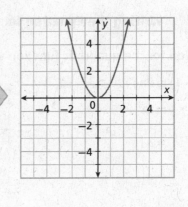

REFLECT

2a. In part A of the previous example, you drew the graph of $g(x) = ax^2$ where $a = 2$. In part A of this example, you drew the graph of $g(x) = ax^2$ where $a = -2$. How do the two graphs compare? How does the graph of $g(x) = -2x^2$ compare with the graph of $f(x) = x^2$?

_____

_____

2b. In part B of the previous example, you drew the graph of $g(x) = ax^2$ where $a = \frac{1}{2}$. In part B of this example, you drew the graph of $g(x) = ax^2$ where $a = -\frac{1}{2}$. How do the two graphs compare? How does the graph of $g(x) = -\frac{1}{2}x^2$ compare with the graph of $f(x) = x^2$?

_____

_____

2c. Summarize your observations about the graph of $g(x) = ax^2$.

Value of a	Vertical stretch or shrink?	Reflection across x-axis?
$a > 1$	Vertical stretch	No
$0 < a < 1$		
$-1 < a < 0$		
$a = -1$		
$a < -1$		

Writing Equations from Graphs A function whose graph is a parabola with vertex $(0, 0)$ always has the form $f(x) = ax^2$. To write the rule for the function, you can substitute the x- and y-coordinates of a point on the graph into the equation $y = ax^2$ and solve for a.

3 EXAMPLE Writing the Equation for a Quadratic Function

Write the equation for the quadratic function whose graph is shown.

Use the point $(2, -1)$ to find a.

$$y = ax^2$$

$$\boxed{} = a\left(\boxed{}\right)^2$$

$$\boxed{} = a\left(\boxed{}\right)$$

$$\boxed{} = a$$

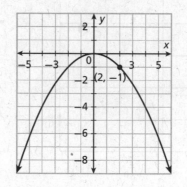

The equation for the function

is _____.

REFLECT

3a. Without actually graphing the function whose equation you found, how can check that your equation is reasonable?

_____

_____

_____

3b. Error Analysis Knowing that the graph of $f(x) = ax^2$ is a parabola that has its vertex at $(0, 0)$ and passes through the point $(-2, 2)$, a student says that the value of a must be $-\frac{1}{2}$. Explain why this value of a is not reasonable.

_____

_____

_____

© Houghton Mifflin Harcourt Publishing Company

Graph each quadratic function.

1. $f(x) = 3x^2$

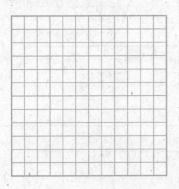

2. $f(x) = -\frac{3}{4}x^2$

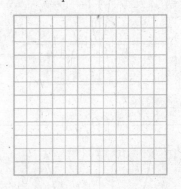

3. $f(x) = 0.6x^2$

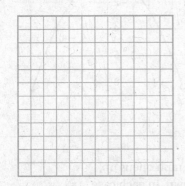

4. $f(x) = -1.5x^2$

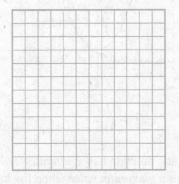

5. $f(x) = \frac{1}{5}x^2$

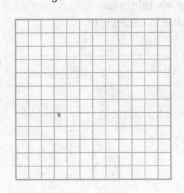

6. $f(x) = -2.5x^2$

7. $f(x) = 4x^2$

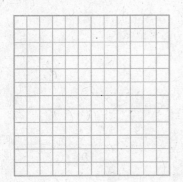

8. $f(x) = -0.2x^2$

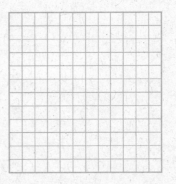

Write the equation for each quadratic function whose graph is shown.

9.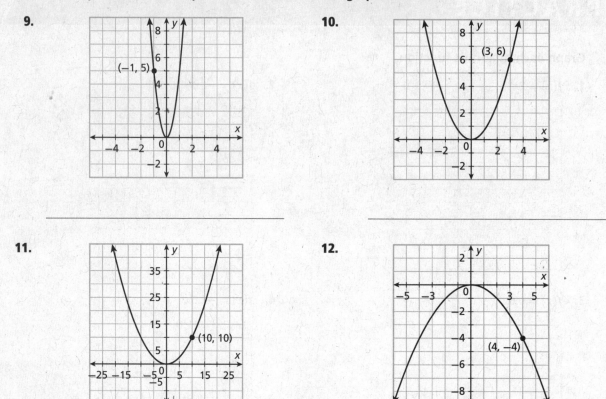

Points shown: $(-1, 5)$

_____

10.

Points shown: $(3, 6)$

_____

11.

Points shown: $(10, 10)$

_____

12.

Points shown: $(4, -4)$

_____

13. A quadratic function has a *minimum value* when the function's graph opens up, and it has a *maximum value* when the function's graph opens down. In each case, the minimum or maximum value is the y-coordinate of the vertex of the function's graph. Under what circumstances does the function $f(x) = ax^2$ have a minimum value? A maximum value? What is the minimum or maximum value in each case?

_____

_____

14. A function is called *even* if $f(-x) = f(x)$ for all x in the domain of the function. Show that the function $f(x) = ax^2$ is even for any value of a.

_____

© Houghton Mifflin Harcourt Publishing Company

7-3

Combining Transformations of the Graph of $f(x) = x^2$

COMMON
CORE

CC.9-12.A.CED.2*,
CC.9-12.F.IF.2,
CC.9-12.F.IF.4*,
CC.9-12.F.IF.7a*,
CC.9-12.F.BF.1*,
CC.9-12.F.BF.3

Essential question: *How can you obtain the graph of $g(x) = a(x - h)^2 + k$ from the graph of $f(x) = x^2$?*

1 **ENGAGE**   Understanding How to Graph $g(x) = a(x - h)^2 + k$

The sequence of graphs below shows how you can obtain the graph of $g(x) = 2(x - 3)^2 + 1$ from the graph of the parent quadratic function $f(x) = x^2$ using transformations.

1. Start with the graph of $y = x^2$.

2. Stretch the graph vertically by a factor of 2 to obtain the graph of $y = 2x^2$.

3. Translate the graph of $y = 2x^2$ right 3 units and up 1 unit to obtain the graph of $y = 2(x - 3)^2 + 1$.

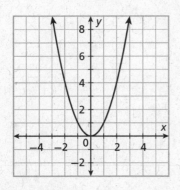 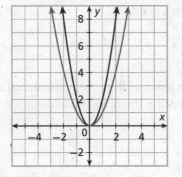 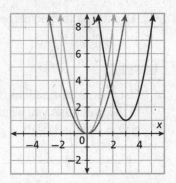

REFLECT

1a. The vertex of the graph of $f(x) = x^2$ is _____, while the vertex of the

graph of $g(x) = 2(x - 3)^2 + 1$ is _____.

1b. If you start at the vertex of the graph of $f(x) = x^2$ and move 1 unit to the right or left,

how must you move vertically to get back to the graph? _____

1c. If you start at the vertex of the graph of $g(x) = 2(x - 3)^2 + 1$ and move 1 unit to the

right or left, how must you move vertically to get back to the graph? _____

1d. Based on your answers to Questions 1a–c, describe how you could graph $g(x) = a(x - h)^2 + k$ directly, without using transformed graphs.

_____

2 EXAMPLE Graphing $g(x) = a(x - h)^2 + k$

Graph $g(x) = -3(x + 1)^2 - 2$.

A Identify and plot the vertex.

Vertex: _____

B Identify and plot other points based on the fact that $f(\pm 1) = 1$ for the parent function $f(x) = x^2$.

If you move 1 unit right or left from the vertex in part A, how must you move vertically to be on the graph of $g(x)$? What points are you at?

_____

C Use the plotted points to draw a parabola.

REFLECT

2a. List the transformations of the graph of the parent function $f(x) = x^2$, in the order that you would perform them, to obtain the graph of $g(x) = -3(x + 1)^2 - 2$.

_____

_____

_____

2b. Before graphing $g(x) = -3(x + 1)^2 - 2$, would you have expected the graph to open up or down? Why?

_____

_____

_____

2c. Suppose you changed the -3 in $g(x) = -3(x + 1)^2 - 2$ to -4. Which of the points that you identified in parts A and B of the example would change? What coordinates would they now have?

_____

_____

_____

© Houghton Mifflin Harcourt Publishing Company

A house painter standing on a ladder drops a paintbrush, which falls to the ground. The paintbrush's height above the ground (in feet) is given by a function of the form $f(t) = a(t - h)^2 + k$ where t is the time (in seconds) since the paintbrush was dropped.

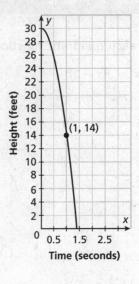

Because $f(t)$ is a quadratic function, its graph is a parabola. Only the portion of the parabola that lies in Quadrant I and on the axes is shown because only nonnegative values of t and $f(t)$ make sense in this situation. The vertex of the parabola lies on the vertical axis.

Use the graph to find an equation for $f(t)$.

A   The vertex of the parabola is $(h, k) = \left(\boxed{}, \boxed{}\right)$.

Substitute the values of h and k into the general equation

for $f(t)$ to get $f(t) = a\left(t - \boxed{}\right)^2 + \boxed{}$.

B   From the graph you can see that $f(1) =$ _____. Substitute 1 for t

and _____ for $f(t)$ to determine the value of a for this function:

$$\boxed{} = a\left(1 - \boxed{}\right)^2 + \boxed{}$$

$$\underline{} = a$$

C   Write the equation for the function: $f(t) =$ _____

REFLECT

3a. Using the graph, estimate how much time elapses until the paintbrush hits

the ground: $t \approx$ _____

3b. Using the value of t from Question 3a and the equation for the height function from part C of the example, find the value of $f(t)$. How does this help you check the reasonableness of the equation?

_____

_____

Graph each quadratic function.

1. $f(x) = 2(x - 2)^2 + 3$

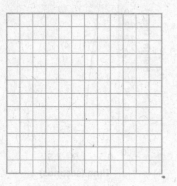

2. $f(x) = -(x - 1)^2 + 2$

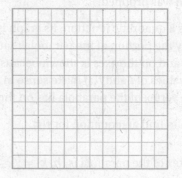

3. $f(x) = \frac{1}{2}(x - 2)^2$

4. $f(x) = -\frac{1}{3}x^2 - 3$

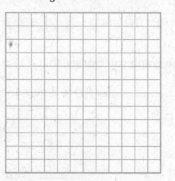

5. A roofer working on a roof accidentally drops a hammer, which falls to the ground. The hammer's height above the ground (in feet) is given by a function of the form $f(t) = a(t - h)^2 + k$ where t is the time (in seconds) since the hammer was dropped.

Because $f(t)$ is a quadratic function, its graph is a parabola. Only the portion of the parabola that lies in Quadrant I and on the axes is shown because only nonnegative values of t and $f(t)$ make sense in this situation. The vertex of the parabola lies on the vertical axis.

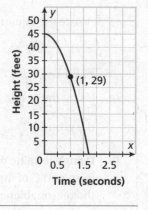

a. Use the graph to find an equation for $f(t)$.

_____

b. Explain how you can use the graph's t-intercept to check the reasonableness of your equation.

_____

_____

Solving Quadratic Equations Graphically

COMMON CORE

CC.9-12.A.CED.1*,
CC.9-12.A.CED.2*,
CC.9-12.A.REI.11*

Essential question: *How can you solve a quadratic equation by graphing?*

1 EXPLORE Finding Intersections of Lines and Parabolas

The graphs of three quadratic functions are shown.

Parabola A is the graph of $f(x) = x^2$.

Parabola B is the graph of $f(x) = x^2 + 4$.

Parabola C is the graph of $f(x) = x^2 + 8$.

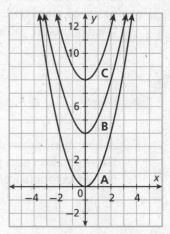

A On the same coordinate grid, graph the function $g(x) = 4$. What type of function is this? Describe its graph.

_____

B At how many points does the graph of $g(x)$ intersect each parabola?

Intersections with parabola A: _____

Intersections with parabola B: _____

Intersections with parabola C: _____

C Use the graph to find the x-coordinate of each point of intersection of the graph of $g(x)$ and parabola A. Show that each x-coordinate satisfies the equation $x^2 = 4$.

_____

D Use the graph to find the x-coordinate of each point of intersection of the graph of $g(x)$ and parabola B. Show that each x-coordinate satisfies the equation $x^2 + 4 = 4$.

_____

REFLECT

1a. Describe how you could solve an equation like $x^2 + 5 = 7$ graphically.

_____

_____

You can solve an equation of the form $a(x - h)^2 + k = c$, which is called a *quadratic equation*, by graphing the functions $f(x) = a(x - h)^2 + k$ and $g(x) = c$ and finding the x-coordinate of each point of intersection.

2 EXAMPLE Solving Quadratic Equations Graphically

Solve $2(x - 4)^2 + 1 = 7$.

A Graph $f(x) = 2(x - 4)^2 + 1$.

What is the vertex? _____

If you move 1 unit right or left from the vertex, how must you move vertically to be on the graph of $f(x)$? What points are you at?

_____

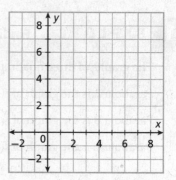

B Graph $g(x) = 7$.

C At how many points do the graphs of $f(x)$ and $g(x)$ intersect? If possible, find the x-coordinate of each point of intersection exactly. Otherwise, give an approximation of the x-coordinate of each point of intersection.

_____

_____

D For each x-value from part C, find the value of $f(x)$. How does this show that you have found actual or approximate solutions of $2(x - 4)^2 + 1 = 7$?

_____

_____

_____

REFLECT

2a. If you solved the equation $4(x - 3)^2 + 1 = 3$ graphically, would you be able to obtain exact or approximate solutions? Explain.

_____

_____

2b. For what value of c would the equation $4(x - 3)^2 + 1 = c$ have exactly one solution? How is that solution related to the graph of $f(x)$?

_____

_____

© Houghton Mifflin Harcourt Publishing Company

While practicing a tightrope walk at a height of 20 feet, a circus performer slips and falls into a safety net 15 feet below. The function $h(t) = -16t^2 + 20$, where t represents time measured in seconds, gives the performer's height above the ground (in feet) as he falls. Write and solve an equation to find the elapsed time until the performer lands in the net.

A Write the equation that you need to solve. _____

B You will solve the equation using a graphing calculator. Because the calculator requires that you enter functions in terms of x and y, use x and y to write the equations for the two functions that you will graph. _____

C When setting a viewing window, you need to decide what portion of each axis to use for graphing. What interval on the x-axis and what interval on the y-axis are reasonable for this problem? Explain.

_____

_____

_____

D Graph the two functions, and use the calculator's trace or intersect feature to find the elapsed time until the performer lands in the net. Is your answer exact or an approximation?

_____

REFLECT

3a. Although the graphs also intersect to the left of the y-axis, why is that point irrelevant to the problem?

_____

3b. The distance d (in feet) that a falling object travels as a function of time t (in seconds) is given by $d(t) = 16t^2$. Use this fact to explain the model given in the problem, $h(t) = -16t^2 + 20$. In particular, explain why the model includes the constant 20 and why $-16t^2$ includes a negative sign.

_____

_____

_____

3c. At what height would the circus performer have to be for his fall to last exactly 1 second? Explain.

_____

_____

_____

Solve each quadratic equation by graphing. Indicate whether the solutions are exact or approximate.

1. $(x + 2)^2 - 1 = 3$

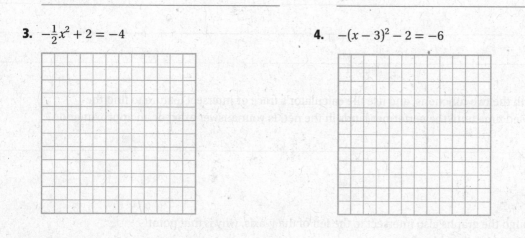

_____

2. $2(x - 3)^2 + 1 = 5$

_____

3. $-\frac{1}{2}x^2 + 2 = -4$

_____

4. $-(x - 3)^2 - 2 = -6$

_____

5. As part of an engineering contest, a student who has designed a protective crate for an egg drops the crate from a window 18 feet above the ground. The height (in feet) of the crate as it falls is given by $h(t) = -16t^2 + 18$ where t is the time (in seconds) since the crate was dropped.

  a. Write and solve an equation to find the elapsed time until the crate passes a window 10 feet directly below the window from which it was dropped.

  _____

  b. Write and solve an equation to find the elapsed time until the crate hits the ground.

  _____

  c. Is the crate's rate of fall constant? Explain.

  _____

  _____

  _____

  _____

Solving Quadratic Equations Using Square Roots

7-5

COMMON CORE

CC.9-12.A.CED.1*,
CC.9-12.A.REI.4b

Essential question: *How can you solve a quadratic equation using square roots?*

1 ENGAGE   Understanding Square Roots

You know that $2^2 = 4$ and $(-2)^2 = 4$. The numbers 2 and -2 are called the *square roots* of 4.

If $x^2 = a$, then x is a **square root** of a. Every positive number a has two square roots. This is illustrated in the diagram using the graph of $y = x^2$ and letting $y = a$. Notice that one square root of a is positive and is written $\sqrt{a}$, while the other is negative and is written $-\sqrt{a}$. The symbol $\sqrt{}$ is called a *radical sign*, and the number underneath the radical sign is called the *radicand*.

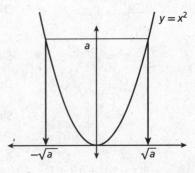

When the radicand is a perfect square, you can simplify a square root. For instance, because 4 is a perfect square, you can write the square roots of 4 as $\pm\sqrt{4} = \pm 2$.

When the radicand is not a perfect square, you may still be able to simplify a square root using one of these properties:

Product Property of Radicals: For nonnegative a and b, $\sqrt{ab} = \sqrt{a} \cdot \sqrt{b}$.

Quotient Property of Radicals: For nonnegative a and positive b, $\sqrt{\frac{a}{b}} = \frac{\sqrt{a}}{\sqrt{b}}$.

For instance, because 12 has 4 as one of its factors, you can use the product property to write the square roots of 12 as $\pm\sqrt{12} = \pm\sqrt{4 \cdot 3} = \pm\sqrt{4} \cdot \sqrt{3} = \pm 2\sqrt{3}$.

REFLECT

1a. Does 0 have any square roots? Why or why not?

_____

1b. Does a negative number have any square roots? Why or why not?

_____

1c. Explain how you would simplify the square roots of $\frac{5}{4}$.

_____

Solving a quadratic equation algebraically involves isolating the squared expression in the equation. Once you have the equation in the form $(x - h)^2 = c$, you can use the definition of a square root to write $x - h = \pm\sqrt{c}$ and finish solving for x.

2 EXAMPLE Solving Quadratic Equations Algebraically

Solve each quadratic equation.

A $2x^2 - 7 = 9$ Equation to be solved

$$\frac{\quad}{}$$ Add 7 to both sides.

$2x^2 = \boxed{}$ Simplify.

$\dfrac{2x^2}{\boxed{}} = \dfrac{\boxed{}}{\boxed{}}$ Divide both sides by 2.

$x^2 = \boxed{}$ Simplify.

$x = \boxed{}$ Definition of a square root

$x = \boxed{}$ Simplify the square roots.

B $-3(x - 6)^2 + 19 = 7$ Equation to be solved

$$\frac{\quad}{}$$ Subtract 19 from both sides.

$-3(x - 6)^2 = \boxed{}$ Simplify.

$\dfrac{-3(x - 6)^2}{\boxed{}} = \dfrac{\boxed{}}{\boxed{}}$ Divide both sides by -3.

$(x - 6)^2 = \boxed{}$ Simplify.

$x - 6 = \boxed{}$ Definition of a square root

$x - 6 = \boxed{}$ $x - 6 = \boxed{}$ Simplify the square roots.

or

$x = \boxed{}$ $x = \boxed{}$ Add 6 to both sides.

REFLECT

2a. How can you check the solutions of a quadratic equation?

_____

_____

© Houghton Mifflin Harcourt Publishing Company

A person standing on a second-floor balcony drops keys to a friend standing below the balcony. The keys are dropped from a height of 10 feet. The height (in feet) of the keys as they fall is given by the function $h(t) = -16t^2 + 10$ where t is the time (in seconds) since the keys were dropped. The friend catches the keys at a height of 4 feet. Write and solve an equation to find the elapsed time before the keys are caught.

$-16t^2 + 10 =$ ▭　　　　　Write the equation to be solved.

▭ ▭
—— ——　　　　　Subtract 10 from both sides.

$-16t^2 =$ ▭　　　　　Simplify.

$\dfrac{-16t^2}{▭} = \dfrac{▭}{}$　　　　　Divide both sides by −16.

$t^2 =$ ▭　　　　　Simplify. Express the right side as a decimal.

$t =$ ▭　　　　　Definition of a square root

$t \approx$ ▭　　　　　Use a calculator to approximate the square roots.

The elapsed time before the keys are caught is about _____.

REFLECT

3a. Although the equation that you solved has two solutions, one of them is rejected. Why?

_____

3b. The exact positive solution of the equation is $t = \dfrac{\sqrt{6}}{4}$. Explain how to obtain this result, and show that it gives the same approximate solution.

_____

_____

3c. Suppose the friend decides not to catch the keys and lets them fall to the ground instead. What equation must you solve to find the elapsed time until the keys hit the ground? What is that elapsed time?

_____

1. Write the square roots of 64 in simplified form. _____

2. Write the square roots of 32 in simplified form. _____

3. Write the square roots of $\frac{8}{9}$ in simplified form. _____

4. Explain why the square roots of 37 cannot be simplified.

_____

Solve each quadratic equation. Simplify solutions when possible.

5. $x^2 = 18$

_____

6. $-4x^2 = -20$

_____

7. $x^2 + 4 = 10$

_____

8. $2x^2 = 200$

_____

9. $(x - 5)^2 = 25$

_____

10. $(x + 1)^2 = 16$

_____

11. $2(x - 7)^2 = 98$

_____

12. $-5(x + 3)^2 = -80$

_____

13. $0.5(x + 2)^2 - 4 = 14$

_____

14. $3(x - 1)^2 + 1 = 19$

_____

15. To study how high a ball bounces, students drop the ball from various heights. The function $h(t) = -16t^2 + h_0$ gives the height (in feet) of the ball at time t measured in seconds since the ball was dropped from a height h_0.

   a. The ball is dropped from a height $h_0 = 8$ feet. Write and solve an equation to find the elapsed time until the ball hits the floor.

_____

   b. Does doubling the drop height also double the elapsed time until the ball hits the floor? Explain why or why not.

_____

_____

   c. When dropped from a height $h_0 = 16$ feet, the ball rebounds to a height of 8 feet and then falls back to the floor. Find the total time for this to happen. (Assume the ball takes the same time to rebound 8 feet as it does to fall 8 feet.)

_____

FOCUS ON MODELING
Modeling with Quadratic Functions

Essential question: *How can you model a car's gas mileage using a quadratic function?*

COMMON CORE

CC.9-12.N.Q.1*,
CC.9-12.N.Q.2*,
CC.9-12.A.CED.2*,
CC.9-12.F.IF.2,
CC.9-12.F.IF.4*,
CC.9-12.F.BF.1*

The Center for Transportation Analysis in the Oak Ridge National Laboratory publishes *Transportation Energy Data Book*, which gives data about the transportation industry. One of the book's many data sets is the gas mileage of cars driven at steady speeds. The gas mileage (in miles per gallon) for a particular year, make, and model of car is shown in the table.

As you can see, the gas mileage varies with the speed of the car. How can you predict the car's gas mileage when the car is driven at a speed of 35 miles per hour?

Speed (mph)	Gas mileage (mpg)
40	23.0
50	27.3
55	29.1
60	28.2
70	22.9

1 **Identify the variables and graph the data.**

A Identify the independent and dependent variables in this situation. State the units associated with each variable.

_____

_____

B Explain why it makes sense to use *s* for the independent variable and *m(s)* for the dependent variable.

_____

_____

C On the scatter plot given on the next page, label the axes with the quantities they represent and indicate the axis scales by showing numbers for select grid lines. Then plot the ordered pairs of data from the table.

D Sketch a parabola that you think best fits the plotted points. (You will not be able to make the parabola pass through all the points. Instead, you should try to draw the parabola so that some points fall above it and some below it.) Explain why a parabola is a reasonable curve to fit to the data.

_____

_____

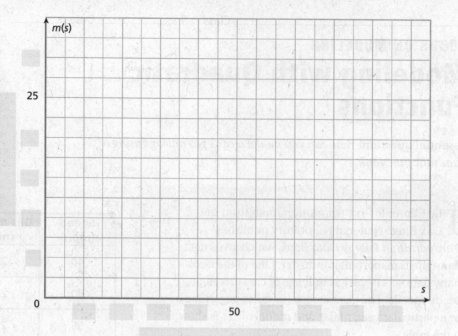

1a. Does your parabola open up or down? What are the coordinates of your parabola's vertex?

_____

1b. Describe the general characteristics of the plotted points. In particular, describe the following:

- the speeds for which the gas mileage is increasing,

- the speeds for which the gas mileage is decreasing,

- and the speed at which the gas mileage has its maximum value.

_____

_____

1c. Based on your answer to Question 1b, would you say that your parabola is reasonable? Explain. If you decide that your parabola is not reasonable, describe how you can redraw it to make it reasonable.

_____

_____

_____

2 **Write the equation for the model.**

A Using the coordinates of the vertex of your parabola, write the equation for a function of the form $m(s) = a(s - h)^2 + k$.

$$m(s) = a\left(s - \right)^2 + $$

B The next step is to find the value of a. Does your parabola open up or down? What does this fact tell you about the value of a?

_____

C Choose a point on your parabola other than the vertex. For your chosen point, what is the value of s? What is the value of $m(s)$?

_____

_____

D Substituting the values of s and $m(s)$ from Step C into the equation from Step A results in an equation containing only the unknown a. Solve the equation to find a.

$$a = \underline{}$$

E Write the equation of the function that models the data.

$$m(s) = \left(s - \right)^2 + $$

REFLECT

2a. Use your model to complete the third column of the table. Compare the predicted gas mileages to the actual ones.

_____

_____

_____

Speed	Actual gas mileage	Predicted gas mileage
40	23.0	
50	27.3	
55	29.1	
60	28.2	
70	22.9	

2b. In Step 2C, suppose you chose a different point on your parabola. How would that have affected the equation for your model?

_____

_____

_____

3 Make a prediction.

A Using only the given data and not your model, predict what the gas mileage for the car is when it travels at a speed of 35 miles per hour. Explain your reasoning.

_____

_____

_____

B Using the equation of your model from Step 2E, predict what the gas mileage for the car is when it travels at a speed of 35 miles per hour.

_____

_____

REFLECT

3a. At a speed of 35 miles per hour, the car's actual gas mileage is 21.2 miles per gallon. Compare this value with your two predictions.

_____

EXTEND

1. Identify the *s*-intercepts of your model. Interpret them in the context of the problem. Would you expect the actual data to support this interpretation? Explain.

_____

_____

_____

_____

2. Suppose that when the car was driven at a steady speed, its gas mileage was 25 miles per gallon. Describe how you can use your model to find the car's speed. Is only one speed or more than one speed possible? Explain, and then find the speed(s).

_____

_____

_____

3. A student found that the gas mileage data for a different car from the same year can be modeled by the function $m(s) = -0.007(s - 40)^2 + 25.5$ where s is the car's speed. Compare this model with the one that you found in Step 2E.

_____

_____

Name _____ Class _____ Date _____

MULTIPLE CHOICE

1. Which is the parent quadratic function?

A. $f(x) = x^2$ **C.** $f(x) = (x - h)^2 + k$

B. $f(x) = ax^2$ **D.** $f(x) = a(x - h)^2 + k$

2. The graph of which function is stretched vertically and reflected in the x-axis as compared to the parent quadratic function?

F. $g(x) = 2x^2$ **H.** $g(x) = 0.4x^2$

G. $g(x) = -2x^2$ **J.** $g(x) = -0.4x^2$

3. The graph of $g(x) = (x - 2)^2 + 3$ can be obtained from the graph of $f(x) = x^2$ using which transformation?

A. Translate -2 units horizontally and 3 units vertically.

B. Translate 3 units horizontally and -2 units vertically.

C. Translate 2 units horizontally and 3 units vertically.

D. Translate 2 units horizontally and -3 units vertically.

4. Which function has a maximum value?

F. $f(x) = -x^2$ **H.** $f(x) = x^2 - 5$

G. $f(x) = (x - 10)^2$ **J.** $f(x) = (x + 100)^2$

5. A parabola has its vertex at $(10, 5)$. One point on the parabola is $(12, 8)$. Which is another point on the parabola?

A. $(8, 12)$ **C.** $(12, -8)$

B. $(-12, 8)$ **D.** $(8, 8)$

6. How many real solutions does the equation $2(x - 1)^2 + 5 = 3$ have?

F. No solution   **H.** Two solutions

G. One solution   **J.** Three solutions

7. What are the solutions of $(x + 9)^2 = 16$?

A. -4 and 4 **C.** -3 and 3

B. 5 and 13 **D.** -13 and -5

8. Nick made the table below while preparing to graph a quadratic function. What is the vertex of the function's graph?

x	f(x)
1	9
2	6
3	5
4	6
5	9

F. $(0, 0)$ **H.** $(3, 5)$

G. $(1, 9)$ **J.** $(5, 9)$

9. The graph of $f(x) = 9x^2 + 3$ has what vertex?

A. $(9, 3)$ **C.** $(0, 3)$

B. $(3, 0)$ **D.** $(9, -3)$

10. The graph of which function is shown?

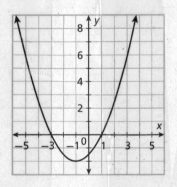

F. $f(x) = \frac{1}{2}(x - 1)^2 - 2$

G. $f(x) = \frac{1}{2}(x + 1)^2 - 2$

H. $f(x) = 2(x - 1)^2 + 2$

J. $f(x) = 2(x + 1)^2 - 2$

11. a. Graph $g(x) = -2x^2 + 3$.

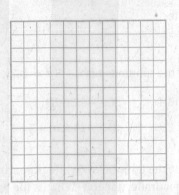

b. Describe the transformations that you would have to perform on the graph of $f(x) = x^2$ to obtain the graph of $g(x)$.

_____

_____

_____

c. If the graph of $g(x)$ is translated 1 unit to the right to obtain the graph of $h(x)$, what is the equation for $h(x)$?

_____

_____

12. a. Find the approximate solutions of $(x + 1)^2 + 2 = 7$ by graphing $f(x) = (x + 1)^2 + 2$ and $g(x) = 7$.

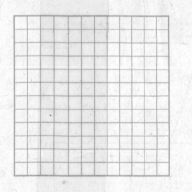

_____

b. Find the exact solutions of $(x + 1)^2 + 2 = 7$ by using square roots.

_____

13. Nicole is bouncing on a trampoline. Her height h (in feet), measured from the surface of the trampoline to the soles of her feet, is given by $h(t) = -16(t - 0.5)^2 + 4$ where t is the time (in seconds) since a bounce began.

a. On the coordinate grid below, add the axis labels and draw the graph of $h(t)$.

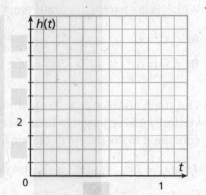

b. Explain the relevance of the statement $h(1) = 0$ in the context of the situation.

_____

c. What is the maximum height of the bounce? At what time does it occur?

_____

d. Suppose you want to know the time(s) at which Nicole was 3 feet above the trampoline during the bounce. Describe how you can obtain this information from the graph and by using algebra. Then find the time(s).

_____

_____

_____

_____

_____

_____

Quadratic Functions of the Form $f(x) = ax^2 + bx + c$

Unit Focus

Quadratic functions are examined further in this unit. You will explore several ways to solve quadratic equations of the form $ax^2 + bx + c = 0$. You will graph quadratic functions of the form $f(x) = ax^2 + bx + c$ and use them to model real-world situations.

Unit at a Glance

COMMON CORE

Lesson		Standards for Mathematical Content
8-1	Multiplying Binomials	CC.9-12.A.SSE.2, CC.9-12.A.APR.1
8-2	Solving $x^2 + bx + c = 0$ by Factoring	CC.9-12.A.SSE.3, CC.9-12.A.SSE.3a, CC.9-12.A.REI.4, CC.9-12.A.REI.4b, CC.9-12.F.IF.8, CC.9-12.F.IF.8a
8-3	Solving $ax^2 + bx + c = 0$ by Factoring	CC.9-12.A.SSE.3a, CC.9-12.A.CED.1*, CC.9-12.A.REI.4, CC.9-12.A.REI.4b, CC.9-12.F.IF.8a, CC.9-12.F.BF.1a*
8-4	Solving $x^2 + bx + c = 0$ by Completing the Square	CC.9-12.A.REI.4, CC.9-12.A.REI.4a, CC.9-12.A.REI.4b
8-5	Solving $ax^2 + bx + c = 0$ by Completing the Square	CC.9-12.A.REI.4, CC.9-12.A.REI.4a, CC.9-12. A.REI.4b
8-6	Deriving the Quadratic Formula	CC.9-12.A.REI.4, CC.9-12.A.REI.4a, CC.9-12.A.REI.4b
8-7	Using the Quadratic Formula	CC.9-12.A.CED.1*, CC.9-12.A.REI.4, CC.9-12.A.REI.4b
8-8	Graphing Functions of the Form $f(x) = ax^2 + bx + c$	CC.9-12.F.IF.4*, CC.9-12.F.IF.5*, CC.9-12.F.IF.7a*, CC.9-12.F.IF.8a, CC.9-12.F.BF.1*
8-9	Solving Systems of Linear and Quadratic Equations	CC.9-12.A.CED.2*, CC.9-12.A.REI.4, CC.9-12.A.REI.4b, CC.9-12.A.REI.7, CC.9-12.F.IF.4*
8-10	Modeling with Quadratic Functions	CC.9-12.A.SSE.3a, CC.9-12.A.REI.4a, CC.9-12.A.REI.4b, CC.9-12.F.IF.4*, CC.9-12.F.IF.6*, CC.9-12.F.IF.8a

Test Prep

Unpacking the Common Core State Standards

Use the table to help you understand the Standards for Mathematical Content that are taught in this unit. Refer to the lessons listed after each standard for exploration and practice.

COMMON CORE Standards for Mathematical Content	What It Means For You
CC.9-12.A.SSE.2 **Use the structure of an expression to identify ways to rewrite it.** Lesson 8-1	When working with quadratic expressions in different forms, you will need to recognize how the forms are related in order to transform expressions from one form to another.
CC.9-12.A.SSE.3 **Choose and produce an equivalent form of an expression to reveal and explain properties of the quantity represented by the expression.** **CC.9-12.A.SSE.3a** **Factor a quadratic expression to reveal the zeros of the function it defines.** Lessons 8-2, 8-3, 8-10	You will learn to find the zeros of the quadratic function $f(x) = ax^2 + bx + c$ by factoring the quadratic expression and setting each factor equal to 0.
CC.9-12.A.APR.1 **Understand that polynomials form a system analogous to the integers, namely, they are closed under the operations of addition, subtraction, and multiplication; add, subtract, and multiply polynomials.** Lesson 8-1	You will learn to multiply binomials using the distributive property and FOIL. You will use this knowledge to help you factor polynomials.
CC.9-12.A.CED.1 **Create equations and inequalities in one variable and use them to solve problems.*** Lessons 8-3, 8-7	You will learn how to create quadratic functions for projectile motion problems. You will then set a function equal to 0 and solve the resulting quadratic equation to determine when a projectile hits ground or water.
CC.9-12.A.CED.2 **Create equations in two or more variables to represent relationships between quantities; graph equations on coordinate axes with labels and scales.*** Lessons 8-9, 8-10	You will graph quadratic functions of the form $f(x) = ax^2 + bx + c$ by rewriting them in vertex form $f(x) = a(x - h)^2 + k$ and graphing them using the vertex and symmetry.

COMMON CORE Standards for Mathematical Content	What It Means For You
CC.9-12.A.REI.4 Solve quadratic equations in one variable. **CC.9-12.A.REI.4a** Use the method of completing the square to transform any quadratic equation in x into an equation of the form $(x - p)^2 = q$ that has the same solutions. Derive the quadratic formula from this form. **CC.9-12.A.REI.4b** Solve quadratic equations by inspection (e.g., for $x^2 = 49$), taking square roots, completing the square, the quadratic formula and factoring, as appropriate to the initial form of the equation. Recognize when the quadratic formula gives complex solutions and write them as $a \pm bi$ for real numbers a and b. Lessons 8-2, 8-3, 8-4, 8-5, 8-6, 8-7, 8-9, 8-10	You will solve quadratic equations of the form $ax^2 + bx + c = 0$ several different ways including factoring, completing the square, and using the quadratic formula. Although some methods of solving quadratic equations have limitations, you can use the quadratic formula to solve any quadratic equation. As you will see, the derivation of the quadratic formula depends on the method of completing the square.
CC.9-12.A.REI.7 Solve a simple system consisting of a linear equation and a quadratic equation in two variables algebraically and graphically. Lesson 8-9	You will solve systems of linear and quadratic equations algebraically by setting a linear expression equal to a quadratic expression and solving for x. You will also solve the systems graphically, both by hand and by using technology.
CC.9-12.F.IF.2 Use function notation, evaluate functions for inputs in their domains, and interpret statements that use function notation in terms of a context. Lesson 8-10	You will evaluate and interpret functions that model projectile motion.
CC.9-12.F.IF.4 For a function that models a relationship between two quantities, interpret key features of graphs and tables in terms of the quantities, and sketch graphs showing key features given a verbal description of the relationship.* Lessons 8-8, 8-9, 8-10	For a quadratic function that models projectile motion, you will determine the vertex of the function's graph, which gives the projectile's maximum height, as well as the graph's intercepts, which give the projectile's initial height and time in the air.
CC.9-12.F.IF.5 Relate the domain of a function to its graph and, where applicable, to the quantitative relationship it describes.* Lessons 8-8 (Also 8-10)	You will analyze quadratic functions that model real-world situations and interpret their graphs including understanding which portion of the graph makes sense in the given situation.
CC.9-12.F.IF.6 Calculate and interpret the average rate of change of a function (presented symbolically or as a table) over a specified interval. Estimate the rate of change from a graph.* Lesson 8-10	You will calculate the average velocity for a projectile and analyze how the projectile's average velocity changes.

UNIT 8

© Houghton Mifflin Harcourt Publishing Company

COMMON CORE Standards for Mathematical Content	What It Means For You
CC.9-12.F.IF.7 Graph functions expressed symbolically and show key features of the graph, by hand in simple cases and using technology for more complicated cases.* **CC.9-12.F.IF.7a Graph** linear and **quadratic functions and show intercepts, maxima, and minima.*** Lesson 8-8 (Also 8-10)	You will graph quadratic functions of the form $f(x) = ax^2 + bx + c$ and relate that form to the intercept form and the vertex form of a quadratic function.
CC.9-12.F.IF.8 Write a function defined by an expression in different but equivalent forms to reveal and explain different properties of the function. **CC.9-12.F.IF.8a Use the process of factoring and completing the square in a quadratic function to show zeros, extreme values, and symmetry of the graph, and interpret these in terms of a context.** Lessons 8-2, 8-3, 8-8, 8-10	You will graph quadratic functions of the form $f(x) = ax^2 + bx + c = 0$ by factoring them to find intercepts and by completing the square to find the vertex.
CC.9-12.F.IF.9 Compare properties of two functions each represented in a different way (algebraically, graphically, numerically in tables, or by verbal descriptions). Lesson 8-10	You will compare two quadratic functions modeling projectile motion to see which projectile goes higher and stays in the air longer.
CC.9-12.F.BF.1 Write a function that describes a relationship between two quantities.* **CC.9-12.F.BF.1a Determine an explicit expression**, a recursive process, or steps for calculation **from a context.*** Lessons 8-3, 8-8, 8-10	You will write a model for the height of a projectile using the quadratic function $h(t) = -16t^2 + vt + h_0$ for situations where you know the projectile's initial vertical velocity v and initial height h_0.

UNIT 8

Multiplying Binomials

8-1

COMMON
CORE

CC.9-12.A.SSE.2,
CC.9-12.A.APR.1

Essential question: *How can you use the distributive property to multiply binomials?*

A **monomial** is a number, a variable, or the product of a number and one or more variables raised to whole number powers, such as 5, x, $-8y$, and $3x^2y^4$. A **polynomial** is a monomial or a sum of monomials. Each monomial in the expression is called a **term**. A polynomial with two terms is a **binomial**. You can multiply two binomials by using algebra tiles.

1 EXPLORE Multiplying Two Binomials Using Algebra Tiles

To use algebra tiles to multiply $(2x + 1)(x + 3)$, first represent $2x + 1$ vertically along the left side of an algebra tile diagram and $x + 3$ horizontally along the top. Then use x^2-tiles, x-tiles, and 1-tiles to complete the diagram, as shown below.

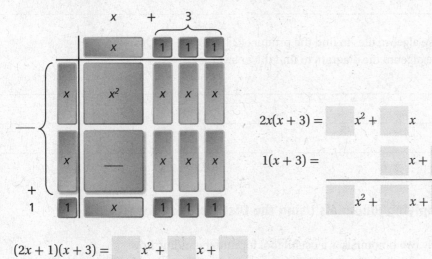

$$2x(x + 3) = \boxed{}\, x^2 + \boxed{}\, x$$

$$1(x + 3) = \boxed{} \quad x + \boxed{}$$

$$\overline{\qquad x^2 + \qquad x + \qquad}$$

$$(2x + 1)(x + 3) = \boxed{}\, x^2 + \boxed{}\, x + \boxed{}$$

The product is a **trinomial**, a polynomial with three terms.

REFLECT

1a. Look at the algebra tile diagram. What two terms in the original binomials combine to form the x^2-term in the trinomial? How do they combine (by multiplying, by adding, or by subtracting)?

_____

1b. Look at the algebra tile diagram. What two terms in the original binomials combine to form the constant term in the trinomial? How do they combine (by multiplying, by adding, or by subtracting)?

_____

1c. Look at the algebra tile diagram. Show how the terms of the original binomials combine to form the x-term in the trinomial.

_____

1d. You can verify that the expressions are equivalent by substituting a value for x into both expressions and simplifying to show that they are equal. Verify that the expressions are equivalent. Use $x = 4$.

_____

_____

_____

1e. Suppose you want to use algebra tiles to find the product $(2x + 1)(x + 2)$. Describe how you can modify the algebra tile diagram to find the product.

_____

_____

1f. Suppose you want to use algebra tiles to find the product $(2x + 2)(x + 3)$. Describe how you can modify the algebra tile diagram to find the answer.

_____

_____

_____

2 ENGAGE Multiplying Binomials Using the Distributive Property

Using algebra tiles to multiply two binomials is a useful tool for understanding how the two binomials are being multiplied. However, it is not a very practical method for everyday use. Using the distributive property is.

To multiply $(2x + 1)(x + 3)$ using the distributive property, you distribute the binomial $x + 3$ to each term of $2x + 1$. Then you distribute the monomial $2x$ to each term of $x + 3$ as well as the monomial 1 to each term of $x + 3$.

$$(2x + 1)(x + 3) = 2x(x + 3) + 1(x + 3)$$
$$= 2x^2 + 6x + x + 3$$
$$= 2x^2 + 7x + 3$$

Notice that the product found using algebra tiles in the Explore is the same as the product found here using the distributive property. Thus, the two methods are equivalent.

To multiply $(4x - 7)(3x + 6)$ using the distributive property, you should think of $4x - 7$ as $4x + (-7)$ and therefore keep the negative sign with the 7.

$$(4x - 7)(3x + 6) = 4x(3x + 6) - 7(3x + 6)$$
$$= 12x^2 + 24x - 21x - 42$$
$$= 12x^2 + 3x - 42$$

This method of using the distributive property to multiply two binomials is referred to as the FOIL method. The letters of the word FOIL stand for **First**, **Outer**, **Inner**, and **Last** and will help you remember how to use the distributive property to multiply binomials.

You apply the FOIL method by multiplying each of the four pairs of terms described below and then simplifying the resulting polynomial.

- **First** refers to the first terms of each binomial.
- **Outer** refers to the two terms on the outside of the expression.
- **Inner** refers to the two terms on the inside of the expression.
- **Last** refers to the last terms of each binomial.

Now multiply $(7x - 1)(3x - 5)$ using FOIL. Again, think of $7x - 1$ as $7x + (-1)$ and $3x - 5$ as $3x + (-5)$. This results in a positive constant term of 5 because $(-1)(-5) = 5$.

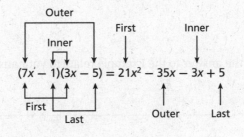

$$(7x - 1)(3x - 5) = 21x^2 - 38x + 5$$

Notice that the trinomials are written with variable terms in descending order of exponents and with the constant term last. This is a standard form for writing polynomials: Starting with the variable term with the greatest exponent, write the other variable terms in descending order of their exponents, and put the constant term last.

REFLECT

2a. Refer back to the Explore. Using the tiles, you multiplied $2x$ by $\left(x + \boxed{}\right)$ and then multiplied 1 by $\left(x + \boxed{}\right)$. You are using the _____ property.

2b. In FOIL, which of the products combine to form the x-term?

_____

2c. In FOIL, which of the products combine to form the constant term?

_____

2d. In FOIL, which of the products combine to form the x^2-term?

_____

2e. Two binomials are multiplied to form a trinomial. When is the constant term of the trinomial positive? When is it negative?

_____

_____

© Houghton Mifflin Harcourt Publishing Company

Multiply $(12x - 5)(3x + 6)$ using the FOIL method.

First   Inner

$$(12x - 5)(3x + 6) = \boxed{}\, x^2 + \boxed{}\, x - \boxed{}\, x - \boxed{}$$

Outer   Last

$(12x - 5)(3x + 6) = $ _____

REFLECT

3a. How does the final x-term in the answer to the Example relate to your answer to Question 2b? Explain.

_____

_____

3b. How does the final constant in the answer to the Example relate to your answer to Question 2c? Explain.

_____

3c. How does the final x^2-term in the answer to the Example relate to your answer to Question 2d? Explain.

_____

3d. Suppose the problem in the example were $(12x - 5)(3x + 2)$. Would the x^2-term in the product change? Would the x-term change? Would the constant term change? Explain your reasoning.

_____

_____

_____

_____

_____

3e. Multiply $(12x - 5)(3x + 2)$.

_____

The special products $(ax + b)^2$, $(ax - b)^2$, and $(ax + b)(ax - b)$ can all be found using the FOIL method. The products $(ax + b)^2$ and $(ax - b)^2$ are called *squares of binomials* and the product $(ax + b)(ax - b)$ is called the *sum and difference product*.

4 **EXAMPLE**   **Multiplying Special Cases**

A   Multiply $(2x + 5)^2$ using FOIL.

$$(2x + 5)^2 = (2x + 5)(2x + 5) = \underline{\hspace{5cm}}$$

$$= \underline{\hspace{5cm}}$$

B   Multiply $(2x - 5)^2$ using FOIL.

$$(2x - 5)^2 = (2x - 5)(2x - 5) = \underline{\hspace{5cm}}$$

$$= \underline{\hspace{5cm}}$$

C   Multiply $(2x - 5)(2x + 5)$ using FOIL.

$$(2x - 5)(2x + 5) = \underline{\hspace{5cm}}$$

$$= \underline{\hspace{5cm}}$$

REFLECT

4a.   In the final answer of Part A, which two terms of the trinomial are perfect squares? How can you use the coefficients 2 and 5 to produce the coefficient of x in the product? Generalize these results to write a rule for the product $(ax + b)^2$ in terms of a, b, and x.

_____

4b.   In the final answer of Part B, which two terms of the trinomial are perfect squares? How can you use the coefficients 2 and 5 to produce the coefficient of x in the product? Generalize these results to write a rule for the product $(ax - b)^2$ in terms of a, b, and x.

_____

4c.   In the final answer of Part C, which two terms of the trinomial are perfect squares? What is the coefficient of the x-term and how was it created? Generalize these results to write a rule for the product $(ax - b)(ax + b)$ in terms of a, b, and x.

_____

_____

4d.   In Part C, suppose the product had been $(2x + 5)(2x - 5)$. Would the answer have been different? Explain.

_____

Classify the expression as a monomial, binomial, trinomial, or polynomial. Use the most descriptive term.

1. $3x^2$ _____

2. $3x^2 - 4$ _____

3. $18x^3 + 5x^2 - 2x + 29$ _____

4. $x - 12$ _____

5. $4x + x^2 + 1$ _____

6. $y^2 + 17$ _____

Find each product.

7. $(x + 2)(x + 3)$

_____

8. $(x + 7)(x + 11)$

_____

9. $(x + 4)^2$

_____

10. $(x - 1)(x + 1)$

_____

11. $(2x + 13)(x - 6)$

_____

12. $(2x - 5)(3x + 1)$

_____

13. $(3x - 8)^2$

_____

14. $(9x - 7)(9x + 7)$

_____

15. The *vertex form* of a quadratic function is $f(x) = a(x - h)^2 + k$. Use your knowledge about multiplying binomials to complete the following.

$f(x) = a(x - h)\left(\boxed{} - \boxed{}\right) + k$ Write as a product of two binomials.

$= a\left(x^2 - \boxed{}\, x + \boxed{}^2\right) + k$ Multiply the binomials.

$= ax^2 - \boxed{}\, x + \boxed{} + k$ Distribute the constant a.

Compare this rewritten form to the standard form of a quadratic function, $f(x) = ax^2 + bx + c$. Discuss how b and c relate to the rewritten function. How can you rewrite a quadratic function in vertex form so that it is in standard form?

_____

_____

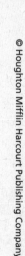

Solving $x^2 + bx + c = 0$ by Factoring

COMMON CORE

CC.9-12.A.SSE.3,
CC.9-12.A.SSE.3a,
CC.9-12.A.REI.4,
CC.9-12.A.REI.4b,
CC.9-12.F.IF.8,
CC.9-12.F.IF.8a

Essential question: *How can you use factoring to solve quadratic equations in standard form when a = 1?*

1 ENGAGE   Factoring Trinomials

You know how to multiply binomials: for example, $(x + 7)^2 = x^2 + 14x + 49$. In this lesson, you will learn how to reverse this process and factor trinomials.

There are several important things you should remember from multiplying binomials.

- Using FOIL, the constant term in the trinomial is a result of multiplying the *last* terms in the two binomials.

- Using FOIL, the *x*-term results from adding the products of the *outside* terms and *inside* terms.

You can factor $x^2 + 10x + 25$ by working FOIL backward. Both signs in the trinomial are plus signs, so you know both binomials are of the form *x plus something*. Therefore, you can set up the factoring as shown below.

$$x^2 + 10x + 25 = (x + \boxed{?})(x + \boxed{?})$$

To find the constant terms in the binomials, use the information above and follow the steps below.

1) The constant term in the trinomial, 25, is the product of the last terms in the two binomials. Factor 25 into pairs. The factor pairs are shown in the table at the right.

Factors of 25	Sum of Factors
1 and 25	26
5 and 5	10 ✓

2) The correct factor pair is the one whose sum is the coefficient of *x* in the trinomial.

3) Complete the binomial expression with the appropriate numbers.

$$x^2 + 10x + 25 = \left(x + \right)\left(x + \right)$$

You should recognize this as one of the special cases presented in Lesson 8-1. It is $(x + 5)^2$. When factoring trinomials, it is convenient to keep the special cases in mind. They are listed below for reference.

$$a^2 + 2ab + b^2 = (a + b)^2 \quad \text{Perfect square trinomial pattern}$$

$$a^2 - 2ab + b^2 = (a - b)^2 \quad \text{Perfect square trinomial pattern}$$

$$a^2 - b^2 = (a + b)(a - b) \quad \text{Difference of squares pattern}$$

Not all trinomials that you need to factor will be one of the special cases. The three-step procedure outlined above works for all factoring problems, not just the special cases.

1a. You want to factor $x^2 - 6x + 8$. What factoring pattern would you set up to begin the process? Explain.

_____

_____

1b. You want to factor $x^2 - 2x - 15$. What factoring pattern would you set up to begin the process? Explain. Would this pattern also work for $x^2 + 2x - 15$? Explain.

_____

_____

_____

_____

2 EXAMPLE Factoring Trinomials

A Factor $x^2 + 3x - 10$.

The constant is negative, so you know one binomial will have a subtraction sign.

$$x^2 + 3x - 10 = (x + \boxed{?})(x - \boxed{?})$$

Complete the table at the right. Note that you are finding the factors of -10, not 10. Since the coefficient of x is positive, the factor with the greater absolute value will be positive (and the other factor will be negative).

Factors of -10	Sum of Factors
-1 and 10	

$$x^2 + 3x - 10 = \left(x + \right)\left(x - \right)$$

B Factor $x^2 - 8x - 48$.

The constant is negative, so you know one binomial will have a subtraction sign.

$$x^2 - 8x - 48 = (x + \boxed{?})(x - \boxed{?})$$

Complete the table at the right. Since the coefficient of x is negative, the factor with the greater absolute value will be negative (and the other factor will be positive).

Factors of -48	Sum of Factors
1 and -48	
2 and	

$$x^2 - 8x - 48 = \left(x + \right)\left(x - \right)$$

REFLECT

2a. Complete the table below. Assume that b, c, p, and q are positive numbers.

Trinomial	Form of Binomial Factors
$x^2 + bx + c$	$\left(x \quad p\right)\left(x \quad q\right)$
$x^2 - bx + c$	$\left(x \quad p\right)\left(x \quad q\right)$
$x^2 - bx - c$ or $x^2 + bx - c$	$\left(x \quad p\right)\left(x \quad q\right)$

For the last row in the table, explain how to determine which factor contains a + sign and which factor contains a − sign.

_____

_____

_____

3 ENGAGE — Understanding the Zero-Product Property and Recognizing Zeros of Quadratic Functions

You already know how to solve simple quadratic equations. For example, you can solve the equation $x^2 = 36$ by using the definition of _____. The solutions of the equation are $x =$ _____ and $x =$ _____.

Another method for solving $x^2 = 36$ involves factoring. Start by subtracting 36 from both sides, resulting in $x^2 - 36 = 0$. This makes the left side of the equation a difference of two squares that can be factored as $\left(x + \quad\right)\left(x - \quad\right)$.

The **zero-product property** states that the product of any group of numbers is 0 if at least one of the numbers is 0 because 0 times any number is 0. Applying the zero-product property to $(x + 6)(x - 6) = 0$ gives the following:

$$x + \boxed{} = 0 \qquad \text{or} \qquad x - \boxed{} = 0$$

$$x = \underline{\quad} \qquad \text{or} \qquad x = \underline{\quad}$$

The solutions of the equation $x^2 - 36 = 0$ are called the **zeros** of the related function $f(x) = x^2 - 36$ because they satisfy the equation $f(x) = 0$. To see this, you can substitute 6 and −6 for x in $f(x) = x^2 - 36$. The result is $f(6) = 0$ and $f(-6) = 0$.

REFLECT

3a. Describe how to use the zero-product property to solve the equation $(x + 4)(x - 12) = 0$. Then identify the solutions.

_____

_____

3b. How can you use your answer to Question 3a to identify the zeros of the function $f(x) = x^2 - 8x - 48$?

_____

_____

You can use the zero-product property to solve any quadratic equation written in standard form, $ax^2 + bx + c = 0$, provided the quadratic expression is factorable. You can also use the zero-product property to find the zeros of any quadratic function $f(x) = ax^2 + bx + c$ whose rule is factorable once you set $f(x)$ equal to 0.

4 EXAMPLE Solving a Quadratic Equation

Find the solutions of $x^2 + 13x = -36$.

A Write the equation in standard form. $\qquad x^2 + 13x \;\boxed{}\; 36 = 0$

B Factor the trinomial. The constant term is positive so its factors are either both positive or both negative. The coefficient of x is positive, so both factors of the

constant term must be _____. The binomial factors will be of the

form $\left(x \;\boxed{}\; p\right)\left(x \;\boxed{}\; q\right)$.

Factors of 36	Sum of Factors
1 and 36	

The factored trinomial is $\left(x + \boxed{}\right)\left(x + \boxed{}\right)$, so the equation

becomes $\left(x + \boxed{}\right)\left(x + \boxed{}\right) = 0$.

C Use the zero-product property.

$$x + \boxed{} = 0 \qquad \text{or} \qquad x + \boxed{} = 0$$

$$x = \underline{\qquad} \qquad \text{or} \qquad x = \underline{\qquad}$$

REFLECT

4a. Suppose the equation was $x^2 - 13x = -36$. Describe how solving the equation would be different than what is shown in the Example. Find the solutions of the equation.

_____

_____

_____

4b. Can the zero-product property be used to solve any quadratic equation? If so, explain why. If not, give an example of an equation that cannot be solved.

_____

_____

5 EXAMPLE — Finding the Zeros of a Quadratic Function

Find the zeros of $f(x) = x^2 - 4x - 12$.

A Set the function equal to 0 and recognize the factoring pattern.

$$x^2 - 4x - 12 = \boxed{}$$

$$\left(x \boxed{} p\right)\left(x \boxed{} q\right) = \boxed{}$$

Explain your choice of factoring pattern.

_____

_____

B Find the factors of -12 that have a sum of -4. Then write the equation in factored form.

Factors of -12	Sum of Factors
1 and -12	

So, the factored form of the equation is $\left(x + \boxed{}\right)\left(x - \boxed{}\right) = 0$.

C Use the zero-product property to solve the equation and identify the zeros.

$$x + \boxed{} = 0 \qquad \text{or} \qquad x - \boxed{} = 0$$

$$x = \underline{} \qquad \text{or} \qquad x = \underline{}$$

So, the zeros of $f(x) = x^2 - 4x - 12$ are _____ and _____.

REFLECT

5a. Show that each zero satisfies $f(x) = 0$.

_____

5b. If you were to graph the function $f(x) = x^2 - 4x - 12$, what points would be associated with the zeros of the function? What is special about these points and their x-coordinates?

_____

_____

PRACTICE

Complete the factorization of the polynomial.

1. $t^2 + 6t + 5 = (t + 5)\left(t + \boxed{}\right)$

2. $z^2 - 121 = (z + 11)\left(z \boxed{} \boxed{}\right)$

3. $d^2 + 5d - 24 = \left(d + \boxed{}\right)\left(d - \boxed{}\right)$

4. $x^4 - 4 = \left(x^2 + \boxed{}\right)\left(\boxed{} - 2\right)$

Factor the polynomial.

5. $y^2 + 3y - 4$

6. $x^2 - 2x + 1$

7. $p^2 - 2p - 24$

8. $g^2 - 100$

9. $z^2 - 7z + 12$

10. $q^2 + 25q + 100$

Solve.

11. $m^2 + 8m + 16 = 0$

12. $n^2 - 10n = 24$

13. $x^2 + 25x = 0$

14. $y^2 - 30 = 13y$

15. $z^2 - 9 = 0$

16. $p^2 = 54 - 3p$

17. $x^2 + 11x - 42 = 0$

18. $g^2 - 14g = 51$

19. $n^2 - 81 = 0$

20. $y^2 = 25y$

Find the zeros of the function.

21. $f(x) = x^2 + 11x + 30$

22. $f(x) = x^2 - x - 20$

23. $f(x) = x^2 + 6x - 7$

24. $f(x) = x^2 + 2x + 1$

Solving $ax^2 + bx + c = 0$ by Factoring

COMMON
CORE

CC.9-12.A.SSE.3a,
CC.9-12.A.CED.1*,
CC.9-12.A.REI.4,
CC.9-12.A.REI.4b,
CC.9-12.F.IF.8a,
CC.9-12.F.BF.1*

Essential question: *How can you use factoring to solve $ax^2 + bx + c = 0$ when $a \neq 1$?*

You have learned how to factor $ax^2 + bx + c$ when $a = 1$ by identifying the correct pair of factors of c whose sum is b. But what if the coefficient of x^2 is not 1?

First, review binomial multiplication. The product $(2x + 5)(3x + 2)$ is found by using FOIL.

$$(2x + 5)(3x + 2) = 6x^2 + 4x + 15x + 10 = 6x^2 + 19x + 10$$
$$\quad\quad\quad\quad\quad \textbf{F} \quad\ \ \textbf{O} \quad\ \ \textbf{I} \quad\ \ \textbf{L}$$

F The product of the coefficients of the **first** terms is a.

$\left.\begin{array}{c}\textbf{O}\\\textbf{I}\end{array}\right\}$ The sum of the coefficients of the **outer** and **inner** products is b.

L The product of the **last** terms is c.

To factor $ax^2 + bx + c$, you need to reverse this process. Start by listing the possible factor pairs of a and c. Then use trial and error to find a sum of b for the outer and inner products.

1 EXAMPLE Factoring $ax^2 + bx + c$

Factor $5n^2 + 11n + 2$.

A First list the possible factor pairs for both a and c. All of the signs of the terms are positive, so the factors of a and c must all be positive.

The only factor pair for a is _____, _____. The only factor pair for c is _____, _____.

B Choose the arrangement of the factor pairs that makes $b = 11$. Check your result by multiplying.

$$5n^2 + 11n + 2 = \left(\ \boxed{\ }\ n + \boxed{\ }\ \right)\left(\ \boxed{\ }\ n + \boxed{\ }\ \right)$$

REFLECT

1a. What other arrangement of factor pairs is possible for a and c? What is the resulting product, and how is it different from $5n^2 + 11n + 2$?

_____

1b. If a is positive, b is negative, and c is positive, what are the signs of the factors of a and c that you are looking for?

1c. If a is positive, b is negative, and c is negative, what are the signs of the factors of a and c that you are looking for?

_____

If a and c have a lot of factors, there are many possible arrangements. One way to quickly check each arrangement is shown below, using the trinomial $5n^2 + 11n + 2$. List the factor pairs of a and c vertically, then multiply diagonally, and add.

Factors of a	Factors of c	Inner and Outer products

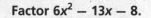

$$1 \diagdown 2 \quad = \quad 10$$
$$5 \diagup 1 \quad = \quad \underline{1}$$
$$11 \leftarrow \text{Sum}$$

If the sum is correct, the factors are read across: $(1n + 2)$ and $(5n + 1)$.

2 EXAMPLE Factoring $ax^2 + bx + c$

Factor $6x^2 - 13x - 8$.

A First list the possible factor pairs for both a and c. Because c is negative, one of the factors of c must be positive, and the other must be negative.

The factor pairs for a are: _____, _____ and _____, _____.

The factor pairs for c are: _____, _____; _____, _____; _____, _____; _____, _____.

B Choose the arrangement of factor pairs that makes $b = -13$. Each factor pair of a can be arranged in two ways with each factor pair of c, so there are 16 possible arrangements. Three are shown below.

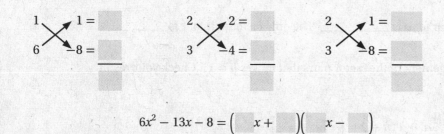

$$6x^2 - 13x - 8 = \left(\,\boxed{}\,x + \boxed{}\,\right)\left(\,\boxed{}\,x - \boxed{}\,\right)$$

REFLECT

2a. If you know the factors of $6x^2 - 13x - 8$, how could you easily factor $6x^2 + 13x - 8$?

_____

2b. What fact about the sign of the sum can you use so that you need to test at most half of the possible arrangements?

_____

To solve a quadratic equation by factoring, first rewrite the equation so one side equals 0, then factor. By the zero-product property, at least one of the factors must equal 0. Set each factor equal to 0 and solve each linear equation separately to find the solutions.

3 EXAMPLE Solving $ax^2 + bx + c = 0$ by Factoring

Solve $7x^2 + 20x = x + 6$ by factoring.

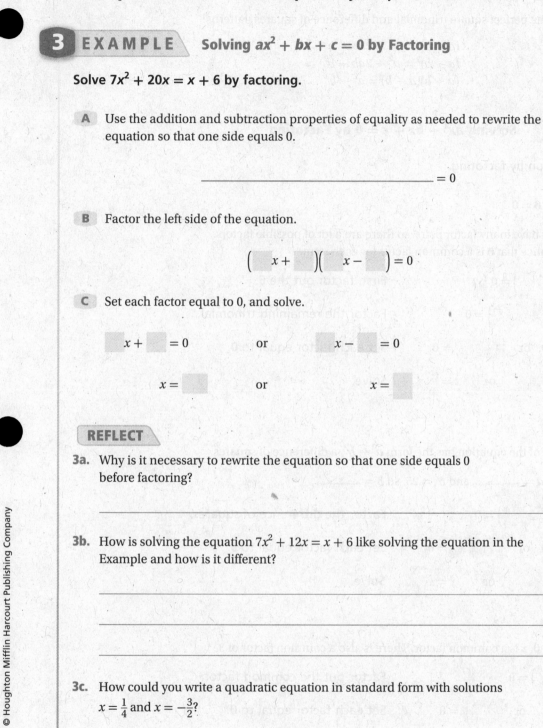

A Use the addition and subtraction properties of equality as needed to rewrite the equation so that one side equals 0.

$$\underline{\hspace{5cm}} = 0$$

B Factor the left side of the equation.

$$\left(\boxed{} \; x + \boxed{} \right)\left(\boxed{} \; x - \boxed{} \right) = 0$$

C Set each factor equal to 0, and solve.

$$\boxed{}\, x + \boxed{} = 0 \qquad \text{or} \qquad \boxed{}\, x - \boxed{} = 0$$

$$x = \boxed{} \qquad \text{or} \qquad x = \boxed{}$$

REFLECT

3a. Why is it necessary to rewrite the equation so that one side equals 0 before factoring?

_____

3b. How is solving the equation $7x^2 + 12x = x + 6$ like solving the equation in the Example and how is it different?

_____

_____

_____

3c. How could you write a quadratic equation in standard form with solutions $x = \frac{1}{4}$ and $x = -\frac{3}{2}$?

_____

_____

_____

Special Cases The following example includes some special cases to consider.

1. Always look for a common factor before you begin. If $c = 0$, then x is a common factor of $ax^2 + bx$.

2. Consider the perfect square trinomial and difference of squares patterns:

$$(a + b)^2 = a^2 + 2ab + b^2$$
$$(a - b)^2 = a^2 - 2ab + b^2$$
$$(a + b)(a - b) = a^2 - b^2$$

4 EXAMPLE Solving $ax^2 + bx + c = 0$ by Factoring

Solve the equation by factoring.

A $12x^2 + 6x - 6 = 0$

Both a and c have many factor pairs, so there are a lot of possible factors. However, notice that 6 is a common factor for each term.

$6\left(\right) = 0$	First, factor out the 6.
$6\left(\right)\left(\right) = 0$	Factor the remaining trinomial.
$ = 0$ or $ = 0$	Set each factor equal to 0.
$x = $ or $x = $	Solve.

B $4x^2 - 25 = 0$

The left side of the equation has the form $a^2 - b^2$, a difference of squares.

$a^2 = 4x^2$, so $a = \underline{}$, and $b^2 = 25$, so $b = \underline{}$.

$\left(\right)\left(\right) = 0$	Factor the difference of squares.
$ = 0$ or $ = 0$	Set each factor equal to 0.
$x = $ or $x = $	Solve.

C $3x^2 + 9x = 0$

Because $c = 0$, x is a common factor. There is also a common factor of 3.

$\left(\right) = 0$	Factor out the common factor.
$ = 0$ or $ = 0$	Set each factor equal to 0.
$x = $ or $x = $	Solve.

4a. Why can you ignore the common factor of 6 in Part A once it is factored out?

_____

4b. Why can't you ignore the common factor of $3x$ in part C?

_____

5 EXAMPLE   Modeling the Height of a Diver

Physics students are measuring the heights and times of divers jumping off diving boards. The function that models a diver's height (in meters) above the water is

$$h(t) = -5t^2 + vt + h_0$$

where v is the diver's initial upward velocity in meters per second, h_0 is the diver's height above the water in meters, and t is the time in seconds. A diver who is 3 meters above the water jumps off a diving board with an initial upward velocity of 14 m/s. How many seconds will it take for the diver to hit the water? That is, when does $h(t) = 0$?

A   Write the equation $h(t) = 0$, substituting in known values. $-5t^2 + \boxed{}\, t + \boxed{} = 0$

B   Factor the left side of the equation. $\left(\boxed{}\right)\left(\boxed{}\right) = 0$

C   Set each factor equal to zero and solve. $t = \underline{\hspace{1cm}}$ or $t = \underline{\hspace{1cm}}$

D   Which value of t makes sense in the context of the problem? Why?

_____

5a. Suppose a diver who is 10 meters above the water jumps off a diving board with an initial upward velocity of 5 m/s. How many seconds will it take for the diver to hit the water? Explain your reasoning.

_____

_____

_____

5b. If an object is dropped, its initial velocity is 0. How would this affect the function that models the object's height?

_____

_____

© Houghton Mifflin Harcourt Publishing Company

Factor.

1. $2x^2 + 15x + 7$

_____

2. $7z^2 - 30z + 27$

_____

3. $8x^2 - 10x - 3$

_____

4. $30d^2 + 7d - 15$

_____

Solve by factoring.

5. $10g^2 + 23g + 12 = 0$

_____

6. $5y^2 - 2y - 7 = 0$

_____

7. $2n^2 + 15 = 11n$

_____

8. $6a^2 + 10a = 3a + 10$

_____

9. $12x^2 - x = 20$

_____

10. $9z^2 - 25 = 0$

_____

11. $36h^2 - 12h + 1 = 0$

_____

12. $12n^2 + 48 = 80n$

_____

13. $18x^2 + 24x = -8$

_____

14. $12y^2 + 3y = 54$

_____

15. A dolphin bounces a ball off its nose at an initial upward velocity of 6 m/s to a trainer lying on a 1-meter high platform. The function $h(t) = -5t^2 + vt$ models the ball's height (in meters) above the water, where v is the initial upward velocity of the ball in meters per second.

  a. Write an equation to find the time when $h(t) = 1$.

$$-5t^2 + \boxed{}\, t = \boxed{}$$

  b. Solve the equation to find the two values for t.

  $t = $ _____ or $t = $ _____

  c. Explain the two values for t in the context of the situation.

  _____

  _____

  _____

Solving $x^2 + bx + c = 0$ by Completing the Square

COMMON CORE

CC.9-12.A.REI.4,
CC.9-12.A.REI.4a,
CC.9-12.A.REI.4b

Essential question: *How can you solve $x^2 + bx + c = 0$ without factoring?*

1 EXPLORE   Completing the Square

The diagram below represents the expression $x^2 + 6x + c$ with the constant term missing.

A Complete the diagram by filling the bottom right corner with 1-tiles to form a square.

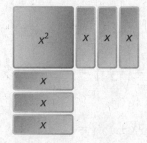

B How many 1-tiles did you add to the expression? _____

C Write the trinomial represented by the algebra tiles for the complete square.

$$\boxed{}\, x^2 + \boxed{}\, x + \boxed{}$$

D You should recognize this trinomial as an example of the special case $(a + b)^2 = a^2 + 2ab + b^2$. Recall that trinomials of this form are called perfect square trinomials. Since the trinomial is a perfect square, you can factor it into two binomials that are the same.

$$\boxed{}\, x^2 + \boxed{}\, x + \boxed{} = \left(\boxed{}\, x + \boxed{}\right)^2$$

REFLECT

1a. Look at the algebra tiles above. The x-tiles are divided equally, with 3 tiles on the right and bottom sides of the x^2-tile. How does the number 3 relate to the total number of x-tiles? How does the number 3 relate to the number of 1-tiles you added?

_____

_____

1b. How would algebra tiles be arranged to form a perfect square trinomial $x^2 + 8x + c$? How many 1-tiles must be added? How is this number related to the number of x-tiles?

_____

_____

Completing the Square Finding the value of c needed to make an expression such as $x^2 + 6x + c$ into a perfect square trinomial is called **completing the square**.

Using algebra tiles, half of the x-tiles are placed along the right and bottom sides of the x^2-tile. The number of 1-tiles added is the square of the number of x-tiles on either side of the x^2-tile.

To complete the square for the expression $x^2 + bx + c$, replace c with $\left(\frac{b}{2}\right)^2$. The perfect square trinomial is $x^2 + bx + \left(\frac{b}{2}\right)^2$ and factors as $\left(x + \frac{b}{2}\right)^2$.

2 EXAMPLE   Completing the Square

Complete the square to form a perfect square trinomial. Then factor the trinomial.

A $x^2 + 12x + c$

Identify b. $b = $ _____

Find c. $c = \left(\frac{b}{2}\right)^2 = \left(\dfrac{\boxed{}}{2}\right)^2 = $ _____

Write the trinomial. $x^2 + \boxed{}\, x + \boxed{}$

Factor the trinomial. $x^2 + \boxed{}\, x + \boxed{} = \left(\boxed{}\right)^2$

B $z^2 - 26z + c$

Identify b. $b = $ _____

Find c. $c = \left(\frac{b}{2}\right)^2 = \left(\dfrac{\boxed{}}{2}\right)^2 = $ _____

Write the trinomial. $z^2 + \boxed{}\, z + \boxed{}$

Factor the trinomial. $z^2 + \boxed{}\, z + \boxed{} = \left(\boxed{}\right)^2$

REFLECT

2a. In Part A, b is positive and in Part B, b is negative. Does this affect the sign of c? Why or why not?

_____

_____

2b. How can you confirm that you have factored each trinomial correctly?

_____

_____

© Houghton Mifflin Harcourt Publishing Company

You have solved quadratic equations by factoring and using the zero-product property. You can also solve quadratic equations by completing the square. This method is especially useful if the quadratic equation is difficult or impossible to factor. To solve a quadratic equation by completing the square, follow these steps:

1. Write the equation in the form $x^2 + bx = c$.

2. Complete the square by adding $\left(\frac{b}{2}\right)^2$ to both sides of the equation.

3. Factor the perfect square trinomial.

4. Apply the definition of a square root.

5. Write two equations, one using the positive square root and one using the negative square root.

6. Solve both equations.

REFLECT

3a. Which property explains why you need to add $\left(\frac{b}{2}\right)^2$ to both sides of the equation?

_____

3b. What would be the first two steps in solving $x^2 + 10x - 11 = 0$ by completing the square?

_____

_____

3c. Could you use another method besides completing the square to solve the equation $x^2 + 10x - 11 = 0$? If so, describe how you would apply the alternate method.

_____

_____

3d. How would you apply the definition of a square root to eliminate the exponent in the equation $(x + 5)^2 = 36$?

_____

_____

3e. Look at step 4 above. Explain why there can be two, one, or zero real solutions of a quadratic equation.

_____

_____

_____

© Houghton Mifflin Harcourt Publishing Company

4 **EXAMPLE** Solving Quadratic Equations by Completing the Square

Solve the equation by completing the square.

A $x^2 - 2x - 1 = 0$

Write the equation in the form $x^2 + bx = c$. _____

Add $\left(\frac{b}{2}\right)^2$ to both sides of the equation. _____

Factor the perfect square trinomial. _____

Apply the definition of a square root. _____

Write two equations. _____

Solve the equations. _____

B $x^2 - 8x + 16 = 0$

Write the equation in the form $x^2 + bx = c$. _____

Add $\left(\frac{b}{2}\right)^2$ to both sides of the equation. _____

Factor the perfect square trinomial. _____

Apply the definition of a square root. _____

Write two equations. _____

Solve the equations. _____

REFLECT

4a. Can you solve either equation by factoring? If so, which method is easier?

_____

_____

_____

4b. Use completing the square to explain why $x^2 - 2x + 3 = 0$ has no solution.

_____

_____

_____

4c. What method would you use to solve the equation $x^2 + 3x - 4 = 0$? Explain why you would choose this method.

_____

_____

_____

1. The diagram represents the expression $x^2 + 4x + c$ with the constant term missing. Complete the square by filling in the bottom right corner with 1-tiles, and write the expression as a trinomial and in factored form.

_____

Complete the square to form a perfect square trinomial. Then factor the trinomial.

2. $m^2 + 10m +$ ▢

_____

3. $g^2 - 20g +$ ▢

_____

4. $y^2 + 2y +$ ▢

_____

5. $w^2 - 11w +$ ▢

_____

Solve the equation by completing the square.

6. $s^2 + 15s = -56$

_____

7. $r^2 - 4r = 165$

_____

8. $y^2 + 19y + 78 = 0$

_____

9. $x^2 - 19x + 84 = 0$

_____

10. $t^2 + 2t - 224 = 0$

_____

11. $x^2 + 18x - 175 = 0$

_____

12. $g^2 + 3g = -6$

_____

13. $p^2 - 3p = 18$

_____

14. $z^2 = 6z - 2$

_____

15. $x^2 + 25 = 10x$

_____

Solving $ax^2 + bx + c = 0$ by Completing the Square

COMMON CORE

CC.9-12.A.REI.4,
CC.9-12.A.REI.4a,
CC.9-12.A.REI.4b

Essential question: *How can you solve $ax^2 + bx + c = 0$ by completing the square when $a \neq 1$?*

You already know how to complete the square to solve equations of the form $x^2 + bx = c$. To solve equations of the form $ax^2 + bx = c$ where $a \neq 1$ by completing the square, you could divide each term by a to eliminate the coefficient of x^2. However, in this lesson you will explore a direct method for solving $ax^2 + bx = c$ where $a \neq 1$ by completing the square.

1 EXPLORE   Completing the Square for $ax^2 + bx$ when $a \neq 1$

A   Refer to the algebra tile diagram shown below. Which expression is represented by the tiles?

_____

Complete the square by filling the bottom right corner with 1-tiles. How many 1-tiles

did you add to the diagram? _____

B   Write the trinomial represented by the algebra tiles for the complete square.

$$\boxed{}\, x^2 + \boxed{}\, x + \boxed{}$$

The trinomial is the square of a binomial. Use the algebra tile diagram to write the trinomial in factored form.

$$\boxed{}\, x^2 + \boxed{}\, x + \boxed{} = \left(\boxed{}\, x + \boxed{}\right)^2$$

1a. The coefficient of x^2 in the trinomial is 4. What is it about the number 4 that makes it possible to arrange the x^2-tiles as shown to complete the square?

_____

1b. When you complete the square for $ax^2 + bx$ with $a \neq 1$, is the number you add $\left(\frac{b}{2}\right)^2$? Why or why not?

_____

Completing the Square when a is a Perfect Square To find the value of c for which $ax^2 + bx + c$ is a perfect square when a is a perfect square, write $ax^2 + bx + c = (mx + n)^2$. Use FOIL to multiply $(mx + n)^2$, and compare the coefficients.

$$ax^2 + bx + c = (mx + n)^2$$
$$= m^2x^2 + 2mnx + n^2$$

Corresponding coefficients must be equal, so $a = m^2$, $b = 2mn$, and $c = n^2$. Thus, $m = \sqrt{a}$ and $n = \frac{b}{2m} = \frac{b}{2\sqrt{a}}$. The constant term, c, is $n^2 = \left(\frac{b}{2\sqrt{a}}\right)^2 = \frac{b^2}{4a}$. (Alternately, $m = -\sqrt{a}$ and $n = -\frac{b}{2\sqrt{a}}$. However, this does not change the overall result, so you need only consider the case of $m = \sqrt{a}$.)

2 EXAMPLE Solving $ax^2 + bx = c$ when a is a Perfect Square

Solve $4x^2 + 8x = 21$ by completing the square.

A Add $\frac{b^2}{4a}$ to both sides of the equation. Since $a =$ ____ and $b =$ ____, $\frac{b^2}{4a} = \frac{\boxed{}^2}{4\left(\boxed{}\right)} = \boxed{}$.

$$4x^2 + 8x + \boxed{} = 21 + \boxed{}$$

B Factor the left side of the equation as a perfect square trinomial.

$$\left(\boxed{}x + \boxed{}\right)^2 = \boxed{}$$

C Apply the definition of a square root. Write two equations, and solve each equation to find the two solutions.

$$\left(\boxed{}x + \boxed{}\right) = \pm\,\boxed{}$$

$$\boxed{}x + \boxed{} = \boxed{} \qquad \text{or} \qquad \boxed{}x + \boxed{} = -\boxed{}$$

$$x = \text{\_\_\_\_} \qquad \text{or} \qquad x = \text{\_\_\_\_}$$

2a. Compare the steps for solving an equation of the form $ax^2 + bx = c$ when $a \neq 1$ and a is a perfect square with solving $x^2 + bx = c$.

_____

_____

_____

2b. Why does a have to be a perfect square for this procedure to work?

_____

_____

Completing the Square when a is Not a Perfect Square To find the value of c for which $ax^2 + bx + c$ is a perfect square when a is not a perfect square, you can multiply each term by a number that makes the coefficient of x^2 be a perfect square. One possible value is a. Remember that when you are solving an equation by completing the square, you need to multiply both sides by a. Then solve in the same manner as before.

3 EXAMPLE Solving $ax^2 + bx = c$ when a is Not a Perfect Square

Solve $2x^2 + 6x = 5$. Leave your answer in exact form.

A The coefficient of x^2 is not a perfect square. Multiply both sides by 2.

$$2(2x^2 + 6x) = 2(5)$$

$$\boxed{} \cdot x^2 + \boxed{} \, x = 10$$

B Add $\dfrac{b^2}{4a}$ to both sides of the equation. In this case, $\dfrac{b^2}{4a} = \dfrac{\boxed{}^2}{4\left(\boxed{}\right)} = \boxed{}$.

$$\boxed{} x^2 + \boxed{} \, x + \boxed{} = 10 + \boxed{}$$

C Factor the left side of the equation as a perfect square trinomial.

$$\left(\boxed{} x + \boxed{}\right)^2 = 19$$

D Apply the definition of a square root. Write two equations, and solve each equation to find the two solutions.

$$\left(\boxed{} x + \boxed{}\right) = \boxed{}$$

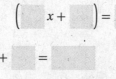

$$\boxed{} \, x + \boxed{} = \boxed{} \qquad \text{or} \qquad \boxed{} \, x + \boxed{} = \boxed{}$$

$$x = \underline{\hspace{2cm}} \qquad \text{or} \qquad x = \underline{\hspace{2cm}}$$

3a. Why is 2 the best value to multiply both sides of the equation by before completing the square? Are other values possible? Explain.

_____

_____

_____

3b. You want to solve $12x^2 - 3x = 51$ by completing the square. What is the smallest whole number you could multiply 12 by? Explain.

_____

_____

PRACTICE

Solve the equation by completing the square.

1. $9z^2 + 48z = 36$

2. $49x^2 + 28x = 60$

3. $121r^2 - 44r = 5$

4. $4x^2 + 20x - 11 = 0$

5. $2x^2 + 9 = 9x$

6. $3x^2 + 4x = 20$

7. A carpenter is making the tabletop shown below. The surface area will be 24 square feet.

a. Write an equation to represent this situation.

_____

b. Solve the equation. Which solution(s) make sense in this situation? Explain.

_____

_____

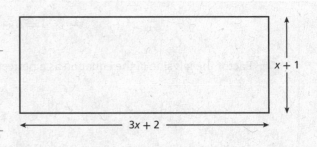

$x + 1$

$3x + 2$

c. What are the dimensions of the tabletop?

_____

Deriving the Quadratic Formula

COMMON CORE

CC.9-12.A.REI.4,
CC.9-12.A.REI.4a,
CC.9-12.A.REI.4b

Essential question: *What is the quadratic formula and how can you derive it from $ax^2 + bx + c = 0$?*

You have learned how to solve quadratic equations by completing the square. In this lesson, you will complete the square on the general form of a quadratic equation to derive a formula that can be used to solve any quadratic equation.

1 EXPLORE Deriving the Quadratic Formula

Solve the general form of the quadratic equation, $ax^2 + bx + c = 0$, by completing the square to find the values of x in terms of a, b, and c.

A Subtract c from both sides of the equation.

$$ax^2 + bx = \boxed{}$$

B Multiply both sides of the equation by $4a$ to make the coefficient of x^2 a perfect square.

$$4a^2x^2 + \boxed{} x = -4ac$$

C Add b^2 to both sides of the equation to complete the square. Then write the trinomial as the square of a binomial.

$$4a^2x^2 + 4abx + b^2 = -4ac + \boxed{}$$

$$\left(\boxed{} \right)^2 = b^2 - 4ac$$

D Apply the definition of a square root and solve for x.

$$\boxed{} = \pm\sqrt{\boxed{}}$$

$$2ax = -\boxed{} \pm \sqrt{\boxed{}}$$

$$x = \underline{}$$

The formula $x = \dfrac{-b \pm \sqrt{b^2 - 4ac}}{2a}$ is called the **quadratic formula**.

For any quadratic equation written in standard form, $ax^2 + bx + c = 0$,

the quadratic formula gives the solutions of the equation.

1a. In Part B, why did you multiply both sides of the equation by $4a$?

_____

_____

1b. In Part C, explain why you added b^2 to each side to complete the square.

_____

_____

1c. Provided the expression under the radical sign, $b^2 - 4ac$, is positive, how many solutions will the quadratic formula give for a quadratic equation? Explain.

_____

_____

1d. If the expression under the radical sign, $b^2 - 4ac$, is 0, how many solutions will the quadratic formula give for a quadratic equation? What if the expression is negative?

_____

_____

1e. Another method of deriving the quadratic formula is to first divide each term by a, and then complete the square. Complete the derivation below. (In this derivation, you will use the quotient property of square roots, which says that $\sqrt{\dfrac{a}{b}} = \dfrac{\sqrt{a}}{\sqrt{b}}$. For a square root of a fraction, this property allows you to simplify the numerator and denominator separately. For instance, $\sqrt{\dfrac{5}{9}} = \dfrac{\sqrt{5}}{\sqrt{9}} = \dfrac{\sqrt{5}}{3}$.)

$ax^2 + bx + c = 0$

$ax^2 + bx = -c$ Subtract c from both sides.

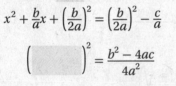   Divide each term by a.

$x^2 + \dfrac{b}{a}x + \left(\dfrac{b}{2a}\right)^2 = \left(\dfrac{b}{2a}\right)^2 - \dfrac{c}{a}$

$\left(\right)^2 = \dfrac{b^2 - 4ac}{4a^2}$ Factor the left side, and write the right side as a single fraction.

$x + \dfrac{b}{2a} = \pm\sqrt{\dfrac{b^2 - 4ac}{4a^2}}$

$x + \dfrac{b}{2a} = \pm\dfrac{\sqrt{b^2 - 4ac}}{\sqrt{4a^2}}$ Apply the quotient property of radicals.

$x + \dfrac{b}{2a} = \pm\dfrac{\sqrt{b^2 - 4ac}}{}$ Simplify the radical in the denominator.

$x = \dfrac{-b \pm \sqrt{b^2 - 4ac}}{2a}$ Solve for x.

© Houghton Mifflin Harcourt Publishing Company

Using the Quadratic Formula

Essential question: *How do you solve quadratic equations using the quadratic formula?*

COMMON
CORE

CC.9-12.A.CED.1*,
CC.9-12.A.REI.4,
CC.9-12.A.REI.4b

1 ENGAGE   Using the Quadratic Formula

You have learned to solve quadratic equations by factoring and by completing the square. Another way to solve quadratic equations is by using the *quadratic formula*.

The standard form of a quadratic equation is $ax^2 + bx + c = 0$. As you saw from Lesson 8-6, if you complete the square on the standard form of the equation and solve for x, you will generate the quadratic formula:

$$x = \frac{-b \pm \sqrt{b^2 - 4ac}}{2a}$$

To solve a quadratic equation by using the quadratic formula, write the equation in standard form, $ax^2 + bx + c = 0$. Then substitute the values of a, b, and c into the quadratic formula, and simplify.

REFLECT

1a. The expression under the radical in the quadratic formula, $b^2 - 4ac$, is called the **discriminant**. If $d = b^2 - 4ac$, how many solutions does a quadratic equation have if $d > 0$? if $d = 0$? if $d < 0$? Justify your answers.

_____

_____

_____

1b. Describe the solutions of a quadratic equation when $b = 0$.

_____

_____

_____

1c. Describe the solutions of a quadratic equation when $c = 0$.

_____

_____

_____

© Houghton Mifflin Harcourt Publishing Company

Use the quadratic formula to solve the quadratic equation.

A $6x^2 + 5x - 4 = 0$

Identify the following. Include negative signs as needed.

$a = $ _____ ; $b = $ _____ ; $c = $ _____

Use the quadratic formula $x = \dfrac{-b \pm \sqrt{b^2 - 4ac}}{2a}$.

$x = \dfrac{-\boxed{} \pm \sqrt{\boxed{}^2 - 4 \cdot \boxed{} \cdot \boxed{}}}{2 \cdot \boxed{}}$ Substitute the values into the quadratic formula.

$= \dfrac{-\boxed{} \pm \sqrt{\boxed{}}}{\boxed{}}$ Simplify the expression under the radical sign.
Simplify the denominator.

$= \dfrac{-\boxed{} \pm \boxed{}}{\boxed{}}$ Evaluate the square root.

Separate the two solutions indicated by the $\pm$ sign, and simplify.

$x = \dfrac{-\boxed{} + \boxed{}}{\boxed{}}$ or $x = \dfrac{-\boxed{} - \boxed{}}{\boxed{}}$

$= \boxed{}$ $= \boxed{}$

B $x^2 + 7 = 4x$

Write the equation in standard form. _____

Identify the following.

$a = $ _____ ; $b = $ _____ ; $c = $ _____

Use the quadratic formula $x = \dfrac{-b \pm \sqrt{b^2 - 4ac}}{2a}$.

$x = \dfrac{-\boxed{} \pm \sqrt{\boxed{}^2 - 4 \cdot \boxed{} \cdot \boxed{}}}{2 \cdot \boxed{}}$ Substitute the values into the quadratic formula.

$= \dfrac{\boxed{} \pm \sqrt{\boxed{}}}{\boxed{}}$ Simplify the expression under the radical sign.
Simplify the denominator.

The discriminant is _____ , so there is _____ solution.

C $5x^2 + 9.8 = -14x$

Write the equation in standard form. _____

Identify the following.

$a =$ _____ ; $b =$ _____ ; $c =$ _____

Use the quadratic formula $x = \dfrac{-b \pm \sqrt{b^2 - 4ac}}{2a}$.

$x = \dfrac{-\boxed{} \pm \sqrt{\boxed{}^2 - 4 \cdot \boxed{} \cdot \boxed{}}}{2 \cdot \boxed{}}$ Substitute the values into the quadratic formula.

$= \dfrac{-\boxed{} \pm \sqrt{\boxed{}}}{\boxed{}}$ Simplify the expression under the radical sign. Simplify the denominator.

$= \dfrac{-\boxed{} \pm \boxed{}}{\boxed{}}$ Take the square root.

The discriminant is _____ , so there is _____ solution.

$x = -\dfrac{\boxed{}}{\boxed{}}$

REFLECT

2a. Is it possible to solve the equation from Part A by factoring? Explain.

_____

_____

2b. Is it possible to solve the equation from Part B by factoring? Explain.

_____

_____

2c. Is it possible to solve the equation from Part C by factoring? Explain.

_____

_____

_____

PRACTICE

State how many real solutions the equation has. Do not solve the equation.

1. $3x^2 + 8x + 6 = 0$ _____

2. $z^2 = 9$ _____

3. $9d^2 + 16 = 24d$ _____

4. $-2x^2 = 25 - 10x$ _____

Solve the equation using the quadratic formula. Round to the nearest hundredth, if necessary.

5. $16 + r^2 - 8r = 0$

6. $3x^2 = 10 - 4x$

7. $2s^2 = 98$

8. $z^2 = 2.5z$

9. $3x^2 + 16x - 84 = 0$

10. $34z^2 + 19z = 15$

11. $6q^2 + 25q + 24 = 0$

12. $7x^2 + 100x = 4$

State what method you would use to solve the equation. Justify your answer. You do not need to solve the equation.

13. $4x^2 + 25 = 20x$

14. $2z^2 = 20$

15. $4x^2 + 25 = 18x$

16. $g^2 - 3g - 4 = 0$

17. A football player kicks a ball with an initial upward velocity of 47 feet per second. The initial height of the ball is 3 feet. The function $h(t) = -16t^2 + vt + h_0$ models the height (in feet) of the ball, where v is the initial upward velocity and h_0 is the initial height. If no one catches the ball, how long will it be in the air?

© Houghton Mifflin Harcourt Publishing Company

Graphing Functions of the Form $f(x) = ax^2 + bx + c$

COMMON
CORE

CC.9-12.F.IF.4*,
CC.9-12.F.IF.5*,
CC.9-12.F.IF.7a*,
CC.9-12.F.IF.8a,
CC.9-12.F.BF.1*

Essential question: *How can you describe key attributes of the graph of $f(x) = ax^2 + bx + c$ by analyzing its equation?*

To graph a function of the form $f(x) = ax^2 + bx + c$, called *standard form,* you can analyze the key features of the graph either by factoring or by completing the square.

1 E X A M P L E   Graphing $f(x) = x^2 + bx + c$

Graph the function $f(x) = x^2 + 2x - 3$ by factoring.

A   You can determine the *x*-intercepts of the graph by factoring to solve $f(x) = 0$:

$f(x) = x^2 + 2x - 3 = \left(x - \boxed{}\right)\left(x + \boxed{}\right)$, so $f(x) = 0$ when $x = $ _____ or

$x = $ _____.

The graph of $f(x) = x^2 + 2x - 3$ intersects the *x*-axis at $\left(\boxed{}, \boxed{}\right)$ and $\left(\boxed{}, \boxed{}\right)$.

B   The axis of symmetry of the graph is a vertical line that is halfway between the two *x*-intercepts and passes through the vertex. The axis of symmetry is $x = \boxed{}$. So, the vertex is $\left(\boxed{}, \boxed{}\right)$.

C   Find another point on the graph and reflect it across the axis of symmetry. Use the point $(2, 5)$. The *x*-value is $\boxed{}$ units from the axis of symmetry, so its reflection is $\left(\boxed{}, \boxed{}\right)$.

D   Use the five points to graph the function.

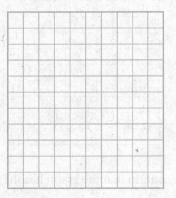

REFLECT

1a.   A useful point to plot is where the *y*-intercept occurs. How can you find the *y*-intercept? What point is the reflection across the axis of symmetry of the point where the *y*-intercept occurs?

_____

_____

If the function cannot be factored, complete the square to rewrite the function in *vertex form*: $f(x) = a(x-h)^2 + k$. Completing the square in this situation is similar to solving equations by completing the square, but instead of adding a term to both sides of the equation, you will both add and subtract it from the function's rule.

2 EXAMPLE Graphing $f(x) = ax^2 + bx + c$

Graph the function $f(x) = -3x^2 + 6x + 1$ by completing the square.

A Complete the square to write the function in the form $f(x) = a(x-h)^2 + k$. Start by disregarding the constant term. Factor -3 from the first two terms, paying close attention to the signs of the terms.

$f(x) = -3\left(\right) + 1$ Factor.

$ = -3\left(+ - \right) + 1$ Complete the square within the parentheses.

$ = -3\left(\left(\right)^2 - \right) + 1$ Factor the first three terms in parentheses using the perfect square trinomial pattern.

$ = -3\left(\right)^2 + + 1$ Distribute the -3.

$ = -3\left(\right)^2 + $ Combine the last two terms.

Write the coordinates of the vertex (h, k). $\left(, \right)$

B Graph the function by plotting another point besides the vertex and reflecting the point across the axis of symmetry. The axis of symmetry is $x = \underline{\hspace{2cm}}$. Since

$f(2) = \underline{\hspace{2cm}}$, the point $\left(2, \right)$ is on the graph. Reflecting this point across the

axis of symmetry gives the point $\left(, \right)$.

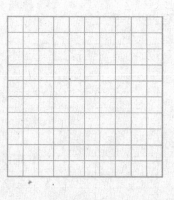

C Based on the fact that $a = -3$, confirm that the graph has the characteristics you

would expect by comparing it with the graph of the parent function, $f(x) = x^2$. The

graph should be a vertical $\underline{\hspace{2cm}}$ of the graph of the parent function as well

as a reflection across the $\underline{\hspace{2cm}}$, which means that the graph should open

$\underline{\hspace{2cm}}$. Does the graph that you drew have these characteristics? $\underline{\hspace{2cm}}$

2a. Why did you add and subtract within the parentheses when completing the square?

_____

_____

_____

2b. Why did you multiply both $(x - 1)^2$ and -1 by -3 in the fourth step? Why did you not multiply 1 by -3 in the same step?

_____

_____

_____

2c. State the domain and range of the function.

_____

2d. Suppose the function were $g(x) = -3x^2 + 6x - 2$ instead of $f(x) = -3x^2 + 6x + 1$. Would you complete the square any differently? Why or why not? What is the vertex form of the function $g(x)$? How does the graph of $g(x)$ compare with the graph of $f(x)$? What are the domain and range of $g(x)$?

_____

_____

_____

_____

2e. It is useful to have a general expression for the vertex form and of the vertex in terms of a, b, and c. Complete the steps below on $f(x) = ax^2 + bx + c$ to write a general expression for the vertex form of a function and of the vertex (h, k) of the function.

$f(x) = a\left(x^2 + \boxed{}\, x\right) + c$ Factor out the a from the first two terms.

$= a\left(x^2 + \boxed{}\, x + \left(\boxed{}\right)^2 - \left(\boxed{}\right)^2\right) + c$ Complete the square within the parentheses.

$= a\left(\left(x + \boxed{}\right)^2 - \dfrac{b^2}{4a^2}\right) + c$ Factor the perfect square trinomial.

$= a\left(x + \boxed{}\right)^2 - \dfrac{b^2}{4a} + c$ Distribute the a.

Write the coordinates of the vertex (h, k). $\left(\boxed{}\, , \boxed{}\right)$

Projectile Motion The height of an object moving under the force of gravity, with no other forces acting on it, can be modeled by the following quadratic function.

$$h(t) = -16t^2 + vt + h_0$$

The variables in the function represent the following quantities:

t is the time in seconds,

$h(t)$ is the height of the object above the ground in feet,

v is the initial vertical velocity of the object in feet per second, and

h_0 is the initial height of the object in feet.

3 EXAMPLE   Graphing a Projectile Motion Model

A person standing at the edge of a 48-foot cliff tosses a ball up and just off the edge of the cliff with an initial upward velocity of 8 feet per second. Graph the function that models the motion of the ball.

A Identify the values of v and h_0 for the projectile motion function.

Initial vertical velocity, $v = $ _____

Initial height, $h_0 = $ _____

B Write the equation for the projectile motion function.

_____

C Complete the square to find the vertex of the function's graph.

$h(t) = -16t^2 + \boxed{} t + \boxed{}$

$ = -16\left(\boxed{} \right) + \boxed{}$ Factor out -16.

$ = -16\left(\boxed{} + \boxed{} - \boxed{} \right) + \boxed{}$ Complete the square.

$ = -16\left(\left(t - \boxed{} \right)^2 - \boxed{} \right) + \boxed{}$ Factor the perfect square trinomial.

$ = -16\left(t - \boxed{} \right)^2 + \boxed{} + \boxed{}$ Distribute the -16.

$ = -16\left(t - \boxed{} \right)^2 + \boxed{}$ Combine the last two terms.

Write the coordinates of the vertex. $\left(\boxed{} , \boxed{} \right)$

© Houghton Mifflin Harcourt Publishing Company

D Graph the function by plotting a couple of points besides the vertex. Because only nonnegative values of t and $h(t)$ make sense for this situation, one point that you should plot is the point where the $h(t)$-intercept occurs. Since $h(0) = $ _____,

the graph starts at the point $\left(0, \boxed{} \right)$. Determining when the ball hits the ground gives you another point that you can plot:

$$h(t) = 0$$

$$-16\left(t - \tfrac{1}{4}\right)^2 + \boxed{} = 0$$

$$-16\left(t - \tfrac{1}{4}\right)^2 = \boxed{}$$

$$\left(t - \tfrac{1}{4}\right)^2 = \boxed{}$$

$$t - \tfrac{1}{4} = \pm\, \boxed{}$$

$$t - \tfrac{1}{4} = \pm\, \boxed{}$$

$$t = \tfrac{1}{4} \pm \boxed{} = \boxed{} \text{ or } \boxed{}$$

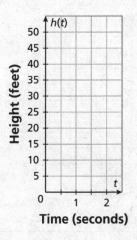

Reject the negative t-value. So, $\left(\boxed{}, 0 \right)$ is another point on the graph.

REFLECT

3a. How long is the ball in the air? When is the ball at its highest? What is its height at that time?

_____

3b. State the domain and range of the function in the context of the situation.

_____

3c. The units of $h(t)$ and h_0 are in feet, the units of t are in seconds, and the units of v are in feet per second. What are the units of the coefficient -16? Explain.

_____

_____

_____

© Houghton Mifflin Harcourt Publishing Company

Write the rule for the quadratic function in the form you would use to graph it. Then graph the function.

1. $f(x) = x^2 + 4x + 3$

_____

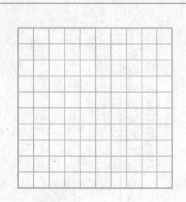

2. $f(x) = x^2 - 6x + 11$

_____

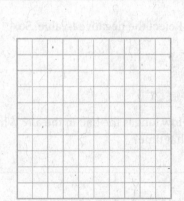

3. $f(x) = -x^2 + 2x - 2$

_____

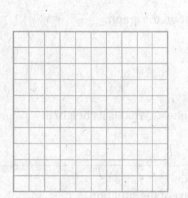

4. $f(x) = \frac{1}{2}x^2 - 4x + 5$

_____

5. A model rocket is launched from a 12-foot platform with an initial upward velocity of 64 feet per second.

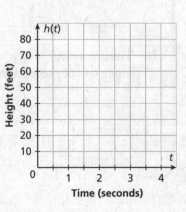

a. Write a quadratic function in standard form that models the height of the rocket.

_____

b. Write the quadratic function in vertex form that models the height of the rocket.

_____

c. Graph the function.

d. State the domain and range of the function in the context of the situation.

_____

Solving Systems of Linear and Quadratic Equations

COMMON
CORE

CC.9-12.A.CED.2*,
CC.9-12.A.REI.4,
CC.9-12.A.REI.4b,
CC.9-12.A.REI.7,
CC.9-12.F.IF.4*

Essential question: *How can you solve a system of equations when one equation is linear and the other is quadratic?*

To estimate the solution to a system of equations, you can graph both equations on the same coordinate plane and find the intersection points. Or you can solve the equations algebraically using substitution or elimination.

1 EXAMPLE **Solving by Graphing and Algebraically**

Solve the system of equations.

$$f(x) = -8x + 48$$
$$g(x) = -2(x - 2)^2 + 32$$

A Solve the system of equations by graphing.

Start by graphing the quadratic function. The vertex is $\left(\boxed{}, \boxed{}\right)$. Describe the transformation of the parent quadratic function that produces the graph of $g(x)$.

_____

_____

To make the graph more accurate, plot the points where the x-intercepts occur. The x-intercepts are the solutions of the equation $g(x) = 0$:

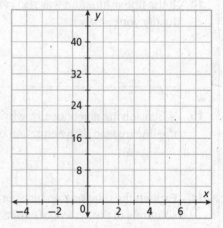

$$-2(x - 2)^2 + 32 = 0$$

$$-2(x - 2)^2 = \boxed{}$$

$$(x - 2)^2 = \boxed{}$$

$$x - 2 = \pm\,\boxed{}$$

$$x = \boxed{} \pm \boxed{} = \boxed{} \text{ or } \boxed{}$$

So, the points $\left(\boxed{}, 0\right)$ and $\left(\boxed{}, 0\right)$ are on the graph. Use these points and the vertex to draw the graph.

Now graph the linear function. The y-intercept is _____, and the slope is _____.

The line and the parabola intersect at two points. Identify the coordinates of those points.

$$\left(\boxed{}, \boxed{}\right) \text{ and } \left(\boxed{}, \boxed{}\right)$$

B Solve the system of equations algebraically.

Write the functions in terms of y.

$$y = -8x + 48$$
$$y = -2(x - 2)^2 + 32$$

Both equations are solved for y, so set the right sides equal to each other and solve for x.

$-8x + 48 = -2(x - 2)^2 + 32$

$-8x + 48 = $ _____   Simplify the right side.

$\underline{8x - 48} = \underline{ 8x - 48}$ Add $8x - 48$ to both sides.

$0 = $ _____   Simplify both sides.

$0 = -2\left(\right)\left(\right)$ Factor the right side.

$x = $ or $x = $ Use the zero-product property to solve for x.

Substitute these values of x into the equation of the line to find the corresponding y-values.

$$y = -8(2) + 48 = \underline{}$$

$$y = -8(6) + 48 = \underline{}$$

The solutions are $\left(, \right)$ and $\left(, \right)$.

REFLECT

1a. If the linear function was $f(x) = 8x + 48$, how many solutions would there be? Justify your answer.

_____

_____

1b. When solving algebraically, why do you substitute the x-values into the equation of the line instead of the equation of the parabola?

_____

1c. Explain the relationship between the intersection points of the graphs and the solutions of the system of equations.

_____

_____

1d. Describe how to check that the solutions are correct.

_____

_____

In the previous example, the system of equations had two solutions. You can use a graph to understand other possible numbers of solutions of a system of equations involving a linear equation and a quadratic equation.

The graph of the quadratic function $f(x) = -x^2 + 10x - 27$ is shown below.

Graph each linear function below on the same coordinate plane as the parabola.

Line 1: $g(x) = 2x - 11$

Line 2: $h(x) = -2x + 14$

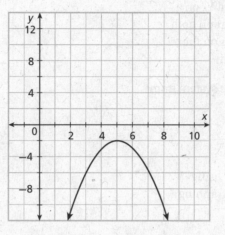

© Houghton Mifflin Harcourt Publishing Company

REFLECT

2a. At how many points do the parabola and Line 1 intersect? _____
   How many solutions are there for the system consisting of the quadratic function and the first linear function? _____

2b. At how many points do the parabola and Line 2 intersect? _____
   How many solutions are there for the system consisting of the quadratic function and the second linear function? _____

2c. A system of equations consisting of one quadratic equation and one linear equation can have _____, _____, or 2 real solutions.

2d. How many solutions does the following system of equations have? Explain your reasoning.

$$f(x) = -x^2 + 10x - 27$$
$$k(x) = -x + 1$$

_____

_____

2e. How many solutions does the following system of equations have? Explain your reasoning.

$$f(x) = -x^2 + 10x - 27$$
$$p(x) = -2$$

_____

_____

You can use the Intersect feature on a graphing calculator to solve systems of equations.

3 **EXAMPLE**   Solving Systems Using Technology

Use a graphing calculator to solve the system of equations.

$$f(x) = -4.9x^2 + 50x + 25$$
$$g(x) = 30x$$

A   Enter the functions as Y_1 and Y_2 on a graphing calculator. Then graph both functions. Sketch the graphs on the coordinate plane at the right.

Estimate the solutions of the system from the graph.

_____

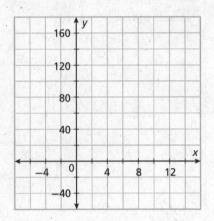

B   Solve the system directly by using the Intersect feature of the graphing calculator.

Press 2nd and CALC, then select Intersect. Press Enter for the first curve and again for the second curve. For Guess?, press the left or right arrows to move the cursor close to one of the intersections, then press Enter again. Repeat, moving the cursor close to the other intersection to find the second solution. Round your solutions to the nearest tenth.

_____

REFLECT

3a. Are the solutions you get using the Intersect feature of a graphing calculator always exact? Explain.

_____

3b. How can you check the accuracy of your estimated solutions?

_____

3c. Use a graphing calculator to solve the system of equations $f(x)$ and $h(x)$ where $h(x) = 30x + 50$. What is the result? Explain.

_____

_____

© Houghton Mifflin Harcourt Publishing Company

Solve the system of equations algebraically. Round to the nearest tenth, if necessary.

1. $f(x) = x^2 - 2$

$g(x) = -2$

_____

2. $y = (x - 3)^2$

$y = x$

_____

3. $y = -2x^2 - 4x + 1$

$y = -\frac{1}{2}x + 3$

_____

4. $f(x) = x^2$

$g(x) = 1$

_____

5. $y = x^2 + 4x - 5$

$y = 3x - 2$

_____

6. $f(x) = -16x^2 + 15x + 10$

$g(x) = 14 - x$

_____

The graph of a system of equations is shown. State how many solutions the system has. Then estimate the solution(s).

7. _____

_____

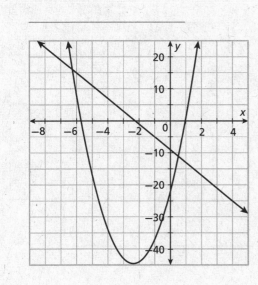

8. _____

_____

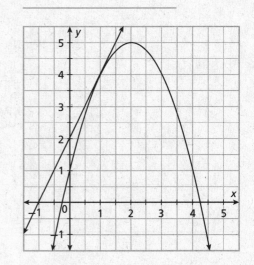

Estimate the solutions to the system of equations graphically. Confirm the solutions by substituting the values into the equations.

9. $f(x) = x^2$

  $g(x) = 1$

_____

10. $y = x^2 - 1$

  $y = 0.5x - 3$

_____

11. $f(x) = -16x^2 + 15x + 10$

  $g(x) = 14 - x$

_____

12. $f(x) = 3(x - 1)^2 + 4$

  $g(x) = -4x + 9$

_____

Solve the system of equations using the Intersect feature of a graphing calculator. Round your answers to the nearest tenth.

13. $y = -x^2 + 6x + 7$

  $y = 2x + 6$

_____

14. $f(x) = -x^2 + x - 2$

  $g(x) = 2x - 3$

_____

FOCUS ON MODELING
Modeling with Quadratic Functions

COMMON
CORE

CC.9-12.A.SSE.3a,
CC.9-12.A.REI.4a,
CC.9-12.A.REI.4b,
CC.9-12.F.IF.4*,
CC.9-12.F.IF.6*,
CC.9-12.F.IF.8a

Essential question: *How can you use quadratic functions to compare the motions of two baseballs that are thrown into the air?*

Franco and Grace each throw a baseball vertically into the air at the same time. Franco throws his baseball while standing on a cliff so that the baseball lands on a beach below. Grace throws her baseball into the air while standing on the beach. The table gives the initial vertical velocity v and the initial height h_0 at which each baseball is thrown. How do the motions of the two baseballs compare?

	Initial Velocity (ft/s)	Initial Height (ft)
Franco's baseball	32	48
Grace's baseball	64	3

1 **Find the maximum height of Franco's baseball.**

A The height in feet of an object thrown into the air with an initial vertical velocity of v feet per second and an initial height of h_0 feet is

$$f(t) = -16t^2 + vt + h_0,$$

where t is the time in seconds. Write a function $f(t)$ that models the height of Franco's baseball.

_____

B To find the maximum height of Franco's baseball, first factor the quadratic expression you wrote in order to find the t-intercepts of the function's graph.

$$-16t^2 + \boxed{}\, t + \boxed{} = -16\left(t^2 - \boxed{}\, t - \boxed{}\right)$$

$$= -16\left(t + \boxed{}\right)\left(t - \boxed{}\right)$$

So, the graph of $f(t)$ intersects the t-axis at $t =$ _____ and at $t =$ _____.
The axis of symmetry of the graph of $f(t)$ is a vertical line that is halfway between the two t-intercepts and passes through the vertex.
The axis of symmetry is the line $t =$ _____ and the vertex is _____.
So, the maximum height of Franco's baseball is _____ feet.

REFLECT

1a. Evaluate $f(t)$ at $t = 0$. What does this value tell you?

_____

1b. Explain how you used the vertex of the graph of $f(t)$ to find the maximum height of Franco's baseball.

_____

_____

1c. How long after Franco's baseball is thrown into the air does it reach its maximum height? How do you know?

_____

_____

1d. What is the domain of $f(t)$? How do the t-intercepts help you determine the domain?

_____

_____

_____

2 **Find the maximum height of Grace's baseball.**

A Write a function $g(t)$ that models the height of Grace's baseball.

_____

B To find the maximum height of Grace's baseball, first complete the square to write the function in vertex form, $g(t) = a(t - h)^2 + k$.

$g(t) = -16t^2 + \boxed{}\, t + 3$ Write the function in standard form.

$= -16(t^2 - \boxed{}\, t) + 3$ Factor -16 from the first two terms.

$= -16\left(t^2 - \boxed{}\, t + \boxed{} - \boxed{}\right) + 3$ Complete the square within the parentheses.

$= -16\left(\left(t - \boxed{}\right)^2 - \boxed{}\right) + 3$ Factor the first three terms in the parentheses using the perfect square trinomial pattern.

$= -16\left(t - \boxed{}\right)^2 + \boxed{} + 3$ Distribute the -16.

$= -16\left(t - \boxed{}\right)^2 + \boxed{}$ Combine the last two terms.

The vertex of the graph of $g(t)$ is _____.

So, the maximum height of Grace's baseball is _____ feet.

REFLECT

2a. Evaluate $g(t)$ at $t = 0$. What does this value tell you?

_____

2b. How long after Grace's baseball is thrown into the air does it reach its maximum height? How do you know?

_____

_____

2c. Explain how you can check that you wrote $g(t)$ correctly in vertex form.

_____

_____

_____

3 Determine when Franco's baseball hits the ground.

A At the moment when Franco's baseball hits the ground and lands on the beach, what must be true about $f(t)$? Why?

_____

B Write an equation you can solve to determine when Franco's baseball hits the ground.

_____

C Show how to solve the equation by factoring.

_____

_____

D Interpret your solutions. When does Franco's baseball hit the ground?

_____

_____

E Use everything you know about $f(t)$ to draw the graph of the function on the coordinate plane at right. Be sure to label the points representing the vertex, where the $f(t)$-intercept occurs, and where the t-intercept occurs.

Explain how the time when Franco's baseball hits the ground is represented in your graph.

_____

_____

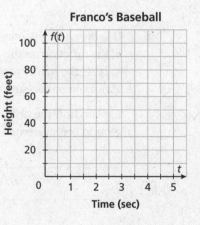

Franco's Baseball

REFLECT

3a. Does Franco's baseball take as much time going up as it does coming down? Why or why not?

_____

_____

4 **Determine when Grace's baseball hits the ground.**

A At the moment when Grace's baseball hits the ground and lands on the beach, what must be true about $g(t)$? Why?

_____

B Write an equation you can solve to find out when Grace's baseball hits the ground.

_____

C Use the quadratic formula to solve the equation.

$a =$ _____; $b =$ _____; $c =$ _____

$t = \dfrac{-b \pm \sqrt{b^2 - 4ac}}{2a}$ Use the quadratic formula.

$t = \dfrac{-\boxed{} \pm \sqrt{\boxed{}^2 - 4 \cdot \boxed{} \cdot \boxed{}}}{2 \cdot \boxed{}}$ Substitute the values of a, b, and c.

$t = \dfrac{-\boxed{} \pm \sqrt{\boxed{}}}{\boxed{}}$ Simplify the expression under the radical. Simplify the denominator.

$t \approx$ _____ or $t \approx$ _____   Use a calculator. Round to the nearest hundredth.

D Interpret your solutions. When does Grace's baseball hit the ground?

_____

_____

E Use everything you know about $g(t)$ to draw the graph of the function on the coordinate plane at right. Be sure to label the points representing the vertex, where the $g(t)$-intercept occurs, and where the t-intercept occurs.

Explain how the time when Grace's baseball hits the ground is represented in your graph.

_____

_____

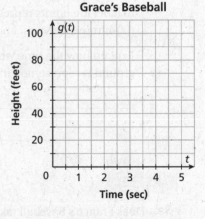

Grace's Baseball

Height (feet) / Time (sec)

REFLECT

4a. A student claims that Grace's baseball takes about the same amount of time going up as it does coming down. Do you agree? Why or why not?

_____

_____

© Houghton Mifflin Harcourt Publishing Company

4b. What is the domain of $g(t)$?

_____

4c. Explain how you can use your graph to estimate when Grace's baseball is at a height of 50 feet.

_____

_____

4d. Explain how you can use your calculator to find more precise estimates of the times when Grace's baseball is at a height of 50 feet.

_____

_____

4e. Why does it make sense that there are two times when Grace's baseball is at a height of 50 feet?

_____

5 Compare the motions of the two baseballs.

A Complete the table to compare the motions of the two baseballs. You have already determined some of the required values. You will need to use your equations and/or graphs to determine others.

	Maximum Height (ft)	Time Spent in the Air (sec)	Total Vertical Distance Traveled (ft)
Franco's baseball			
Grace's baseball			

B Which baseball has greater values in every column of the table? Why do you think this is the case?

_____

_____

REFLECT

5a. How did you find the total vertical distance traveled by each baseball?

_____

_____

_____

1. Complete the table for the motion of Grace's baseball.

Time (sec)	0	1	2	3	4
Height (ft)					

Describe any symmetry in the table. Explain why this makes sense.

_____

_____

2. The average rate of change of the function $g(t)$ over an interval is

$$\frac{\text{change in } g(t)}{\text{change in } t} = \frac{g(t_2) - g(t_1)}{t_2 - t_1}.$$

For example, from $t = 0$ to $t = 1$, the average rate of change of $g(t)$ is $\frac{51 - 3}{1 - 0} = \frac{48}{1}$ or 48 ft/sec. This is the average velocity of the baseball during the first second of its motion. Find the average rate of change of $g(t)$ for the other intervals in the table.

Interval	From $t = 0$ to $t = 1$	From $t = 1$ to $t = 2$	From $t = 2$ to $t = 3$	From $t = 3$ to $t = 4$
Average Rate of Change (ft/sec)	48			

3. When is the average rate of change is positive? When is it negative?

_____

_____

_____

4. Is the average rate of change greater during the first second of the baseball's motion or during the next second of its motion? Explain why this is so.

_____

_____

_____

5. What do you find if you calculate the average rate of change over the interval from $t = 1$ to $t = 3$? Why does this happen?

_____

_____

Name _____ **Class** _____ **Date** _____

MULTIPLE CHOICE

1. What is the product $(2x - 9)(3x + 5)$?

  A. $6x^2 - 17x - 45$

  B. $6x^2 - 21x + 45$

  C. $6x^2 + 10x - 45$

  D. $6x^2 + 37x + 45$

2. What are the solutions of $y^2 - 8y + 7 = 0$?

  F. $-1, -7$ **H.** $-1, -8$

  G. $1, 7$ **J.** $1, 8$

3. What is the factored form of $5z^2 + 9z - 2$?

  A. $(5z - 2)(z + 1)$

  B. $(5z + 2)(z - 1)$

  C. $(5z - 1)(z + 2)$

  D. $(5z + 1)(z - 2)$

4. What number should be added to both sides to complete the square on $r^2 - 5r = 12$?

  F. 6.25   **H.** 36

  G. 25   **J.** 144

5. What is the *best* first step to solve $2x^2 = x + 1$ by completing the square?

  A. Put the equation in standard form.

  B. Divide both sides by 2.

  C. Subtract x from both sides.

  D. Add 0.25 to both sides.

6. To solve the equation below by completing the square, you could multiply both sides of the equation by which number?
$$3x^2 - 7x = 8$$

  F. 3   **H.** -7

  G. $3x$ **J.** 8

7. What are the solutions of the following system of equations?
$$f(x) = x^2 - 4x + 13$$
$$g(x) = x + 9$$

  A. $(0, 4); (0, 13)$

  B. $(0, 10); (4, 13)$

  C. $(1, 10); (4, 13)$

  D. $(2, 9); (0, 9)$

8. What values of a, b, and c should be substituted in the quadratic formula to solve $5x^2 - 3x + 2 = 0$?

  F. $a = 5; b = -3; c = -2$

  G. $a = 5; b = 3; c = -2$

  H. $a = 5; b = 3; c = 2$

  J. $a = 5; b = -3; c = 2$

9. What does it mean if the value under the radical sign in the quadratic formula is negative?

  A. The quadratic equation has one solution.

  B. The quadratic equation has two solutions.

  C. The quadratic equation has no solution.

  D. There is an error in the calculations.

10. The graph of which function is shown?

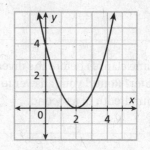

  F. $f(x) = x^2 - 2$

  G. $f(x) = x^2 + 2$

  H. $f(x) = x^2 + 4x + 4$

  J. $f(x) = x^2 - 4x + 4$

FREE RESPONSE

11. Complete the diagram and the equation that represent the binomial multiplication shown by the algebra tiles.

$x + 2$

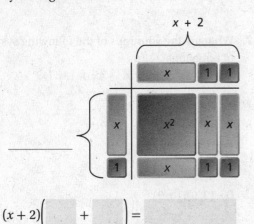

$(x + 2)\left(\boxed{} + \boxed{}\right) = \boxed{}$

12. A diver leaves a 3-foot-high diving board with an initial upward velocity of 11 feet per second. Use the projectile motion model, $h(t) = -16t^2 + vt + h_0$, for the following.

a. Write the function that represents the diver's height as a function of time.

_____

b. Graph the function.

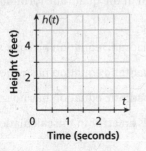

c. What is the diver's maximum height above the water?

_____

d. How much time elapses before the diver enters the water? Round your answer to the nearest hundredth of a second.

_____

e. What is the domain and range of the function in terms of the situation?

_____

13. Solve the quadratic equation. Tell which method you used and explain why.

$$0 = 3x^2 - 4x + 12$$

_____

_____

_____

14. Solve the system of equations algebraically. What do the solutions tell you about the graphs of the two functions?

$$f(x) = -3x^2 + 3x + 4$$
$$g(x) = -6x + 4$$

_____

_____

15. Solve the quadratic equation by completing the square. Show all work. Round solutions to the nearest tenth, if necessary.

$$11 = 2x^2 + 5x$$

_____

_____

_____

_____

_____

_____

_____

Data Analysis

Unit Focus

In this unit you will learn how to display and analyze data. You will begin by calculating statistics that locate the center and measure the spread of a set of numerical data. Then you will see how displaying numerical data in various ways helps you make sense of data, especially when the amount of data is substantial. By comparing data displays for two sets of numerical data, you will be able to draw conclusions about how one set differs from another. Finally, you will learn how to organize and analyze categorical data by using relative frequencies.

Unit at a Glance

COMMON CORE

Lesson		Standards for Mathematical Content
9-1	Measures of Center and Spread	CC.9-12.S.ID.2*
9-2	Data Distributions and Outliers	CC.9-12.S.ID.1*, CC.9-12.S.ID.2*, CC.9-12.S.ID.3*
9-3	Histograms	CC.9-12.S.ID.1*, CC.9-12.S.ID.2*
9-4	Box Plots	CC.9-12.S.ID.1*, CC.9-12.S.ID.2*
9-5	Two-Way Frequency Tables	CC.9-12.S.ID.5*
	Test Prep	

Unpacking the Common Core State Standards

Use the table to help you understand the Standards for Mathematical Content that are taught in this unit. Refer to the lessons listed after each standard for exploration and practice.

COMMON CORE Standards for Mathematical Content	What It Means For You
CC.9-12.S.ID.1 Represent data with plots on the real number line (dot plots, histograms, and box plots).* Lessons 9-2, 9-3, 9-4	You will see how different data displays reveal different aspects of a data set. Data displays are useful in making sense of raw data, such as long lists of numbers.
CC.9-12.S.ID.2 Use statistics appropriate to the shape of the data distribution to compare center (median, mean) and spread (interquartile range, standard deviation) of two or more different data sets.* Lessons 9-1, 9-2, 9-3, 9-4	You will see that there are a variety of statistics that can be used to describe a single data set. You will learn that some statistics are more useful than others in describing certain data sets.
CC.9-12.S.ID.3 Interpret differences in shape, center, and spread in the context of the data sets, accounting for possible effects of extreme data points (outliers).* Lesson 9-2	A real-world data set may include extreme data values. Knowing how to recognize extreme data values is important so that the unusual does not cloud your picture of what is typical.
CC.9-12.S.ID.5 Summarize categorical data for two categories in two-way frequency tables. Interpret relative frequencies in the context of the data (including joint, marginal, and conditional relative frequencies). Recognize possible associations and trends in the data.* Lesson 9-5	In most of this unit, you will focus on analyzing numerical data. However, it is also important to learn how to display and make sense of data that involve categories, such as gender and favorite type of pet.

9-1

Measures of Center and Spread

COMMON
CORE

CC.9-12.S.ID.2*

Essential question: *What statistics can you use to characterize and compare the center and spread of data sets?*

Two commonly used measures of the center of a set of numerical data are the *mean* and *median*. Let n be the number of data values. The **mean** is the sum of the data values divided by n. When the data values are ordered from least to greatest, the **median** is either the middle value if n is odd or the average of the two middle values if n is even. The median divides the data set into two halves. The **first quartile** (Q_1) of a data set is the median of the lower half of the data. The **third quartile** (Q_3) is the median of the upper half.

Two commonly used measures of the spread of a set of numerical data are the *range* and *interquartile range*. The **range** is the difference between the greatest data value and the least data value. The **interquartile range** (IQR) is the difference between the third quartile and first quartile: $\text{IQR} = Q_3 - Q_1$.

1 EXAMPLE   Finding Mean, Median, Range, and Interquartile Range

The April high temperatures (in degrees Fahrenheit) for five consecutive years in Boston are listed below. Find the mean, median, range, and interquartile range for this data set.

$$77 \quad 86 \quad 84 \quad 93 \quad 90$$

A Find the mean.

$$\text{Mean} = \frac{77 + 86 + 84 + 93 + 90}{\rule{1cm}{0.4pt}} = \boxed{} = \boxed{}$$

B Find the median.

Write the data values from least to greatest: _____

Identify the middle value: _____

C Find the range.

$$\text{Range} = 93 - \boxed{} = \boxed{}$$

D Find the interquartile range.

Find the first and third quartiles. Do not include the median as part of either the lower half or the upper half of the data.

$$Q_1 = \frac{\boxed{} + \boxed{}}{2} = \boxed{} \quad \text{and} \quad Q_3 = \frac{\boxed{} + \boxed{}}{2} = \boxed{}$$

Find the difference between Q_3 and Q_1: $\text{IQR} = \boxed{} - \boxed{} = \boxed{}$

1a. If 90°F is replaced with 92°F, will the median or mean change? Explain.

_____

_____

1b. Why is the IQR less than the range?

_____

_____

Standard Deviation Another measure of spread is **standard deviation**. It is found by squaring the deviations of the data values from the mean of the data values, then finding the mean of those squared deviations, and finally taking the square root of the mean of the squared deviations. The steps for calculating standard deviation are listed below.

1. Calculate the mean, $\bar{x}$.

2. Calculate each data value's deviation from the mean by finding $x - \bar{x}$ for each data value x.

3. Find $(x - \bar{x})^2$, the square of each deviation.

4. Find the mean of the squared deviations.

5. Take the square root of the mean of the squared deviations.

2 EXAMPLE   Calculating the Standard Deviation

Calculate the standard deviation for the data from the previous example.

A   Complete the table using the fact that the mean of the data is $\bar{x} = 86$.

Data value, x	Deviation from mean, $x - \bar{x}$	Squared deviation, $(x - \bar{x})^2$
77	$77 - 86 = -9$	$(-9)^2 = 81$
86		
84		
93		
90		

B   Find the mean of the squared deviations.

$$\text{Mean} = \frac{81 + \quad + \quad + \quad + \quad}{\quad} = \frac{\quad}{\quad} = \quad$$

C   Take the square root of the mean of the squared deviations. Use a calculator, and round to the nearest tenth.

Square root of mean $= \sqrt{\quad} \approx \quad$

© Houghton Mifflin Harcourt Publishing Company

2a. What is the mean of the deviations *before* squaring? Use your answer to explain why squaring the deviations is reasonable.

_____

_____

2b. In terms of the data values used, what makes calculating the standard deviation different from calculating the range?

_____

2c. What must be true about a data set if the standard deviation is 0? Explain.

_____

_____

Numbers that characterize a data set, such as measures of center and spread, are called **statistics**. They are useful when comparing large sets of data.

3 EXAMPLE   Comparing Statistics for Related Data Sets

The tables below list the average ages of players on 15 teams randomly selected from the 2010 teams in the National Football League (NFL) and Major League Baseball (MLB). Compare the average ages of NFL players to the average ages of MLB players.

NFL Players' Average Ages		MLB Players' Average Ages	
Team	**Average Age**	**Team**	**Average Age**
Bears	25.8	Astros	28.5
Bengals	26.0	Cardinals	29.0
Broncos	26.3	Cubs	28.0
Chiefs	25.7	Diamondbacks	27.8
Colts	25.1	Dodgers	29.5
Eagles	25.2	Giants	29.1
Jets	26.1	Marlins	26.9
Lions	26.4	Mets	28.9
Packers	25.9	Nationals	28.6
Patriots	26.6	Padres	28.7
Saints	26.3	Pirates	26.9
Seahawks	26.2	Phillies	30.5
Steelers	26.8	Reds	28.7
Texans	25.6	Rockies	28.9
Titans	25.7	Yankees	29.3

A On a graphing calculator, enter the two sets of data into two lists, L_1 and L_2. Examine the data as you enter the values, and record your general impressions about how the data sets compare before calculating any statistics.

_____

_____

_____

B Calculate the statistics for the NFL data in list L_1. Then do the same for the MLB data in L_2. Record the results in the table below. Your calculator may use the following notations and abbreviations for the statistics you're interested in.

Mean: $\bar{x}$

Median: Med

IQR: May not be reported directly, but can be obtained by subtracting Q_1 from Q_3

Standard deviation: σx

```
1-Var Stats
x̄=25.98
Σx=389.7
Σx²=10127.63
Sx=.4798809376
σx=.4636090307
↓n=15
```

	Center		Spread	
	Mean	**Median**	**IQR** $(Q_3 - Q_1)$	**Standard Deviation**
NFL				
MLB				

C Compare the corresponding statistics for the NFL data and the MLB data. Are your comparisons consistent for the two measures of center and the two measures of spread? Do your comparisons agree with your general impressions from Part A?

_____

_____

_____

_____

_____

3a. Based on a comparison of the measures of center, what conclusion can you draw about the typical age of an NFL player and of an MLB player?

_____

3b. Based on a comparison of the measures of spread, what conclusion can you draw about variation in the ages of NFL players and of MLB players?

_____

3c. What do you notice about the mean and median for the NFL? For the MLB?

_____

3d. What do you notice about the IQR and standard deviation for the NFL? For the MLB?

_____

PRACTICE

The numbers of students in each of a school's six Algebra 1 classes are listed below. Find each statistic for this data set.

28   30   29   26   31   30

1. Mean = _____

2. Median = _____

3. Range = _____

4. IQR = _____

5. Find the standard deviation of the Algebra 1 class data by completing the table and doing the calculations below it.

Data value, x	Deviation from mean, $x - \overline{x}$	Squared deviation, $(x - \overline{x})^2$
28		
30		
29		
26		
31		
30		

Mean of squared deviations = _____

Standard deviation ≈ _____

6. Error Analysis Suppose a student in the Algebra 1 class with 31 students transfers to the class with 26 students. The student claims that the measures of center and the measures of spread will all change. Correct the student's error.

_____

_____

_____

7. The table lists the heights (in centimeters) of 8 males and 8 females on the U.S. Olympic swim team, all randomly selected from swimmers on the team who participated in the 2008 Olympic Games held in Beijing, China.

Heights of Olympic male swimmers	196	188	196	185	203	183	183	196
Heights of Olympic female swimmers	173	170	178	175	173	180	180	175

a. Use a graphing calculator to complete the table below.

	Center		Spread	
	Mean	**Median**	**IQR** $(Q_3 - Q_1)$	**Standard deviation**
Olympic male swimmers				
Olympic female swimmers				

b. Discuss the consistency of the measures of center for male swimmers and the measures of center for female swimmers, and then compare the measures of center for male and female swimmers.

_____

_____

_____

c. What do the measures of spread tell you about the variation in the heights of the male and female swimmers?

_____

_____

© Houghton Mifflin Harcourt Publishing Company

Data Distributions and Outliers

Essential question: *Which statistics are most affected by outliers, and what shapes can data distributions have?*

COMMON CORE

CC.9-12.S.ID.1*,
CC.9-12.S.ID.2*,
CC.9-12.S.ID.3*

1 EXAMPLE   Using Line Plots to Display Data

Twelve employees at a small company make the following annual salaries (in thousands of dollars): 25, 30, 35, 35, 35, 40, 40, 40, 45, 45, 50, 60.

A   Create a line plot of the data by putting an X above the number line to represent each data value. Stack the Xs for repeated data values.

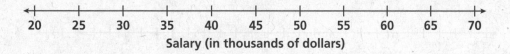

Salary (in thousands of dollars)

B   Complete the table. Round to the nearest hundredth, if necessary.

Mean	Median	Range	IQR	Standard deviation

REFLECT

1a. *Quantitative data* are numbers, such as counts or measurements. *Qualitative data* are categories, such as attributes or preferences. For example, employees' salaries are quantitative data while employees' positions within a company are qualitative data. Is it appropriate to use a line plot for displaying quantitative data, qualitative data, or both? Explain.

_____

_____

1b. The line plot allows you to see how the data are distributed. Describe the overall shape of the distribution of employees' salaries.

_____

1c. When you examine the line plot, do any data values appear to be different than the others? Explain.

_____

Outliers An **outlier** is a value in a data set that is relatively much greater or much less than most of the other values in the data set. Outliers are determined using either the IQR or the standard deviation. Below is one way to determine whether a data value is an outlier.

Determining Whether a Data Value Is an Outlier

A data value x is an outlier if $x < Q_1 - 1.5(IQR)$ or if $x > Q_3 + 1.5(IQR)$.

---

2 EXPLORE Investigating the Effect of an Outlier in a Data Set

Suppose the list of salaries in the previous example is expanded to include the owner's salary, which is $150,000. Now the list of salaries is: 25, 30, 35, 35, 35, 40, 40, 40, 45, 45, 50, 60, 150.

A Create a line plot for the revised data set. Choose an appropriate scale for the number line.

Salary (in thousands of dollars)

B Complete the table. Use a calculator and round to the nearest hundredth, if necessary.

Mean	Median	Range	IQR	Standard deviation

C Complete each sentence by stating whether the statistic increased, decreased, or stayed the same when the data value 150 was added to the original data set. If the statistic increased or decreased, say by what amount.

The mean _____.

The median _____.

The range _____.

The IQR _____.

The standard deviation _____.

© Houghton Mifflin Harcourt Publishing Company

2a. Show that the data value 150 is an outlier, but the data value 60 is not.
Use the inequalities given at the top of the previous page to support your answer.

_____

_____

2b. What effect does the outlier have on the overall shape of the distribution?

_____

2c. For the original data set, you can conclude that the salary of a typical employee
is $40,000 regardless of whether you used the mean or the median. For the
revised data set, you could say that the salary of a typical employee is either
$48,500 or $40,000 depending on whether you used the mean or the median.
Which average salary is more reasonable for the revised data set? Explain
your reasoning.

_____

_____

2d. Based on how the IQR and standard deviation are calculated, explain why the IQR
was only slightly affected by the addition of the outlier while the standard deviation
was dramatically changed.

_____

_____

_____

_____

2e. Because the median and the IQR are based on quartiles while the standard
deviation is based on the mean, the center and spread of a data set are usually
reported either as the median and IQR or as the mean and standard deviation.
Which pair of statistics would you use for a data set that includes one or more
outliers? Explain.

_____

_____

Shapes of Distributions A data distribution can be described as **symmetric**, **skewed to the left**, or **skewed to the right** depending on the general shape of the distribution in a line plot or other data display.

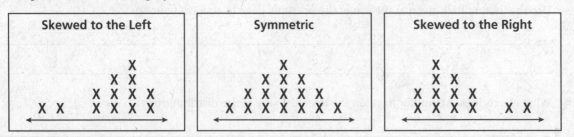

3 EXAMPLE   Comparing Data Distributions

The tables list Sierra's and Jacey's scores on math tests in each quarter of the school year. Create a line plot for each student's scores and identify the distribution as symmetric, skewed to the left, or skewed to the right.

Sierra's Scores			
I	II	III	IV
88	86	92	88
94	90	87	91
91	95	94	91
92	91	88	93
90	94	96	89

Jacey's Scores			
I	II	III	IV
89	76	87	82
83	86	86	85
86	87	72	86
83	88	73	88
87	90	84	89

A Create and examine a line plot for Sierra's scores.

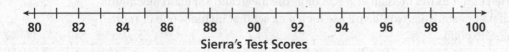

The distribution is centered on one value (91) with the data values to the left of the center balanced with the data values to the right, so the distribution is symmetric.

B Create and examine a line plot for Jacey's scores.

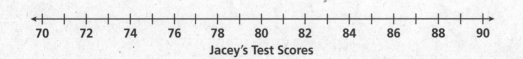

The data values cluster on the right with a few data values spread out to the left of the cluster, so the distribution is skewed to the left.

REFLECT

3a. Find the mean and median for Sierra's test scores. How do they compare?

_____

3b. Will the mean and median in a symmetric distribution always be equal or approximately equal? Explain.

_____

_____

_____

_____

3c. Find the mean and median for Jacey's test scores. How do they compare?

_____

3d. Will the mean and median in a skewed distribution always be different? Explain.

_____

_____

_____

PRACTICE

1. a. Rounded to the nearest $50,000, the values (in thousands of dollars) of homes sold by a realtor are listed below. Use the number line to create a line plot for the data set.

300 250 200 250 350

400 300 250 400 300

200   250   300   350   400
Values of Homes
(in thousands of dollars)

b. Suppose the realtor sells a home with a value of $650,000. Which statistics are affected when 650 is included in the data set?

_____

c. Would 650 be considered an outlier? Explain.

_____

_____

2. In Exercise 1, find the mean and median for the data set with and without the data value 650. Why might the realtor want to use the mean instead of the median when advertising the typical value of homes sold?

_____

_____

3. The table shows Chloe's scores on math tests in each quarter of the school year.

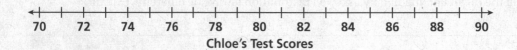

Chloe's Scores			
I	**II**	**III**	**IV**
74	77	79	74
78	75	76	77
82	80	74	76
76	75	77	78
85	77	87	85

a. Use the number line below to create a line plot for Chloe's scores.

70 72 74 76 78 80 82 84 86 88 90
Chloe's Test Scores

b. Complete the table below for the data set.

Mean	Median	Range	IQR	Standard deviation

c. Identify any outliers in the data set. Which of the statistics from the table above would change if the outliers were removed?

_____

d. Describe the shape of the distribution.

_____

e. Which measure of center and which measure of spread should be used to characterize the data? Explain.

_____

4. Give an example of a data set with a symmetric distribution that also includes one or more outliers.

_____

5. Suppose that a data set has an approximately symmetric distribution, with one outlier. What could you do if you wanted to use the mean and standard deviation to characterize the data?

_____

Histograms

COMMON CORE

CC.9-12.S.ID.1*,
CC.9-12.S.ID.2*

Essential question: *How can you estimate statistics from data displayed in a histogram?*

Like a line plot, a histogram uses a number line to display data. Rather than display the data values individually as a line plot does, a histogram groups the data values into adjoining intervals of equal width and uses the heights of bars to indicate the number of data values that occur in each interval.

The number of data values in an interval is called the *frequency* of the interval. A histogram has a vertical frequency axis so that you can read the frequency for each interval. In the histogram at the right, you can see that 3 students had test scores in the interval 60–69, 9 students had test scores in the interval 70–79, and so on.

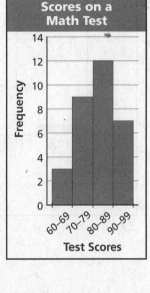

Scores on a Math Test

---

1 EXAMPLE Creating a Histogram

Listed below are the ages of the 100 U.S. senators at the time that the 112th Congress began on January 3, 2011. Create a histogram for this data set.

39, 39, 42, 44, 46, 47, 47, 47, 48, 49, 49, 49, 50, 50, 51, 51, 52, 52, 53, 53, 54, 54, 55, 55, 55, 55, 55, 55, 56, 56, 57, 57, 57, 58, 58, 58, 58, 58, 59, 59, 59, 59, 60, 60, 60, 60, 60, 60, 60, 61, 61, 62, 62, 62, 63, 63, 63, 63, 64, 64, 64, 64, 66, 66, 66, 67, 67, 67, 67, 67, 67, 67, 68, 68, 68, 68, 69, 69, 69, 70, 70, 70, 71, 71, 73, 73, 74, 74, 74, 75, 76, 76, 76, 76, 77, 77, 78, 86, 86, 86

A Create a frequency table. To do so, you must decide what the interval width will be and where to start the first interval. Since the data are ages that run from 39 to 86, you might decide to use an interval width of 10 and start the first interval at 30. So, the first interval includes any Senator who is in his or her 30s.

Use the data to complete the table at the right. When done, be sure to check that the sum of the frequencies is 100.

Age Interval	Frequency
30–39	2

B   Use the frequency table to complete the histogram.

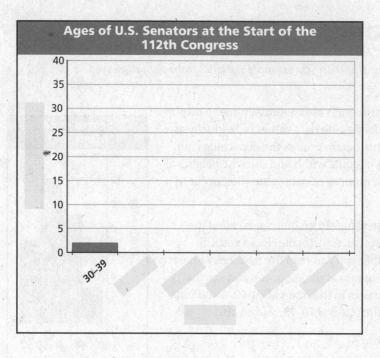

Ages of U.S. Senators at the Start of the 112th Congress

REFLECT

1a. Describe the shape of the distribution. Is it approximately symmetric, skewed to the right, or skewed to the left? Explain.

_____

_____

_____

1b. Estimate the center of the distribution. Explain your reasoning.

_____

_____

1c. Using the histogram alone, and not the data values on the first page of this lesson, estimate the maximum possible range and the minimum possible range. Explain your reasoning.

_____

_____

_____

_____

_____

Although the first page of this lesson listed the ages all 100 senators, suppose you have only the histogram on the second page as a reference. Show how to estimate the mean and the median ages from the histogram.

A Estimate the mean. You know the frequency of each interval, but you don't know the individual data values. Use the midpoint of the interval as a substitute for each of those values. So, for the interval 30–39, you can estimate the sum of the data values by multiplying the midpoint, 35, by the frequency, 2. Complete the calculation below, rounding the final result to the nearest whole number.

$$\text{Mean} \approx \frac{35 \cdot 2 + \boxed{} \cdot \boxed{} + \boxed{} \cdot \boxed{} + \boxed{} \cdot \boxed{} + \boxed{} \cdot \boxed{} + \boxed{} \cdot \boxed{} + \boxed{} \cdot \boxed{}}{}$$

$$= \frac{\boxed{}}{\boxed{}} \approx \boxed{}$$

B Estimate the median. The median is the average of the 50th and 51st data values. In what interval do these values fall? Explain.

_____

_____

The median is the average of the 8th and 9th values in an interval with 37 values, so you can estimate that the median is the sum of the interval's least value and $\frac{8.5}{37} \approx 20\%$ of the interval width, 10. So, what is the estimate?

_____

2a. How do the estimates of the mean and median support the observation that the distribution is approximately symmetric?

_____

_____

2b. Describe how you could estimate the IQR. Then give your estimate.

_____

_____

_____

1. The ages of the first 44 U.S. presidents on the date of their first inauguration are listed below.

   42, 43, 46, 46, 47, 47, 48, 49, 49, 50, 51, 51, 51, 51, 51, 52, 52, 54, 54, 54, 54, 54, 55, 55, 55, 55, 56, 56, 56, 57, 57, 57, 57, 58, 60, 61, 61, 61, 62, 64, 64, 65, 68, 69

   a. Complete the frequency table by organizing the data into six equal intervals.

Age Interval	Frequency
41–45	2

   b. Use the frequency table to complete the histogram.

   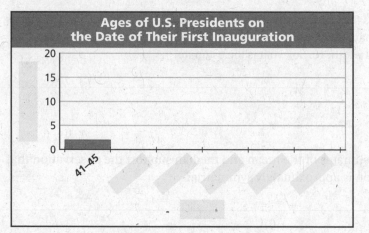

   c. Describe the shape of the distribution. What measures of center and spread would you use to characterize the data? Why?

   _____

   _____

   d. Use the histogram to estimate the median and IQR.

   _____

   _____

2. Describe a way to estimate the standard deviation from a histogram.

   _____

   _____

   _____

Box Plots

Essential question: *How can you compare data sets using box plots?*

COMMON CORE

CC.9-12.S.ID.1*,
CC.9-12.S.ID.2*

1 **EXAMPLE** Interpreting a Box Plot

The table lists the total number of home runs hit at home games by each team in Major League Baseball (MLB) during the 2010 season. The data are displayed in the box plot below the table. Identify the statistics that are represented in the box plot, and describe the distribution of the data.

Home Runs in 2010 MLB Games Played at Home					
Team	**Home Runs**	**Team**	**Home Runs**	**Team**	**Home Runs**
Toronto	146	Tampa Bay	78	Cleveland	64
NY Yankees	115	San Francisco	75	Pittsburgh	64
Chicago Sox	111	Atlanta	74	Houston	63
Colorado	108	Chicago Cubs	74	NY Mets	63
Cincinnati	102	Washington	74	LA Dodgers	61
Milwaukee	100	Baltimore	72	Kansas City	60
Boston	98	Detroit	70	San Diego	59
Arizona	98	LA Angels	69	Minnesota	52
Philadelphia	94	Florida	69	Oakland	46
Texas	93	St. Louis	67	Seattle	35

Home Runs in 2010 MLB Games Played at Home

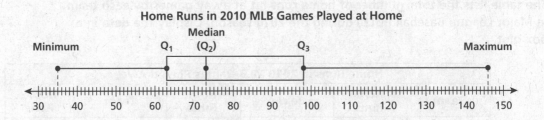

A A box plot displays a five-number summary of a data set. The five numbers are the statistics listed below. Use the box plot to determine each statistic.

Minimum	First Quartile	Median	Third Quartile	Maximum

B A box plot also shows the distribution of the data. Find the range of the lower half and the upper half of the data.

Range of lower half: _____   Range of upper half: _____

The data are more spread out in the upper half than the lower half, so the distribution is skewed to the right.

1a. The lines that extend from the box in a box plot are sometimes called "whiskers." What *part* (lower, middle, or upper) and about what *percent* of the data does the box represent? What part and about what percent does each whisker represent?

_____

1b. Which measures of spread can be determined from the box plot, and how are they found? Calculate each measure.

_____

_____

1c. In the table, the data value 146 appears to be much greater than the other data values. Determine whether 146 is an outlier.

_____

_____

1d. The mean of the data is about 78.5. Use the shape of the distribution to explain why the mean is greater than the median.

_____

_____

_____

2 EXAMPLE   Comparing Data Using Box Plots

The table lists the total number of home runs hit at away games by each team in Major League Baseball (MLB) during the 2010 season. Display the data in a box plot.

Home Runs in 2010 MLB Games Played Away					
Team	Home Runs	Team	Home Runs	Team	Home Runs
Boston	113	Milwaukee	82	Atlanta	65
Toronto	111	Arizona	82	NY Mets	65
Minnesota	90	Tampa Bay	82	Colorado	65
San Francisco	87	Chicago Cubs	75	Cleveland	64
LA Angels	86	Washington	75	Oakland	63
NY Yankees	86	San Diego	73	Pittsburgh	62
Cincinnati	86	Philadelphia	72	Baltimore	61
St. Louis	83	Texas	69	Kansas City	61
Florida	83	Chicago Sox	66	LA Dodgers	59
Detroit	82	Seattle	66	Houston	45

A Find the values for the five-number summary.

Minimum	First Quartile	Median	Third Quartile	Maximum

B Determine whether the data set includes any outliers. Begin by finding the value of each expression below using the fact that the IQR = $Q_3 - Q_1 = 83 - 65 = 18$.

$Q_1 - 1.5(\text{IQR}) = $ _____ $Q_3 + 1.5(\text{IQR}) = $ _____

These values are sometimes called *fences* because they form the boundaries outside of which a data value is considered to be an outlier. Which data values, if any, are outliers for the away-game data? Why?

_____

C The box plot shown below displays the number of home runs hit at home games during the 2010 MLB season. Draw a second box plot that displays the data for away games. The whiskers should extend only to the least and greatest data values that lie within the fences established in Part B. Show any outliers as individual dots.

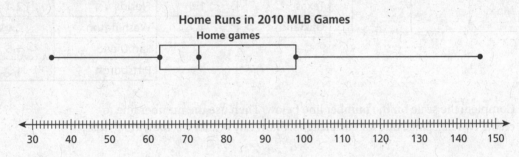

Home Runs in 2010 MLB Games
Home games

REFLECT

2a. Use the box plots to compare the center, spread, and shape of the two data distributions. Ignore any outliers.

_____

_____

_____

_____

1. The table shows the 2010 average salary for an MLB player by team for both the American League (AL) and the National League (NL).

   a. Find the values for the five-number summary for each league.

	AL	NL
Min.		
Q₁		
Median		
Q₃		
Max.		

MLB Players' Average 2010 Salaries (in Millions of Dollars)			
American League		**National League**	
Team	**Salary**	**Team**	**Salary**
New York	8.3	Chicago	5.4
Boston	5.6	Philadelphia	5.1
Detroit	4.6	New York	5.1
Chicago	4.2	St. Louis	3.7
Los Angeles	3.6	Los Angeles	3.7
Seattle	3.5	San Francisco	3.5
Minnesota	3.5	Houston	3.3
Baltimore	3.1	Atlanta	3.1
Tampa Bay	2.7	Colorado	2.9
Kansas City	2.5	Milwaukee	2.8
Cleveland	2.1	Cincinnati	2.8
Toronto	2.1	Arizona	2.3
Texas	1.9	Florida	2.1
Oakland	1.7	Washington	2.0
		San Diego	1.5
		Pittsburgh	1.3

   b. Complete the scale on the number line below. Then use the number line to create two box plots, one for each league. Show any outliers as individual dots.

   MLB Player's Average 2010 Salaries (in Millions of Dollars)

   1.0

   c. Compare the center, spread, and shape of the two data distributions. Ignore any outliers.

   _____

   _____

   _____

   _____

   _____

Two-Way Frequency Tables

Essential question: *How can categorical data be organized and analyzed?*

COMMON CORE

CC.9-12.S.ID.5*

In previous lessons, you worked with numerical data involving variables such as age and height. In this lesson, you will analyze *categorical* data that involve variables such as pet preference and gender.

---

1 **EXAMPLE** Creating a Relative Frequency Table

The frequency table below shows the results of a survey that Jenna took at her school. She asked 40 randomly selected students whether they preferred dogs, cats, or other pets. Convert this table to a *relative frequency* table that uses decimals as well as one that uses percents.

Preferred Pet	Dog	Cat	Other	Total
Frequency	18	12	10	40

A Divide the numbers in the frequency table by the total to obtain relative frequencies as decimals. Record the results in the table below.

Preferred Pet	Dog	Cat	Other	Total
Relative Frequency	$\frac{18}{40} = 0.45$			

B Write the decimals as percents in the table below.

Preferred Pet	Dog	Cat	Other	Total
Relative Frequency	45%			

REFLECT

1a. How can you check that you have correctly converted frequencies to relative frequencies?

_____

_____

1b. Explain why the number in the Total column of a relative frequency table is always 1 or 100%.

_____

_____

In the previous example, the categorical variable was pet preference, and the variable had three possible data values: dog, cat, and other. The frequency table listed the frequency for each value of that single variable. If you have two categorical variables whose values have been paired, you list the frequencies of the paired values in a **two-way frequency table**.

2 EXAMPLE   Creating a Two-Way Frequency Table

For her survey, Jenna also recorded the gender of each student. The results are shown in the two-way frequency table below. Each entry is the frequency of students who prefer a certain pet *and* are a certain gender. For instance, 8 girls prefer dogs as pets. Complete the table.

Preferred Pet / Gender	Dog	Cat	Other	Total
Girl	8	7	1	
Boy	10	5	9	
Total				

A   Find the total for each gender by adding the frequencies in each row. Write the row totals in the Total column.

B   Find the total for each preferred pet by adding the frequencies in each column. Write the column totals in the Total row.

C   Find the grand total, which is the sum of the row totals as well as the sum of the column totals. Write the grand total in the lower-right corner of the table (the intersection of the Total column and the Total row).

REFLECT

2a. Where have you seen the numbers in the Total row before?

_____

2b. In terms of Jenna's survey, what does the grand total represent?

_____

You can obtain the following *relative* frequencies from a two-way frequency table:

- A **joint relative frequency** is found by dividing a frequency that is not in the Total row or the Total column by the grand total.
- A **marginal relative frequency** is found by dividing a row total or a column total by the grand total.

A **two-way relative frequency table** displays both joint relative frequencies and marginal relative frequencies.

3 EXAMPLE Creating a Two-Way Relative Frequency Table

Create a two-way relative frequency table for Jenna's data.

A Divide each number in the two-way frequency table from the previous example by the grand total. Write the quotients as decimals.

Gender \ Preferred Pet	Dog	Cat	Other	Total
Girl	$\frac{8}{40} = 0.2$			
Boy				
Total	$\frac{18}{40} = 0.45$			$\frac{40}{40} = 1$

B Check by adding the joint relative frequencies in a row or column to see if the sum equals the row or column's marginal relative frequency.

Girl row: $0.2 + \underline{\hspace{1cm}} + \underline{\hspace{1cm}} = \underline{\hspace{1cm}}$

Boy row: $\underline{\hspace{1cm}} + \underline{\hspace{1cm}} + \underline{\hspace{1cm}} = \underline{\hspace{1cm}}$

Dog column: $0.2 + \underline{\hspace{1cm}} = 0.45$

Cat column: $\underline{\hspace{1cm}} + \underline{\hspace{1cm}} = \underline{\hspace{1cm}}$

Other column: $\underline{\hspace{1cm}} + \underline{\hspace{1cm}} = \underline{\hspace{1cm}}$

REFLECT

3a. A joint relative frequency in a two-way relative frequency table tells you what portion of the entire data set falls into the intersection of a particular value of one variable and a particular value of the other variable. For instance, the joint relative frequency of students surveyed who are girls *and* prefer dogs as pets is 0.2, or 20%. What is the joint relative frequency of students surveyed who are boys and prefer cats as pets?

_____

3b. A marginal relative frequency in a two-way relative frequency table tells you what portion of the entire data set represents a particular value of just one of the variables. For instance, the marginal relative frequency of students surveyed who prefer dogs as pets is 0.45, or 45%. What is the marginal relative frequency of students surveyed who are girls?

_____

One other type of relative frequency that you can obtain from a two-way frequency table is a *conditional relative frequency*. A **conditional relative frequency** is found by dividing a frequency that is not in the Total row or the Total column by the frequency's row total or column total.

4 **EXAMPLE** Calculating Conditional Relative Frequencies

From Jenna's two-way frequency table you know that 16 students surveyed are girls and 12 students surveyed prefer cats as pets. You also know that 7 students surveyed are girls who prefer cats as pets. Use this information to find each conditional relative frequency.

A Find the conditional relative frequency that a student surveyed prefers cats as pets, given that the student is a girl.

Divide the number of girls who prefer cats as pets by the number of girls. Express your answer as a decimal and as a percent.

_____

B Find the conditional relative frequency that a student surveyed is a girl, given that the student prefers cats as pets.

Divide the number of girls who prefer cats as pets by the number of students who prefer cats as pets. Express your answer as a decimal and as a percent.

_____

REFLECT

4a. When calculating a conditional relative frequency, why do you divide by a row total or a column total and not by the grand total?

_____

_____

_____

4b. You can obtain conditional relative frequencies from a two-way *relative* frequency table. For instance, in Jenna's survey, the relative frequency of girls who prefer cats as pets is 0.175, and the relative frequency of girls is 0.4. Find the conditional relative frequency that a student surveyed prefers cats as pets, given that the student is a girl.

_____

© Houghton Mifflin Harcourt Publishing Company

Jenna conducted her survey because she was interested in the question, "Does gender influence what type of pet people prefer?" If there is no influence, then the distribution of gender within each subgroup of pet preference should roughly equal the distribution of gender within the whole group. Use the results of Jenna's survey to investigate possible influences of gender on pet preference.

A Identify the percent of all students surveyed who are girls: _____

B Determine each conditional relative frequency.

Of the 18 students who prefer dogs as pets, 8 are girls.
Percent who are girls, given a preference for dogs as pets: _____

Of the 12 students who prefer cats as pets, 7 are girls.
Percent who are girls, given a preference for cats as pets: _____

Of the 10 students who prefer other pets, 1 is a girl.
Percent who are girls, given a preference for other pets: _____

C Interpret the results by comparing each conditional relative frequency to the percent of all students surveyed who are girls.

The percent of girls among students who prefer dogs is fairly close to 40%, so gender does not appear to influence preference for dogs.

The percent of girls among students who prefer cats is much greater than 40%. What conclusion might you draw in this case?

_____

The percent of girls among students who prefer other pets is much less than 25%. What conclusion might you draw in this case?

_____

REFLECT

5a. Suppose you analyzed the data by focusing on boys rather than girls. How would the percent in Part A change? How would the percents in Part B change? How would the conclusions in Part C change?

_____

_____

5b. For pet preference to be completely uninfluenced by gender, about how many girls would have to prefer each type of pet? Explain.

_____

_____

© Houghton Mifflin Harcourt Publishing Company

Antonio surveyed 60 of his classmates about their participation in school activities as well as whether they have a part-time job. The results are shown in the two-way frequency table below. Use the table to complete the exercises.

Job \ Activity	Clubs Only	Sports Only	Both	Neither	Total
Yes	12	13	16	4	
No	3	5	5	2	
Total					

1. Complete the table by finding the row totals, column totals, and grand total.

2. Create a two-way relative frequency table using decimals.

Job \ Activity	Clubs Only	Sports Only	Both	Neither	Total
Yes					
No					
Total					

3. Give each relative frequency as a percent.

   a. The joint relative frequency of students surveyed who participate in school clubs only and have part-time jobs: _____

   b. The marginal relative frequency of students surveyed who do not have a part-time job: _____

   c. The conditional relative frequency that a student surveyed participates in both school clubs and sports, given that the student has a part-time job: _____

4. Discuss possible influences of having a part-time job on participation in school activities. Support your response with an analysis of the data.

_____

_____

_____

Name _____ Class _____ Date _____

MULTIPLE CHOICE

For Items 1–3, use the line plots below.

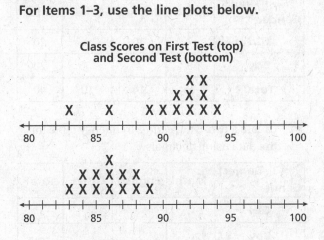

Class Scores on First Test (top)
and Second Test (bottom)

For Items 4–6, use the histograms below.

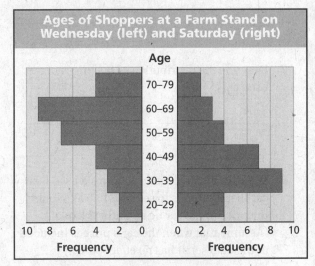

Ages of Shoppers at a Farm Stand on
Wednesday (left) and Saturday (right)

1. How do the medians of the two sets of test scores compare?

   A. The median for the first test is greater than the median for the second test.

   B. The median for the first test is less than the median for the second test.

   C. The medians for the first and second tests are equal.

   D. The relationship cannot be determined.

2. For which test is the median greater than the mean?

   F. First test only

   G. Second test only

   H. Both tests

   J. Neither test

3. Which measure of center is appropriate for comparing the two sets of test scores?

   A. The median only

   B. The mean only

   C. Either the median or the mean

   D. Neither the median nor the mean

4. Which distribution is skewed toward older ages?

   F. Only the Wednesday distribution

   G. Only the Saturday distribution

   H. Both distributions

   J. Neither distribution

5. How do the spreads of the two distributions compare?

   A. The spread for the Wednesday data is much greater than the spread for the Saturday data.

   B. The spread for the Wednesday data is much less than the spread for the Saturday data.

   C. The spreads are roughly equal.

   D. The relationship cannot be determined.

6. Which measure of spread is appropriate for comparing the sets of ages?

   F. The interquartile range only

   G. The standard deviation only

   H. Either the interquartile range or the standard deviation

   J. Neither the interquartile range nor the standard deviation

For Items 7–10, use the box plot below.

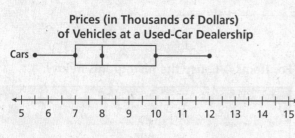

Prices (in Thousands of Dollars)
of Vehicles at a Used-Car Dealership

7. Describe the distribution of the prices of the used cars.

_____

_____

8. Suppose the dealership acquires a used luxury car that it intends to sell for $15,000. Would the price of the car be an outlier? Explain. (Assume that when the car's price is included in the data set, it has no effect on Q_3.)

_____

_____

9. The dealership also sells used SUVs. The prices (in thousands of dollars) of the SUVs are listed below. Add a box plot for the SUVs to the data display above.

    6, 6, 7.5, 7.5, 8, 9, 11, 11, 11, 13, 14, 15

10. Compare the distribution of prices for the used SUVs with the distribution of prices for the used cars.

_____

_____

_____

_____

_____

Derrick surveyed 40 of his classmates by asking each of them whether his or her favorite subject is math, English, or another subject. He also recorded the gender of each classmate surveyed. He recorded his results in the two-way frequency table below. Use the table to complete Items 11–15.

Gender \ Subject	Math	English	Other	Total
Girl	7	10	3	20
Boy	9	4	7	20
Total	16	14	10	40

11. Create a two-way *relative* frequency table for the data using decimals.

Gender \ Subject	Math	English	Other	Total
Girl				
Boy				
Total				

12. Find the joint relative frequency of surveyed students who are girls and prefer English.

_____

13. Find the marginal relative frequency of surveyed students who prefer math.

_____

14. Find the conditional relative frequency that a surveyed student prefers another subject, given that the student is a girl.

_____

15. Discuss possible influences of gender on favorite subject.

_____

_____

_____

_____

_____

© Houghton Mifflin Harcourt Publishing Company

Correlation of *On Core Mathematics* to the Common Core State Standards

Standards	Algebra 1	Geometry	Algebra 2
Number and Quantity			
The Real Number System			
CC.9-12.N.RN.1 Explain how the definition of the meaning of rational exponents follows from extending the properties of integer exponents to those values, allowing for a notation for radicals in terms of rational exponents.			Lesson 1-2
CC.9-12.N.RN.2 Rewrite expressions involving radicals and rational exponents using the properties of exponents.			Lesson 1-2
CC.9-12.N.RN.3 Explain why the sum or product of two rational numbers is rational; that the sum of a rational number and an irrational number is irrational; and that the product of a nonzero rational number and an irrational number is irrational.			Lesson 1-1
Quantities			
CC.9-12.N.Q.1 Use units as a way to understand problems and to guide the solution of multi-step problems; choose and interpret units consistently in formulas; choose and interpret the scale and the origin in graphs and data displays.*	**Lessons 1-1, 1-2, 1-3, 1-5, 1-6, 2-3, 2-8, 3-6, 4-2, 4-3, 7-6**		Lesson 2-6
CC.9-12.N.Q.2 Define appropriate quantities for the purpose of descriptive modeling.*	**Lessons 1-3, 1-4, 2-3, 2-8, 3-6, 7-6**		
CC.9-12.N.Q.3 Choose a level of accuracy appropriate to limitations on measurement when reporting quantities.*		Lesson 9-1	
The Complex Number System			
CC.9-12.N.CN.1 Know there is a complex number i such that $i^2 = -1$, and every complex number has the form $a + bi$ with a and b real.			Lesson 1-3
CC.9-12.N.CN.2 Use the relation $i^2 = -1$ and the commutative, associative, and distributive properties to add, subtract, and multiply complex numbers.			Lesson 1-3
CC.9-12.N.CN.3(+) Find the conjugate of a complex number; use conjugates to find moduli and quotients of complex numbers.			Lesson 1-4

(+) Advanced   * = Also a Modeling Standard

Standards	Algebra 1	Geometry	Algebra 2
CC.9-12.N.CN.7 Solve quadratic equations with real coefficients that have complex solutions.			Lesson 1-5
CC.9-12.N.CN.9(+) Know the Fundamental Theorem of Algebra; show that it is true for quadratic polynomials.			Lesson 3-10
Algebra			
Seeing Structure in Expressions			
CC.9-12.A.SSE.1 Interpret expressions that represent a quantity in terms of its context.* **a.** Interpret parts of an expression, such as terms, factors, and coefficients. **b.** Interpret complicated expressions by viewing one or more of their parts as a single entity.	Lessons 1-1, 1-2, 1-3, 2-8		Lessons 2-6, 3-5, 3-11, 4-4, 4-5, 9-4, 9-5
CC.9-12.A.SSE.2 Use the structure of an expression to identify ways to rewrite it.	Lessons 1-2, 1-3, 2-1, 2-2, 8-1		Lessons 3-9, 3-10
CC.9-12.A.SSE.3 Choose and produce an equivalent form of an expression to reveal and explain properties of the quantity represented by the expression. **a.** Factor a quadratic expression to reveal the zeros of the function it defines. **b.** Complete the square in a quadratic expression to reveal the maximum or minimum value of the function it defines. **c.** Use the properties of exponents to transform expressions for exponential functions.	Lessons 8-2, 8-3, 8-10		Lessons 2-4, 2-5, 6-4, 6-6
CC.9-12.A.SSE.4 Derive the formula for the sum of a finite geometric series (when the common ratio is not 1), and use the formula to solve problems.			Lessons 9-4, 9-5
Arithmetic with Polynomials and Rational Expressions			
CC.9-12.A.APR.1 Understand that polynomials form a system analogous to the integers, namely, they are closed under the operations of addition, subtraction, and multiplication; add, subtract, and multiply polynomials.	Lessons 4-6, 8-1		Lessons 3-5, 3-6, 3-7, 3-8
CC.9-12.A.APR.2 Know and apply the Remainder Theorem: For a polynomial $p(x)$ and a number a, the remainder on division by $x - a$ is $p(a)$, so $p(a) = 0$ if and only if $(x - a)$ is a factor of $p(x)$.			Lesson 3-8
CC.9-12.A.APR.3 Identify zeros of polynomials when suitable factorizations are available, and use the zeros to construct a rough graph of the function defined by the polynomial.			Lesson 3-9
CC.9-12.A.APR.4 Prove polynomial identities and use them to describe numerical relationships.			Lesson 3-6

(+) Advanced   * = Also a Modeling Standard

© Houghton Mifflin Harcourt Publishing Company

Standards	Algebra 1	Geometry	Algebra 2
CC.9-12.A.APR.5(+) Know and apply the Binomial Theorem for the expansion of $(x + y)^n$ in powers of x and y for a positive integer n, where x and y are any numbers, with coefficients determined for example by Pascal's Triangle. (The Binomial Theorem can be proved by mathematical induction or by a combinatorial argument.)			Lesson 3-7
CC.9-12.A.APR.6 Rewrite simple rational expressions in different forms; write $a(x)/b(x)$ in the form $q(x) + r(x)/b(x)$, where $a(x)$, $b(x)$, $q(x)$, and $r(x)$ are polynomials with the degree of $r(x)$ less than the degree of $b(x)$, using inspection, long division, or, for the more complicated examples, a computer algebra system.			Lesson 4-3
CC.9-12.A.APR.7(+) Understand that rational expressions form a system analogous to the rational numbers, closed under addition, subtraction, multiplication, and division by a nonzero rational expression; add, subtract, multiply, and divide rational expressions.			Lessons 4-4, 4-5
Creating Equations			
CC.9-12.A.CED.1 Create equations and inequalities in one variable and use them to solve problems.*	Lessons 1-4, 2-3, 5-5, 6-5, 7-4, 7-5, 8-3, 8-7		Lessons 3-11, 4-6, 6-7, 7-4
CC.9-12.A.CED.2 Create equations in two or more variables to represent relationships between quantities; graph equations on coordinate axes with labels and scales.*	Lessons 2-3, 2-5, 2-8, 3-6, 4-2, 4-3, 4-5, 4-6, 5-1, 5-5, 5-6, 5-8, 6-1, 6-2, 6-3, 6-4, 6-5, 6-6, 7-1, 7-2, 7-3, 7-4, 7-6, 8-9, 8-10		Lessons 2-3, 2-4, 2-5, 2-6, 3-9, 3-11, 4-1, 4-2, 4-3, 4-7, 5-1, 5-2, 5-3, 5-5, 5-6, 6-2, 6-3, 6-4, 6-5, 6-6, 7-5, 8-9
CC.9-12.A.CED.3 Represent constraints by equations or inequalities, and by systems of equations and/or inequalities, and interpret solutions as viable or nonviable options in a modeling context.*	Lessons 1-4, 2-3, 2-8, 3-6		Lessons 2-6, 3-11, 9-5
CC.9-12.A.CED.4 Rearrange formulas to highlight a quantity of interest, using the same reasoning as in solving equations.*	Lesson 2-5		Lesson 7-5
Reasoning with Equations and Inequalities			
CC.9-12.A.REI.1. Explain each step in solving a simple equation as following from the equality of numbers asserted at the previous step, starting from the assumption that the original equation has a solution. Construct a viable argument to justify a solution method.	Lessons 2-1, 2-2, 2-4		
CC.9-12.A.REI.2 Solve simple rational and radical equations in one variable, and give examples showing how extraneous solutions may arise.			Lessons 4-6, 5-7
CC.9-12.A.REI.3 Solve linear equations and inequalities in one variable, including equations with coefficients represented by letters.	Lessons 2-1, 2-2, 2-3, 2-4		

(+) Advanced   * = Also a Modeling Standard

© Houghton Mifflin Harcourt Publishing Company

Standards	Algebra 1	Geometry	Algebra 2
CC.9-12.A.REI.4 Solve quadratic equations in one variable. **a.** Use the method of completing the square to transform any quadratic equation in x into an equation of the form $(x - p)^2 = q$ that has the same solutions. Derive the quadratic formula from this form. **b.** Solve quadratic equations by inspection (e.g., for $x^2 = 49$), taking square roots, completing the square, the quadratic formula and factoring, as appropriate to the initial form of the equation. Recognize when the quadratic formula gives complex solutions and write them as $a \pm bi$ for real numbers a and b.	**Lessons 7-5, 8-2, 8-3, 8-4, 8-5, 8-6, 8-7, 8-9, 8-10**		Lesson 1-5
CC.9-12.A.REI.5 Prove that, given a system of two equations in two variables, replacing one equation by the sum of that equation and a multiple of the other produces a system with the same solutions.	**Lesson 3-4**		
CC.9-12.A.REI.6 Solve systems of linear equations exactly and approximately (e.g., with graphs), focusing on pairs of linear equations in two variables.	**Lessons 3-1, 3-2, 3-3, 3-4, 3-6**		
CC.9-12.A.REI.7 Solve a simple system consisting of a linear equation and a quadratic equation in two variables algebraically and graphically.	**Lesson 8-9**	Lesson 8-7	
CC.9-12.A.REI.10 Understand that the graph of an equation in two variables is the set of all its solutions plotted in the coordinate plane, often forming a curve (which could be a line).	**Lessons 2-6, 2-7**		
CC.9-12.A.REI.11 Explain why the x-coordinates of the points where the graphs of the equations $y = f(x)$ and $y = g(x)$ intersect are the solutions of the equation $f(x) = g(x)$; find the solutions approximately, e.g., using technology to graph the functions, make tables of values, or find successive approximations. Include cases where $f(x)$ and/or $g(x)$ are linear, polynomial, rational, absolute value, exponential, and logarithmic functions.*	**Lessons 4-5, 5-5, 5-8, 6-5, 7-4**		Lessons 4-6, 5-7, 6-7, 7-4
CC.9-12.A.REI.12 Graph the solutions to a linear inequality in two variables as a half-plane (excluding the boundary in the case of a strict inequality), and graph the solution set to a system of linear inequalities in two variables as the intersection of the corresponding half-planes.	**Lessons 2-6, 2-7, 3-5, 3-6**		
Functions			
Interpreting Functions			
CC.9-12.F.IF.1 Understand that a function from one set (called the domain) to another set (called the range) assigns to each element of the domain exactly one element of the range. If f is a function and x is an element of its domain, then $f(x)$ denotes the output of f corresponding to the input x. The graph of f is the graph of the equation $y = f(x)$.	**Lessons 1-5, 1-6, 4-2, 4-7, 5-2**		Lesson 8-3

(+) Advanced   * = Also a Modeling Standard

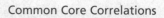© Houghton Mifflin Harcourt Publishing Company

Standards	Algebra 1	Geometry	Algebra 2
CC.9-12.F.IF.2 Use function notation, evaluate functions for inputs in their domains, and interpret statements that use function notation in terms of a context.	**Lessons 1-5, 1-6, 4-1, 4-2, 4-7, 5-1, 6-1, 6-2, 6-3, 6-4, 6-6, 7-1, 7-2, 7-3, 7-6, 8-10**		Lessons 2-1, 2-2, 2-3, 2-4, 2-5, 2-6, 3-4, 4-1, 4-2, 4-3, 4-7, 5-1, 5-2, 5-3, 5-5, 5-6, 6-1, 6-2, 6-3, 6-4, 6-5, 7-1, 7-5, 8-9, 9-1
CC.9-12.F.IF.3 Recognize that sequences are functions, sometimes defined recursively, whose domain is a subset of the integers.	**Lessons 4-1, 5-1**		Lesson 9-1
CC.9-12.F.IF.4 For a function that models a relationship between two quantities, interpret key features of graphs and tables in terms of the quantities, and sketch graphs showing key features given a verbal description of the relationship.*	**Lessons 4-3, 4-4, 4-5, 5-3, 5-4, 6-1, 6-6, 7-1, 7-2, 7-3, 7-6, 8-8, 8-9, 8-10**		Lessons 2-6, 3-11, 4-1, 4-2, 4-3, 4-7, 5-5, 5-6, 6-2, 6-3, 6-6, 7-5, 8-9
CC.9-12.F.IF.5 Relate the domain of a function to its graph and, where applicable, to the quantitative relationship it describes.*	**Lessons 1-5, 1-6, 4-1, 4-2, 5-1, 5-2, 5-8, 6-1, 6-6, 7-1, 8-8**		Lessons 2-6, 3-11
CC.9-12.F.IF.6 Calculate and interpret the average rate of change of a function (presented symbolically or as a table) over a specified interval. Estimate the rate of change from a graph.*	**Lessons 4-3, 4-5, 8-10**		Lessons 2-6
CC.9-12.F.IF.7 Graph functions expressed symbolically and show key features of the graph, by hand in simple cases and using technology for more complicated cases.* **a.** Graph linear and quadratic functions and show intercepts, maxima, and minima. **b.** Graph square root, cube root, and piecewise-defined functions, including step functions and absolute value functions. **c.** Graph polynomial functions, identifying zeros when suitable factorizations are available, and showing end behavior. **d.** (+) Graph rational functions, identifying zeros and asymptotes when suitable factorizations are available, and showing end behavior. **e.** Graph exponential and logarithmic functions, showing intercepts and end behavior, and trigonometric functions, showing period, midline, and amplitude.	**Lessons 4-1, 4-3, 4-5, 5-1, 5-2, 5-3, 5-8, 6-1, 6-2, 6-3, 6-4, 6-6, 7-1, 7-2, 7-3, 8-8**		Lessons 2-1, 2-2, 2-3, 2-4, 2-5, 2-6, 3-1, 3-2, 3-3, 3-4, 3-9, 3-11, 4-1, 4-2, 4-3, 4-7, 5-1, 5-2, 5-3, 5-4, 5-5, 5-6, 6-1, 6-2, 6-3, 6-4, 6-5, 6-6, 6-7, 7-1, 7-2, 8-5, 8-6, 8-7, 8-8, 8-9
CC.9-12.F.IF.8 Write a function defined by an expression in different but equivalent forms to reveal and explain different properties of the function. **a.** Use the process of factoring and completing the square in a quadratic function to show zeros, extreme values, and symmetry of the graph, and interpret these in terms of a context. **b.** Use the properties of exponents to interpret expressions for exponential functions.	**Lessons 8-2, 8-3, 8-8, 8-10**		Lessons 2-4, 2-5, 6-4, 6-6
CC.9-12.F.IF.9 Compare properties of two functions each represented in a different way (algebraically, graphically, numerically in tables, or by verbal descriptions).	**Lessons 4-2, 8-10**		Lesson 4-7

(+) Advanced   * = Also a Modeling Standard

On Core Mathematics Algebra 1

Common Core Correlations

Standards	Algebra 1	Geometry	Algebra 2
Building Functions			
CC.9-12.F.BF.1 Write a function that describes a relationship between two quantities.* **a.** Determine an explicit expression, a recursive process, or steps for calculation from a context. **b.** Combine standard function types using arithmetic operations. **c.** (+) Compose functions.	Lessons 1-6, 2-3, 2-8, 4-5, 4-6, 4-9, 5-5, 5-6, 5-8, 6-1, 6-2, 6-3, 6-4, 6-6, 7-1, 7-2, 7-3, 7-6, 8-3, 8-8, 8-10		Lessons 2-6, 3-5, 3-11, 4-1, 4-2, 4-3, 4-4, 4-5, 4-7, 5-5, 5-6, 6-2, 6-3, 6-4, 6-6, 7-5, 8-9, 9-1, 9-2, 9-3
CC.9-12.F.BF.2 Write arithmetic and geometric sequences both recursively and with an explicit formula, use them to model situations, and translate between the two forms.*	Lesson 4-1		Lessons 9-2, 9-3
CC.9-12.F.BF.3 Identify the effect on the graph of replacing $f(x)$ by $f(x) + k$, $kf(x)$, $f(kx)$, and $f(x + k)$ for specific values of k (both positive and negative); find the value of k given the graphs. Experiment with cases and illustrate an explanation of the effects on the graph using technology.	Lessons 4-4, 5-4, 6-2, 6-3, 6-4, 7-1, 7-2, 7-3		Lessons 2-1, 2-2, 2-3, 3-1, 3-2, 3-3, 4-1, 4-2, 5-4, 6-2, 6-3, 6-4, 6-5, 7-2, 8-7, 8-8, 8-9
CC.9-12.F.BF.4 Find inverse functions. **a.** Solve an equation of the form $f(x) = c$ for a simple function f that has an inverse and write an expression for the inverse. **b.** (+) Verify by composition that one function is the inverse of another. **c.** (+) Read values of an inverse function from a graph or a table, given that the function has an inverse. **d.** (+) Produce an invertible function from a non-invertible function by restricting the domain.	Lesson 4-7		Lessons 5-1, 5-2, 5-3, 5-5, 5-6
CC.9-12.F.BF.5(+) Understand the inverse relationship between exponents and logarithms and use this relationship to solve problems involving logarithms and exponents.			Lessons 7-1, 7-3
Linear, Quadratic, and Exponential Models			
CC.9-12.F.LE.1 Distinguish between situations that can be modeled with linear functions and with exponential functions.* **a.** Prove that linear functions grow by equal differences over equal intervals, and that exponential functions grow by equal factors over equal intervals. **b.** Recognize situations in which one quantity changes at a constant rate per unit interval relative to another. **c.** Recognize situations in which a quantity grows or decays by a constant percent rate per unit interval relative to another.	Lessons 5-2, 5-3, 5-6, 5-7, 5-8		
CC.9-12.F.LE.2 Construct linear and exponential functions, including arithmetic and geometric sequences, given a graph, a description of a relationship, or two input-output pairs (include reading these from a table).*	Lessons 4-5, 4-6, 5-1, 5-2, 5-3, 5-5, 5-8		Lessons 6-2, 6-3, 6-4, 6-5, 9-2, 9-3

(+) Advanced   * = Also a Modeling Standard

Standards	Algebra 1	Geometry	Algebra 2
CC.9-12.F.LE.3 Observe using graphs and tables that a quantity increasing exponentially eventually exceeds a quantity increasing linearly, quadratically, or (more generally) as a polynomial function.*	Lesson 5-7		Lessons 6-1, 6-6
CC.9-12.F.LE.4 For exponential models, express as a logarithm the solution to $ab^{ct} = d$ where a, c, and d are numbers and the base b is 2, 10, or e; evaluate the logarithm using technology.*			Lesson 7-4
CC.9-12.F.LE.5 Interpret the parameters in a linear or exponential function in terms of a context.*	Lessons 4-4, 4-5, 4-6, 4-9, 4-10, 5-2, 5-3, 5-6, 5-8		Lessons 6-4, 6-5
Trigonometric Functions			
CC.9-12.F.TF.1 Understand radian measure of an angle as the length of the arc on the unit circle subtended by the angle.			Lesson 8-2
CC.9-12.F.TF.2 Explain how the unit circle in the coordinate plane enables the extension of trigonometric functions to all real numbers, interpreted as radian measures of angles traversed counterclockwise around the unit circle.			Lesson 8-3
CC.9-12.F.TF.3(+) Use special triangles to determine geometrically the values of sine, cosine, tangent for $\pi/3$, $\pi/4$ and $\pi/6$, and use the unit circle to express the values of sine, cosines, and tangent for x, $\pi + x$, and $2\pi - x$ in terms of their values for x, where x is any real number.			Lesson 8-3
CC.9-12.F.TF.4(+) Use the unit circle to explain symmetry (odd and even) and periodicity of trigonometric functions.			Lessons 8-5, 8-6
CC.9-12.F.TF.5 Choose trigonometric functions to model periodic phenomena with specified amplitude, frequency, and midline.*			Lesson 8-9
CC.9-12.F.TF.8 Prove the Pythagorean identity $\sin^2(\theta) + \cos^2(\theta) = 1$ and use it to calculate trigonometric ratios.			Lesson 8-4
Geometry			
Congruence			
CC.9-12.G.CO.1 Know precise definitions of angle, circle, perpendicular line, parallel line, and line segment, based on the undefined notions of point, line, distance along a line, and distance around a circular arc.		Lessons 1-1, 1-4, 1-5, 9-4	
CC.9-12.G.CO.2 Represent transformations in the plane using, e.g., transparencies and geometry software; describe transformations as functions that take points in the plane as inputs and give other points as outputs. Compare transformations that preserve distance and angle to those that do not (e.g., translation versus horizontal stretch).		Lessons 2-1, 2-2, 2-3, 2-4, 2-5, 2-6, 5-1, 5-2	

(+) Advanced   * = Also a Modeling Standard

Standards	Algebra 1	Geometry	Algebra 2
CC.9-12.G.CO.3 Given a rectangle, parallelogram, trapezoid, or regular polygon, describe the rotations and reflections that carry it onto itself.		Lesson 4-1	
CC.9-12.G.CO.4 Develop definitions of rotations, reflections, and translations in terms of angles, circles, perpendicular lines, parallel lines, and line segments.		Lessons 2-2, 2-5, 2-6	
CC.9-12.G.CO.5 Given a geometric figure and a rotation, reflection, or translation, draw the transformed figure using, e.g., graph paper, tracing paper, or geometry software. Specify a sequence of transformations that will carry a given figure onto another.		Lessons 2-2, 2-5, 2-6, 3-1	
CC.9-12.G.CO.6 Use geometric descriptions of rigid motions to transform figures and to predict the effect of a given rigid motion on a given figure; given two figures, use the definition of congruence in terms of rigid motions to decide if they are congruent.		Lessons 2-2, 2-5, 2-6, 3-1	
CC.9-12.G.CO.7 Use the definition of congruence in terms of rigid motions to show that two triangles are congruent if and only if corresponding pairs of sides and corresponding pairs of angles are congruent.		Lessons 3-2, 3-3	
CC.9-12.G.CO.8 Explain how the criteria for triangle congruence (ASA, SAS, and SSS) follow from the definition of congruence in terms of rigid motions.		Lesson 3-3	
CC.9-12.G.CO.9 Prove geometric theorems about lines and angles.		Lessons 1-6, 1-7, 2-3, 2-4	
CC.9-12.G.CO.10 Prove theorems about triangles.		Lessons 3-5, 3-6, 3-7, 3-8, 3-9	
CC.9-12.G.CO.11 Prove theorems about parallelograms.		Lessons 4-2, 4-3, 4-4, 4-5	
CC.9-12.G.CO.12 Make formal geometric constructions with a variety of tools and methods (compass and straightedge, string, reflective devices, paper folding, dynamic geometry software, etc.).		Lessons 1-1, 1-4, 1-5	
CC.9-12.G.CO.13 Construct an equilateral triangle, a square, and a regular hexagon inscribed in a circle.		Lesson 7-3	
Similarity, Right Triangles, and Trigonometry			
CC.9-12.G.SRT.1 Verify experimentally the properties of dilations given by a center and a scale factor: **a.** A dilation takes a line not passing through the center of the dilation to a parallel line, and leaves a line passing through the center unchanged. **b.** The dilation of a line segment is longer or shorter in the ratio given by the scale factor.		Lesson 5-1	

(+) Advanced   * = Also a Modeling Standard

© Houghton Mifflin Harcourt Publishing Company

Standards	Algebra 1	Geometry	Algebra 2
CC.9-12.G.SRT.2 Given two figures, use the definition of similarity in terms of similarity transformations to decide if they are similar; explain using similarity transformations the meaning of similarity for triangles as the equality of all corresponding angles and the proportionality of all corresponding pairs of sides.		Lessons 5-3, 5-4	
CC.9-12.G.SRT.3 Use the properties of similarity transformations to establish the AA criterion for two triangles to be similar.		Lesson 5-4	
CC.9-12.G.SRT.4 Prove theorems about triangles.		Lessons 5-6, 5-7	
CC.9-12.G.SRT.5 Use congruence and similarity criteria for triangles to solve problems and prove relationships in geometric figures.		Lessons 3-4, 4-2, 4-3, 4-4, 4-5, 5-5, 5-6, 5-7	
CC.9-12.G.SRT.6 Understand that by similarity, side ratios in right triangles are properties of the angles in the triangle, leading to definitions of trigonometric ratios for acute angles.		Lessons 6-1, 6-2, 6-3	
CC.9-12.G.SRT.7 Explain and use the relationship between the sine and cosine of complementary angles.		Lessons 6-2, 6-3	
CC.9-12.G.SRT.8 Use trigonometric ratios and the Pythagorean Theorem to solve right triangles in applied problems.		Lesson 6-4	
CC.9-12.G.SRT.9(+) Derive the formula $A = 1/2\ ab \sin(C)$ for the area of a triangle by drawing an auxiliary line from a vertex perpendicular to the opposite side.		Lesson 6-5	
CC.9-12.G.SRT.10(+) Prove the Laws of Sines and Cosines and use them to solve problems.		Lessons 6-6, 6-7	
CC.9-12.G.SRT.11(+) Understand and apply the Law of Sines and the Law of Cosines to find unknown measurements in right and non-right triangles (e.g., surveying problems, resultant forces).		Lessons 6-6, 6-7	
Circles			
CC.9-12.G.C.1 Prove that all circles are similar.		Lesson 5-3	
CC.9-12.G.C.2 Identify and describe relationships among inscribed angles, radii, and chords.		Lessons 7-1, 7-5	
CC.9-12.G.C.3 Construct the inscribed and circumscribed circles of a triangle, and prove properties of angles for a quadrilateral inscribed in a circle.		Lessons 7-2, 7-4, 7-6	
CC.9-12.G.C.4(+) Construct a tangent line from a point outside a given circle to the circle.		Lesson 7-5	

(+) Advanced   ∗ = Also a Modeling Standard

© Houghton Mifflin Harcourt Publishing Company

Standards	Algebra 1	Geometry	Algebra 2
CC.9-12.G.C.5 Derive using similarity the fact that the length of the arc intercepted by an angle is proportional to the radius, and define the radian measure of the angle as the constant of proportionality; derive the formula for the area of a sector.		Lessons 9-4, 9-5	Lesson 8-1
Expressing Geometric Properties with Equations			
CC.9-12.G.GPE.1 Derive the equation of a circle of given center and radius using the Pythagorean Theorem; complete the square to find the center and radius of a circle given by an equation.		Lesson 8-1	
CC.9-12.G.GPE.2 Derive the equation of a parabola given a focus and directrix.		Lesson 8-2	
CC.9-12.G.GPE.4 Use coordinates to prove simple geometric theorems algebraically.		Lessons 1-2, 1-3, 3-7, 3-8, 3-9, 8-1, 8-6	
CC.9-12.G.GPE.5 Prove the slope criteria for parallel and perpendicular lines and use them to solve geometric problems (e.g., find the equation of line parallel or perpendicular to a given line that passes through a given point).		Lessons 8-4, 8-5	
CC.9-12.G.GPE.6 Find the point on a directed line segment between two given points that partitions the segment in a given ratio.		Lesson 8-3	
CC.9-12.G.GPE.7 Use coordinates to compute perimeters of polygons and areas of triangles and rectangles, e.g., using the distance formula.*		Lesson 9-2	
Geometric Measurement and Dimension			
CC.9-12.G.GMD.1 Give an informal argument for the formulas for the circumference of a circle, area of a circle, volume of a cylinder, pyramid, and cone.		Lessons 9-3, 9-5, 10-2, 10-3, 10-4	
CC.9-12.G.GMD.2(+) Give an informal argument using Cavalieri's principle for the formulas for the volume of a sphere and other solid figures.		Lessons 10-2, 10-5	
CC.9-12.G.GMD.3 Use volume formulas for cylinders, pyramids, cones, and spheres to solve problems.*		Lessons 10-2, 10-3, 10-4, 10-5, 10-6	
CC.9-12.G.GMD.4 Identify the shapes of two-dimensional cross-sections of three-dimensional objects, and identify three-dimensional objects generated by rotations of two-dimensional objects.		Lesson 10-1	

(+) Advanced   * = Also a Modeling Standard

Standards	Algebra 1	Geometry	Algebra 2
Modeling with Geometry			
CC.9-12.G.MG.1 Use geometric shapes, their measures, and their properties to describe objects (e.g., modeling a tree trunk or a human torso as a cylinder).*		Lessons 9-2, 9-3, 10-2	
CC.9-12.G.MG.2 Apply concepts of density based on area and volume in modeling situations (e.g., persons per square mile, BTUs per cubic foot).*		Lessons 9-2, 10-2, 10-5	
CC.9-12.G.MG.3 Apply geometric methods to solve design problems (e.g., designing an object or structure to satisfy physical constraints or minimize cost; working with typographic grid systems based on ratios).*		Lessons 5-5, 10-6	
Statistics and Probability			
Interpreting Categorical and Quantitative Data			
CC.9-12.S.ID.1 Represent data with plots on the real number line (dot plots, histograms, and box plots).*	Lessons 9-2, 9-3, 9-4		Lessons 10-2, 10-3
CC.9-12.S.ID.2 Use statistics appropriate to the shape of the data distribution to compare center (median, mean) and spread (interquartile range, standard deviation) of two or more different data sets.*	Lessons 9-1, 9-2, 9-3, 9-4		
CC.9-12.S.ID.3 Interpret differences in shape, center, and spread in the context of the data sets, accounting for possible effects of extreme data points (outliers).*	Lesson 9-2		Lesson 10-2
CC.9-12.S.ID.4 Use the mean and standard deviation of a data set to fit it to a normal distribution and to estimate population percentages. Recognize that there are data sets for which such a procedure is not appropriate. Use calculators, spreadsheets, and tables to estimate areas under the normal curve.*			Lesson 10-4
CC.9-12.S.ID.5 Summarize categorical data for two categories in two-way frequency tables. Interpret relative frequencies in the context of the data (including joint, marginal, and conditional relative frequencies). Recognize possible associations and trends in the data.*	Lesson 9-5		
CC.9-12.S.ID.6 Represent data on two quantitative variables on a scatter plot, and describe how the variables are related.* a. Fit a function to the data; use functions fitted to data to solve problems in the context of the data. b. Informally assess the fit of a function by plotting and analyzing residuals. c. Fit a linear function for a scatter plot that suggests a linear association.	Lessons 4-9, 4-10, 5-6, 5-8		Lessons 5-5, 5-6, 6-6

(+) Advanced   * = Also a Modeling Standard

© Houghton Mifflin Harcourt Publishing Company

Standards	Algebra 1	Geometry	Algebra 2
CC.9-12.S.ID.7 Interpret the slope (rate of change) and the intercept (constant term) of a linear model in the context of the data.*	**Lessons 4-9, 4-10**		
CC.9-12.S.ID.8 Compute (using technology) and interpret the correlation coefficient of a linear fit.*	**Lessons 4-8, 4-10**		
CC.9-12.S.ID.9 Distinguish between correlation and causation.*	**Lesson 4-8**		
Making Inferences and Justifying Conclusions			
CC.9-12.S.IC.1 Understand statistics as a process for making inferences about population parameters based on a random sample from that population.*			Lesson 10-1
CC.9-12.S.IC.2 Decide if a specified model is consistent with results from a given data-generating process, e.g., using simulation.*			Lesson 10-3
CC.9-12.S.IC.3 Recognize the purposes of and differences among sample surveys, experiments, and observational studies; explain how randomization relates to each.*			Lesson 10-7
CC.9-12.S.IC.4 Use data from a sample survey to estimate a population mean or proportion; develop a margin of error through the use of simulation models for random sampling.*			Lessons 10-5, 10-6
CC.9-12.S.IC.5 Use data from a randomized experiment to compare two treatments; use simulations to decide if differences between parameters are significant.*			Lesson 10-8
CC.9-12.S.IC.6 Evaluate reports based on data.*	**Lesson 4-8**		Lesson 10-7
Conditional Probability and the Rules of Probability			
CC.9-12.S.CP.1 Describe events as subsets of a sample space (the set of outcomes) using characteristics (or categories) of the outcomes, or as unions, intersections, or complements of other events ("or," "and," "not").*		Lesson 11-1	
CC.9-12.S.CP.2 Understand that two events A and B are independent if the probability of A and B occurring together is the product of their probabilities, and use this characterization to determine if they are independent.*		Lesson 11-7	
CC.9-12.S.CP.3 Understand the conditional probability of A given B as P(A and B)/P(B), and interpret independence of A and B as saying that the conditional probability of A given B is the same as the probability of A, and the conditional probability of B given A is the same as the probability of B.*		Lessons 11-6, 11-7	

(+) Advanced   * = Also a Modeling Standard

Standards	Algebra 1	Geometry	Algebra 2
CC.9-12.S.CP.4 Construct and interpret two-way frequency tables of data when two categories are associated with each object being classified. Use the two-way table as a sample space to decide if events are independent and to approximate conditional probabilities.*		Lessons 11-6, 11-7, 11-10	
CC.9-12.S.CP.5 Recognize and explain the concepts of conditional probability and independence in everyday language and everyday situations.*		Lessons 11-6, 11-7	
CC.9-12.S.CP.6 Find the conditional probability of *A* given *B* as the fraction of *B*'s outcomes that also belong to *A*, and interpret the answer in terms of the model.*		Lesson 11-6	
CC.9-12.S.CP.7 Apply the Addition Rule, $P(A \text{ or } B) = P(A) + P(B) - P(A \text{ and } B)$, and interpret the answer in terms of the model.*		Lesson 11-5	
CC.9-12.S.CP.8(+) Apply the general Multiplication Rule in a uniform probability model, $P(A \text{ and } B) = P(A)P(B|A) = P(B)P(A|B)$, and interpret the answer in terms of the model.*		Lesson 11-8	
CC.9-12.S.CP.9(+) Use permutations and combinations to compute probabilities of compound events and solve problems.*		Lessons 11-3, 11-4	
Using Probability to Make Decisions			
CC.9-12.S.MD.6(+) Use probabilities to make fair decisions (e.g., drawing by lots, using a random number generator).*		Lessons 11-2, 11-9	
CC.9-12.S.MD.7(+) Analyze decisions and strategies using probability concepts (e.g., product testing, medical testing, pulling a hockey goalie at the end of a game).*		Lesson 11-10	

(+) Advanced   * = Also a Modeling Standard

© Houghton Mifflin Harcourt Publishing Company